MW01408871

Economic Foundations of International Law

Economic Foundations of International Law

Eric A. Posner
and
Alan O. Sykes

The Belknap Press of
Harvard University Press

Cambridge, Massachusetts, and London, England | 2013

Copyright © 2013 by the President and Fellows of Harvard College
All rights reserved
Printed in the United States of America

Library of Congress Cataloging-in-Publication Data

Posner, Eric A.
    Economic foundations of international law / Eric A. Posner and Alan O. Sykes.
      p. cm.
    Includes bibliographical references and index.
    ISBN 978-0-674-06699-1 (alk. paper)
    1. International law—Economic aspects.   I. Sykes, A. O.   II. Title.
    KZ1252.P67   2012
    341'.1—dc23   2012012120

For Emlyn, Nathaniel, and Jacob
—*E. P.*

For Maureen, Maddie, and Sophie
—*A. S.*

Contents

I Basics
1. Introduction   *3*
2. Fundamentals of International Law   *6*
3. Economic Analysis of International Law—the Essentials   *12*

II General Aspects of International Law
4. Sovereignty and Attributes of Statehood   *39*
5. Customary International Law   *50*
6. Treaties   *63*
7. International Institutions   *79*
8. State Responsibility   *113*
9. Remedies   *126*
10. The Intersection between International Law and Domestic Law   *139*

III Traditional Public International Law
11. Treatment of Aliens, Foreign Property, and Foreign Debt   *155*
12. The Use of Force   *163*
13. The Conduct of War   *190*
14. Human Rights   *198*
15. International Criminal Law   *209*

IV The Environment
16. International Environmental Law   *225*
17. The Law of the Sea   *233*

V International Economic Law

    18. International Trade   *263*

    19. International Investment, Antitrust, and Monetary Law   *288*

Notes   *329*
Acknowledgments   *355*
Index   *357*

Economic Foundations of International Law

I

Basics

1

Introduction

Recent years have witnessed a torrent of new writing that uses concepts from economics to analyze international law. The economic or rational choice approach to public international law assumes that states are rational, self-interested agents that use international law in order to address international externalities and obtain the other benefits of international cooperation. This approach also emphasizes that because no external enforcement agent such as a world government exists, international law must be self-enforcing. States must believe that if they violate international law, other states will retaliate or in other ways respond negatively. This self-enforcement constraint is the major analytic distinction between international law and domestic law, where it is usually safe to assume that parties can rely on the government to enforce the law.

Although the economic approach to international law is only about ten years old, a large literature has already accumulated.[1] Many of the earliest works focused on the question of compliance, asking what reason rational states have for complying with international law. Since then, scholars have turned their attention to substantive areas of law—human rights, the law of the sea, the laws of war, environmental law, and so forth—and general themes such as the role of adjudication and of international organizations. The purpose of this book is to gather together and build on many of the ideas from this body of work and to present them in a manner suitable as an introduction for students and as a reference work for scholars. We mainly have in mind law students and law professors, but we hope that political scientists, economists, and other scholars who work in international relations will find this book useful as well.

Some background about the intellectual antecedents of this work will be helpful. Most scholars who write about international law take a doctrinal approach, in which they analyze legal sources for the purpose of determining what the law is. Where scholars ventured outside the doctrinal realm, they tended to be influenced by currents in legal philosophy and legal history. Most international law scholars ignored the revolution in (domestic) legal scholarship of the 1960s and 1970s, which introduced social science methods, and in particular economic methods, to legal scholarship. Only international trade scholars, in the spirit of their enterprise, imported economic ideas into their field. Economic analysis of public international law began only in the 1990s and, after a slow start, accelerated in the early 2000s.

A parallel stream of scholarship has been produced by political scientists. International relations theorists discovered rational choice in the 1980s, much earlier than international law scholars. Their earliest work, however, focused not on international law but on more general questions of international cooperation.[2] In the late 1990s, political scientists turned their attention to international law, and since then a great deal of writing on this topic has emerged.[3] The work of international lawyers influenced by economics and political scientists overlaps but is not identical. Political scientists (like economists) are oriented to producing descriptive hypotheses about how states and other international actors behave and testing them using statistical methods. Much political science scholarship tries to test which of the different schools of international relations (realism, constructivism, and so forth) best explains international behavior, a topic of little interest for lawyers. Lawyers are oriented to normative argument and also tend to examine international law in a more fine-grained way, focusing on particular rules and doctrines rather than general institutional patterns.

This book focuses on the law-oriented literature. In addition to summing up prior work, we hope to produce a springboard for future scholarship. International law is a vast subject, and its importance is increasing. It is sufficient to point to the major role of international law in the conflicts and wars that emerged from the 9/11 terrorist attack and in international efforts to address climate change. These are two of the most important issues of our time. "Globalization" has become a cliché, but it is undeniable that interactions among states have increased enormously over the last twenty years, and this has produced urgent questions for international law. This book provides an intellectual framework for thinking about these questions in a rigorous way.

The book aims for breadth, not depth. Given the scope of the topic, we can address international law only by simplifying it for analytic purposes. Readers who seek a more comprehensive and precise introduction to international legal doctrine should consult a standard treatise on international law.[4]

This book has five parts. In this, Part I, we provide a brief introduction to economics, international law, and the economic approach to international law.

In Part II, we survey the general structural and institutional features of international law. In Part III, we focus on some traditional international law topics such as the treatment of aliens, the laws of war, and human rights. Part IV addresses international environmental law, and Part V addresses international economic law.

2

Fundamentals of International Law

International law is the system of laws that governs the relationships of states. States make international law by entering treaties with each other and by recognizing customary norms. International law creates obligations primarily for states: states comply with or violate international law. The one exception to this proposition is international criminal law, a body of law that states have created but that imposes duties on individuals.

What Is a State?

The state is the central agent of international law. Putting aside complexities that we will address later, states make international law; they decide whether to comply with or violate international law; they are the victims of international law violations; and they demand and pay reparations on account of international law violations. But what is a state? We can start with the legal definition of the *state* in international law: "Under international law, a state is an entity that has a defined territory and a permanent population, under the control of its own government, and that engages in, or has the capacity to engage in, formal relations with other such entities."[1] One might begin by noting that every state has a territory defined by borders with a population within those borders, but we immediately see difficulties. The people who "belong" to the state ("citizens," "subjects," "nationals") do not necessarily stay within the borders, and foreigners may come onto the state's territory. To be more precise, then, the state has some set of rules that identify the people in the subset of the world population that have certain substantial rights and obligations under domestic law—including, nowadays, the right to enter the state's territory after leaving and the right to remain in the state.

But there is more to be said about the population. One can identify territories without populations (like Antarctica) and populations without territories—the

Kurds, the Palestinians, Jews before the establishment of Israel. Certain groups of people identify with each other along religious, ethnic, or territorial lines: they think of themselves as having special obligations to each other, as belonging together, and with a right to inhabit some specific territory usually. The Kurds are scattered across a territory that includes parts of Turkey, Iraq, Iran, and other countries, but they do not have a state because they lack something more. Not all Jews believe that there must be a Jewish state, but many do, those living in Israel especially. At one time, it was thought that all national or ethnic groups were entitled to their own specific territory where they have historical ties. This idea lives on under the rubric of "self-determination," a concept that can be found in various international documents including human rights treaties. But it turns out that the idea is not practical: there are too many different national and ethnic groups, which, thanks to intermarriage and migration, overlap in complex ways, with many people disagreeing about who belongs in what group; plus, people occupying territories to which some other group has historical ties rarely yield to those claims, often claiming, with varying degrees of accuracy, that they have historical ties to the land as well. We will discuss this problem in more detail in Chapter 5.

There are two more criteria in the legal definition of a state. A state must have a government: some institution must maintain order among the people who live on the state's territory. Some states lack governments; they are called "failed states." Today, Somalia is an example of a failed state. Last, states must enjoy the recognition of other states. This criterion is crucial. Otherwise, certain self-governing population-territory packages that are not states would seem to be states: Quebec is an example.

Sources of Law

We have discussed some of the complications that surround the idea that states are the primary agents of international law. As always, the analogies and disanalogies to domestic law are instructive. People make law through their representatives; states make law directly. We do not need to worry about individuals breaking apart or merging; states, by contrast, break apart and merge. Yet states, unlike individuals but like corporations, are indefinitely lived. The persistence of states contributes to the stability of the international system, yet their susceptibility to failure, breakup, and reconfiguration can play havoc with it.

Nonetheless, the state is the starting point for understanding international law. States make international law, and they are bound by it. Hence, when international lawyers try to figure out what international law is, they begin by looking at the activities of states—treaties, of course, but also custom and the various official statements that states make through their governments. The method for examining these phenomena comes under the doctrine of "sources."

When a lawyer seeks to determine what domestic law is, the method is straightforward. In the United States, one starts with statutes and judicial opinions. There is rarely any doubt whether a particular rule is a matter of federal statutory law or not—one just consults the U.S. Code—but if doubt arises, a set of constitutional rules guides one to the answer. The statute must emerge from Congress, after a vote, and usually with presidential consent. A number of other constitutional rules may deprive the statute of validity; these one learns by reading judicial opinions. One also consults judicial opinions for interpretations of statutes and for the common law. Again, various straightforward rules allow one to distinguish legally authoritative documents (statements issued by a duly constituted court or panel, after a vote, involving a case or controversy) from other documents (for example, speeches of judges, articles written by judges, and so forth). In a well-functioning domestic legal system, the method for determining the source of law is transparent.

In international law, matters are more complicated. Let us begin with the doctrine:

(1) A rule of international law is one that has been accepted as such by the international community of states
    (a) in the form of customary law;
    (b) by international agreement; or
    (c) by derivation from general principles common to the major legal systems of the world.
(2) Customary international law results from a general and consistent practice of states followed by them from a sense of legal obligation.
(3) International agreements create law for the states parties thereto and may lead to the creation of customary international law when such agreements are intended for adherence by states generally and are in fact widely accepted.
(4) General principles common to the major legal systems, even if not incorporated or reflected in customary law or international agreement, may be invoked as supplementary rules of international law where appropriate.[2]

The two main sources of law are treaties and custom. A state that has ratified a treaty is bound by it. Customary international law is essentially the customary behavior of states. As we discuss in the next section, to discern customary international law, the lawyer must examine the statements and behavior of states—with the statements contained in all manner of official documents and practice just a matter of observation. Other sources are even more vague. The decisions of international tribunals may, but need not, be sources of law. The decisions of domestic courts that address international law may be a source of international law. The common constitutional and legal norms of states may be a source of international law. So may be the writings of scholars.

Why are the sources of international law more complicated than the sources of domestic law? The beginning of an answer is that there is no international constitution that determines how international law is made. International institutions, such as the United Nations, largely lack legislative power, and international courts do not fit into a neat hierarchy, so they may deliver conflicting interpretations of even the most basic principles of international law. But why is there no international constitution, and why are there no international institutions such as a legislature? A simplistic but adequate answer for present purposes is that people will allow themselves to be governed by nation states but not international institutions, in part because people do not trust each other across vast areas of territory, or do not identify with each other, or do not feel bound to each other—these are all roughly synonymous ideas. States rarely yield sovereignty to international institutions; they do not trust such institutions for the same reason that national populations do not trust people who live in other states.

As we noted above, however, states do gain by cooperating with each other. International law just is the manifestation of interstate cooperation when states choose to use legal forms to govern their cooperation. International cooperation can be fluid. States often write down the terms of their cooperation in treaties, but they often do not. When they do not, cooperation can take place in a more informal way, reflected in custom or just in oral promises or in promises that are written down but not formally designated as law. The process of identifying these often implicit rules of conduct is akin to identifying the customs and social norms that govern a community of individuals. One starts by looking at how people behave and what they say, and one makes inferences on the basis of these actions and statements. Similarly, international lawyers attempt to infer from the statements and practices of states how those states cooperate with each other, which in part involves predicting how states will react in light of new, often unforeseen events.

Oliver Wendell Holmes famously said that the law is a prediction of what judges do, and one might just as well say that international law is a prediction of what states do. One needs a theory to make such predictions. In the case of international law, the formal method directs one to look for indications of state consent—explicit, in treaties; implicit, in custom. But in reality one tries to figure out what states' interests are and how states overcome conflicts so that they can jointly advance their interests. The indicia of state consent help in this process—consent reveals a state's perceived interest in a particular setting. So do the other sources of law—the internal legal rules, the general principles, and so on—help one understand the interests of states, as well as their capacities, and the limits on cooperation. More important still is an understanding of how states behave; what history has suggested they can and cannot do; how much they can cooperate and the limits of cooperation.

Bodies of Law

We have discussed the doctrine of sources: it is a doctrine, or really a set of doctrines, that cuts across the many different substantive bodies or fields of international law. Other rules of general applicability include the law of state responsibility (which governs the conditions under which states are liable for the actions of individuals), the law of remedies (which governs the remedies that states must offer to states that they have wronged), and the law of treaties (the set of rules for interpreting and enforcing treaties). Then there are bodies of law that are organized by substance: international environmental law, including the law of the sea and the various treaties addressing climate change; international humanitarian law (the rules governing the use of violence during hostilities); the law of use of force (the rules governing when states may go to war); international economic law, including trade and investment law; international human rights law; laws governing the treatment of aliens, including tourists, business people, and refugees; and much else.

Institutions

International law lacks most of the institutions of domestic law, including a legislature, an executive with general powers to enforce the law, a hierarchically organized judiciary, a significant bureaucracy, and an army. But many international legal institutions exist. The United Nations contains a General Assembly, which cannot make law but serves as a forum for discussion and signal sending, and a Security Council, which is an executive agency with the power to enforce the peace. States have set up a number of courts, some of them temporary, including the International Court of Justice, the International Criminal Court, and the World Trade Organization (WTO) dispute settlement mechanism. And there are countless other institutions—committees, commissions, organizations, bodies—which typically have no formal legal power to make, adjudicate, or enforce the law but in practice have some influence on the development of the law and its application in particular cases. These institutions are not hierarchically organized, so there is no boss at the top who can command them to cooperate or bring them into line. Nor is there a clearly defined sovereign who can revise or reorganize them through constitutional change. The untidiness of the international legal structure no doubt accounts for skepticism among some commentators about its efficacy, but it would be a mistake to assume that these institutions have no power at all.

3

Economic Analysis of International Law—the Essentials

As explained in Chapter 2, public international law is created by two or more states, by custom or more commonly by treaty, to govern interaction among those states. With few exceptions (such as international investment law and international criminal law), only states have the right to invoke and enforce public international law, and only states are bound by it. Thus, states are the key actors in public international law.

But what exactly is a "state" from the standpoint of economics? Why do states exist? What do they want from each other, and why do they need a body of "law" to govern their interaction? Indeed, absent a world government to compel states to obey the law, what good is having a body of law anyway? These are the most basic questions that economic analysis of public international law must confront, and we will begin our treatment of them in this chapter after introducing some basic economic terms.

Background Concepts and Terminology

Many readers might be put off by economic theory, with its forbidding array of mathematical equations and impenetrable jargon. But that would be a mistake. Economic theory makes progress by simplifying human behavior, not by making it more complex, and the basics of economics are easy to understand.

Economists assume that individuals act in their rational self-interest. This assumption is obviously a simplification; human behavior is much more complex. But it provides a useful starting point for thinking about difficult problems. A person is assumed to have a set of goals (called *preferences*) and limited resources (called the *budget constraint*). He uses those resources to satisfy his preferences to the extent possible. In order to satisfy his preferences, a person must frequently buy goods and services. He buys that bundle of goods and services that best satisfies his preferences given his budget constraint. If prices change, the person's behavior will change predictably. For example, if the price of tomatoes rises, then the person will (normally) buy fewer tomatoes and use the money he saves to buy something else that he prefers. In theory, the consumer makes purchases of any good up to the point where the *marginal cost* of the good—the price paid for the last increment—is just equal to the *marginal benefit* of consuming an additional increment of the good.

Law and economics was born when economists realized that the law, in effect, raises or lowers the cost of certain behavior. Criminal law raises the cost of criminal activity and so should reduce its incidence. However, much of the law has a different purpose—it facilitates behavior that makes people better off. For example, contract law eases the process of entering agreements for the exchange of goods and services. Exchanges make people better off because they trade something they value less for something they value more. When people make exchanges, they incur certain *transaction costs*—the costs of negotiating, writing down the agreement, and so forth. Contract law reduces transaction costs by supplying *default terms* that (in theory) parties would agree to if they negotiated over them—for example, the market rate of interest for a loan.

Economists evaluate legal institutions by using two normative criteria. Under the Pareto criterion, a law is desirable if it makes at least one person better off without making anyone else worse off. Under the Kaldor-Hicks criterion, a law is desirable even though it produces losers as well as winners, as long as winners gain more than the losers lose. For example, a vaccine program might cause health problems for a few people while benefiting a large number of people by protecting them from a serious disease. The program satisfies the Pareto criterion if the people who are harmed can be identified and fully compensated out of the gains from the people who benefited. The program satisfies the Kaldor-Hicks criterion even if this compensation does not occur as long as the monetized value of the health gains for the winners is greater than the monetized loss of health for the losers. When economists talk about *efficiency*, they have one or the other criterion in mind. Efficiency in both cases is a useful standard for evaluating laws and other government projects, but we agree with most scholars that it is not the only relevant criterion. An equitable *income distribution* is certainly among the other considerations that most people regard as important. That said, one must always ask what is the best *policy instrument* for achieving a more equitable income distribution. Inefficient laws are often inferior to other policies relating to taxation.[1]

A central problem in modern life is that when people act, they often create *externalities*. Negative externalities arise when a person engages in an action that is privately beneficial but that harms others: for example, a factory that pollutes. Positive externalities arise when a person engages in an action that benefits others: for example, the construction of a beautiful house that increases the property values of neighbors. A central role of government is both to deter negative externalities and encourage positive externalities. A simple way to do so is to tax activities that cause negative externalities and subsidize activities that cause positive externalities. These taxes can be efficient if they cause the agent to "internalize" the effects of his actions on others. A person who pollutes but is fined an amount equal to the harm caused by the pollution will continue to pollute only if his private benefits exceed the costs to others.

Commentators often refer to the related concept of a *public good*. Technically, a public good is a good the consumption of which by one person has no effect on the ability of other people to consume it. National defense is (roughly) a public good because when one citizen enjoys the benefit of an effective defense, another person's ability to do the same is generally unaffected. By contrast, when a person eats food, no other person can eat the same food—food is not a public good.

The creation of public goods and the control of externalities generally are subject to *collective action problems.* Consider an externality like pollution. Where a government exists, it can simply pass a law that taxes or sanctions polluters. But where a government does not exist, the only way to stop the pollution is through action by individuals to discourage it. The problem is that each person has an incentive to free ride on the efforts of others. If a group consists of one hundred people, for example, each person might think that if ninety-nine other people sanction the polluter, that will be sufficient to end the pollution, in which case the person in question need not expend any effort himself to sanction the polluter. But if everyone thinks in this way, no one will sanction the polluter. Domestic polities overcome the collective action problem in many domains by creating governments with the responsibility to act on behalf of all people affected by a problem. But international institutions are much weaker, and so in many cases where states face collective problems, they cannot overcome them or can overcome them only with great difficulty.

We have so far spoken of individuals, but rational-choice models can be applied to collective bodies as well. Corporations, for example, are groups of people but are so constructed that they frequently act approximately as though they were single agents. A manager is placed at the helm and given contractual incentives to cause the corporation to maximize profits. In this book, our main focus is the state, which is the primary agent in international law. States also often seem to act as though they were individual agents, but what exactly states maximize, and whether they are rational, is a more complex question than the case of corporations. We will address these issues in Chapter 8.

The Theory of Statehood

The world is now divided into just under 200 states. Each state is "sovereign" over its own territory and is nominally equal to every other state under international law (although this notion is quite misleading, as we will see at many places in this book).

What accounts for this form of organization? One can certainly imagine alternatives. One could imagine, for example, a single global state: all law would be domestic law and international law would not exist. The ancient Greeks lived in city-states, which had relations with each other much as states do today; but the Greeks did not regard non-Greek states, such as Persia, as having equal status. In the Middle Ages and early modern period, people lived in kingdoms, duchies, cities, and other entities, which often had complicated horizontal and vertical relationships with other such entities. And of course the world has seen various periods of colonialism, in which more powerful states have conquered less powerful states and turned them into "colonies," only to grant them independence later.

The current "equilibrium," so to speak, with its emphasis on states that have sovereignty over their own territory but not others, has an economic explanation. In a well-functioning state, the people benefit from policies of their government that apply within its territory. If overlapping jurisdictions exist,[2] or superior colonial powers control a territory, the danger arises that people with control over policy will adopt measures that affect other people who have no control over policy, transferring wealth from the group with little or no control to the group in control and destroying valuable resources in the process. Government "by the people" who are most directly affected by government policy tends to abate this exploitation of weaker groups by giving the citizens most affected by policy the capacity to identify the officials responsible for particular policies and to reward and sanction them. These observations also suggest why modern states are typically reluctant to submit (voluntarily) to the authority of other states.

Of course, dysfunctional arrangements toward minorities or weaker groups can and do arise within a state. States historically split up when a minority group—often an ethnic minority—claims that its interests are not adequately represented by those in power and successfully launches an insurgency that results in secession. "We want a state of our own" or "we have the right to self-determination" is the typical rallying cry.

Such disintegration of states hints at the reason why the world is not concentrated into a smaller number of states or perhaps a single world state. Well-functioning states have governments that produce goods and services for people who live in them—national security, crime control, enforcement of property and contract rights, infrastructure, environmental protection, and so forth. A single world state does not exist in part because a government of that scale would have a great deal of trouble figuring out what goods and services best meet the local interests of everyone around the world, and people would have a great deal of trouble trying to monitor the government to ensure that it acts in their interest. Instead, we have nearly 200 nation-states that, more or less, are responsive to the groups of people who live in them. These groups are sometimes homogenous; even when they are not—as in the United States, Indonesia, and Nigeria—they are more homogenous than the world population as a whole is.

This point can be made a bit more precisely.[3] Suppose that the main function of states is to supply certain goods and services that are not supplied by (or not readily supplied by) the private market; these include national security, environmental protection, and enforcement of contract and property rights. We will sometimes refer to such things as "public goods," even though we acknowledge that they often do not meet the technical definition of a public good in economics.[4]

These goods and services are supplied more cheaply per capita at larger scales. If the cost of defending a certain territory from enemies is X, and everyone must pay taxes to finance defense, then in a larger population the tax per person will be lower than in a smaller population. Scale economies imply that larger states have advantages over smaller states.

But governance becomes more difficult as the population increases. The reason is that the population is likely to be more diverse and thus less able to agree on the nature of the public goods that the state should supply. Although the government can solve this problem to some degree by taxing the beneficiaries of public goods and making transfers to those who do not benefit from them, taxing and transferring is costly and distorts people's behavior. Accordingly, heterogeneity costs put a limit on the size of the state. The larger the population, the larger are the heterogeneity costs and hence the greater is the cost of governance.

The optimal size of a state balances the benefits of scale economies as the number of citizens increases against the growing costs of governance. A state should stop growing when the marginal benefit to a representative citizen from adding another citizen due to scale economies falls below the marginal cost to a representative citizen of higher governance costs due to greater heterogeneity. This simple theory suggests why a single world state does not exist and why, alternatively, billions of household-sized states do not exist.

What the theory does not fully explain is the diversity in state size. Iceland has a population of 300,000; India and China have populations greater than one billion (and India has an extraordinarily diverse population in ethnic, religious, and linguistic terms). Factors such as geographic barriers and historical antagonisms surely matter. These too can be interpreted to be consistent with the theory—geographic barriers and historical antagonisms are simply factors that add (perhaps dramatically) to the costs of trying to govern a more heterogeneous population.

The Role of International Law

We have now suggested why the world is divided into sovereign states rather than integrated into a single global state with one world government. The next step is to introduce a role for public international law, which concerns the relations among these sovereign states.

In the abstract, one might imagine a world of sovereign states that do not interact with each other. In each state, people produce goods and services that are consumed entirely by people in the same state; no one leaves one state and visits another state, and no state (or citizen) takes actions that affect the citizens of other states. International law would play no role, other than perhaps to embody a common understanding that no state has any business interfering with what happens in other states.

The modern world is quite different. The people living in different states interact with each other in many ways, and the actions taken by one state often affect people in other states. Therein lies a range of opportunities for broader international cooperation.

International Externalities

As we will argue throughout this book, the gains from international cooperation arise primarily from the fact that actions in or by one state have implications for the well-being of citizens in other states. In such settings, we will say that actions create an *international externality*. In economic parlance, many of these externalities are *nonpecuniary,* in that they do not travel through the price system—cross-border pollution is an example. Others are *pecuniary,* in that the effect on others is felt because of a change in prices.[5] The effects of import tariffs on the prices received by foreign exporters are an example.

Economic theory suggests that international cooperation can be valuable in the presence of international externalities. The basic theoretical point can be made quite simply. Let us assume that states behave as if they have a set of preferences regarding the outcomes of their interaction. The specific assumptions that may be made in this regard are myriad and need not detain us. States may be assumed to maximize economic welfare,[6] or to maximize a social welfare function that weighs the welfare of certain constituencies more heavily than others. The preferences of the "state" may be assumed to be those of its political leaders, who may maximize votes, campaign contributions, or their personal welfare (as in the case of a dictator). Other variations can be imagined depending on the context, and the basic point to be made does not turn on any particular assumption about the nature of state preferences beyond the possibility that actions by one state may affect the perceived well-being of other states.

The assumption that states have well-defined preferences and act rationally to maximize their welfare in relation to those preferences is concededly simplistic. States represent an aggregation of many different actors, whose preferences may well be at odds. The actor with the power to choose among alternatives may change over time, and the constraints imposed on actors with the power to make choices can change over time (in the United States, think of the president as the actor with the power to make choices on international matters, subject to constraints imposed by Congress). Even when it is plausible to assume that a pertinent decision maker has a preference ordering over the available alternatives at a point in time, therefore, the notion that the "preferences" of the "state" are stable over time may be quite problematic. Although one must acknowledge this problem, it is not fatal to these sorts of simple theories. Economic analysis of international law proceeds much like other areas of economic analysis, which embrace their own simple assumptions about the objectives of corporations, bureaucracies, and other large institutions. Here, as in those other areas, the test is not whether the assumptions are fully descriptive of behavior but whether they yield useful insights with empirical purchase.

Beyond the assumption that states behave as if they have preferences, the only further key assumption is that states "care" primarily or exclusively about their own welfare or interests (or those of their own citizens) and less or not at all about the welfare or interests of other states and their citizens. The result is a divergence between the national interest and the global interest that will produce *inefficiency* in the absence of international cooperation. By inefficiency here, we mean that a state of affairs will arise without cooperation whereby all nations are worse off (in terms of their own preferences) than they could be if the externality problem were addressed through cooperation.

The basic intuition for this result is as follows, which we elaborate in a (rare, we promise) technical footnote for more technically inclined readers.[7] Consider two states (more than two would not change the basic point), and suppose that each state has control over policy instruments of some sort—trade policy, human rights policy, environmental policy, it does not matter. Let the welfare of each state be affected by the policies of the other (that is, an international externality is present). Absent cooperation, however, each state cares only about its own welfare and chooses its policy instruments to maximize its own welfare without regard to the effect on the other nation. A *noncooperative equilibrium* (sometimes called a *Nash equilibrium*) arises when each state is content with its own policy choice given the policy choice by the other.

The noncooperative equilibrium will be inefficient due to the international externality, for reasons that are most easily seen by example. Suppose that the externality is pollution that crosses the border (perhaps air pollution borne by the wind) and that the policy instrument is a pollution control measure. Each state will choose its pollution control measure in relation to the costs of pollution control and the benefits from pollution control. In particular, each will choose a level of pollution control such that the marginal benefits are equal to the marginal costs from a national perspective. In so doing, it ignores the fact that the other state also benefits from its pollution control measure. Thus, when the marginal costs of pollution control equal the marginal benefits from the national perspective, marginal costs are less than marginal benefits from a global perspective (which takes account of the additional benefit to the other nation). Accordingly, additional expenditures on pollution control will increase global economic welfare, up to the point where the marginal costs spent in each state equal the sum of the marginal benefits to both states. Absent some form of cooperation, however, the two nations have no incentive to undertake these higher levels of expenditures.

This reasoning generalizes to other types of international externalities. The broad lesson is that, in the absence of cooperation, states will do too little to abate harmful international externalities (like those associated with pollution, high tariffs or human rights violations), and cooperation to enhance measures to abate such externalities can bring mutual gains. Likewise, states will tend to engage in too little of any behavior that yields beneficial externalities (such as preserving biodiversity or rainforests), and cooperation to encourage such behavior can bring mutual gains.

Domestic Commitment

As noted, we believe that most international law may be understood as an effort to orchestrate cooperation in the face of international externalities, but that is not the only possible explanation for international law. A small literature suggests that international law is sometimes useful for states because it constrains them in ways that are valuable domestically rather than to other states.

At first blush, this proposition seem odd—if the actions of states do not affect other states through externalities, why would any state either seek or accept constraints on its behavior under international law? Constraints on behavior would seem to be a detriment, and if they are not addressing international externalities, what is the point of them?

The answer lies in the notion of a *time consistency* problem. Suppose that, at some point in time, a government wishes to pursue some course of action without fail. But it also knows that political circumstances may evolve at a subsequent point in time such that it will have difficulty sticking to its preferred course of action. It may then value international law as a hands-tying device that forces it to pursue its desired course of action.

As just one example, a new democracy, whose officials are fearful of a return to authoritarianism, might wish to enlist other states to coerce its government to remain democratic in the future. To do so, it might agree to certain democratic reforms under a human rights treaty and subject itself to a threat of external sanctions if it fails to respect them.[8]

A common difficulty with such theories, however, concerns the credibility of the sanction for deviating from international law. If the behavior that international law constrains has no adverse consequences for other nations, why would other nations expend the resources to punish it? Domestic commitment theories of international law thus require some other elements to achieve plausibility, such as the possibility that the punishment for violation is actually beneficial to states that punish.

When Is International Cooperation Possible?

The fact that international cooperation is potentially valuable does not ensure that it will occur. The checkered history of international cooperation on security matters and greenhouse gas emissions suggests how challenging it can be to achieve anything useful.

In thinking about the question of when cooperation will arise successfully, perhaps the starting point for analysis is the insights of Nobel laureate economist Ronald Coase.[9] One would expect international agreements to exhaust potential joint gains from solving externality problems only to the degree that those gains remain after all transaction costs of achieving them have been accounted for (which must be understood broadly to include not only monetary costs of achieving agreement but all factors that affect the political acceptability of agreement). To understand the universe of international agreements (and the areas in which they are absent), one must therefore ask not simply whether there are benefits to cooperation but also whether the transaction costs of international agreements to address them are low enough to permit agreements to go forward. A variety of considerations will affect the magnitude of transaction costs.

Trivially, agreement can arise only if some agreement lies in what economists term the *core* of the bargain—each state that becomes party to an agreement must perceive itself better off than by refusing to participate (or by breaking off with others into a smaller numbers agreement in the multilateral case). We also sometimes refer to this concept as the state's *participation constraint*. It is easy to imagine settings in which cooperation is potentially valuable yet where the bargaining options are too limited to allow an agreement in the core. For example, imagine two states, one of which contains a monopoly producer and exporter of widgets and the other of which is a consumer of widgets with no monopoly power over any tradable good or service. The monopolist exploits its market power with the familiar deadweight economic losses associated with monopoly,[10] although much of its monopoly profit comes as a transfer from consumers abroad. Global economic welfare would increase if each state pursued a sensible antimonopoly policy. But if the two states try to strike a bilateral agreement that merely requires each of them to adopt an antimonopoly policy, the state with the export monopolist may well object that such an agreement leaves it worse off than without it (would members of the Organization of Petroleum Exporting Countries want an enforceable agreement to end all cartels, for example?).

Two obvious and related solutions to the problem suggest themselves. The first is monetary side payments from one state to the other. This device is sometimes employed in practice, usually in the form of a promise of monetary aid to a state that cooperates on some issue (U.S. aid to Pakistan associated with its quiet assistance in Afghanistan is illustrative).

Second, and probably more common in practice, the scope of bargaining can be expanded to include other issues (or other states, a point explored later). The state that enjoys a widget monopoly may be willing to forego monopoly rents in exchange for valued concessions on security issues, environmental matters, and so on. The general lesson is that issue linkage in international negotiations can greatly expand the scope of possible agreements. A likely modern example is the Agreement on Trade Related Aspects of Intellectual Property (TRIPs) in the WTO. Developing nations, which are to a great degree consumers rather than producers of intellectual property, were induced to agree to strengthen their intellectual property laws in ways that would confer considerable rents on foreign rights holders in exchange for concessions on other trade issues, such as textiles and agriculture.

It is too optimistic, however, to imagine that either monetary side payments or issue linkage will always eliminate the problem of an empty core. Take the monopoly hypothetical above and consider the monetary side payment option. If an antimonopoly agreement is to lie in the core, the consuming state must make a monetary payment to the state with the monopolist that is large enough to induce it to give up its monopoly rents. Such a payment may leave little gain to the consuming nation in relation to the transaction costs of negotiation. As for issue linkage, an expansion in the scope of negotiations inevitably increases their cost and draws in a greater number of domestic political constituencies with an interest in the outcome. The resulting increase in the costs of international negotiation and of domestic political deliberation may be great enough to undermine the process. Nevertheless, many international agreements display a great deal of issue linkage in their formation.

Moving beyond the problem of ensuring that an agreement lies in the core, the transaction costs of reaching an international agreement turn importantly on the complexity of the issues to be addressed. Some agreements entail reasonably simple commitments (such as the ban on nuclear testing in the Nonproliferation Treaties). Others require highly complex commitments spanning a wide array of issues. The WTO is again illustrative. To make its central commitments on tariff reductions valuable, signatories must disable themselves from turning to substitute instruments of protection. The result is hundreds of pages of treaty text addressing quotas, import licensing restrictions, balance of payments policy, domestic tax and regulatory policy, state trading and monopolies, and many other subjects. Complexity can be said to increase not only as the detail involved in specifying the proper behavior of a state increases but also as the optimal behavior across states becomes more variable. Both dimensions of complexity raise the costs of agreement not only because desired behavior becomes more costly to describe and memorialize but because enforcement may become more difficult as the number and variety of possible violations multiply.

A third important factor affecting the transaction costs of reaching and enforcing an international agreement is the number of countries involved in it. Even holding constant the complexity of the commitments (which of course may increase as more states participate), greater numbers of states add to the negotiation costs of reaching agreement. Logistical costs increase because of the larger numbers, and delays may develop as states hold back on what they offer to achieve agreement, hoping to free ride on inducements offered by other states. A free rider problem may also manifest itself in the enforcement mechanism. Imagine that breach of agreement requires some action by nonbreaching parties to punish the party in breach. If these actions are costly, each state may prefer that others do the punishing, and unless some coordination mechanism can be designed to overcome the problem, the threat of punishment may lose credibility. This observation suggests an important distinction between situations in which punishment requires actions that the punishers view as costly to themselves and situations in which the opportunity to punish another state is welcomed. An example of the first may be military force. A state that employs military force risks the lives of its troops and consumes monetary resources, and most states will be happy to have others undertake the task if they can perform it as well. By contrast, imagine an environmental agreement limiting emissions of some pollutant in each state, enforced by a threat of mutual defection. Here, should another state defect, a punishing state might well benefit economically from the opportunity to defect itself, and there may be no free rider problem in enforcement.

These last observations suggest some further principles. If externality problems can be handled adequately on a bilateral basis, such arrangements will tend to be preferred to multilateral arrangements. The case for agreements involving larger numbers of states maps directly onto the case for international agreements in the first instance—multilateral cooperation is potentially desirable mainly when bilateral cooperation itself creates externalities for third states. The caveat is that if a multitude of bilateral agreements would all look about the same, it may be more economical to create one multilateral agreement that sets out the same principles in a single document.

A related point is that when bilateral or small numbers agreements create externalities, an expansion of the number of states participating in an agreement will increase not simply the costs of agreement but also the benefits. Hence, the international community may move toward large-scale multilateral agreements despite their higher cost.

Finally, not only does the number of states involved affect the costs of achieving and enforcing agreement, but the size distribution of states may also matter. In particular, the presence of a few large states may help at least on the enforcement problem. If punishment is seen as costly to the punishers, the free rider problem will be less acute when some states are large enough to capture a considerable portion of the joint gains from enforcing the agreement. It may then be in their private interest to act as enforcers even if smaller states will free-ride. This possibility suggests a constructive role in some contexts for what political scientists term a "hegemon," a powerful state that enforces its will in an environment populated by other smaller and less powerful states.

International Law as Contract

When nations come together and agree to cooperate using international law, the situation is much analogous to private actors coming together and cooperating by creating a contract. Indeed, from an economic standpoint, the international agreements that create international law are contracts, albeit between states rather than individuals. Accordingly, there are great similarities between the problem of designing an optimal contract and the problem of crafting an optimal body of international law. A few illustrations follow, and we will draw further on the contract analogy throughout this book.

International Law as an Incomplete Contract

Some areas of international law address simple matters about which optimal behavior changes little over time. But many areas address complex matters in an environment subject to uncertainty. For familiar reasons, international law in the latter category is likely to be incomplete as to certain behaviors and contingencies. States may then benefit from various devices to fill the gaps in their agreement. Specialized tribunals may supply useful default rules in some cases, as may overarching treaties on interpretation, such as the Vienna Convention on Treaties. As in the literature on default rules for private contracts, one can ask what the guiding principle should be in designing them.[11] Should they replicate what the parties would have negotiated expressly if they had addressed the matter, penalize a party that has withheld pertinent information, or something else?

The Contractibility of Desired Behavior

It is a commonplace in the literature on optimal contracting to suppose that some behavior is noncontractible, usually because the behavior in question cannot be observed by other parties, or at least cannot be verified by a court. The same class of problems arises under many international agreements regarding everything from hidden nontariff trade barriers to cheating on nonproliferation commitments. Treaties may then employ the familiar types of (generally second-best) solutions. Treaty obligations may be conditioned on verifiable behavior that is correlated with the unverifiable behavior, as in the classic principal-agent models where payoffs must be conditioned on observable outcomes rather than unobservable effort. Alternatively, provisions may be designed to encourage decision makers to internalize the externalities from their choices and thereby to eliminate the divergence between privately and socially optimal behavior.

Renegotiation, Modification, and Efficient Breach

Treaties are often negotiated under conditions of uncertainty. A variety of shocks may cause particular commitments to become inefficient or may leave some signatory worse off than it would be by exiting. Some treaties will address the problem simply by providing for a short duration,[12] or for the possibility of withdrawal,[13] normally after a period of notice (the Strategic Arms Limitation Talks [SALT] treaty, for example). But many treaties address a broad range of issues, and changed circumstances may justify only a modification of the bargain, not a complete end to it. Accordingly, treaties may contain provisions providing for the renegotiation of parts of the bargain or may specify contingencies under which states may deviate from their prior commitments. A treaty may provide that a party can breach its obligations at a price, which if set correctly can facilitate *efficient breach*—defined as a breach for which the benefits to the breaching party exceed the costs to all nonbreaching parties.

The challenge of allowing efficient adaptation to changing circumstances raises a number of interesting questions. For example, is it best to force adjustment to changing circumstances to occur through renegotiation? One difficulty here, especially in a multilateral treaty, is the problem of holdouts—states that refuse to accede to efficient changes in behavior in the hope of extracting surplus from other states. Bargaining breakdowns can occur, and efficient adaptations may be stifled. Does that problem argue for allowing breach at a "compensatory price," without the need to secure permission in advance through renegotiation? How is the price for breach to be set? These issues relate to the choice between a *property rule* and a *liability rule* to govern deviation from the original bargain.[14]

In addition to the problem of facilitating efficient adjustments to changed circumstances, treaties must confront the fact that efforts to modify the bargain may be opportunistic. In the event that a party deviates from its commitments and then offers to renegotiate, will it be in the interest of the other parties at that point in time to hold it to the original bargain, and will they have the ability to do so, or will they capitulate to new terms that extract some of their surplus? In many important contexts, therefore, a treaty designer must worry whether the agreement is *renegotiation-proof*. This problem is usually related to the presence of sunk costs (costs that cannot be recovered once incurred). After states have made sunk investments in reliance on an agreement, the returns to those investments may be vulnerable to expropriation during opportunistic renegotiation.

This is but a partial listing of the issues that international agreements must confront and that have direct parallels in optimal contracting problems. Economically oriented scholars will find many fruitful applications to international law of the ideas developed in the contract literature.

Enforcement and Dispute Resolution

States contemplating an international agreement often confront another set of problems that is absent for parties to conventional contracts. Private actors commonly rely on state enforcers to hold them to their commitments. An award of damages in contract can be enforced through a seizure of the promisor's assets or an injunction backed by threat of imprisonment. By contrast, although the use of military force and the seizure of assets are surely seen occasionally in international relations, such devices are not part of the enforcement arsenal for many international agreements. Indeed, the observation that much of international law is not backed by a credible threat of military force or other strong coercive measures has led many commentators to question whether international law is "law" at all.

Such skepticism is misplaced for at least three reasons. First, states that join international agreements can and do create international regimes where strong coercive measures are possible—witness the occasional deployment of troops after UN authorization through the years or the various episodes of UN sanctions that have affected the economic vitality of rogue states. International law should not be viewed as hopelessly weak because of a limited enforcement regime that is imposed on it exogenously. Instead, one must recognize that the choice of enforcement regime is endogenous. There is much that states can do, if they wish, to make their commitments more credible. One must therefore ask why some international legal commitments carry much greater punishments for breach than others, and whether weaker regimes of enforcement are inadequate to their task or are instead chosen precisely because nothing more is necessary.[15]

Second, governments, especially democratic governments, are constrained by public opinion, and it is possible that public opinion (or influential interest groups) care about compliance with certain international obligations or agreements.[16] For example, it is a commonplace that exporters will pressure their government to comply with trade agreements so that importing nations will not retaliate by raising tariff barriers against the exporters. What is less clear is that people or groups care about international law per se, as opposed to the various bargains that are embodied in international law. But either way, public opinion creates some pressure toward compliance with international law.

Third, although parties to private contracts can often appeal to state enforcers, in many settings they cannot. Litigation costs may swamp the benefits of an appeal to the courts when the monetary stakes are modest. Transnational contracts can confront difficult issues of securing personal jurisdiction in the event of a dispute, enforcing awards, and securing unbiased decision makers. Such problems have led economic scholars to recognize that there are valuable mechanisms for making contractual commitments credible that do not rely on the existence of a third-party enforcer with coercive powers. The term for such arrangements is a *self-enforcing agreement*.[17]

Even when these mechanisms cannot achieve the "first-best," they can often accomplish a great deal, and so too at the international level. We thus offer a brief catalog of the mechanisms that are available for the enforcement of international agreements that do not rely on the coercive powers of third-party enforcers.

Mutual Threats of Defection

International agreements that address externalities often have many of the qualities of a repeated prisoner's dilemma game.[18] Each party makes commitments that it would prefer not to make, other things being equal, in exchange for valuable commitments from others that result in mutual gains.

Consider our earlier example in which two states choose their desired level of pollution control with respect to pollution that crosses the border. Each state would like to undertake pollution control measures to the point that the marginal benefit is equal to the marginal cost from a national perspective. But such a calculus neglects the benefit of pollution control to the other state. An appropriate cooperative agreement between them requires each to increase its pollution control efforts.

This strategic environment is a prisoner's dilemma. Each state would prefer that the other state enhance its pollution control efforts in accordance with an appropriate cooperative agreement, yet each would also prefer, other things being equal, to limit its own pollution control efforts to the point that marginal benefit and marginal cost are equal from the national perspective. In other words, state 1 is better off if state 2 adheres to a cooperative agreement while state 1 cheats on its obligations. Of course, if both states cheat and the agreement falls apart, they are both worse off than they would be if both kept their commitments.

This general strategic structure is depicted in Figure 3.1.

	Player 2 Cooperate	Player 2 Defect
Player 1 Cooperate	3 / 3	1 / 4
Player 1 Defect	4 / 1	2 / 2

Figure 3.1

Each pair of numbers represents the payoffs for each player: the first number in each pair is the row player 1's payoff; the second number is the column player 2's payoffs. If both players cooperate, each receives 3, for a joint payoff of 6 (the top, left cell). If both players defect, each receives 2, for a joint payoff of 4 (the bottom, right cell). If one player tries to cooperate, but the other player defects, the defector receives 4 and the cooperator receives 1 (the remaining pairs).

In the classic prisoner's dilemma, the assumption is that each player decides what strategy to pick without any opportunity to coordinate with the other player—the analogy is to two criminal co-conspirators being interrogated in separate rooms (hence the name of the game). To understand why the parties have an incentive to defect under these conditions, take the perspective of the row player. If player 2 cooperates (the first column), player 1 receives a higher payoff from defecting (4) than from cooperating (3). If player 2 defects (the second column), player 1 again receives a higher payoff from defecting (2) than from cooperating (1). Thus, whatever player 2 does, player 1 will defect (defection is the "dominant strategy"). Player 2 faces symmetric payoffs and therefore will act identically. The players end up doing worse (receiving a payoff of 2) than they would if they cooperated (receiving a payoff of 3).

The classic prisoner's dilemma is a single-play game, however, and thus misses an important element of people's (and states') interactions: time. In the repeated prisoner's dilemma, the two agents play the game over and over again with no fixed final play. This introduces a new element: if one player defects in one round, the other can punish the first player by defecting rather than cooperating in the next round. The threat of retaliation by each agent can deter the other agent from cheating.

To see why, imagine that each player decides to play the *grim strategy,* which provides that a player cooperates in the first round and then cooperates in every later round unless the other player cheated in the immediately preceding round. If defection occurs, the first player defects in the next round and permanently thereafter. If player 2 plays this strategy, then player 1 faces the following payoffs if she also plays the grim strategy: 3, 3, 3, 3, . . . Compare now another possible strategy—cheat in every round. If player 1 plays this strategy when player 2 plays the grim strategy, she receives payoffs of 4, 2, 2, 2, . . . , because player 2 will retaliate by cheating in every round after the first. Player 1 will prefer the grim strategy as long she does not discount future payoffs too much (as long as the gain from moving the payoff from 3 to 4 in round one does not outweigh the reduced payoff from 3 to 2 in all future rounds). The same analysis shows that player 1 will prefer the grim strategy as long as she does not discount the future too much. Sustained cooperation, with each player playing the grim strategy, turns out to be a noncooperative (Nash) equilibrium of the infinitely repeated prisoner's dilemma game.

Mutual play of the grim strategy is not the only possible equilibrium, nor is cooperation a certainty. Game theory simply suggests that cooperation is possible as long as the game has no fixed ending (otherwise, defection would become a dominant strategy in the last period and cooperation would unravel from there) and that the players have low enough *discount rates* that the current gains from defection do not loom too large in relation to the long-term gains from cooperation. Some well-known empirical research suggests that the "tit-for-tat" strategy, whereby a period of defection by one party is met by a subsequent period of defection by others, can be a successful enforcement device, even if the theoretical literature notes that this strategy is not *subgame perfect.*[19]

The analysis of the two-player repeated prisoner's dilemma thus indicates that two nation states can cooperate successfully over time. The analysis can be extended to any number of players. Imagine that some large number of states—five or ten or thirty—share a body of water that contains a fishery. The states could enter a treaty that limits fishing to the sustainable yield. It is possible, theoretically, for the cooperative outcome to occur. Each state must retaliate against any state that overfishes, and also against any state that fails to retaliate against a state that overfishes, and also against any state that fails to retaliate against any state that fails to retaliate against a state that overfishes, and so on. The problem is that as the number of states increases, the information necessary to play the jointly maximizing strategy increases exponentially; at some point, it becomes unrealistic to expect that states can produce the cooperative outcome. However, it is difficult to say what this point is.

Regardless of the number of players, threats of mutual defection are more likely to sustain cooperation when defection by one party can be detected readily by others. It is also important that parties be able to agree on what constitutes defection and hence that the rules of the game be clear. Otherwise, what one party claims to be a justifiable punishment for defection by another party may itself be viewed by others as opportunistic defection.

Another important factor that aids cooperation in international agreements is absent from classic models of the prisoner's dilemma. Under the usual assumptions about the way the game is played, the parties cannot communicate with each other during a "period" of play and can discover what the other party has done only after each has made a simultaneous move. Parties to international agreements, by contrast, can remain in close communication with each other at all times. Depending on the context, any movement toward defection may be easy to detect. Indeed, any plans for defection may be public knowledge and even the subject of public debate long before defection actually occurs. Consequently, defection may become punishable more quickly. From an analytic standpoint, improved communication shortens the "periods" during which the repeated game is played and has a tendency to reduce the short-term gains from defection.

International Sanctions (Unilateral or Multilateral)

Reciprocal defection from a cooperative arrangement is not the only way for breaches of international law to be punished. A party that violates its human rights commitments, for example, might become subject to trade sanctions or even a punitive military strike. Let us thus define a *sanction* as a costly measure, other than retaliatory defection, taken by a state aggrieved by breach of international law. Sanctions may be undertaken unilaterally or in coordinated fashion by a number of states.

So defined, a key feature of sanctions is that they impose costs on the states that employ them. The strategic setting thus differs importantly from that of a repeated prisoner's dilemma, in which retaliatory defection can benefit a state after another has already defected. The question of whether to carry out a sanction under these conditions is sometimes termed the "punisher's dilemma."

Sanctions too have received considerable study, both theoretical and empirical. The theoretical literature is rather technical, and so we will provide a brief and simplified account of it. One well-known model considers a two-country framework, with one country as the "target" of sanctions and one as the "sender."[20] The sender makes a demand on the target, which can then balk or comply. If the target balks, the sender can impose a sanction that is costly both to itself and to the target. Equilibria exist in which the threat to impose the sanction succeeds and the target complies as long as discount rates are not too high. The sender's threat to impose the costly sanction is credible because a reputation for toughness is valuable to it in the future. The equilibria that sustain compliance are not "renegotiation-proof," however, as following an incident of balking it would be in the two countries' interest to forget about past transgressions, so that in the simplest case the only renegotiation-proof equilibrium is unpunished balking.

We can consider a more complex case in which compliance is a matter of degree. Renegotiation-proof equilibria then do emerge in which the threat of sanction induces some level of compliance. The degree of compliance will be greater, other things being equal, the less costly the sanction is to the sender. A high degree of compliance can be exacted if, for example, the sender can extract reparations from the target to cover the cost of the sanction. Further complications arise when there is more than one "sender" country. Depending on the distribution of costs and benefits from acting, some countries may free ride on the sanctions efforts of others, and it is possible that no country will take action.

Turning from theory to empirics, the historical efficacy of sanctions has also received considerable study. Any such study must come with an important caveat—we cannot observe sanctions that were never imposed because the mere threat of them achieved desired compliance all along, and we cannot observe cases in which sanctions were not imposed because they were perceived to be futile. Cases where they are actually employed, therefore, must represent intermediate instances where states were uncertain about their efficacy or were simply building a reputation for toughness. That said, one notable study has reviewed the use of sanctions in about 200 cases since World War I.[21] It found that sanctions succeeded about one-third of the time. Sanctions were more likely to succeed, inter alia, when the policy change sought by sanctions was relatively modest, when the sanctions were more costly to the target, and when the sanctions were less costly to the sender.

Bribes

Punishment for breach is not the only way to sustain cooperation; states might also offer bribes to induce cooperative behavior. It is often argued, for example, that developed countries should compensate developing countries for cooperation in reducing greenhouse gas emissions.

The obvious problem with bribes is that states may not wish to offer them, for a variety of reasons. Even if cooperation is valuable on balance, bribes reduce the gains from cooperation to states that pay them, and when coupled with other transaction costs of cooperation, it may become impossible to satisfy those states' participation constraints. Bribes also raise a free rider problem in a multilateral setting where it is not obvious how much any particular nation should offer.

A further concern is that in any regime where "carrots" are offered to induce cooperation, states may react strategically to extract larger "carrots."[22] Suppose that there are two "types" of potential recipients of bribes, those whose private optima in the absence of a bribe are relatively close to the desired cooperative behavior (good types) and those whose private optima in the absence of a bribe are relatively far from the desired cooperative behavior (bad types). They all signal their type by engaging in some level of the behavior in question (cutting down the rain forest, for example). A possible outcome is a "pooling equilibrium" in which the good types mimic the bad types to extract larger bribes. Such a development is potentially unfortunate, of course, because it raises the costs of securing cooperation and may lead to perverse signaling behavior that exacerbates the underlying problem.

Reputation

It is often said that states care about their reputations and that they generally avoid violating international law because they fear the reputational consequences. This view is intuitive.[23] If a state repeatedly violates its treaty obligations, why would other states bother entering new treaties with it?

In game theoretic terms, reputation refers to other states' beliefs about a particular state's *type*.[24] Suppose, for example, that some states discount the future very little ("good types") and other states discount the future a great deal ("bad types"). It is possible that a state's valuation of future payoffs reflects internal institutional arrangements that are hard for other states to observe and understand. If so, the type of a state is hidden information, which other states can infer only by observing its behavior. A state that repeatedly violates treaties reveals itself as a bad type; other states will respond by breaking off relations with it.

Why would other states care about whether the state in question discounts the future a lot? As we saw in our discussion of the repeated prisoner's dilemma, states that excessively discount the future will not cooperate. Accordingly, states that want to cooperate care about the discount rates of potential cooperative partners. Having a good reputation means being known as a cooperator, that is, a state with a low discount rate.

Concerns about reputation could explain why states comply with international law. Some interesting work shows that states go to great lengths to avoid being criticized in public, and it is hard to understand why they would care about criticism if it did not potentially weaken their ability to cooperate with other states (or possibly create doubts in the mind of the local population about the competence of their government).[25] No one really knows how important reputation is for states, however, and thus how much it accounts for compliance with international law.

There are a few reasons to be skeptical of the importance of reputation. It is unclear whether reputation for cooperation in one issue area (say, international trade) carries over to other issue areas (say, security pacts). Likewise, it is unclear whether reputation cuts across political officials either cross-sectionally or intertemporally. If the Commerce Department cheats on a trade obligation, will military allies care? If the Bush administration cheats on an environmental obligation, will anyone care later during the Obama administration?[26]

Finally, the notion that states infer the "type" of another state from past behavior seems dubious if the other state is a transparent democracy. If a state wishes to predict whether the United States will stick to its commitments under some treaty, it would be well advised to listen to speeches by U.S. officials, read the Congressional Record and the Federal Register, and generally follow proposed legislation and regulations. The notion that it learns much more from past behavior is questionable. The importance of reputation is more plausible for more autocratic, less transparent regimes.

Hostage Exchange and Bond Posting

The paradigm example of the hostage exchange involves a hypothetical peace treaty between warring kings. Each king sends a son to live in the other kingdom, with the understanding that if either king attacks the other kingdom his son will be killed. Both kings value their sons' lives more than any possible gains from aggression, and so peace is sustained. A possible difficulty with the hostage exchange mechanism, of course, is that the reciprocal threats to the hostages may not be credible. It may not be in the interest of the king who is attacked to kill the attacker's son, for example, if he knows that his own son will then be killed.

The exchange of human hostages threatened with death is rather unseemly by modern standards, of course, and we do not observe it in international agreements. But analogous situations may arise, as when foreign nationals or their assets travel and become subject to the jurisdiction of other states. When such movements are reciprocal, a situation akin to a hostage exchange may arise implicitly—perhaps the modern rules of ambassadorial immunity are sustained through such a mechanism.

A related mechanism is bond posting. Each party posts a bond that is large enough to exceed its potential gains from cheating on the agreement. Should cheating occur, the bond is forfeited. Compliance with the agreement then becomes an equilibrium as long as cheating will be detected with sufficient probability in relation to the size of the bond. Bond posting differs from hostage exchange in that it generally relies on a third-party arbiter to determine whether breach of agreement exists, but the arbiter need not possess any coercive powers beyond the capacity to declare that one party has forfeited its bond to another. If the arbiter is trusted by all parties, and they cannot interfere with the exercise of the arbiter's authority, then a bond posting mechanism can do quite well in encouraging compliance. Interestingly, formal bond posting arrangements seem quite rare in international law, perhaps in part because of the challenges of finding a trustworthy neutral arbiter.

Dispute Resolution as an Information Revelation Mechanism

All of the enforcement devices noted above rely on the ability of states to detect violations of international agreements. Sometimes violations are obvious, as when a nuclear test occurs within the territory of a signatory to a nonproliferation treaty. But sometimes violations are surreptitious, and in other cases disagreement may arise over what constitutes a violation. In response, a number of devices may be employed to improve on the information possessed by parties to an international agreement.

If violations are surreptitious, a need may arise for investigators to examine suspected violations or to conduct routine inspections for compliance. Parties may place greater confidence in neutral investigators who are not linked to disputants, and a role for an institution with independent investigators may emerge. UN weapons inspectors and WTO dispute panels are useful illustrations of this possibility.

Even in cases where pertinent behavior is observable by other states without investigators, a mechanism may be needed to resolve factual and legal disputes regarding alleged violations. None of the mechanisms outlined above can work well unless states know whether observed conduct is compliant or deviant. Here, a role emerges for a formal tribunal to conduct legal analysis. Related, it may be valuable for violations to be publicized extensively. Tribunals and their decisions, if public, can also serve this role. Requirements for centralized reporting of violations, even in the absence of a tribunal, can serve a valuable publicity function.

Pure Coordination Problems

Not all interactions among states are repeated prisoner's dilemmas. A few have the structure of a repeated *coordination game*. The standard example is the driving game, depicted in Figure 3.2.

		Player 2	
		Left	Right
Player 1	Left	1 / 1	0 / 0
	Right	0 / 0	1 / 1

Figure 3.2

Imagine that no traffic laws govern the roads in a particular area. Drivers approach each other and must decide whether to pass on the left or pass on the right. If each driver chooses right, they pass safely and receive payoffs of 1. If each driver chooses left, again they pass safely and receive payoffs of 1. But if they fail to coordinate, they crash and receive payoffs of zero.

The game has two equilibria: both parties passing on the right and both parties passing on the left.[27] If player 2 plays left, player 1 can do no better than play left. If player 2 plays right, player 1 can do no better than play right. It is not obvious how the norm gets started in the first place, but once it gets started, it should be stable.

Coordination games are not extensive in international law, but a few types of interaction may involve coordination problems. When the cooperation problem involves nothing more than the selection of a compatibility standard, for example, such as railroad gauges, fax machine protocols, television broadcast standards, or units of measurement, the strategic setting is mainly that of a coordination game.[28] If states have little difficulty informing each other of the standard that they will employ before the game begins, and when states are essentially indifferent among the options as in the driving game, a stable cooperative choice should result. States sometimes incorporate these compatibility standards in treaties. The treaties are robustly self-enforcing; once states agree on a particular standard, no state has an interest in deviating.

Some compatibility issues become quite thorny, however, when states have preferences over the different possible standards and are not simply interested in achieving coordination. If state A's nationals have a patent on standard 1, while state B's nationals have a patent on standard 2, for example, the states may sacrifice coordination and its attendant efficiencies to appease their own constituents. The history of incompatible broadcast television standards is illustrative.[29]

II

General Aspects of International Law

4

Sovereignty and Attributes of Statehood

As discussed in Chapter 2, states are the primary agents in international law. They make international law and they thereby create for themselves the legal obligation to comply with international law. In this way, states bear the same relationship to international law that persons bear to domestic law. But states are different from persons in many ways. The very nature of a state—whether a particular group of people who live in a territory compose a state or not—can be ambiguous. States, unlike persons (but like domestic corporations), can break up and have successors, who inherit some of the predecessor's legal rights and obligations. These peculiar features of states are the subject of this chapter.

Sovereignty

Sovereignty is a vexed term that incites passions on all sides. It has a core meaning in international law but in practice is used in many ways.

If you recall our discussion of the state, you will remember that a state consists of a territory with a significant and permanent population and with a government that has the capacity to conduct international relations.[1] *Sovereignty* refers to this independence, and so, roughly, being a state is the same thing as having sovereignty. A sovereign state controls its territory, which means that no other state or entity has a right to exert control on that same territory.

One might think of sovereignty, then, as analogous to a person's basic right to control over his or her body. Without ever losing control of one's body, one can enter contracts and become liable for failing to act as promised. Note that the law almost never forces people to keep their promises by performing a particular physical action—in this sense, one never loses control over one's body (except if one commits a crime).

Similarly, sovereignty exists even when states enter treaties. Normal treaties do not result in a loss of sovereignty even though the state promises to act in some way. States retain the ultimate right to bar people from their territory even if those people simply want to collect assets that the state owes them as a result of a treaty or other legal obligation.

States can lose their sovereignty in a number of ways. If a state is conquered and annexed, it no longer has sovereignty—even if the conquest is illegal. If a state merges with another state, then both states lose their sovereignty and are replaced by a new sovereign state consisting of the formerly independent states. Sometimes, a state can endure without sovereignty: when Kuwait was conquered by Iraq in 1991, the world insisted that Kuwait continued to exist as a state because it did not recognize the conquest; but it would have been odd to say that Kuwait remained sovereign since its people no longer controlled the territory.

Governments frequently use the term sovereignty in a more capacious sense, to refer to a more general claim to noninterference. One state might try to influence another state in many ways: by trading with it, by beaming radio broadcasts into it, by condemning it in international gatherings, by eavesdropping on leaders' telephone conversations. The government of the state at the receiving end of these efforts may complain of interference with its sovereignty—referring here to the ways that one state can exert influence over the population and territory of another state by using methods short of an actual border trespass. But international law does not generally recognize these activities as violations of sovereignty in the legal sense. If someone scolds you for eating fatty foods, you might resent his interference and tell him to mind his own business, but he hasn't broken any law. So it is with states.

States sometimes decline to join international organizations on the ground that these organizations can make rules and issue orders that would violate the states' sovereignty. Sometimes they swallow their pride and join anyway. In these discussions, the narrow and broader meanings of sovereignty are often mixed. One can reasonably say that all states except the five permanent members of the Security Council lost some sovereignty when they joined the United Nations. The UN charter gives the Security Council the power to order military attacks on other states, and at least in theory, such states have no legal right to resist authorized incursions on their territory. Because the five permanent members have vetoes, they take no such risk. One might say that a state loses sovereignty when it joins the UN charter because of this theoretical loss of power even though it is never likely to occur. The loss of sovereignty is limited, moreover; the state remains supreme with respect to all other activities on its territory. The merging of states into the European Union has the same quality.

The notion that sovereignty is lost in these instances must be qualified, however, by the fact that membership in such organizations is voluntary. Thus, whatever "loss of sovereignty" attends accession, the attendant benefits of accession are presumably great enough to offset the costs (at least in the eyes of the government officials who control that decision). Otherwise, states would not accede. As long as those government officials act in accordance with the national interest, therefore, the loss of sovereignty is not an objection to membership.

Where does this leave us? Sovereignty means that states have an obligation not to interfere with each other's affairs. In the narrowest sense firmly incorporated in the law, this principle means that states cannot send people or things onto the territory of other states without permission. States that do so violate the law. In the broader sense, states cannot seek to influence policies, especially the internal policies, of other states, with threats, or other forms of interference, or by trying to work around the government (supporting insurgents or the political opposition or the like). Usually, when a state violates the sovereignty of another state, one can identify a particular rule of international law that has been violated—for example, the rule prohibiting the use of military force. Thus, the accusation that a state has violated the sovereignty of another state is usually redundant, another way of saying that the state has violated a rule of international law in such a way that impinges on the victim state's control over its territory.

What accounts for the centrality of sovereignty? As we discussed in Chapter 3, the world could be organized in other ways. There could be a single world government, or there could be overlapping jurisdictions, as existed in the Middle Ages. As we explained, the most plausible explanation for the persistence of the state system in modern times is that the world population as a whole is too diverse and spread out to be amenable to effective government. If the world population is to be divided into pieces, then the natural way to do so is along territorial lines (rather than, say, religious or ethnic lines), because the most valuable cooperative activities like trade, agriculture, and manufacturing are generally spatially confined. If states could have control over each other, then populations in one state could make decisions that predominantly affect other people, which would create externalities and conflict.

Recognition of States

States have traditionally exercised the prerogative to recognize or to refuse to recognize other states. Recall our definition of a state: it implies that whenever you can identify a self-governing population in a defined territory that is not subject to rule by some superior political entity, a state exists. On one theory—known as the *declarative theory*—a state indeed exists in such circumstances.[2]

Other states, however, can refuse to recognize that state, which as a practical matter just means that they do not do business with that state, or at least they pretend not to. Under the *constitutive theory,* a state legally comes into existence only when a sufficient number of other states recognize it as such.[3] No state has a right under international law to demand recognition from other states.[4] Recognition is a matter of foreign policy rather than law.

A few examples will help clarify the distinction. In 1991, Croatia declared independence from Yugoslavia. Germany quickly recognized Croatia as a state. Under the declarative theory, Germany's recognition did not cause Croatia to become a state; it just meant that Germany would establish relations with Croatia, whether or not it was really a state. Other states regarded Croatia as a renegade province of Yugoslavia, to be returned to the fold in due course. Under the constitutive theory, Croatians could declare themselves independent until blue in the face, but Croatia was not a state until a sufficient number of other states recognized it as such.

An unusual example is Vatican City and its government, the Holy See. Vatican City possesses only 0.44 square kilometers of territory and has a population of less than 1,000.[5] Yet it receives ambassadors from other states and has entered treaties with other states.[6] Scholars have justified the legal status of the Vatican on various grounds, but the real reason the Vatican is a state or quasi-state is that other states have policy reasons to treat it as such.

Taiwan presents another unusual case. In 1949, the nationalists of China, led by Chiang Kai-shek, fled mainland China for Taiwan. The communists under Mao took control of the mainland. The United States treated the nationalists as the true government of China, so that, in effect, the mainland was just lost territory controlled (for the time being) by an insurgency. Eventually, the United States could not ignore Mao's China, the People's Republic, and established diplomatic relations with it. For Mao, *Taiwan* was the renegade province. The two states—the United States and China (the People's Republic)—entered into an agreement under which the United States recognized a single China governed by the communist government and China agreed not to take over Taiwan by force but instead to wait for a peaceful reincorporation into the Chinese state.

This deal rested on a fiction, and it created an anomalous situation. Henceforth, Taiwan was no longer a state—it was just a province of China, just as Illinois is a part of the United States. It was no longer a state because other states refused to recognize it as a state. But, of course, Taiwan remained a self-governing entity—a state under the declarative theory and a not-quite state under the constitutive theory. The United States and other countries have continued to maintain relations with Taiwan, so it is a state in fact but not in law.

These fictions can give rise to tricky problems. If the nationalist government of China entered a treaty back in the 1960s that the communist government did not enter, should we consider Taiwan a party to that treaty, or not? There is no definitive answer here; states work through these problems as they arise. Depending on the situation, other states might think it in their interest to consider the treaty valid or invalid.[7]

The distinction between the declarative and constitutive theory makes little difference in practice. When a self-governing population in a defined territory that is not subject to rule by some superior political entity comes into existence, the question boils down to whether some other state continues to claim control over it or not. If not, then other states will recognize the new state because the state offers a market for foreign exports, or resources, or territory from which military operations can be launched, and if other states want to obtain the benefit of these opportunities, they will have to recognize the state first so that they can deal with it through its government. This new state may not be optimal from an economic perspective—it may be too small or too large or badly shaped—but no entity has the power or interest in ensuring that all states have an optimal size and shape. Here we see an externality problem: it might be easier for other states to cooperate with a few large states than a lot of small states, but the people who decide to break up a state have no incentive to take into account these costs. Other states will try to influence the process with bribes and threats of military force, but it will be difficult for them to cooperate, and free riding is likely to prevent them from ensuring that breakups occur only in the optimal conditions along the optimal lines.

If another state claims control over the territory in question, then other states must decide whether they place a greater value on a possible cooperative relationship with the putative new state or on the maintenance of a relationship with the state that claims control, a relationship that may be disrupted if the new state is recognized. These are policy questions that, in practice, are not governed by international law. The sorts of nationalist and economic forces that cause states to break apart and reform can rarely be controlled by other states, and so little attempt has been made to formulate laws limiting the recognition of states that could address the externality problems described above.

Recognition of Governments

All states have governments, which consist of institutions—legislatures, courts, and so forth—that manage the state, that is, that regulate the people who live in the state and adopt policy toward other states. We distinguish "government" and "governments": a successful state has a continuous government, in the sense of a set of institutions that regulate it; but particular governments come and go. In the United States, we generally identify the government with the president (for example, the Obama administration, the Bush administration). In some countries, the government refers to the party or coalition of parties with a majority in parliament; this party or coalition of parties governs the state. Governments turn over because people tire of their leaders or their leaders die or retire; yet in any successful state, continuity is maintained. Governments generally honor the commitments of earlier governments; that makes it possible for the state to act in the long term—to make promises (for example, to pay back a long-term loan) without which other countries or people might be reluctant to act in ways that benefit the state (for example, by lending money to it).

All of this is important for domestic law and is usually thought to be an aspect of internal or constitutional organization. But government matters for international law. When a state (that is, the government of a state) wants to enter a treaty with another state, it must know who to deal with; it must be able to identify the government and the relevant officials—the head of state, the foreign minister, an ambassador, whomever. If the U.S. government seeks to enter a treaty with China, it must talk to the Chinese government. Only that government can enter a treaty that binds China and hence succeeding Chinese governments. If a Chinese person attacks a U.S. tourist, the consequences under international law are different if the Chinese person is a government official (a possible international law violation) and if the person is a private citizen (probably not an international law violation).

We will discuss later—under the topic of state responsibility—how one knows whether a state acts or not for international law purposes. For present purposes, one should understand that a government at time 1 binds the government at time 2 under virtually all circumstances. This can sometimes seem unfair. Suppose that the first government borrows an enormous amount of money from foreign governments and banks and then squanders that money on an ill-conceived project or luxuries for government officials. International law says that the second government must pay back the debt, even though this means taxing people who did not benefit from the loan.

The legal explanation for this rule is that the first government acted merely as an agent for the state. The state at time 1 and the state at time 2 are the same entity. So the same state repays the loan as it takes out initially. The same rule applies to domestic corporations, but here the rule does not have harsh results because people can always choose not to be shareholders of corporations; one rarely has a choice whether to belong to a state. But if governments could not act as agents of the state and hence bind future governments, then international law would not be possible. This is what happens when treaties are ratified and customary international law develops. Most states, most of the time, do borrow funds for good reasons, and so if they could escape repaying just because the government turns over, creditors would not lend in the first place, and so governments would be deprived of needed capital. And although some people have argued that governments should not be bound to loans used for bad purpose by earlier authoritarian regimes, this doctrine—known as the doctrine of odious debt—has not caught on. We will talk about this rule in Chapter 11

Just as states can choose whether to recognize other states or not, they can choose to recognize other governments or not. The China/Taiwan problem offers a useful illustration. As noted above, before the United States entered diplomatic relations with mainland China, the United States officially regarded the territory of China—both mainland and Taiwan—as the territory of a single state. However, it recognized the nationalists in Taiwan, not the communists in Beijing, as the government of China. This mattered. If the United States needed to enter a treaty with China, it had to go to the Taiwanese government. But because the Taiwanese government had no power over the mainland, the United States could not effectively enter a treaty that affected what happened on the mainland. As mainland China became more and more powerful, this state of affairs could not endure. If the United States needed the people on the mainland to act in a certain way—to respect American intellectual property rights, for example—it would have to deal with the people who control them, the communist party government located in Beijing.

The United States—and most other countries—did not recognize the Taliban as the government of Afghanistan. The Taliban came to power in a civil war in the 1990s and governed most of Afghan territory prior to the U.S.-led invasion after the 9/11 attack. Most countries refused to recognize the Taliban government because they objected to the harshness of its rule and its relationship with Al Qaida. They hoped that by withholding aid, trade, and the other benefits of international cooperation, they could either pressure the Taliban to change its policies or encourage another, more humane and cooperative, government to come to power. Saudi Arabia, the United Arab Emirates, and Pakistan did recognize the Taliban. This gave them an advantage: they could cooperate with the Afghan government while other countries could not.

The countries that refused to recognize the Taliban government did recognize Afghanistan as a state. The Kurds would like to have their own state and, in some areas, have a government, but other countries refuse to recognize a Kurdish government and a Kurdish state. The difference in the two settings is that where a state is recognized, other countries imply that they will wait until a government is formed before doing business with the state; in the meantime, however, they will not claim sovereignty over the territory of that state. They will ignore it rather than interfere with it.

Other examples can be cited. The United States refused to recognize the communist government of Russia after 1917 because that government refused to comply with certain international legal obligations of the predecessor government. Refusal to recognize seems like an abstraction, but in practice it means refusal to trade, lend, and engage in other cooperative endeavors—it is a form of economic sanctioning. The United States subsequently recognized the Soviet government when the policy of isolation was no longer sustainable. After the military intervention in Libya in 2011, a split arose among states that recognized the rebel government and those that did not. The choice came down not to law but to whether one expected the rebel government to prevail. Early recognition (which means withdrawal of recognition of the Gaddafi government) both improves the rebels' chances of success and may bring with it rewards if the rebel government comes to power, but the risk is that Gaddafi's government will prevail and then refuse to do business with states that threw their support to the rebels.

The recognition of governments, like the recognition of states, is mostly a matter of policy. But in some quarters one finds a claim that states may recognize a government only if that government meets certain criteria—chiefly, that it obeys human rights.[8] We see here an attempt to formalize the sorts of considerations that caused many states not to recognize the Taliban as the government of Afghanistan. But in reality states cannot afford to withhold recognition from governments that violate human rights. Except in extreme cases, it is too important to be able to cooperate with other states, even those with harsh, authoritarian governments—and, indeed, many, perhaps most governments are authoritarian and pretty harsh. A climate treaty, for example, will not succeed unless China and Russia—two states with harsh, authoritarian governments—participate. The West also needs these countries to help contain North Korea and Iran. Withholding recognition of governments that enjoy the loyalty of the local population, or at least are able to control them, is a luxury that states cannot afford.

Nonetheless, we can understand the popular view that governments should not recognize governments that do not comply with human rights or even governments that are not democratic. The idea here is that every state cares at least a little about the political structure in other states. This concern may be based on pragmatic considerations (for example, the view that democracies do not fight other democracies) or altruistic ideals (for example, people in countries with good governments will be better off). States that take this view face a collective action problem. To overcome the collective action problem, they may seek to create an international rule that denies recognition to governments that violate human rights. The problem is that merely creating a rule does not overcome the collective action problem but instead defers it to the question of enforcement. We will discuss this issue in more detail in Chapter 14.

Succession

Governments succeed each other routinely; states, less so. State succession occurs in the relatively unusual situation where an existing state breaks apart or sheds a territory whose people form a state. The major causes of state succession in our times have been the collapse of empires: the Austro-Hungarian, Russian, and Ottoman empires during and after World War I; the French, British, Dutch, and Portuguese empires after World War II. The Spanish empire had collapsed much earlier, in the nineteenth century. Each empire left in its wake a rump state—the former imperial master—and dozens of shards, states thrown together from the tribes that formerly had been ruled, though in some cases the empires left behind relatively coherent states—the United States, Canada, Australia, South Africa, New Zealand.

More recent years have witnessed the collapse of the Soviet Union—an empire itself, which emerged from the ashes of the Russian empire. In 1990–1991, the Soviet Union broke into Russia, Armenia, Azerbaijan, Belarus, Estonia, Georgia, Kazakhstan, Kyrgyzstan, Latvia, Lithuania, Moldova, Tajikistan, Turkmenistan, Ukraine, and Uzbekistan. At roughly the same time, Yugoslavia broke into Serbia, Croatia, Slovenia, Bosnia-Herzegovina, and Macedonia; Serbia then lost Montenegro and Kosovo.[9] Meanwhile, Czechoslovakia split into the Czech Republic and Slovakia; Eritrea separated from Ethiopia; and East Timor left Indonesia. Table 4.1 provides an overview of the new states that have emerged over the last forty years.

States also merge and expand through conquest. The North American former colonies that joined into the United States merged consensually. Some states form through a combination of the two—Germany and Italy are examples. The merger and breakup of states remind us that states are not natural units but human creations. People living in a state can gain from merger with another state because merger creates a larger internal market and other public goods; but people living in large states often chafe at the demands of the central government, believing it unable or unwilling to take seriously their interests.

Table 4.1. Recent Successions

Year	Successor State(s)	Original State	Notes
2011	South Sudan	Sudan	Civil war followed by referendum
2002	East Timor	Indonesia	Civil war
1993	Eritrea	Ethiopia	Civil war
1992	Czech Republic and Slovak Republic	Czechoslovakia	Consensual
1991	Serbia and Montenegro, Slovenia, Croatia, Macedonia, Bosnia-Herzegovina, etc.	Yugoslavia	Civil war
1991	Ukraine, Turkmenistan, etc.	USSR	Consensual
1990	Namibia	South Africa	Consensual
1971	Bangladesh	Pakistan	Civil war

The fluidity of the state is a problem for international law, where the state is the primary agent. If state X belongs to a treaty, and then the state breaks up into states A and B, what happens next? Can states A and B claim that the treaty is void because they did not "consent" to it? If not, how are the obligations divided between A and B?

International law provides few answers to these questions. In practice, other states renegotiate treaties and other obligations with the successor states, A and B in this example. If state X had debt, then the debt will be divided between A and B, on the basis of population, territory, or some other measure of relative wealth or power. If a treaty affects the territory of just A and not B, then only A will remain a party. In practice, states remain in treaties because those treaties serve their interests. This is true even though international law allows for a "clean slate" rule for newly independent states,[10] pursuant to which successor states are not obliged to remain a party to treaties of the predecessor state. However, this theory has not really prevailed. If X had a reason to belong to a treaty, then chances are that its successors will as well. Successor states that use the breakup of their predecessor as an excuse for not repaying debts incurred by the predecessor for the benefit of the general population, including people living in the successor states, will have trouble finding creditors in the future. Moreover, because most treaties allow parties to withdraw, or are interpreted to do so even if not, the successors can terminate their obligations if they do not want to retain them. So what seems like a huge problem for international law turns out to be not much of a problem at all.

There is an important lesson here. The "clean slate" doctrine is a problem only in a world in which states are anxious to evade their legal responsibilities and will do so at the first chance given to them. But that is not how international relations work. States enter treaties and remain in them only when doing so advances their interests. The reason that states pay their debts is not that there is a legal obligation to do so. States pay their debts because if they did not, they would be shut out of the credit market in the future. Thus, if a state had an interest in entering a treaty, its successor or one of its successors usually will have an interest in staying in that treaty, whatever its formal legal obligations.

5

Customary International Law

One of the two main sources of international law is custom, the other being treaties. Customary international law is defined as the "general and consistent practice of states followed by them from a sense of legal obligation."[1] Before we examine this definition, we should make some general comments about the function of customary international law.

States often appear to observe rules of law even when no treaty supplies them. This type of behavior occurs today, but the easiest examples to understand come from the past; today, most of these norms of customary international law have been codified in treaties. Here are some examples:

- Ambassadorial immunity: The ambassador may not be charged with a crime, or in any way harassed or harmed. She must be given protection. If she does something wrong, the only remedy is expulsion from the country and declaring her persona non grata.
- Freedom of the seas: No state may exercise jurisdiction over the high seas. All vessels, of whatever nationality, may travel on the high seas without obstruction from foreign naval or coast guard vessels, with narrow exceptions.
- The territorial sea: States may exercise jurisdiction over the area of the seas near their coasts. They may, for example, forbid ships to carry contraband in that area and can stop and search them.
- Protection of foreign property: A state may not seize the property of an alien unless pursuant to generally applicable law, which requires that the seizure is for a public purpose, is not discriminatory, and adequate compensation is paid.[2]
- Laws of war: Enemy soldiers who surrender may not be slaughtered. The flag of truce may not be used as a subterfuge to conceal an attack, though other forms of trickery (for example, ambushes) are permitted.

Many more examples could be given. As noted above, these rules have made their way into treaties and so nowadays one would look first to treaties rather than at customary international law to resolve disputes over these issues. However, treaties are often vague, and then customary international law might come into play, and sometimes the relevant states have not ratified the relevant treaties, in which case again customary international law applies.

How can we make sense of these rules of customary international law? Why would states, which normally act in their self-interest, agree to rules that seem to provide for the common good? And if states can agree to customary rules that provide for the common good, why are they so limited? The laws of war, for example, provide rather minimal protections, so although they might be better than nothing, they could certainly go further. And, finally, if states can follow rules of law that are not set out in treaties, then why bother to draft treaties in the first place?

To answer these questions, let us focus on the rule of ambassadorial immunity. Start by recalling that states have sovereignty: they can refuse to permit foreigners on their soil. Consider a hypothetical story about, say, France and Spain, that takes place in the distant past. The two countries share a border. They have not had friendly relations, but the governments of both states come to realize that they would do better if they could maintain peace, and permit trade and migration, than if they continue hostilities. They begin by exchanging ambassadors. The function of the ambassador is to serve as a representative of a foreign government. Once an ambassador is in place, constructive interaction between the states becomes easier. This was particularly true before the invention of telegraphs, telephones, and the other machinery of modern communication, but it remains true today. The ambassador from France, who resides in Madrid, can help resolve disputes between traveling merchants from France and the government of Spain—for example, when the merchants inadvertently break a law they do not understand. The French ambassador can also explain to the King of Spain what the French government wants and needs—for example, return of prisoners of war, or extradition of escaped criminals, or access across Spain's territory. The Spanish ambassador can do the same thing with respect to the French government. Of course, for all this to work, the ambassador must reside on foreign territory, normally in the capital city so that he or she is close to government officials.

The exchange of ambassadors is evidently in the joint interest of the two states: each state is better off than it would be if the ambassadors were not exchanged, because the ambassadors facilitate various types of cooperative arrangements. For this system to work, it is important that each government respect the person and possessions of the foreign ambassador. One might wonder why a government would not do so, given the advantages of having a foreign ambassador on one's territory, but there are many reasons why a government might be tempted to detain or harm a foreign ambassador or fail to protect him. Suppose, for example, the foreign ambassador commits espionage and has some secret documents in his possession. Or he causes a car accident and kills someone. Or his government has committed some outrage against the honor of the state and a mob is baying for revenge. In the old days, a government might respond to a hostile communication from a foreign country by lopping off the ambassador's head and impaling it on a pike. But if a state cannot commit to protect ambassadors, then other states will not send over their ambassadors onto the territory of the first state, and the advantages of ambassadorial exchange will not be obtained.

The exchange of ambassadors is just one of many examples of the ways that states can gain by cooperating with each other. States can also enjoy mutual gains by protecting each other's citizens and respecting their property, keeping out of each other's territorial seas, and much else. Cooperation is always advantageous, but it is not always possible. If states act in their national interests, then one might think that they will harass ambassadors when that is useful for them, and thus that they will not exchange ambassadors in the first place. The states must somehow promise or agree to give ambassadors immunity—and that means protecting them from mobs and declining to harass them. Because of the risk that criminal process can be abused, states have also promised not to prosecute ambassadors suspected of crimes; instead, they can only be expelled. But why do states keep these promises?

The answer is that states that do not keep their promises and follow the rules risk retaliation from states that are harmed by their actions.[3] In narrow, two-state interactions, this process is easy to understand. If France harms Spain's ambassador, then Spain might harm France's ambassador—who is on site, after all—or take some other action against France, including declaring war. If France expropriates the property of a Spanish citizen, then Spain might expropriate the property of a French citizen. Or, also bad for France, people from Spain might stop making investments in France. If France and Spain are at war, and France harms POWs from Spain, then Spain might harm POWs from France. If French vessels fish in Spain's territorial sea, then Spain might encourage local vessels to fish in France's territorial sea.

The norms of customary international law can be understood as the rules that describe the cooperative behavior of states in the absence of a treaty. The absence of a treaty can make it hard to figure out the content of these rules but the process resembles common law reasoning. Suppose that Spain arrests the French ambassador's son for drunk driving. Does that violate the rule of ambassadorial immunity? If there is relevant precedent—suppose that in the past France and Spain extended ambassadorial immunity to the ambassador's family—then France will cite this precedent and argue that Spain has broken the rules. The implicit consequence is that France will act likewise and Spain will lose protection for its ambassador's family. If there is no relevant precedent, then Spain's behavior will help set it. In future, France may arrest family members of Spain's ambassador in similar circumstances, citing Spain's prior behavior. In this way, precedents are built up, rules are induced, and with the passage of time, cooperation can be smooth and easy. The limits of ambassadorial immunity—whether it extends to the ambassador's family, or his secretary, or his staff, or foreign workers at the embassy—will be determined by the states, and the limits will reflect their joint interest. It may be the case that states do not trust each other, in which case they are likely to limit immunity to a small group of people; otherwise, they might be willing to assume that the foreign state will ensure that its entourage does not commit crimes or cause other problems, in which case broad immunity will be granted.

This type of analysis is repeated over and over between pairs of states. Because most states benefit in similar ways from exchanges of ambassadors, the customs that emerge between one pair of states likely mirror the customs that emerge between other pairs of states. When this happens, states can look at other state pairs for precedents, and gradually the norm of customary international law comes to be seen as universal rather than as bilateral. At the same time, because the interests and needs of states constantly change, it is predictable that the customs will vary at the margin, both over time and between states, and so the universal norms of ambassadorial immunity might form a relatively small core that is constant across states—while a penumbra of other rules apply as between some states and not others.

Similar stories can be told about the other rules. Cooperation is possible because states fear retaliation if they break the rules. But cooperation is limited because the sanction is weak. Self-help—the refusal to keep a promise that the other side does not keep—does not always work. We should add that customary international law norms will always be efficient as between the states that adopt them, in the sense that cooperative activity will always generate a surplus that makes each state better off. But cooperation between two states may harm a third state, so it would be wrong to say that customary international law is always efficient taking into account all countries.[4] In addition, the norms agreed to by states will not necessarily be superior to possible alternative norms, and so states may gain by negotiating treaties that supersede existing norms of customary international law.

State Practice and Consent

Let us return to the definition of customary international law: "Customary international law results from a general and consistent practice of states followed by them from a sense of legal obligation."[5] The state practice requirement refers to the actual conduct of state; the consent or *opinio juris* requirement refers to the attitude of the state. Both of these criteria have given commentators no end of trouble.

Let us use as our example the norm of customary international law at issue in the Paqueta Habana,[6] a case decided by the U.S. Supreme Court in the wake of the Spanish-American war. The U.S. navy had seized two coastal fishing vessels as prizes in that war. Under the laws of war that existed at the time, navies could seize both naval warships and private merchant ships and sell them at auctions, with proceeds distributed in part to the crew. These rules no doubt simply reflected military practice. In an era when it was difficult to raise capital to pay for navies during wartime, states would reward sailors with loot so that wages could be kept meager. Yet the owners of the fishing vessels argued that a norm of customary international law protects coastal fishing vessels from the prize system. What was special about coastal fishing vessels? Unlike foreign naval vessels, they pose no threat to one's naval forces. And unlike foreign deep-sea fishing vessels owned by commercial operations, they were most likely to be owned and operated by ordinary fishermen, a "poor and industrious" class of people, according to the Supreme Court. The exception for coastal fishing vessels, then, was designed to protect ordinary people from some of the brutality of war—it was the type of humanitarian rule that would become more common with the ratification of the Geneva Conventions later in the twentieth century.

But the norm asserted by the owners of the vessels could be a rule of international law only if it satisfied the state consent and state practice requirements. The owners had to prove that states in fact recognized the norm as a rule of customary international law.

To address this question, the court surveyed hundreds of years of history, focusing on treaties, the decisions of domestic courts, authoritative statements issued by governments, and the writings of scholars. It concluded that the alleged norm existed. Of course, there was no relevant treaty in this case. Such a treaty would have had to be ratified by the United States and Spain, and it would have needed to contain the rule protecting coastal fishing vessels. But the fact that the United States had entered treaties with the coastal fishing vessel norm with other states (such as Prussia) at least showed that the United States had, from time to time, believed that such a norm might make sense, as did the fact that other states had entered such treaties with each other. As we noted earlier, states often have similar interests, and evidence that their interests converge in certain respects can be found in their earlier practices, including the practices of entering treaties. All states go to war from time to time; those wars often involve naval battles; the coastal fishing vessel exception to the prize system in various treaties showed that many states believe that, on balance, they gain more from the exception (their own citizens are protected from the depredations of the enemy) than they lose (their own sailors will not have access to this type of plunder). If some states have these interests and can cooperate in this respect, then maybe it is true for all states, including the United States.

This type of reasoning, nowhere spelled out in the Paqueta Habana but everywhere implicit, applies to other types of evidence as well. If domestic courts of various countries have released coastal fishing vessels to their owners, then those courts must believe that the coastal fishing vessel exception serves the interests of their states. If foreign governments announce that they will abide by this exception, then they must believe the same. If foreign states not only say that they will not seize coastal fishing vessels but also in fact refrain from seizing coastal fishing vessels, then the inference that this rule reflects their interests is that much stronger. The fact that the United States had, at various times, engaged in this practice must have further impressed the justices.

This type of reasoning should be familiar. In our everyday lives, we similarly try to figure out what the customs and norms are, and we do so by observing how other people talk and behave. If you start a new business, you will want to know what is customary—for example, whether you should perform "extras" (extra work not specified in the contract) free of charge or only for compensation. To learn what is customary, you can ask people, of course, but these people know what is customary only because they have observed the custom. Custom can be inferred from practice and words. Practice alone is not enough because sometimes people do things for reasons other than custom. Some people might perform extras for free not because that is customary but because they want to distinguish themselves from what is customary—to offer a better service in order to attract customers.

Consent

Customary law requires not only a regularity in behavior but a sense that this regularity reflects a general norm to which states have consented. In standard doctrine, the consent idea usually refers to the verbal description by a state of its motives for complying with a rule. In the Paqueta Habana, the Supreme Court noted that although the British navy had in certain conflicts adopted a policy of not seizing coastal fishing vessels, the British government said that this policy was adopted as a matter of "comity" rather than "law."[7] The government in this way announced that it did not recognize, or "consent" to, a legal norm protecting coastal fishing vessels even though in a particular military conflict it chose not to seize those vessels. Why make such a distinction? The British government must have believed that refraining from seizing coastal fishing vessels would not always be in its interest—even if other states reciprocated—and so giving such a norm the force of law could undermine its interests in the future. In the particular war or wars in question, the government may have believed that naval resources were better used for other purposes (for example, to maintain a blockade or to chase after more dangerous foreign naval vessels) or that such a policy would minimize the hostility of local populations in case of occupation or otherwise appease foreign opinion in neutral states that might join the enemy if their populations were aroused. Whatever the case, one must distinguish between (1) granting immunity to coastal fishing vessels because doing so serves a state's unilateral interest in a particular conflict and (2) granting immunity to coastal fishing vessels because doing so serves a state's interest in all foreseeable conflicts, conditional on other states acting in reciprocal fashion. Only in the latter case can a norm of customary international law come into existence, for only in the latter case does such a norm serve the interests of states. When a state adopts a policy in the first case, it will want to make sure that other states do not believe that it adopts the policy for the second reason. From this observation follows the importance of stating that the government does not consent to a norm of international law but acts for other reasons.

The doctrinal requirement that states consent to a norm of customary international law is, as lawyers like to say, "flexible"—meaning that decision makers do not always seem to take it seriously. Indeed, the weakness of this requirement has given rise to a subsidiary rule known as the "persistent objector exception." This rule refers to cases where nearly all states express their approval of a developing norm of international law. A state that keeps silent is held to be bound to that rule unless it persistently objects—that is, repeatedly makes known that it does not agree to that rule. The persistent objector exception would not make sense if state consent—or at least overt, verbally expressed state consent, as opposed to implicit, state consent—were really necessary. And this suggests that state consent is not always necessary for the purpose of finding customary international law.[8] We see why below.

Practice

If the consent requirement is met, and thus states (at least in theory) announce their adherence to a norm of customary international law, then why should a pattern of state practice be required as well? After all, the usual theory of international law is that states are bound if they consent to be bound. If states enter a treaty, and thereby signal their consent to a set of new obligations, they cannot escape those obligations merely by refusing to keep them and then arguing that no state practice supports the treaty. The idea of a treaty is to create a new pattern of state practice as between the states that enter the treaty.

The best answer to this question reverts to our argument above. Customary international law refers to patterns of cooperative behavior between states. When trying to determine whether a norm of customary international law exists, we are really trying to figure out what is optimal and sustainable between states. The pattern must be optimal in the sense of being in the interest of the states involved; the pattern must be sustainable in the sense that ordinary reciprocal behavior—the threat of retaliation if the other state violates the rules—is adequate for maintaining the pattern of cooperation. And here is the key point: the states themselves—meaning the government officials and judges and others who determine or announce the policy of states—may not know what is optimal and sustainable when they announce the states' consent to a norm of customary international law. We learn whether they are right only when we subsequently observe the behavior of states. If states find it impossible to adhere to the norms that they previously consented to, they will act differently, the state practice requirement will not be satisfied, and thus there is no point in recognizing the existence of a norm of customary international law.

Customary International Law without Consent and Practice: Jus Cogens

Jus cogens is Latin for "compelling law." Jus cogens norms are norms of customary international law that bind states regardless of their consent and regardless of state practice.[9] The standard list of jus cogens norms include rules against genocide, slavery, torture, and aggressive war. However, the extent to which states really agree about the content of jus cogens norms is murky.

How can norms of customary international law exist without state consent and practice? One can answer this question from several angles. Initially, observe that states have agreed that jus cogens norms exist; thus, one might say that these norms are, in fact, grounded in consent. Jus cogens norms are mentioned in a number of treaties, including the Vienna Convention on the Law of Treaties.[10] Yet at the same time, the Vienna Convention and other instruments say that states cannot, as between themselves, agree to derogate from the requirements of jus cogens norms. This is a distinctive feature of the jus cogens norm. Two states can agree to deviate from an ordinary norm of customary international law—for example, they can renegotiate the division of a body of water that is otherwise controlled by customary international law. However, they cannot decide to reestablish the slave trade.

Even though consent and practice are not "required" for jus cogens norms, the jus cogens norms no doubt reflect the interests of most states. It is hard to imagine how they could not. If states agreed that the jus cogens norms did not serve their interests, deviation from them would become routine whether or not one thinks that in some sense they continue to exist as law. The fact that the international community accepts the concept of jus cogens norms is powerful evidence that these norms are seen as valuable by most states most of the time.

Yet deviations from these norms may often be seen in practice. Torture exists in many states. States rarely announce that torture is official policy, but their security services practice it or it is otherwise tolerated. Under the traditional view of customary international law, the absence of state practice means that no norm can exist. Yet no one seems to be prepared to say that the norm against torture does not exist. What is going on?

One possibility is that states have different ideas about what torture means, and so states that appear to be engaging in torture may not agree that they are. Another possibility is that states both want to recognize a law against torture—there is indeed a treaty that recognizes the norm against torture under customary international law[11]—but want to retain the option to break the law in "exigent circumstances" and are willing to take the consequences, whatever they might be. A third possibility is that states may wish to deceive their populations. Public opinion opposes torture, and states might want to appease public opinion while secretly engaging in torture where doing so advances their perceived interests.

Some scholars approach jus cogens norms from a different direction. These norms, they argue, are morally compelled and enter international law not because states consent to them but because international law can be valid law only if it reflects fundamental moral norms. In earlier centuries, this type of reasoning was more common than it is today. Commentators believed in what they called *natural law*—a common morality binding all human beings—and argued that international law reflected natural law principles. In the nineteenth century, natural law reasoning was abandoned in favor of positivism—the view that international law is created entirely by states, which may or may not choose to incorporate moral norms into international law. It is from the positivist conception that the fundamental premise of state consent emerges. If states make international law, then international law must reflect their consent.

Natural law reasoning made a comeback after World War II. Many of the Nazis' worst atrocities did not violate international law—there was no law against genocide, for example. As a result, many people felt uneasy about punishing the Nazis. If the Nazis did not violate a law against genocide, how could they be tried and punished for committing genocide? Natural law reasoning could supply the answer—international law really did (implicitly) incorporate a rule against genocide because genocide violates natural law, which is itself part of international law.

Natural law reasoning has a lot of problems. People living in different states disagree about morality, and if international law is to reflect morality, whose morality should it reflect? If people cannot agree on moral rules, then they will not agree about the rules of international law, in which case the many benefits of international law—its capacity to maintain a modicum of order and advance joint interests—will be lost. For the most part, therefore, governments have shown no inclination to abandon the positivist underpinnings of international law. Treaties and norms of customary international law are valid even if some commentators object to them on moral grounds; claimed universal moral norms that are not embodied in treaties or custom are not valid law.

Bilateral versus Multilateral

Customary international law comes in two flavors: multilateral and bilateral. Most of the examples we have discussed so far involve multilateral norms—that is, they bind all states except those that persistently object to them. Bilateral norms bind only two states. They frequently govern territorial matters. In *Right of Passage over Indian Territory (Portugal v. India)*,[12] for example, the International Court of Justice (ICJ) addressed whether Portugal had a right of passage through Indian territory, so that it could send supplies to a colony surrounded by Indian territory. To answer this question, the ICJ examined the history of relations between Portugal and Britain, whose territory India had inherited when it won independence. Britain had in fact routinely permitted Portugal to send supplies across British territory and had appeared to acknowledge that Portugal had a legal right to do so. However, the British did not give Portugal a right to send military forces across British territory; Britain had insisted that it had the discretion to deny such passage. Hence Portugal had a customary right to send civilians and nonmilitary supplies but not military forces to its isolated colonial enclaves. No other states were involved; this was a bilateral norm of customary international law.

Is Customary International Law Binding? How Customary International Law Changes

In 1945, President Harry Truman declared that the United States would exercise sovereignty over its continental shelf.[13] The continental shelf is an underwater landmass that juts miles outward into the ocean. It is loaded with minerals, and because the seabed on the shelf is in relatively shallow water, these minerals can be extracted. By contrast, minerals in the seabed at the bottom of the ocean cannot be extracted in economical fashion, at least not today; they certainly could not when Truman made his announcement.

Technological change during the twentieth century brought within reach the minerals in the continental shelf. But prior to Truman's announcement, no one believed that a state's sovereignty extended over the continental shelf. This meant that foreign deep-sea mining companies could drill for oil off the U.S. coast (albeit not in territorial waters) without first obtaining a license from the United States. The United States would not be able to regulate this activity in order to protect the maritime environment and to prevent duplicative and inefficient extraction. By asserting sovereignty over the continental shelf, the United States made clear that it would regulate mining activities in this area. It implicitly suggested that other states could do the same with respect to their continental shelves.

The new U.S. policy may well have made good economic sense, but it was a clear violation of international law. The freedom of the seas extended over the continental shelf up to the limits of the territorial waters—a portion of the ocean occupying a narrower band of twelve miles hugging the coast. Other states could have argued that Truman's announcement violated international law or at least portended a violation that would occur the moment the U.S. Coast Guard blocked a foreign company from setting up an oil platform off the U.S. coast.

But they did not. Foreign states did not argue that the United States violated international law and demand a remedy.[14] Instead, foreign states with coastlines claimed sovereignty over the continental shelf that jutted from their coasts. In this way, states appeared to consent to a new legal regime—one that gave all states control over mineral extraction from their portion of a continental shelf—and states acted consistently with this norm. A norm of customary international law was born.

This course of events might seem puzzling. Why did foreign states acquiesce in the U.S. violation; why didn't they demand a remedy? If the answer is that the United States had simply shifted international law in a desirable direction, then what force does law have in the first place? Why can't states routinely violate customary international law and ward off objections by claiming that they are merely trying to change customary international law in a way that benefits everyone?

To answer this question, recall the theory of customary international law that we described earlier. Customary international law refers to patterns of cooperative behavior. When states refrain from pursuing short-term interests, they can sometimes become mutually better off over the long term. Before Truman's announcement, states believed that they did best if they retained control only over the territorial seas, where they could guard against smuggling and regulate traffic. There was no need to exert control over the continental shelf because no one could exploit the minerals in it. When technology changed, it became clear that states would do best if they had control over both their territorial sea and the continental shelf. The exogenous shock—the development of technology—changed the content of the optimal law: what had before been adequate was no longer adequate, and a new regime suggested itself.

But how could states get from point A to point B? A literal-minded approach to the consent and practice doctrines would suggest that the rules could change only when all states consent to a change and then adjust their practice accordingly. But customary international law is decentralized: there is no clear mechanism for changing it. States sometimes call conventions and send delegates who try to negotiate changes in international law, but this procedure is cumbersome and does not always work. The simple expedient of violating the old rule and announcing a new rule avoids these obstacles—but only if other states agree to the change.

Thus, we might say that Truman took a risk that other states would reject his proposal, which would have caused diplomatic difficulties. The administration could then have withdrawn the policy or addressed foreign states' opposition in some other way. If it did not, it would have run the risk that at a later point conflict would occur, as foreign states attempted to exploit resources on the U.S. continental shelf while the U.S. Coast Guard tried to stop them. Happily for the

United States, other states did not oppose the new U.S. policy—perhaps because they believed that the new rule was superior to the old rule.

There is thus no conflict between the idea that customary international law is binding and the idea that it can change as a result of violation. If a state violates a norm of customary international law, and other states acquiesce, then the law loses its force. If they do not, the law retains its force. In domestic law, we see a similar phenomenon. People break all kinds of laws, but the government does not enforce all laws equally. It pursues some law violators more aggressively than others and often refrains from bringing charges if the law violation does not seem serious. For example, governments stopped enforcing anti-sodomy laws long before they were repealed; in many places, governments do not seriously enforce laws against euthanasia or hiring illegal immigrants. As a result, these laws lose much of their force. In extreme cases, courts may even refuse to enforce laws that for a long time have not been enforced. Popular opinion influences government behavior and can effect an implicit repeal.[15]

6

Treaties

A treaty is a legal agreement between or among states. States can also make nonlegal agreements; the difference between a legal agreement and a nonlegal agreement just seems to be whether states declare that the treaty is legally binding, that is, creates legal obligations. We will talk about nonlegal agreements ("soft law") later.

Most treaties are bilateral treaties: two states enter the agreement and the agreement binds just the two of them. A typical extradition treaty, for example, binds two states, which agree to send back to the country of origin certain types of suspected criminals if requested to do so. Treaties can also have multiple parties. Some multilateral treaties are the result of efforts by a small group of states to cooperate with each other. The North American Free Trade Agreement (NAFTA), for example, is a treaty between the United States, Canada, and Mexico that obliges each country to reduce trade barriers. Another type of multilateral treaty has a universal orientation. The United Nations has sponsored treaties that are open to all states—not just a small group. Human rights treaties fall into this category. Their sponsors hope that all states will enter these treaties, thus establishing certain universal rules of international law.

What Are Treaties For?

Treaties are just vehicles for cooperation between states. When states do not cooperate, they impose negative externalities on each other (for example, pollution) or fail to create public goods (for example, fisheries). Cooperation enables states to overcome these problems. As we saw in Chapter 5, cooperation can emerge in a decentralized fashion and is embodied in customary international law. When states refrain from seizing each other's coastal fishing vessels during a naval conflict, they cooperate by sacrificing a short-term benefit (the value of the enemy's fishing vessels) in return for a long-term benefit (the value of being protected from the same action). Norms can arise in a decentralized fashion because unilateral announcements and practice can sufficiently indicate a state's interest in cooperation, leading other states to reciprocate.

But decentralized cooperation is hazardous even in ideal circumstances. First, the content of a norm can be obscure. What is a coastal fishing vessel, anyway? How is it different from fishing vessels that are not coastal? The coastal fishing vessel norm applied only to vessels used for catching fresh fish and not salted fish or cod,[1] and there were always numerous ill-defined exceptions—for coastal fishing vessels used to carry spies and contraband, for example. But what if the private operator of a coastal fishing vessel conveys information to the enemy; does that count as spying? When states disagree about the content of customary international law, they can end up in legal disputes. One state acts innocently by its own lights—it seizes a large merchant ship that it does not regard as a coastal fishing vessel—and the other states accuses it of violating the law.

Second, customary international law can be hard to change. As we saw earlier, there is no institution that can modify customary international law when it is overtaken by technological changes and other developments. States have little choice but to violate it or unilaterally declare a departure from the norm, but this can give rise to disputes and retaliation.

Against this background, the advantages of treaty making are easy to see. States that can gain by cooperation need to be able to set down in some detail the nature of their cooperative activity: which actions will be considered obligatory and which not. The treaty might contain mechanisms so that it can be modified as conditions change.[2] Indeed, treaties often provide that a party can withdraw after giving notice. The notice requirement protects the expectations of the other party, while the right to withdraw makes it easy to demand modifications if conditions change.

Consider the extradition treaty. When a criminal suspect crosses a border and takes refuge in a foreign state, the state from which he fled has a strong interest in obtaining his return so that he can be tried and convicted. Otherwise, people will have weaker incentives to comply with the law. If they know that they can easily avoid punishment by leaving the country, then domestic criminal sanctions will hold less sway over them. Meanwhile, the foreign country will usually have little interest in providing refuge to a criminal. That person is likely to cause trouble at some point in the future. At the same time, the foreign country may wish to accept law-abiding immigrants, including those out of political favor abroad, and those individuals may be hesitant to migrate if they know that they are vulnerable to deportation if their government claims they are criminals. The same consideration applies in reverse when criminals or alleged criminals from the foreign state travel to the first state.

The extradition treaty resolves these competing interests. Each state obtains the right to the return of fleeing criminals. At the same time, both states agree to procedural protections so that innocent people are not mistakenly returned. In addition, the right to extradition is limited in certain ways, so that one state need not acquiesce in policies that it disapproves. States that oppose the death penalty make sure that the extradition treaty gives them the right to refrain from extraditing people subject to the death penalty unless they are given assurances that that penalty will not be administered. States also refuse to agree to extradite people who have committed "political" crimes—such as criticism of the foreign government—and people whose crimes are trivial. It is clear that these rules could evolve in a decentralized way only with great difficulty and over a long period of time; the treaty format allows states to negotiate an agreement that reflects their joint interests with a degree of precision.

These points carry over to multilateral treaties.[3] A bilateral trade treaty benefits its two parties by reducing trade barriers and thus enhancing trade. A trade treaty with three or more parties produces the same benefits but for more states. Whether states choose to enter bilateral or multilateral treaties depends in part on the type of strategic problem that they seek to solve. If two states disagree about the location of a portion of the border between them, then a treaty that resolves that disagreement and specifies the location need have only two parties—those with the border. Where three states border a lake, and the states wish to limit pollution of that lake and prevent overfishing, a treaty will need to have all three states as parties. If only two states agree to reduce fishing, for example, then they will simply put themselves at a disadvantage with respect to the third state, which might increase its own fishing and thus eliminate the benefits of the treaty. A treaty that limited greenhouse gas emissions will need to have virtually all major emitting states as parties. If just a few countries reduce emissions, industry may migrate to nonparties, so that aggregate global emissions will continue apace. The treaty parties will have done little for the climate while injuring their own economies.

The problem with multilateral treaties is that as the number of parties increases, the incentives to cheat or free ride increase as well. When two states share a lake governed by a treaty regime that they have created, and one state violates the treaty by polluting the lake, the other state can simply withdraw from the treaty. Now the lake will be as polluted as ever; the second state will have gained nothing by polluting. To avoid this outcome, it will refrain from polluting in the first place. When dozens of states surround an ocean and all engage in overfishing, the logic of retaliation is weaker. The problem is that one state that engages in overfishing may be difficult to detect, and the other states will free ride on each other rather than invest in detection technologies. But if all states believe that they can overfish without detection, then they will do so, and the treaty regime will collapse. This is not to say that a multilateral treaty regime cannot succeed but only that success is difficult.

Many multilateral treaty regimes appear to work effectively because they set up a common framework within which bilateral cooperation takes place. The trade regime has this feature. The WTO provides a forum in which trade negotiations can take place and a set of institutions for resolving disputes can arise. But in the end, a state must rely on itself to impose a retaliatory trade sanction if it is the victim of a trade violation. States refrain from violations in large part because they fear retaliation from the victimized partner, not because WTO members will impose sanctions on them collectively (although many members may become less willing to negotiate with a persistent violator in the future).

The final group of treaties consists of the universal treaties that are usually sponsored by the United Nations. These treaties are the most problematic from the standpoint of enforcement. Because the treaties are open to all states, all states can join them, but not all states have a hand in their negotiation. States separate into blocs with similar interests; these blocs negotiate with each other. States whose interests in the treaty regime do not naturally align with other states find themselves frozen out. So do poor states and other states that do not have the capacity to launch a sophisticated diplomatic campaign. As for the remaining states, their interests may diverge so much that the resulting treaty will be vague and hortatory. When states cannot agree on details, they agree on general propositions that different states will be able to interpret in different ways once the treaty is in force. Finally, states try to protect themselves by issuing reservations, declarations, and understandings;[4] these statements may unilaterally adjust their obligations under the treaty or advance idiosyncratic interpretations. All of the forces conspire to produce weak, ambiguous treaties that many states either do not join or do not take seriously. The problem of collective enforcement further exacerbates these problems.

The human rights treaties illustrate these problems with particular clarity. Most of them have been ratified by most states, but there is a fair amount of variation. The provisions of the treaties are predictably vague. The wealthier and more sophisticated states, especially the wealthy democracies, have issued numerous reservations, declarations, and understandings that undercut their obligations and throw the meaning of many treaty provisions in doubt. Authoritarian states enter these treaties but do not seem to take them seriously and are rarely sanctioned if they violate them. Empirical research has thrown into doubt the efficacy of these treaties.[5]

Nonetheless, many government officials and commentators of various stripes continue to support the universal treaty. For some people, these treaties offer the best hope for an international "rule of law." In this setting, this term means a world in which states are all bound by a single legal system consisting of rules that apply equally, much as we have in domestic law. Bilateral treaties and multilateral treaties with closed membership are regarded with suspicion from this standpoint. They seem like efforts by states or small groups of states to obtain advantages at the expense of the rest of the world. Many such treaties impose unequal burdens or seem to create clubs where some states have special powers over others. A universal treaty, whatever its defects, can never do that, because states are (in theory) allowed in on equal terms; indeed, some of these treaties put more burdens on the wealthier and more powerful states. Environmental and trade treaties, for example, sometimes release poorer states from obligations—under the rubric of "common but differentiated responsibilities." The question is whether such a vision can survive the realities of the state system, a system where power inequalities are rife and states act in their interest.

Treaty Interpretation, Validity, Termination

Treaties are like contracts, and there is a law of treaties that resembles the law of contracts. The law of treaties governs such contract-law-like topics as how states enter treaties; how treaties are interpreted; when states are excused from performance; and how treaties are terminated. The law of treaties exists in customary international law—it reflects the ways that states have addressed treaty-related problems over the centuries—but it also has been codified in the Vienna Convention on the Law of Treaties.[6] The United States has not ratified the Vienna Convention, but most states have, and the United States recognizes it as reflecting customary international law.

Anyone who has taken a first-year contracts course in law school should have little trouble understanding treaty law. There are important differences, of course, but the broad contours of the two bodies of law resemble each other. For that reason, our discussion of treaty law will be brief.

Entering Treaties: Consent

Just as individuals must consent to a contract, states must consent to a treaty. But because states are more sophisticated than individuals are—states have diplomatic staffs—the types of disputes over information, fraud, and the like that one sees in contract law rarely arise between states. States can rarely make a plausible argument that their consent to a treaty is invalid because they did not understand the treaty or have sufficient information about the state of the world.

But some states have tried to argue that treaties are invalid if entered under duress. This argument seems sensible, given that the opposite of consent is coercion. But the argument turns out to be weaker than it first appears. The borders of most, if not all, states reflect some past war. The location of the border may well reflect the victor dictating terms to a vanquished state. Could the latter state turn around and claim that the treaty is invalid because it was coerced, by the use of military force, into accepting disadvantageous terms? If it could, then no peace treaty could ever be enforceable.

Some states have suggested that if a rich country threatens to cut off trade or withdraw foreign aid if a poor state does not enter a particular treaty, then that treaty is invalid. Again, such a rule would have perverse results. The rich state is perfectly free to cut off trade privileges or foreign aid unilaterally. If a poor state cannot "pay" the rich state not to do so by offering it something that the rich states wants by treaty, then the poor state is likely to be made worse off.

One might try to distinguish "coercive" peace treaties and "noncoercive" peace treaties; presumably, the latter are less harsh than the former. But no one has proposed any general principles for distinguishing the two, and it is hard to think of any. Nor have any peace treaties been deemed invalid because of coercion.

Signature and Ratification

Entry to a treaty usually takes two steps. The states negotiate and sign the treaty; subsequently, they ratify the treaty. In some cases, only one step is necessary. Other states negotiate a treaty but provide that additional states may join the treaty after the original states have ratified it. These additional states— states that were not party to the original negotiations or came into existence afterward—simply ratify (or accede to or approve of) the treaty at a later time.

The two-step process needs little explanation. States do not, and should not, enter treaties unless sufficient political support exists at home. The executive or a delegate usually negotiates the treaty and signs it, but then some time is needed for the state to ratify because at this point broader political support must be found. In most states, this involves approval of the legislature such as parliament; in the United States, typically the Senate consents to a treaty and then the president formally ratifies it. A one-step process would require the larger body to participate in the negotiations, which is impractical. We see various domestic analogies, such as mergers and other major contracts between corporations, which are negotiated and signed by an executive and then later ratified by a board of directors or shareholders. However, in both parliamentary and presidential systems (and likewise in the corporate setting), there are circumstances where it is generally accepted that the executive can enter a treaty without obtaining subsequent ratification—usually, when there is some explicit or implicit prior authorization.

The two-step process raises a question about the legal status of the treaty between signature and ratification. The Vienna Convention says that the state must not act inconsistently with the object of the treaty while waiting for ratification,[7] but what if ratification never occurs? Does the state remain bound in perpetuity to respect the object of the treaty that it never formally consented to? It seems unlikely; certainly, there are no examples. The rule does give executives an incentive not to negotiate treaties that the legislature will not approve, but such a rule can prevail only if states on the other side object strenuously to the failure to ratify or to the failure of the state to act consistently with the object of the treaty. But it is hard to imagine holding a state to a treaty, or even its object, if it has no legal remedy against the treaty parties if they violate the treaty because that state itself does not belong to the treaty. President Clinton signed the Kyoto Accord but did not make a serious effort to obtain the consent of the Senate (which in the meantime had issued a unanimous declaration rejecting the treaty). It seems hardly plausible that the United States has since then acted consistently with the "object" of the treaty, yet although other nations have complained about the failure of ratification, they have not argued that the United States has violated international law.

In 2002, the Bush administration purported to "unsign" the United States from the Rome Statute that created the International Criminal Court.[8] The announcement is best interpreted as an indication that the Bush administration itself had no intention of ratifying the treaty. As a matter of international law, such an act would hardly have any meaning other than to make clear that the United States would not even act consistently with the object of the treaty, whatever that might mean.

Termination

If you imagine that treaties are like contracts, you might think that a treaty party could never unilaterally terminate a treaty or withdraw from a treaty, which hardly seems much different from breach. In fact, treaty terminations are ubiquitous.[9] Treaties frequently give the parties a right to withdraw, typically upon notice; the Vienna Convention adds that even in the absence of a withdrawal term, such a term can be derived from the parties' intentions or implied from the "nature" of the treaty.[10] The ease with which states can exit treaties explains why so little law exists on remedies for violation of treaties; violation can be easily avoided through lawful termination.

What accounts for the ease of termination? A possible answer is that in the absence of external enforcement mechanisms, nothing prevents states from breaching treaties aside from fear of retaliation and generalized concerns about reputation. A treaty is best understood as the terms of cooperation *as long as states are willing to cooperate;* when one state no longer sees gains from cooperating with the other, it will exit the treaty. If there are reputational costs from overtly breaching a treaty, the state that wishes to escape the relationship can renegotiate with the other state so that the two states can publicly announce that the treaty has been suspended or renegotiated. The avoiding state makes a side payment to the other state in order to secure its consent to mutual termination of the treaty; the other state might also be happy enough to avoid being seen as the victim of a treaty violation, since that might signal to other states that it is weak or has little to offer. In this way, the two states internalize a positive externality that would otherwise benefit foreign states, which would learn not to trust the state engaged in the violation. In a similar way, employers prefer obtaining a resignation from incompetent employees to firing them. The employee avoids the stigma of being fired, and the employer avoids the possibility of a lawsuit, while future employers are deprived of information that the employee is incompetent.

Reservations, Declarations, Understandings, and Objections

Universal multilateral treaties appeal to many international lawyers because they seem to promote the "rule of law," creating norms that apply equally to all states, regardless of their size and strength. This agenda, whatever its merits, has faltered over the tendency of states to issue reservations, declarations, and understandings when they ratify or accede to the treaties. These statements modify the terms of the treaties in ways that affect different states differently or muddy the treaties' meanings.

A reservation is a statement that a term of the treaty does not apply to the reserving state. Consider, for example, the Convention on the Prohibition of Military or Any Other Hostile Use of Environmental Modification Techniques, which went into force in 1978.[11] This treaty prohibits states from using "environmental modification techniques," such as technologies that disrupt weather patterns, as a method of warfare. Among other things, the treaty provides that all parties must render support to countries that are victims of such techniques.

Switzerland issued a reservation providing that it would not engage in actions that went beyond its traditional position of neutrality, presumably meaning that it would not cooperate in a war against a country that uses environmental modification techniques against its enemy.

Declarations and understandings are less problematic. Understandings are claims about the proper interpretation of an ambiguous term of the treaty. Declarations are often one-sided commitments, which might be made in connection with the ratification of a treaty but can also be made independently. Declarations are also sometimes used to explain how states will comply with their treaty obligations. For example, U.S. declarations often say that the treaty is not self-executing, meaning that it will be enforced by the executive branch, not domestic courts, except to the degree that the treaty is implemented into domestic law through legislation. For bilateral treaties, reservations are generally unacceptable and are best seen as counteroffers.

Let us focus on reservations.[12] A first question is how they can be acceptable in the first place. If treaties require the consent of states, and reservations can be issued after the negotiations are completed, and without the acquiescence of the other states, then in principle they should be invalid or the treaty as a whole should be invalid. This was the rule at one time, but states came to realize that bans on reservations could make it impossible for a large number of parties to negotiate an acceptable treaty. To be sure, some treaties, such as the Law of the Sea treaty,[13] ban reservations. But states have acquiesced in the practice of reservation when the treaty does not say otherwise.

Still, reservations pose problems. Consider a treaty that eliminates trade barriers between states X, Y, and Z. Could state X, by reservation, withdraw its obligation to reduce barriers, so that it benefits from Y's and Z's trade barrier reductions while incurring no cost? Two rules prevent this outcome.[14] First, all reservations have reciprocal effect. In our example, X's reservation would automatically eliminate Y's and Z's obligation to eliminate barriers against X's goods; but their obligations between each other—Y's obligation to reduce barriers against Z's goods and vice versa—would remain in force. Second, a state may not use reservations to undermine the core objective of the treaty, which is what happens in our example. Reservations can be used at the margins and usually apply only to a small subset of a treaty's obligations.

The second rule is easy enough to understand; the rationale of the first rule is more complex.[15] The reciprocity rule imposes a cost on the reserving state: while it benefits by avoiding an obligation, it also loses the benefit that results from other states having an obligation to it. This cost prevents states from issuing reservations too enthusiastically, as they surely would if reciprocity did not occur. But why not ban reservations altogether? One answer is that it is too costly for states to negotiate all of the reservations that would be necessary to persuade multiple states to join a treaty regime. The traditional consent rule is just too strong when hundreds of states are involved in negotiations and they all have different interests. Another answer is that the need for a reservation may not become apparent until negotiations are over and obstacles to ratification emerge in the domestic political process of various signatories. The ability to enter reservations then avoids the need for costly renegotiation.

However, as noted above, sometimes states do, by treaty, ban the use of reservations. The Law of the Sea treaty and the Montreal Protocol on Substances That Deplete the Ozone Layer[16] have such a provision; so does the International Criminal Court treaty.[17] States in these cases must have believed that reservations would have been used too freely to subvert deals that were incorporated in the treaty instrument. Clearly, the policy toward reservations involves a tradeoff. A ban on reservations may, by increasing transaction costs, prevent parties from reaching a deal. Allowing reservations may prevent parties from reaching a deal by creating the risk that the deal will not stick. The greater risk will depend on the circumstances, including the efficacy of the reciprocity rule at protecting the value of the bargain. For example, when a state gives up a claim about the territorial sea in order to obtain a concession regarding the treatment of undersea resources, it will fear that other states will make reservations about undersea resources. The state in question does not benefit from the reciprocity rule because reservations by others regarding undersea resources simply allow it to impose similar restrictions; this opportunity is no compensation for its loss of the claim regarding the territorial sea.

Human Rights Treaties

Reservations have also played a prominent role in human rights treaties. Many people have complained that the United States only grudgingly enters these treaties and then undercuts core obligations with reservations. Consider, for example, the U.S. reservations for the International Covenant on Civil and Political Rights (ICCPR),[18] which (1) hold that provisions banning war propaganda and hate speech cannot compel the U.S. to violate the first amendment of the U.S. Constitution; (2) retain the right to execute people who commit crimes as juveniles despite a contrary provision in the ICCPR; (3) limit the ICCPR's ban on cruel, inhuman, and degrading punishment to the restrictions imposed by the fifth, eighth, and fourteenth amendments of the U.S. Constitution; (4) reject a provision in the ICCPR that requires offenders to be subject to lighter sanctions if they are legislated after the offense; and (5) permit the United States in certain circumstances to treat juveniles as adults despite contrary provisions in the ICCPR.

In fact, most liberal democracies issue numerous reservations when entering human rights treaties. Oddly, the authoritarian states do not. What is going on?

When states negotiate human rights treaties, they start off with different views about how the relevant human rights should be defined. Some states believe that the death penalty violates human rights; others do not. Some states believe that bans on radical political parties violate human rights; others do not. Negotiations, however, are dominated by liberal states that are committed to human rights, and the deal reflects a compromise. The liberal states that believe in more limited rights protect themselves by issuing reservations, so that, in effect, the final deal has a common core to which all adhere, while various groups of states agree to sets of more generous rights. None of these states necessarily change domestic law. They do not enter the treaties in order to change their own law; they enter the treaties in order to obtain changes in the law of other states.

Authoritarian states avoid ratifying human rights treaties or do so reluctantly, usually in order to obtain foreign aid, appease domestic constituents, or obtain some other benefit. They do not bother issuing reservations because they do not expect to comply with the treaty. It may be that their ratifications do some good—for example, giving internal dissidents more bargaining power—but the evidence is slim.

The reciprocity rule does little to protect the bargain in the case of human rights treaties. If one state issues a reservation saying that it can ban political parties that oppose the constitution, then the reciprocity rule would seem to indicate that other states would be able to ban their radical political parties. But that does not create a cost for the reserving state: if it believes that banning radical political parties is justified, then it will not care if other states also ban radical political parties. Accordingly, although human rights treaties are often subject to reservations, they are generally not thought to trigger the reciprocity principle.

Reservations When Obligations Are Not Bilateral

The human rights treaty is just an example of a more general case that poses problems for reservations: the treaty that generates a single public good that treaty members share, as opposed to treaties that create a set of bilateral cooperative surpluses.

Consider a multilateral extradition treaty that provides that each state will extradite fugitives if conditions A, B, and C are met. The treaty has three parties, X, Y, and Z. Let us suppose that condition C is controversial—for example, it allows extradition for capital crimes. Z objects to the death penalty and so issues a reservation with respect to C. Thus, X and Y will extradite fugitives accused of capital crimes to each other; but X and Z, and Y and Z, will not.

This treaty creates three bilateral relationships and cooperative surpluses for each pair. The cooperative surplus is higher for X-Y than for X-Z and Y-Z because it encompasses more types of fugitives, but, as we have argued, X and Y have no reason to complain about Z's reservation. If the parties had separately negotiated three bilateral treaties, the result would have been the same. The multilateral negotiation, followed by Z's reservation, reduced transaction costs, making everyone better off.

Now consider a treaty that requires X, Y, and Z to reduce discharges of three types of chemicals—A, B, and C—into a lake. This time Z issues a reservation with respect to chemical C. Suppose that X and Y regard a lake polluted with A and B to be no better than a lake polluted with A, B, and C: their first choice is a clean lake; otherwise, they are unwilling to incur the expense of curtailing their own pollution. Meanwhile, Z greatly benefits if it can discharge C and, while it would prefer a clean lake to a dirty lake, taking into account all of its costs it prefers a lake polluted with C to a clean lake. Here, Z's reservation eliminates the benefit that X and Y would receive from the treaty. Unlike in the prior case, X and Y would not enter the treaty at all if Z's reservation were permitted.

The law needs to distinguish the first type of reservation—which adjusts one of many bilateral bargains encompassed in a multilateral treaty—and the second type, which undermines a public good. A rule does just this in general terms by prohibiting reservations that are "incompatible with the object and purpose of the treaty."[19] Whether states actually apply the rule in this way (or at all) is another question.

Objections to Reservations

States can and do issue objections to the reservations of other states, adding another layer of complexity to the analysis. For example, the United States made a reservation to Article IX of the Convention on the Prevention and

Punishment of the Crime of Genocide in 1988, stating that "before any dispute to which the United States is a party may be submitted to the jurisdiction of the International Court of Justice . . . the specific consent of the United States is required in each case."[20] The Netherlands made a declaration rejecting this reservation by stating that the "reservation was incompatible with the object and purpose of the Convention and that it did not consider states making such reservations parties to the Convention."[21] Meanwhile, other states did not reject the U.S. reservation. What was the legal effect of the Netherlands' objection? One view is that the objection means that the Netherlands cannot be a party to the treaty, but clearly states regard the Netherlands as a party. Perhaps we should hold that the United States cannot be a party as long as the Netherlands objects to its reservation, but that does not seem to be the view of states either. One might think that the right approach is to determine whether the reservation really undermines the treaty and to hold it invalid if it does, but then it is not clear what the legal significance of the Netherlands' objection is.

International lawyers have not resolved these disputes. In practice, states enter reservations and objections—and then nothing happens. The treaties enter into force, and then we have to wait and see what happens when (say) the Netherlands insists that the United States use the International Court of Justice. It is hard to say as a general proposition how these disputes are resolved—they are rare and are probably resolved through negotiation.

It is easy to see why some legal consequence should be given to objection. If objections are not permitted, then states may reserve excessively, thus undoing the deal that the states had believed that they negotiated. The prospect of objections might deter states from reserving excessively. The problem, however, is that states can also strategically object, so as to prevent a state from reserving when doing so follows from the valid transaction cost–reducing function of reservations. If states know that their reservations may be invalid, then they may not sign the treaty in the first place.

Let us distinguish more carefully valid and invalid reasons for reserving. A state might issue a reservation because its preferences are idiosyncratic and thus not reflected in the terms of the treaty. Such a reservation effectively creates a somewhat different deal between that state and all other treaty parties—one where the obligations are more limited than those contained in the treaty itself. This reservation is valid and the reciprocity rule ensures that it does not create unfairness. A state might also reserve in order to give itself an advantage. Here, the set of obligations that disappear was more valuable to other states than the set of obligations that remain, and the other states agreed to the treaty in the first place because the gain from the first set of obligations was large enough to offset the loss created for them by the second set of obligations. This reservation is invalid, and the reciprocity rule is not adequate for resolving the problem.

The second type of reservation—where the obligations are "asymmetric" to use Fon and Parisi's term—should be invalid.[22] And perhaps the rule against reservations that undermine the objective of the treaty reflects this goal. If other states formally object to the reservation, now we would need further to distinguish valid objections to asymmetric reservations and invalid objections to symmetric reservations. One might argue that if the consequence of objection is that the objecting state leaves the treaty, then the objecting state will object only when the reservation is invalid. Otherwise, the state would prefer to stay in the treaty. However, the objection surely creates costs as well, namely, the uncertainty about who remains party to the treaty.

All of this is enough to make one's head spin, and it is reassuring that states do not spend much time arguing about these questions.

Soft Law

Numerous international documents do not create or reflect law because they are not formal sources of law. Although these documents reflect promises or agreements to which states consent, states do not consent to these promises or agreements being legally binding.[23] Examples include the following:

- Multilateral treaties that do not create binding commitments, either because the parties say so or because the obligations are not specific, indicating an aspiration or goal rather than a rule. The Universal Declaration of Human Rights is an example.
- Statements issued by international organizations that have not been given authority to make legally binding statements. The UN General Assembly, for example, issues resolutions by majority rule, but by the terms of the UN Charter, the General Assembly (unlike the Security Council) cannot issue resolutions that have legal force. Dozens of UN committees and commissions are in a similar position.
- Bilateral agreements between states that are designated as "political" or otherwise nonlegal. For example, two states might agree to conduct joint military exercises, or to share green technology, or to share logistical capacity while responding to a natural disaster in a third country, while not agreeing that their agreements are legally binding.

These nonlegal agreements pose basic questions about how international law works. To see why, consider the domestic versions of soft law. Two firms negotiate a merger. Initially, they agree to a nonbinding letter of intent, which provides explicitly that it does not create legal obligations. The executives then consult their boards, and sometimes the shareholders vote. If all goes well, the two sides subsequently enter a legally binding contract. One might ask why the parties bother to enter the letter of intent if it is not legally binding, and the answer must be that reputational sanctions come into play if one party decides not to go through with the deal for a strategic reason—for example, as a threat in order to extract a better deal, rather than because of legitimate objections from the board or shareholders. By "reputational sanctions," we mean a nonlegal sanction that nevertheless penalizes actors because other actors are less willing to deal with them in the future. As reputational sanctions are not always adequate to deter opportunism, however, the legal contract is used to consummate the deal.

When we turn our attention back to international law, we see that the basic distinction between reputational and legal sanctions is harder to maintain. If a state violates a (legally valid) treaty, the usual sanction is simply retaliation or injury to the state's reputation (we will have much more to say about this later). If a state violates a nonlegal agreement, the sanction is the same. So why do states bother to make this distinction? There is no obvious answer.

However, there is a possible explanation for the nonlegal output of the General Assembly and other institutions, and for this phenomenon an alternative explanation is necessary. Again, a domestic analogy might help. Legislative bodies, like the U.S. Congress, frequently issue nonlegal resolutions. These resolutions often express a "sense of Congress" about some issue of the day—for example, that the United States should withdraw troops from Iraq, or that regulatory agencies should devote more resources to cleaning up the Great Lakes, or some such thing. These resolutions have no legal effect, but they may have political effect. They make clear to political officials such as the president, and to relevant interest groups and others, that Congress has a particular view on some issue. Some people might be influenced by Congress's views, but, more important, everyone will infer that if Congress cares enough about the issue to pass a resolution, then at some point in the future it might pass a law. That information is valuable, and potentially regulated parties and other government organs might adjust their behavior in response to it.[24]

The General Assembly, in particular, has been a valuable source of information about the political stances of states. States can make arguments there—for example, that rich countries should supply more foreign aid, or that countries should be able to expropriate foreign-owned property if they provide compensation, and so on—and a majority vote on the issue confirms at least that substantial world opinion (or at least the opinion of governments) supports a particular position. This position will not become law until all relevant states consent to it, but in the meantime information about the views of other states may help people to adjust to a future in which the legal regime has changed.

7

International Institutions

States benefit from elaborate domestic institutions that make, interpret, and enforce the law. Legislatures, executives, administrative agencies, courts, police, and other institutions translate public preferences into outcomes. No one thinks that a state can merely legislate and then assume that people will follow the law. Even people inclined to follow the law may disagree about its interpretation, and of course many people are not inclined to follow the law.

Yet international law rests on only a handful of weak international institutions. No international legislature or executive exists—with the very limited exception of the UN Security Council. A handful of international courts exist but most of them are weak and frequently ignored. A small number of institutions, like the World Trade Organization and the International Labor Organization, help coordinate negotiations and standard setting. The World Bank provides development aid, and the International Monetary Fund (IMF) provides financial assistance, but these institutions have narrow missions and are closely controlled by powerful states. Within the umbrella of the United Nations, there are numerous institutions that perform various useful functions—the World Health Organization is a prominent example. These institutions mainly gather information and coordinate activity among countries that want to participate; they have no coercive powers.

The institutional deficiency poses serious problems for international cooperation. If a global problem needs a legal solution—say, the problem of global warming—then people cannot apply to a legislature, one that could simply pass a law regulating emissions after debate and a majority vote. Instead, states must send delegates to conferences in the hope that they can agree on a treaty. Because states can be subject to international law only if they agree to it, a valid globally applicable treaty requires unanimous consent. Yet unanimity in anything is extremely rare; given the diversity of interests among states, unanimity usually requires a watering down of obligations plus hefty side payments that states are not always willing to make.

The absence of an international legislature accounts for the continued importance of customary international law. But states frequently disagree about the norms of customary international law. They also disagree about the meaning of treaties. Courts, such as the International Court of Justice, are needed to resolve these disagreements, but courts cannot normally take cases without the consent of states. Naturally, states that fear that they will lose a case are reluctant to give their consent to adjudication. Here again a robust legal system is foiled by the requirement of consent.

Finally, ordinary states have a domestic executive that uses force to implement the law. The international system has no executive; it depends on states to follow the law and to pressure each other when they do not. But states have a great deal of trouble forcing other states to follow the law. The problem is not just that weak states cannot coerce powerful lawbreakers. It turns out that powerful states cannot coerce weak lawbreakers. Consider the difficulties posed by medium-sized and small states like Iran, North Korea, Zimbabwe, Myanmar, and Sudan. The weakest of states—the failed states like Somalia—can be the most difficult of all to affect through coercion. Short of occupying and running a state—and no one wants to do that because of the risks and costs—a failed state cannot be deterred by the threat of sanctions because it has no government that can control the population.

International Delegation

Why, then, do states not create better international institutions? Scholars use the term *international delegation* to refer to the process of such institution building. A state "delegates" power to an international institution by yielding to it authority over some domain of government action.[1] Delegations can be legislative, executive, or judicial.

For an example of legislative delegation, consider the EU treaties that give European institutions—the Council, the Commission, the Parliament—the power to enact competition policy (antitrust law). The laws issued by these institutions apply to businesses in the member states and take precedence over those member states' domestic competition laws. If European countries wanted to implement regional competition policy without using European institutions, they would constantly have to enter new treaties that modify the law in response to changing conditions. Treaty making and amendment are extremely cumbersome, requiring unanimity. By contrast, the European institutions, like the legislative institutions of national governments, use voting rules (majority, supermajority: with each member state's voting power based on the size of its population) that fall well short of unanimity and enjoy the support of a permanent bureaucracy. Additional treaties give these EU institutions authority over various other areas of policy.

Legislative delegation at the international level, however, is exceedingly rare. The Security Council occasionally engages in behavior that looks like legislation: it adopts a policy and incorporates rules into a legally binding resolution. For example, it has issued some rules that restrict terrorist financing. Various bodies, such as the International Labor Organization, can propose rules, but states are free to reject them. Maybe these rules sometimes enter customary international law but usually not. Likewise, the General Assembly can issue resolutions that seem to set down rules of conduct, but these rules are not law unless they enter customary international law, and this requires widespread, perhaps universal, consent. Powerful institutions (by international standards) such as the World Trade Organization do not make law (except in the interstices of the treaty text); they merely provide forums for state-to-state negotiation and a bureaucracy for expertise and logistical support. The World Bank and the IMF set policies that states are free to ignore, though at a price, of course. These institutions have influence because states must comply with those policies in order to receive financial assistance, but they do not have lawmaking power.[2]

The best example of judicial delegation also comes from the European Union. The European Court of Justice (ECJ) has the power to resolve disputes arising under European law—the treaties and the secondary law created by the legislative institutions. Normally, domestic courts would have this power. If, for example, someone alleges that the German government violates European law, a German court would decide the case. But Germany has delegated this judicial power to the ECJ. If the ECJ decides that Germany has violated European law, then German domestic courts will normally defer to the ECJ's decision—as well as to the ECJ's interpretations of European law in cases not involving Germany.

Judicial delegation at the international level is also extremely rare. The International Court of Justice has jurisdiction over certain interstate disputes, but there is little evidence that national judiciaries treat its rulings as legally binding. The U.S. Supreme Court has explicitly rejected the argument that the ICJ's rulings bind American courts.[3] Many other international courts exist, and it is hard to generalize about them, but it is safe to say that judicial delegation has either not occurred or is of little practical importance outside the field of international trade, which indeed has a highly judicialized dispute resolution mechanism. Moreover, governments decide whether to comply with the ruling of an international court. If they do not, they violate international law, but noncompliance is always an option.

Delegation of executive power to an international institution has been even less common; indeed, it is hard to think of a pure example. States have delegated certain administrative tasks to international agencies. Again, the European Union is the strongest example. The Commission has certain powers that we think of as executive. It can investigate allegations of misconduct and impose fines and other penalties. But it cannot directly enforce its will; for that, it must rely on the law enforcement agencies of the member states. Similarly, the UN Security Council can investigate breaches of the peace and issue legally binding orders to states that threaten security. But although its founders hoped that it would someday have its own army, states never gave it one. So the Security Council must rely on states to carry out its will by deploying military forces. Execution of the law in the end relies on guns, and states very rarely put guns in the hands of international organizations. The occasional international peacekeeping force is a very limited exception.

The most common type of international organization is the committee or commission. These institutions have a mixture of legislative, executive, and judicial power that is so watered down as to bear little resemblance to the real thing. When states enter ambitious multilateral treaties, they often establish committees, councils, or commissions to which member states send delegates. Human rights treaties frequently create such organizations, but so do many other types of treaties. The delegates will meet periodically and discuss compliance and other issues related to the treaty. They discuss and propose amendments, for example, and they issue resolutions proposing rules that seem justified by the general policy goals of the treaty. States are free to follow or disregard these rules. The delegates will also issue interpretations of the treaty. They may also send agents or groups to investigate allegations that a state party has violated the treaty—subject, of course, to the state in question giving permission. No one knows how much effect committees, commissions, and councils have on international relations; we suspect that it is marginal.

The Benefits and Costs of Delegation: Domestic

The scarcity of international delegation has puzzled many scholars because the benefits of international delegation seem obvious. Indeed, delegation within nations is ubiquitous, and we can start with the analysis as it exists in the domestic setting.

In the United States, Congress delegates power to administrative agencies like the Environmental Protection Agency when it passes laws with vague goals—protect the public, increase safety, reduce pollution—along with authority to issue regulations that flesh out those goals. Because the goals are so vague, the agency has de facto policymaking authority, on which it draws when issuing regulations that impose specific rules—so many parts per million of such-and-such particle may be emitted into the air, for example. Courts may review these regulations, but because the legal limits on the agency's actions are so vague, the courts usually defer to the agency's policy judgments.

Delegation serves three purposes. First, it frees up Congress's time for other matters. If Congress had to determine every standard for every type of pollutant, it would have no time to do anything else. Delegation is required by the vastness of modern governance. Second, it allows for the accumulation of knowledge in a specialist bureaucracy. Agencies can be expert in a way that Congress, always dependent on outside advice, cannot be. Third, and more controversially, delegation may promote impartiality in government. Because agency officials are appointed rather than elected, agencies are insulated from public pressure, it is argued, so they can take the long view. Many people disagree with this last argument, however; agencies may be susceptible to pressures from interest groups, which overwhelm them with studies and reports and offer agency officials lucrative positions in the regulated industry when they leave office.

The costs of delegation are twofold. First, if agencies are insulated from public pressure, they can go off on frolics. An agency official who issues regulations that serve her own personal ideological interest, or the interest of some regulated industry that she hopes will give her a job, cannot easily be disciplined. Political superiors, including Congress, may have trouble evaluating the regulation—that is why an agency exists in the first place. These costs are known as "agency costs." Second, the technocratic attitudes of agencies fit uneasily with democratic aspirations. Elected officials are supposed to regulate those who elect them; many people suspect that Congress hands over the most difficult issues to agencies so as to duck the brickbats that come flying whenever politicians take a controversial position.

Although the academic debate continues, delegation is a settled fact in modern governance. In the United States, the success of the New Deal put the question to rest. Today, we live under an immense bureaucracy that has obtained its powers from congressional delegation.

The Benefits and Costs of Delegation: International

Why doesn't this logic carry through to the international plane? If states could, by treaty, delegate certain powers to an international agency, then the states could turn their attention to other things while the agency regulates. The agency would accumulate expertise, pooling knowledge drawn from officials from all over the world. And because the agency would be insulated from popular pressures within states, and thus from the periodic xenophobic eruptions from which all states suffer, it could act independently, with the global interest in mind.

This is the argument for international delegation. Outside of the European Union, however, it has been rejected. The only explanation is that states do not trust international agencies to act in their interest: agency costs are overwhelmingly high.[4] To see why, compare international delegation with domestic delegation. When Congress sets up an agency, it expects the ranks of the agency to be drawn from its constituents—or, really, members of the U.S. political elite. Congress has a say in appointments and retains control over the agency by virtue of its appropriations power and its ability to reverse agency decisions and modify its organization by statute. Although the interests of agency officials will not be perfectly aligned with those of Congress, Congress has many tools for disciplining the agency.

Now imagine an international Environmental Protection Agency with authority to issue regulations governing activities that pollute the high seas and the atmosphere. If established by treaty, then states will be able to discipline the agency only by treaty—which requires unanimous consent. This means that the agency can do whatever it wants, as long as it pleases one state that can exercise a veto on proposals for amendment. In addition, the agency officials will come not from one country but from many different countries and will have political preferences that reflect their national origins. Because values and interests across countries are much more heterogeneous than the values and interests within a country, the world as a whole will have much more trouble agreeing on the mission of an international agency than a particular national legislature will have in agreeing on the mission of a domestic agency. These two problems feed on themselves. If the world cannot agree on much, it will not be able to agree on how to discipline a wayward agency. The agency therefore will do what it wants. To forestall such an outcome, nations refrain from delegating power to an agency in the first place.[5]

These are, of course, empirical conjectures and some people will disagree with them. And we will see some cases where international agencies—especially courts—are established. In these cases, the benefits of international delegation evidently outweigh the costs, at least in the eyes of states that engage in it.

The United Nations

Predecessors

World War I killed millions of people and convinced leaders that the somewhat relaxed attitude toward war in the nineteenth century could no longer be sustained. In the nineteenth century, most people believed that states had a legal right to go to war; war was just an element of Great Power politics. After the Napoleonic Wars, wars between the major states were relatively rare, and those that did occur were not nearly as devastating as those of the twentieth century would be. Technology changed all this. The railroad gave states the power to mobilize enormous masses of troops and quickly move them to the front. Advances in metallurgy, ballistics, automation, and chemistry yielded artillery pieces, machine guns, powerful bombs, and poison gas—which could kill many more people in a short time span than the weapons of the past. Technological change does not always favor killing (as opposed to defense), but in the late nineteenth and early twentieth centuries it did. The U.S. Civil War hinted at these developments, but battles in which tens of thousands died did not become routine until World War I.

The increased destructiveness of war persuaded people that war should be ruled out, or used only as a last resort, and only for the purpose of preventing a more devastating war. The Treaty of Versailles ended World War I in the West and provided the groundwork for the League of Nations. The rules of the League of Nations did not outlaw war, but they did require states to seek peaceful means to resolve their disputes and empowered the League—an institution to which all states would send delegates—to impose sanctions on states that breached the peace and even to authorize the use of military force against them.

Scholars debate whether the League system helped resolve disputes in the 1920s, but everyone agrees that it failed to prevent World War II. The United States is often blamed for failing to ratify the Treaty of Versailles and hence declining to join the League of Nations. The League responded ineffectually to Japan's invasion of Manchuria in 1931 and Italy's invasion of Abyssinia in 1935. In both cases, the major powers did not have an interest in sanctioning the aggressors. It is costly to impose sanctions—if they cannot trade with you, you also cannot trade with them. And although the major powers objected to both invasions, the victims of the invasions were just not important for those powers' security needs.

Origins of the United Nations

The failure of the League of Nations system gave rise to redoubled efforts to construct an international organization that could advance collective security. The United Nations, named after the victorious allies in World War II, was the result. World War II confirmed the devastation of World War I, but the Holocaust set it apart as a uniquely grotesque event in human history. The lesson seemed to be that not only must states prevent war, they must also prevent other states from committing atrocities against their own populations.

The wartime U.S. president, Franklin Delano Roosevelt, had a vague notion that the United States and the Soviet Union would act as the world's policemen, albeit in some kind of formal institutional structure, modeled on the League of Nations but with more teeth. The organization that emerged from negotiations in San Francisco in 1945 bore traces of this conception but would evolve into a more complex institution.

The United Nations consists of three main institutions: the Security Council, the General Assembly, and the secretariat. The secretary general has administrative authority and a bully pulpit but no formal legal power. The General Assembly consists of delegates from every member state—there were 193 as of 2011, nearly all of the nations of the world. The General Assembly can issue resolutions, but these resolutions have no legal force. The Security Council has fifteen members; it is the only institution within the United Nations that has the power to issue legally binding orders. There are also numerous agencies, such as the United Nations Children's Fund, that can collect information, make proposals, and the like, but that also have no legal authority.

Security Council

Of the fifteen seats on the Security Council, five are permanent and ten rotate. The permanent members are the United States, Russia, China, France, and the United Kingdom. The rotating seats are distributed on a regional basis—so every region of the world always has some representation on the Security Council. Regional groups select the member among themselves, though this is subject to a pro forma vote by the General Assembly.

The Security Council makes decisions by a supermajority vote—nine of the fifteen members must agree. Each of the permanent members holds a veto.

Thus, the Security Council cannot act against the interests of any of the permanent members; it can act against the interests of any other state unless that state has found a patron among the permanent members.

These rules have a simple explanation. Roosevelt anticipated not a global government or parliament or some such thing but a concert of Great Powers, which would jointly keep the peace. He envisioned "four policemen"—the United States, China, Britain, and the Soviet Union. France, still an empire and nominally a powerful state even after its defeat during World War II, was later added. At the time, China was divided by civil war; later Taiwan would be given the China seat, and still later that seat would be turned over to mainland China, which continues to hold it.

It is striking that virtually every state has agreed to this system. States do not lightly yield sovereignty to international institutions; the Security Council is probably the only clear example at the international level (as opposed to the regional level, where the European Union has considerably greater powers). States other than the permanent members have agreed that they can be bound to a legal order without their consent—in contradiction to the normal unanimity rule that prevails in international law, as we have seen. But the end of World War II was a unique period in international relations. All the major states had been devastated, except the United States, which could not be allowed to retreat into isolation as it had done after World War I. The United States and the Soviet Union had extraordinary prestige. Modern military technology, culminating in the atom bomb, would complete the destruction of World War II if global war recurred.

But the Security Council did not live up to its promise. During the cold war, which began within a few years of the end of World War II and ended around 1989, the Security Council could never reach a consensus on an issue of significance. The reason was very simple. During the cold war, the United States and the Soviet Union regarded each other as enemies. They fought through proxies, with each country forming alliances with whatever other countries that it could. A potential breach of peace could occur in any number of circumstances—a country could be threatened by a neighbor or by an insurgency. But inevitably the United States and the Soviet Union took opposite sides, so that Security Council action in favor of one side would always be against the interests of one of the two superpower rivals. Thus, one or the other would veto or threaten to veto resolutions that could keep the peace, and so Security Council involvement in major disputes almost never occurred.

There was one exception, the Korean War of 1950–1953. When North Korea invaded South Korea, the United States secured a Security Council Resolution that condemned the invasion and authorized countries to use force to repel it. The Soviet Union had walked out in protest of the failure to give the China seat of the Security Council to the People's Republic of China, the Soviet Union's communist ally. Taiwan, a U.S. ally, held the seat. The Soviets would not repeat this error.

But it can be doubted whether the error made much of a difference. The founders of the UN appeared to have expected states to give the Security Council its own army, so that it could independently use force against states that breach the peace. That never happened. No state was willing to put troops under international—meaning, in practice, foreign—command. So a Security Council resolution could not mobilize force against a threat to the peace. It could at best confer some legitimacy on one side of a conflict.

But it could not even do that until the end of the cold war. In the meantime, numerous conflicts occurred, while the Security Council sat by helplessly. These included three wars between India and Pakistan; numerous wars between Israel and its neighbors; a large number of conflicts in Africa; Soviet actions in several of its satellites and Afghanistan; U.S. actions in Cuba, Vietnam, Grenada, and other places; a war between Britain and Argentina; a British and French adventure in the Middle East; a war between China and Vietnam and between Vietnam and Cambodia; and various border conflicts between the Soviet Union and China. There were also countless insurgencies and civil wars, often with cross-border effects, and frequently involving atrocities on a wide scale—in none of these conflicts did the Security Council play any serious role.

With the end of the cold war, it seemed that the Security Council might fulfill the role it had been given. In 1990, Iraq invaded Kuwait. This time the Security Council condemned the invasion and authorized the use of military force against Iraq. A coalition led by the United States launched an air attack and brief ground war against Iraq in 1991, ejecting Iraqi forces from Kuwait and inflicting heavy damage.

The United States and other Western countries had numerous reasons for opposing the Iraqi invasion. What was new was that the Soviet Union did not exercise its veto. The Soviet Union was in the midst of a difficult transition, trying to dismantle its authoritarian political system and communist economic system, and highly reliant on the West for assistance. It gained nothing from Iraq's adventures and did not want to antagonize the West.

The Security Council also set the parameters for the ensuing isolation of Iraq. The resolution ending the war merely suspended hostilities until Iraq revealed and destroyed its weapons of mass destruction. The resolution also ordered Iraq to pay reparations to Kuwait and respect the human rights of its people. The Security Council maintained sanctions on Iraq when that country failed to comply and for the next decade managed the sanctions regime.

But the legacy of the Iraq War for the Security Council was mixed. Iraq did not at first cooperate in the dismantling of its weapons of mass destruction (WMD), and it continued to cause trouble—for example, attempting to assassinate George H. W. Bush, the U.S. president during the Iraq War. The Security Council kept the pressure on Iraq, but it could do little more than tinker with the sanctions regime, which both imposed hardships on Iraqi civilians and proved leaky and ineffective at pressuring the Iraqi regime. An exception under which Iraq could trade oil for food and medicine gave rise to a corruption scandal involving UN officials.

Although it was revealed later that the Iraqis did dismantle, or at least suspend, their WMD programs in response to pressure in the latter half of the 1990s, they did not admit to having done so, nor did they allow inspectors the unrestricted access that would have been necessary to verify that the programs had ended. No one knows why; perhaps Saddam Hussein hoped to keep his enemies (such as Iran) guessing, or perhaps lower-level officials never informed him of what they were doing. In any event, the perceived failure of the sanctions regime contributed to the U.S. and British decisions to go to war against Iraq again in 2003.

The Security Council did not authorize the 2003 invasion of Iraq. France and Russia made clear that they opposed the move. The United States and Britain claimed legal authority under the 1991 Security Council resolution that suspended hostilities on condition that Iraq eliminate its WMD programs. Since Iraq had failed to do so, hostilities could continue. Critics argued that the Security Council had reserved for itself the exclusive right to determine whether Iraq had complied with the earlier resolution. The critics had a point. The United States sidelined the Security Council by adopting a highly aggressive interpretation of its earlier resolutions. It is hard to imagine nations like China, Russia, and even France repeating this mistake in the future.

As the central institution for responding to breaches of the peace, the Security Council is hardly more credible today than it was during the cold war. But it has found a niche. Starting in 1948, UN peacekeeping operations have been established in various conflict-ridden states in the developing world. Rather than forging consensus or initiating military operations for the purpose of countering states that pose threats to others, states put peacekeeping operations in place after agreeing on a settlement. UN soldiers—who are simply soldiers contributed by various UN member states—engage in policing operations in places where civilian law enforcement has failed, or maintain safe zones for refugees, or guard the borders between hostile forces.

What accounts for the disappointing performance of the Security Council? The answer lies in its weak structure. A collective body that must act under a supermajority rule will have trouble coming to agreement, especially when the members have divergent interests. During the cold war, the United States and the Soviet Union rarely could cooperate because of their mutual suspicion. After the cold war, some convergence in the interests of the major countries occurred, and this has permitted greater cooperation, such as the authorization to intervene in Libya in 2011. However, nations still disagree a great deal about security matters, and so the Security Council can do very little. But then why did nations set up such a weak structure in the first place? The answer is that when principals have divergent interests, they will not delegate authority to a strong agent because the agent cannot be trusted to act in their joint interests.

Security Council Reform

Some people have pinned their hopes on reform. The structure of the Security Council—in particular, the existence of permanent members with the veto—reflects great power politics that are sixty years out of date. France and Britain are no longer leading nations. Germany is bigger and wealthier than both. So is Japan. Regional balance argues for the inclusion of India (the second most populous country), Brazil (the most populous country and leading economy in South America), an African country such as Nigeria (most populous) or South Africa (largest economy), and perhaps Indonesia (another vast country).

The reform proposals, however, have been a flop; and the reasons why are illuminating. Some reformers advocate elimination of the veto on the ground that it unfairly gives a handful of states the power to block action. The veto holders, for obvious reasons, oppose this proposal. And nations cannot agree who should be given special status as a permanent member. China opposes Japan's membership because of long-standing hostility between those nations. Pakistan opposes India. Argentina and Mexico oppose Brazil. Italy opposes Germany. Various compromise proposals that create a new tier of membership—permanent or with longer terms but no veto—have also failed.

Why can't states agree? Increasing the number of vetoes will further encumber decision making and at some point make it impossible. Eliminating vetoes will put powerful states at the mercy of weaker states—something they will never tolerate. And no country will willingly permit a regional or global rival to obtain additional institutional powers that it currently lacks. The problem boils down to agency costs. States do not trust other states to act in their interests; since the Security Council is just an agglomeration of the interests of the permanent members and those members who happen to rotate on, its expansion will just put those states left off at a greater disadvantage, while weakening the power of permanent members, which would therefore veto any such reform. Thus, we are trapped in the status quo distribution of power.

General Assembly

The General Assembly has the look and feel of an ordinary national legislature; it just has none of a legislature's powers. The General Assembly consists of delegates of each member state. Each state has one vote, with majority rule. Resolutions issued by the General Assembly have no legal effect.

It is not surprising that the powerful states that established the United Nations, and finance it, have refused to agree to a system of one state, one vote, for legally binding orders. The two largest states in the world, China and India, have populations over one billion. A few dozen states have populations in the tens and hundreds of millions. Many states are much smaller, with the smallest having less than 20,000.[6] The majority of states contain much less than a majority of the world's population, and if they had the power to bind other states, they would no doubt use that power to transfer the world's wealth in their direction.

That leaves the question of what function the General Assembly is supposed to accomplish. It does give small states a voice. A resolution that has the consent of 120 small, poor states may make more of an impression than 120 diplomatic notes. A resolution can help influence the development of customary international law just because it can provide a relatively clear indication of the attitudes of a multitude of states. The General Assembly has a role in the election of judges for the International Court of Justice and members of the Security Council—institutions that do have legal power—and in determining the composition of other bodies. But little more can be said.

From time to time, various states have argued that the General Assembly does or should have legal power. At one time, the United States claimed that the General Assembly could take over the Security Council's function when that institution was frozen by the veto and the United States had more allies; in more recent years, others have taken up this position (while the United States has abandoned it). Because powerful states will never yield power to the larger group of weak states, do not expect this proposal to bear fruit.

The European Union

Existing international institutions tend to be weak, but that is not inevitable. If the gains from international cooperation were high enough, and governance and other heterogeneity costs were low enough, then people might prefer strong international institutions. The history of state building supports this conjecture. Most states are constructed from smaller self-governing states that unified. England and Scotland merged in 1707. The United States is the product of a long period of integration, which included the ratification of a constitution in 1788 and the elimination of secessionist tendencies in the South after a brutal civil war that lasted from 1861 to 1865. Several dozen German states merged in the nineteenth century, as did a number of Italian states. In all of these cases, the populations of the states that merged acquiesced in the delegation of substantial government authority from the original states to the merged state.

Today, the chief examples of such processes can be found in Europe. Some commentators have argued that if European countries, which, after all, have a long history of bloodshed, can delegate authority to regional institutions, then countries around the world can delegate authority to international institutions. We cannot in this book fully address European institutions, but we will briefly address them here to illustrate two important themes: how states can overcome externalities through cooperation and how delegation to institutions can advance cooperation.[7]

A Brief Overview

The European Union consists of twenty-seven member states, a majority of the states in Europe and nearly all of its major economies. It originated in the 1950s as two organizations, the European Coal and Steel Community (ECSC) and the European Economic Community (EEC), which initially had only six members—France, Germany, Italy, the Netherlands, Belgium, and Luxembourg. The ECSC regulated the coal and steel industries in those countries, while the EEC lowered tariff barriers and brought about a customs union. Over the years, additional members joined these institutions, and the institutions were given a number of additional powers. The main accomplishment of the European system, which became known as the European Union in 1993, was to integrate the economies of Europe and maintain political peace among the countries. In 2009, the EU was given a "constitution," which for the most part formalized existing understandings.

The major institutions of the EU include the Council of Ministers, the European Commission, the European Parliament, and the European Court of Justice. (Another institution known as the European Council, which consists of the heads of state, sets general policy.) Governance is complex, with the rules depending on the area of policy, but speaking very roughly, it works as follows. The European Commission, which serves as the EU's bureaucracy, proposes legislation (usually), based on the policy priorities set by the European Council. Both the Council of Ministers, in which each state has a seat, and the Parliament, whose members are directly elected by European citizens, play a role in approving the legislation, based on various voting rules (which essentially require a supermajority). European legislation is generally implemented by the member states, but the Commission and other agencies have enforcement authority as well. The European Court of Justice has jurisdiction over disputes arising under European law.

Scholars have devoted a great deal of effort to ascertaining whether the system is essentially one of intergovernmentalism (states are bound only to laws to which they consent) or supranationalism (states can be bound to laws to which they do not consent).[8] Clearly, the EU is nothing like a nation-state—most Europeans identify with the countries in which they live, not with Europe as such; the member states pursue independent foreign policies outside of trade, recent efforts to set up a foreign minister for the EU and a president of the European Council notwithstanding; and much of domestic policy (including tax rates and spending) remains discretionary as well. Yet the EU is not a mere confederation or conglomeration of states. From the standpoint of international law, the EU looks decidedly supranationalist: there are no international institutions that feature comparable levels of delegation from member states to institutions with government-like powers. The key distinction is that, by contrast to most international organizations, in various policy areas no single state can veto outcomes approved by a supermajority of other states in the European system. International delegation has thus occurred to a greater degree.

Gains and Limits

Thanks to its institutions, the EU has accomplished a great deal. The EU has created a common market, that is, there are no trade barriers; the economies are subject to a common set of regulations (albeit with a degree of permitted variation); people are free to move from country to country; a common agricultural policy prevails; its competition, intellectual property, and privacy laws have greatly affected the behavior of multinational organizations; and so on. The EU has successfully combined the bargaining power of its members so that it can counter American, Japanese, and Chinese trade policies. And the EU has played a large role in pacifying and unifying peripheral countries in Europe by dangling the economic carrot of membership in return for commitments to respect human rights, resolve conflicts peacefully, and in general act as good world citizens.

Moreover, the European institutions are generally respected (with the possible exception of the Parliament, which has failed to win much public support). The European Commission is a highly regarded bureaucracy, and the European Court of Justice is usually obeyed by the member states.

The EU faces some significant problems. As noted, most ordinary Europeans feel little loyalty to European institutions, and thus if significant strains arise, the national governments could well reassert themselves. European leaders failed at several attempts to advance European integration in the last decade or so. Notably, a treaty establishing a European constitution was rejected by voters in France and the Netherlands in 2005; a watered-down version that effected many of the same changes but avoided the language of constitutionalism was rejected by voters in Ireland before finally being ratified in 2009. Most countries did not subject either treaty to a referendum, so the rejections by French, Dutch, and Irish voters underlined the lack of significant popular support for deepening integration.

Turkey poses an acute embarrassment: by all rights, it should be admitted into the EU, but if it were, a Muslim country would be the second largest member state, with proportionate influence, and this possible outcome sits uneasily with many Europeans. The eurozone debt crisis, which we will discuss in Chapter 19, has put a great deal of stress on European solidarity. The debt crisis has highlighted the weakness of European institutions other than the central bank. And the Europeans have failed to create a common foreign policy. To a large extent, the EU exists at the sufferance of the member states, unlike a normal country, like the United States, whose states are fully subordinate to the national government, in fact if not always in theory.

Significance for International Law

These problems do not undermine the claim that the EU is the prime example of international delegation. Its member states successfully created a set of institutions that internalize externalities as they arise, and so the states do not need to renegotiate their relationship every time a new issue arises. Some commentators have argued that if European countries can engage in international delegation of such depth and significance, then other countries should be able to do so as well, and indeed that something like a world government (in the limited sense that the EU is a kind of supranational government) ought to be possible.

And yet broad international delegation of this type is no more likely today than it was fifty or a hundred years ago. Why not? The major factors behind European integration do not apply to the world as a whole. European integration began only a few years after the end of World War II and cannot be understood outside this context. European countries, France in particular, sought ways to bind Germany economically and politically to the other countries, so that a third world war would be impossible. Germany, in return, needed a route back to international respectability, and European integration provided such a path.

Also recall our discussion of heterogeneity costs in Chapter 3. The European countries resemble each other a great deal more than other countries resemble each other. A common set of values binds these countries together: most of them subscribe to basic Western norms supporting political freedom, religious tolerance, women's rights, and redistribution to the poor. Thus, none of the countries take much of a risk that European institutions will compel them to act against their values. Although it is difficult to quantify such things, it seems likely that Europeans share roughly similar valuations for major public goods—such as environmental protection, security, food safety, and so forth. (A major problem revealed by the eurozone debt crisis is that monetary integration may be impossible without fiscal integration, which voters in wealthier countries have so far opposed lest they end up transferring wealth to the poorer countries in the periphery like Greece.) Thus, heterogeneity costs in Europe, or at least in the core European countries (which are also the largest), are low.[9]

As for the benefits of integration, at least the leaders and elites in Europe believe that peace is the chief public good that has resulted from integration. Economic benefits have been large as well, although it is not clear how much larger they would have been beyond what was achieved from the general relaxation of international trade barriers through the General Agreement on Tariffs and Trade (GATT) and the WTO.

In sum, Europeans faced low heterogeneity costs and large benefits from integration; this permitted them to engage in partial international delegation, albeit far less than what would be necessary to create a new state. The rest of the world faces significantly higher heterogeneity costs; and it is not clear how to judge the benefits to be gained from global delegation to government institutions. The inability of the European public to warm to the EU government also sounds warning bells. If this is a problem for Europe, it would be a far worse problem for the world. For the foreseeable future, then, major international delegation is most unlikely.

International Adjudication

Aside from the Security Council and the World Trade Organization, which we will discuss in Chapter 18, the most consequential international organizations are (or appear to be) courts. Table 7.1 shows many of them.

The International Court of Justice enjoys the most prominence. It was created by the founders of the United Nations, and all UN member states—virtually all states—may use the ICJ. The ICJ handles general state-to-state disputes involving any issue of international law. But states have hived off many areas of international law for other tribunals. The WTO dispute settlement mechanism handles trade disputes arising under the WTO/GATT system. The Law of the Sea Tribunal hears law-of-the-sea cases. The International Criminal Court holds trials of people accused of international crimes. Unlike the other courts, the ICC does not hear state-to-state cases but cases brought by an independent prosecutor (also set up by the ICC treaty) against persons.

The ICC is not the first international criminal tribunal. It descends from the Nuremberg Tribunal, which was created after World War II to prosecute Nazis (a similar tribunal was set up in Tokyo to try Japanese war criminals). In between, a variety of ad hoc international criminal tribunals have been used to address particular conflicts—the International Criminal Tribunal for the Former Yugoslavia, the International Criminal Tribunal for Rwanda, and various hybrid tribunals combining international and national elements in Cambodia, Sierra Leone, and elsewhere. Most of these proceedings are ongoing or winding down. The founders of the ICC hoped to put international criminal justice on a more stable footing by creating a permanent tribunal that could take the place of the ad hoc tribunals that were being constantly reinvented.

Regional courts also exist. Human rights courts exist for Latin America, Europe, and Africa. There are also various trade courts, including the NAFTA tribunal. Also of great importance, but frequently overlooked, is international arbitration.

Arbitration

The simplest form of international dispute resolution is arbitration. Because of its simplicity, it is easy to understand and provides a starting point for analyzing international courts.

Table 7.1. Selected International Courts

Court	Established	State Parties
International Court of Justice (ICJ)	1945	193 parties to ICJ statute; 66 filed declarations of acceptance of compulsory jurisdiction.
International Tribunal for the Law of the Sea (ITLOS)	1982	161 parties to UNCLOS; 14 accepted compulsory jurisdiction.
Dispute Settlement System of the World Trade Organization (WTO)	1994	153
International Criminal Court (ICC)	1998	114
International Criminal Tribunal for the Former Yugoslavia (ICTY)	1993	Created by United Nations
International Criminal Tribunal for Rwanda (ICTR)	1993	Created by United Nations
European Court of Human Rights (ECHR)	1950/1994	47
Inter-American Court of Human Rights	1969	25
African Court on Human and People's Rights (AfCHR)	1998	25
European Court of Justice	1952	27
Court of Justice of the Andean Community (TJAC)	1979	5
Central American Court of Justice (CACJ)	1907	3
Court of Justice of the Common Market for Eastern and Southern Africa (COMESA)	1993	19

Note: The number of state parties has been updated where possible through July 2011.
Source: Cesare P. R. Romano et al., *PICT Research Matrix,* http://www.pict-pcti.org/matrix/Matrix-main.html (accessed Aug. 11, 2009).

The Structure of Arbitration

International arbitration resembles domestic arbitration.[10] In both settings, the parties either begin with a dispute, which they later decide to submit to arbitration, or they have an existing agreement (a treaty or contract) that stipulates that arbitration will occur in case of dispute. Often, each party selects an arbitrator (sometimes more than one, but always an equal number); the selected arbitrators or a neutral party then select a third arbitrator (or arbitrators). The arbitration agreement will usually provide instructions to the arbitration panel, telling them exactly which issues to decide and imposing other constraints, for example, on the remedy. Each party hires a lawyer or agent to argue its case before the arbitration panel; the panel decides by majority rule. The arguments and opinions are frequently secret; the procedures may be ad hoc.

Arbitrators, in domestic and international settings, are private individuals: they have no power to coerce the losing party to pay an award. In domestic arbitration, the victor can usually persuade a court to issue an order enforcing an award. In international arbitration, this is virtually impossible. The losing party must decide whether to comply with the arbitration award or not; it often does. In some cases, states have agreed in advance to arrangements that allow the awards to be enforced by national courts against their available assets.

It should be clear, then, that arbitration takes place mainly between countries that are already inclined to cooperate with each other. As noted, the two states will often have to consent to arbitrate in the first place; and the losing state will have to consent to pay the award. Arbitration will rarely settle disputes between states on the verge of war. But it is still a valuable procedure for a range of more modest but still important disputes.

The Theory of Arbitration

What explains the structure of arbitration? Why do states appoint arbitrators, who then appoint another arbitrator or group of arbitrators? To understand these questions, recall that disputes arise because of information asymmetries—each state has information about its interests, the sources of law, or the facts, which the other state lacks. Consider a border dispute: each state knows how much value it attaches to the disputed area and not necessarily how much value the other state attaches to the disputed area; or each state holds an interpretation of treaties, based on its own interpretation of the relevant materials; or each state has records of land use that hint where the border was located at an earlier time. The states are jointly better off if the information is aggregated but do not have an incentive to disclose their private information unilaterally. An impasse results; information is not disclosed, and the territory remains disputed and hence not efficiently exploited.

Arbitration can help overcome this problem. The arbitrator is typically given both fact-finding authority and the authority to interpret ambiguous elements of the law. By adopting rules and presumptions, the arbitrator may be able to compel states to disclose information. For example, the arbitrator might infer from state X's refusal to turn over land use records that those records contain information that favor state Y's claims. State X must either turn over those records or risk losing the case. The arbitrator can also help resolve legal ambiguities by drawing on the expertise of international lawyers.

One important benefit of arbitration is that the final order (if public) enables other states—those not involved in the arbitration—to evaluate the behavior of the states involved. Without arbitration, it will be difficult for other states to evaluate the factual claims of states X and Y, and—to some extent—even the legal claims, especially if they are based on some bilateral treaty between X and Y, or local customs, with which other states are unfamiliar. Once the arbitral order is issued, other states learn that state X or Y violated international law, and they will also learn whether state X or Y cares enough about international law to bring its behavior in line with the conclusion of the arbitrator. For X and Y, then, arbitration raises the stakes and hence the probability of resolution and compliance.

But all this depends on the arbitration panel being neutral. The panel must determine the facts as they exist, and not in such a way that benefits one side or the other. And the panel must evaluate the law in the same way. It is tempting to think that arbitrators must be people of good will and hence that there is no reason to believe that they would act otherwise, but the careful design of arbitration procedures shows that states are not willing to make this assumption.

Indeed, states generally assume that the arbitrators they directly appoint will be biased in their favor. Often, unless the agreement to arbitrate forecloses this option (as in the WTO), state X appoints a national of X—a government official or someone else in the legal or political elite—and state Y appoints a national of Y. Typically, X's arbitrator will vote in favor of X, and Y's arbitrator will vote in favor of Y. The third arbitrator—the one jointly appointed by X's and Y's arbitrators—holds the key to impartiality.

Now, X's arbitrator would prefer the third arbitrator to prefer X, and Y's arbitrator would prefer the third arbitrator to prefer Y. They both might try to appoint nationals of their own states. But this cannot happen because the two arbitrators must agree on the third. The only type of arbitrator they could agree on is one who is not likely to be biased in favor of X (for Y's arbitrator would reject such a person) and one who is not likely to be biased in favor of Y (for X's arbitrator would reject such a person). A person who satisfies these conditions must be neutral between X and Y (but not necessarily other states that might have an interest in the outcome, an issue to which we will return).

This simple device for achieving impartiality is the core of the arbitration system. However, it need not always succeed. X's and Y's arbitrators might blunder, of course, and end up agreeing to a third arbitrator who is not impartial. Worse, the states never know whether X and Y might have blundered, so they may doubt whether the panel as a whole is neutral. This uncertainty also affects the ability of other states to evaluate the behavior of the states in question. Still, on average, the arbitration system will do better than the alternative—diplomatic negotiation that leads to an impasse—because it does inject information into the process where, as we have seen, the reason for impasse in the first place is insufficient information about facts, law, and the interests of the states.

The Limits of Arbitration

Arbitration is only a partial solution to the problem of international disputes. The main limitation of arbitration is that it is voluntary. States not inclined to arbitrate will not arbitrate. Consider a predatory state, one that seeks to conquer others or bully them in other ways. Such a state would not agree to arbitrate the disputes it starts with other states because it knows it would lose a fair arbitration.

There are domestic analogies. Two merchants who frequently interact with each other may well agree to arbitrate their disputes because they want to continue to do business even though they disagree about one or more of their contracts. A thief, by contrast, has no reason to agree to arbitrate the theft with the victim. Indeed, a merchant who expects to go out of business may refuse to arbitrate existing contractual disputes; why bother if he does not plan to continue doing business with the people on the other side? For such cases, a mandatory judicial system is required. The victim (or a representative such as the state) can force the perpetrator into court and obtain a judgment that can be enforced, through violence if necessary.

The idea of mandatory international dispute resolution caught fire in the twentieth century. But this idea is puzzling. If international law rests on the consent of states, then states would have to consent to mandatory dispute resolution. What would it mean to consent to something mandatory? Couldn't states withdraw their consent if they decide they prefer not going through with a judicial proceeding? Or might the negative consequences of such an action be greater than any possible benefit? We will consider these questions below.

Another disadvantage of arbitration is that every new arbitration involves significant start-up costs. States have to agree to arbitrate, draw up the instructions, and hire arbitrators; the arbitrators may have to agree to procedures, and so forth. Over time, some of these processes may be routinized, but a permanent arbitration or even court system can avoid these start-up costs. Let a permanent group of arbitrators or judges be appointed, with fixed terms, a courthouse, and an established set of procedures. Let them publish their opinions so that a jurisprudence can evolve, in a clearer or more systematic way than with traditional arbitrations (which often result in secret opinions).

These twin concerns—with mandatory jurisdiction and with institutional regularity—produced a push toward judicialization. The twentieth century would be the century of international courts.

International Court of Justice

The central international court, though not necessarily the most important, is the ICJ. The ICJ was not actually the first international court. That honor goes to the misnamed Permanent Court of International Justice (PCIJ), which was created after World War I but proved unable to resolve, or even play any positive role in, the disputes that would lead up to World War II. The "Permanent" in the PCIJ's name might seem a hubristic gesture, one for which its founders received their comeuppance, but it reflected the commitment to moving beyond ad hoc arbitration and replacing it with a regular judicial system. The ICJ would be the PCIJ's successor and would have the same basic structure and organization but a more modest name.

Structure

The ICJ has its own statute, the Statute of the ICJ, but this treaty was drafted at the same time as the UN Charter, and was incorporated in the UN Charter. Thus, people often refer to the ICJ as the "judicial organ" of the United Nations, that is, a kind of judicial branch in a larger international government whose policy apparatus is contained in the Security Council and the General Assembly. All UN members are thus "members" of the ICJ—but as we will see, being a member of the ICJ is not the same thing as being subject to its jurisdiction.

The ICJ has jurisdiction over disputes between states. It cannot hear a case brought by (or against) an individual. It also has advisory jurisdiction—the power to give legal advice to the General Assembly, the Security Council, and certain other international organizations. All issues of international law fall within the ICJ's ambit—any treaty dispute, any dispute over customary international law.

To address the problem of imposing mandatory jurisdiction when international law requires consent, the ICJ Statute offers three approaches. First, it allows (say) two states with a dispute to consent to jurisdiction. These are called "special agreement" cases and do not represent an innovation over arbitration. Second, the ICJ Statute allows states to provide by treaty that disputes will be resolved by the ICJ. States that have a dispute under a treaty therefore are bound to use the ICJ—but then only as long as they do not withdraw from the treaty. Third, the statute has an optional clause that permits states to consent to "mandatory" jurisdiction by issuing a declaration to that effect. This last provision was the most important; but by the same token, it was the most controversial. That is why the provision had to be put into an optional clause rather than in the body of the statute. Still, the drafters hoped that all states would eventually declare consent to mandatory jurisdiction.

The court sits in The Hague. It has fifteen judges who serve nine-year terms. The five permanent members of the Security Council—Britain, China, France, the United States, and Russia—by tradition always have a national on the bench. The other ten judges are appointed on a regional basis—with judges from major countries such as Japan serving disproportionally. When a state appears before the court as a litigant and it does not have a judge among the nationals, it is entitled to appoint an ad hoc judge to the bench for the case. The procedures combine common law and civil law practice. The common law incorporates an oral tradition, the civil law a written tradition—with the unhappy result, exacerbated by language differences, of lawyers reading their briefs at great length to a somnolent bench. In a nod to the common law tradition, judges write lengthy opinions and issue dissents and concurrences.

The ICJ's Performance

The ICJ has resolved some important disputes, especially involving borders. But its performance has fallen well short of the expectations or at least hopes of its founders. It has heard a little over a hundred cases in its existence and many of these petered out without any resolution. Usage of the court has remained about constant—a couple of cases per year—but the number of states that could potentially use it has more than tripled. Major powers have increasingly shown reluctance to use the court. And states have shown decreasing enthusiasm about both mandatory jurisdiction and treaties that confer jurisdiction on the ICJ in case of dispute. Finally, compliance with ICJ judgments, while inherently hard to measure, does not seem high.[11]

Limits

What accounts for the disappointing performance of the ICJ? First, it appears that states lost faith in the ability of the ICJ to decide cases impartially. With the arbitration model in mind, we can see why this might have happened. In arbitration, the impartiality of the decision maker is guaranteed because both sides must agree on it. A court by its nature cannot supply a guarantee. States could be sure that one judge favored them, but the other fourteen, fifteen, or sixteen would be people they did not pick. The Soviet Union and its allies must have realized early on that their view of international law would not pass muster with a Western-dominated court. In later years, the United States and the West have come to a similar realization about a court filled with judges from developing countries.

Second, it seems doubtful that the ICJ could serve the information-forcing function that states seek. The ICJ is a rather clumsy institution; it is not in a good position to engage in fact-finding. As is always the case with courts, the judges are generalists; arbitration panels, by contrast, may be filled with specialists. And states do not want to lose control over the development of international law. International law is stable only as long as it serves states' interests. If an independent agency like the ICJ can resolve ambiguities in the law, then it can make law, often in ways that states do not like.

International Criminal Tribunals

International criminal tribunals conduct trials of individuals accused of violating international criminal law. They differ from the ICJ and other international tribunals because they do not formally involve state-to-state disputes. Before the first international criminal tribunals were established, states prosecuted individuals for violating international criminal law on occasion—either using domestic courts or military commissions or tribunals set up to prosecute soldiers and civilians who violated the laws of war. For example, states had long prosecuted pirates in national courts for violating international (and domestic) criminal law. And during wars, belligerents tried captured enemy soldiers who were suspected of having committed war crimes. The idea of an international tribunal—one involving the participation of several states—did not bear fruit until the end of World War II, when the allies put into place the Nuremberg Tribunal to prosecute Nazis and the Tokyo Tribunal to prosecute Japanese. The experiment would not be repeated until the 1990s.

International Criminal Tribunal for the Former Yugoslavia

The collapse of the Soviet Union ended the cold war and eliminated the cold war rivalry that interfered with international efforts to create and enforce an international criminal law. It also set off a chain reaction of other events, including the collapse of Yugoslavia, which began in 1991 and has still not fully exhausted itself. Yugoslavia was cobbled together after World War I out of pieces of the Austro-Hungarian and Ottoman empires.[12] It was held together after World War II by its leader, Osip Broz Tito, who used an iron fist but also paid careful attention to the demands of the various nationalities that composed the state—Serbs, Croats, Bosnians, and so forth. When Tito died in 1980 and the Soviet Union collapsed shortly thereafter, these groups no longer saw any reason to stick together. Long-standing ethnic and nationalist rivalries had been suppressed but not eliminated, and they burst forth with extraordinary violence when the center no longer held.

Nationalists in each state set to work expelling members of other ethnic groups—a process that was called ethnic cleansing in the media—and seizing control over border areas where ethnicities were mixed. Paramilitaries as well as newly constituted national armies were used (Serbia inherited the Yugoslav army). Ethnic cleansing involved kicking people out of their homes, often using murder and other forms of intimidation in order to persuade people to leave without resistance. It also involved the setting up of concentration camps, torture, and wholesale slaughter of civilians. After much dithering, the United States and European countries managed to intervene with military force and broker a settlement at a 1995 conference in Dayton, Ohio. The Dayton settlement essentially created or ratified borders and provided for various types of international governance that remain with us to this day.

In the meantime, the UN Security Council had set up the International Criminal Tribunal for the Former Yugoslavia (ICTY). Some thought this effort a futile gesture by an institution that was unable to take action to stop the hostilities, especially given the absence of any mechanism for arresting those whom the tribunal's prosecutor indicted. But eventually the various states were pressured to turn over suspects—at first a multitude of small fry (concentration camp commanders, for example) but eventually some big fish (generals and civilian leaders). For the states concerned, that would be the ticket for international respectability and everything that comes with it—foreign aid, trade concessions, and potential admission to the European Union.

The ICTY has two components. Despite its name, it includes a prosecutor's office as well as a court. The court has a trial division and an appellate division. The prosecutor has a great deal of independence. Many thousands of people committed or were complicit in international crimes; only a few of them can be prosecuted. Thus, the prosecutor has had to make the sensitive decision as to who is important enough to warrant prosecution and who is not. The trial court conducts regular trials; the appellate court reviews its judgments. The court has jurisdiction over various international crimes—genocide, torture, war crimes,

crimes against humanity (these categories overlap to a large extent)—that were committed by the belligerents in the former Yugoslavia. Echoing the Nuremberg precedent forbidding prosecutions of allied soldiers, no trials of North Atlantic Treaty Organization (NATO) personnel were permitted.

International Criminal Tribunal for Rwanda

On April 6, 1994, the president of Rwanda was killed when his airplane was shot down. His assassination sparked a three-month orgy of violence—an authentic genocide in which thousands of members of the Hutu majority slaughtered somewhere between 500,000 and one million members of the Tutsi minority as well as their moderate Hutu supporters. The United Nations dithered, as did the rest of the world; the violence ended when a Tutsi militia located in neighboring Uganda intervened and toppled the Hutu government. The Security Council established the International Criminal Tribunal for Rwanda (ICTR), modeled on the ICTY, to prosecute and try the genocidaires.

The ICTR, like the ICTY, was given jurisdiction over various international crimes—genocide, crimes against humanity, and violations of the Geneva Conventions.[13] The situation in Rwanda was different, however, from that which prevailed in Yugoslavia. In Yugoslavia, each national group—Serbs, Croats, Bosnian Muslims—sought to protect their nationals; the ICTY extracted indicted suspects only with difficulty and obtained many minor criminals as well as leaders. This gave the overall impression of arbitrariness, and each side accused the ICTY of favoring the other sides. In Rwanda, the newly installed Tutsi-dominated government had ample incentive to prosecute Hutu genocidaires and arrested and warehoused thousands of them. Because of limited resources, the ICTR could handle only a small number of them, again creating an impression of arbitrariness.

The Verdict on the ICTY and ICTR

Both the ICTR and ICTY exceeded the expectations of skeptics who did not believe that they could accomplish anything. But their performance was mixed.

The two tribunals tried and convicted a number of bad people who did awful things. But the Rwandans would surely have been punished in any event—with less process, maybe, but some kind of justice would have been done. Both tribunals convicted so few people relative to the thousands of wrongdoers as to suggest more symbolism than substance. They did not do justice in the sense of ensuring that all or even most or even many of the wrongdoers were punished.

They operated at enormous expense—billions of dollars that could have been used for reconstruction.[14] They may have performed in a professional manner,[15] but they did not appear to contribute to reconciliation. It seems unlikely that, given the vast expense and limited output, these tribunals have served as deterrents elsewhere in the world, where atrocities continue as always.

As is always the case when an institution falls short of expectations, one can do two things: give up on it or improve it. States decided on the latter course. The successor of the ICTY and the ICTR would be the International Criminal Court.

International Criminal Court

Supporters of an International Criminal Court (ICC) believed that a permanent institution would advance the values underlying the ICTY and ICTR but in a more efficient and just way. A permanent court has obvious advantages: it does not need to be reinvented for every new crisis. But the main appeal of such a court was, for its most ardent supporters, the possibility that it would apply equally to the citizens of all states, big and small, strong and weak. An international criminal court would spring into action whenever international crimes take place, regardless of who commits them and why.[16] By contrast, the ICTY and ICTR could take jurisdiction over nationals of weak countries only, and only after the powerful countries agreed to such a course of action in the Security Council.

But this was also a stumbling block. The strong countries had a different vision for the ICC. It would sit in reserve, ready for action, but it could not initiate prosecutions and trials. It would have to await the call of the Security Council, which alone would have the power to authorize the ICC to launch an investigation. This system would have had some obvious advantages for the permanent five members of the Security Council. Their nationals could never be prosecuted by the ICC because those countries would veto any such proposal. The ICC would be a sword put at their disposal, one that could never be turned against them.

The universalism of the most enthusiastic supporters of the ICC butted up against the great power politics of the United States. The enthusiasts had their way but lost the support of the United States—as well as big countries like China and Russia, which never had much enthusiasm for an international court in the first place.

The ICC, like the ICTY and ICTR, consists of two separate institutions—a prosecutor's office and a judicial chamber, with a pre-trial court, trial court, and an appellate panel. The prosecutor has a fair amount of discretion to bring charges, though these are subject to review of the court. The court's jurisdiction extends to war crimes, crimes against humanity, genocide, and aggressive war. The court has jurisdiction over crimes committed by nationals of member states, crimes referred by the Security Council, and crimes committed on the territories of member states. The United States has objected forcefully to the latter provision, fearing that its soldiers could be picked up if suspected of committing international crimes while on peacekeeping missions or, for that matter, on military missions. To forestall such an outcome, it has cajoled and threatened various countries into agreeing not to turn over U.S. citizens to the court.

The ICC treaty (called the Rome Statute) has a provision known as complementarity, according to which the ICC obtains jurisdiction only if the state that has control over a suspect fails to prosecute him in good faith. So the ICC remains as a backstop, able to intervene only if people commit international crimes and the relevant state fails to prosecute them. This was a gesture to the sovereignty of states, but it did not appease the United States, which did not want its decisions about when or whether to prosecute to be second-guessed by an international institution over which it had no control. The ICC's defenders argued that the United States could be trusted to prosecute U.S. soldiers or civilians who commit international crimes. Recent years, however, have revealed that this is not always the case. The Obama administration has chosen not to investigate and prosecute those complicit in the torture of members of Al Qaida (although the Bush administration did prosecute soldiers involved in the Abu Ghraib prison abuses).

The ICC was supposed to be a court of last resort for international crimes, one that would ensure that dictators and their henchmen would not escape punishment for their atrocities. So far, it has not fulfilled this mission, but it is very early. Instead, it has turned out to be a kind of supplier of in-kind foreign aid, in the form of institutional capacity and expertise. At the request of Uganda, the Democratic Republic of Congo, and the Central African Republic, it has launched investigations and in some cases filed charges against members of insurgencies in those countries. These were not governments that committed atrocities and refused to prosecute; these were governments that were helpless—they could not prosecute even though they wanted to do so. The Security Council, with U.S. cooperation, asked the ICC to investigate atrocities in Sudan, which it did. It indicted Omar al-Bashir, the president of Sudan, for his involvement in genocide. Rather than hand him over to the ICC, the Sudanese government has increased its harassment of humanitarian relief groups. Lacking the ability to enter Sudan and arrest al-Bashir, the court must wait for other states to pressure Sudan to turn him over. As of this writing, this has not happened. Indeed, most African countries have announced that they will not do so. It is possible, though, that in due course international pressure on host countries will restrict his ability to travel internationally. As of June 2011, al-Bashir had canceled plans to attend a forum in Malaysia, allegedly as a result of pressure exerted by Amnesty International.[17] However, whether such pressure will yield results when applied to more powerful countries is doubtful: the ICC warrant did not discourage China from welcoming him,[18] and more recently from encouraging other nations to normalize relations with Sudan.

As the hostilities between pro-Gaddafi forces and the Libyan rebels broke out in 2011, accusations surfaced that Gaddafi's forces had committed international crimes against civilians. In February, the Security Council passed a resolution condemning the actions of the Libyan government and referring the matter to the ICC. A few days later, the ICC prosecutor announced the commencement of an investigation against Gaddafi and members of his inner circle. But Libyan resistance forces murdered Gaddafi rather than turn him over to the ICC.

Does the ICC have a future? The universalistic aspirations of its supporters are a long way from being realized. Most states have ratified the Rome Statute, but the ICC has limited resources and cannot investigate all the atrocities being committed around the world. Most of the major powers have refused to ratify the Rome Statute. And the ICC does not address the basic problem with international criminal prosecutions. When states are willing to prosecute international crimes committed by their nationals, the ICC is not necessary. When states are unwilling to launch such prosecutions, the ICC has no capacity to compel them to turn over indicted suspects. Other states rarely have an incentive to use military, economic, or diplomatic pressure against states that fail to cooperate in international criminal prosecutions. They care more about maintaining good military and economic relations with those states than ensuring that international criminal justice is done. The ICC will surely maintain some role—but probably a modest role, as a court-in-waiting that can offer its services to governments that request them and to the Security Council when it has an interest in using it.

The World Trade Organization

The WTO dispute resolution mechanism is the most elaborate and successful of the international adjudication systems. It is a successor to the GATT system, which was essentially a structured system of arbitration. We will discuss the WTO in Chapter 18.

Other Tribunals

Law of the Sea Tribunal

In 1994 the United Nations Convention on the Law of the Sea went into force. The dispute resolution provisions of the Law of the Sea convention are complex. States are permitted to choose among the newly established International Tribunal for the Law of the Sea (ITLOS), the International Court of Justice, and two types of arbitration; they are also permitted to opt out of mandatory dispute resolution for a set of disputes. The ICJ has not heard a law of the sea case. ITLOS has so far heard few cases, most of them involving challenges to bonds demanded for the release of ships seized in territorial waters.

Regional Human Rights Courts

The three regional human rights courts are the European, Inter-American, and African systems. The Inter-American and African systems have a commission and a court. The commission monitors compliance with regional human rights treaties and typically plays an intermediary role between petitioners and the court—screening and providing assistance. The court has jurisdiction over the regional treaty and can issue legally binding judgments against member states. The most developed of the regional systems is the European system, which has forty-seven member states. Its busy court (an earlier commission was dropped) sees almost 50,000 new applications each year,[19] and it has issued thousands of judgments.

The various regional human rights courts have the power to issue legally binding judgments. Of these, only the European Court of Human Rights (ECtHR) has enjoyed a substantial degree of success. In thousands of cases, the ECtHR has awarded judgments—typically fines accompanied by orders to national governments requiring them to modify laws that violate the Convention. However, the extent to which the ECtHR has affected the behavior of states is unknown.[20] There is no doubt that some advanced European states have changed their laws when required to by the ECtHR. However, Russia has slid back into authoritarianism since it joined the ECtHR in 1998, and a general view is that while states like Russia will pay penalties (which are typically small), they do not reliably change their laws (or enforce changes in the law) in response to adverse judgments. The sheer size of its jurisdiction—many hundreds of millions of people across Europe and parts of Asia—limits the impact of this forty-seven-judge court, which today has an enormous backlog of cases, resulting in long delays.

The ECtHR is a regional institution, not an international one, and it no doubt derives much of its power from the fact that most of its members belong to the EU and most of the remaining members want to belong to the EU.

Committees, Commissions, and Quasi-Tribunals

There are countless international bodies that do not have adjudicatory powers but serve advisory or monitoring roles. A frequently mentioned example is the International Labor Organization, a UN-affiliated body that sets labor standards. These standards are not legally binding, and there is controversy over whether they have had any influence.

The World Health Organization (WHO) is another such body. It, too, has no legal authority, but it serves as a repository of expert opinion and resources about health issues. Despite its lack of legal authority, it plays a prominent role in efforts to contain outbreaks of infectious diseases that may, or do, cross borders. It monitors conditions in states (subject to their permission, which is not always forthcoming) and so can make recommendations about how to minimize the spread of a pandemic, which are credible and likely to be followed.

A basic problem in this setting is that states often want to delay reporting an outbreak of disease until the last minute. At its earliest stages, states (particularly developing states) prefer to try to contain the outbreak without alerting foreign countries, which might result in loss of tourism and trade. If they succeed, then they do not lose revenues. However, if they fail, the disease will spread. Other countries would do better from an earlier alert, so that they can take precautions against the spread of the disease—by, for example, closing their borders to people from the state in which the disease originates. The WHO has no mechanism for forcing states to divulge disease outbreaks at the optimal stage; however, because it possesses and offers expertise, those states will seek help at some point, whereupon the WHO can issue a general alert. This is not optimal, but it may well be the best that is possible, and it is far better than a system where the WHO did not exist. A general lesson here is that an international body with highly limited legal powers may nonetheless generate public goods.

In the area of human rights, institutions flourish. The Human Rights Council, which replaced the Commission on Human Rights in 2006, monitors human rights in UN member states and issues resolutions condemning human rights violations (which, however, have no legal force). In addition, the main human rights treaties established bodies charged with the task of monitoring compliance with the treaties, interpreting them, and developing them. These bodies include the Human Rights Committee (created by the International Covenant for Civil and Political Rights); the Committee on Economic, Social and Cultural Rights (created by the International Covenant for Economic, Social and Cultural Rights); the Committee Against Torture (created by the Convention Against Torture); the Committee on the Elimination of Racial Discrimination (created by the Convention on the Elimination of All Forms of Racial Discrimination); the Committee on the Elimination of Discrimination Against Women (created by the Convention on the Elimination of All Forms of Discrimination against Women); and the Committee on the Rights of the Child (created by the Convention on the Rights of the Child). A number of other UN institutions have human rights-related responsibilities—for example, the UN High Commissioner for Refugees. A High Commissioner for Human Rights has the task of coordinating these different agencies and publicizing human rights abuses.

The Commission on Human Rights had some significant accomplishments; it drafted the Universal Declaration of Human Rights, for example. But by the first decade of the twenty-first century, it had lost a great deal of support. Chief among the complaints was that a large fraction of its fifty-three member states were routine human rights abusers, such as Libya and Sudan, and that the Commission rarely criticized human rights abusers, focusing most of its attention on Israel. Thanks to some modest changes in election procedures, the Human Rights Council has fewer rights-abusing members than the Commission did (though still a substantial minority), but its record is no better. It continues to focus its attention on Israel and a handful of other countries (Sudan and Myanmar) and to ignore most other human rights–abusing countries. Consistent with the interest of developing states, the Council avoids singling out states for criticism as much as possible and instead has instituted a toothless universal periodic review procedure. This procedure results in a document that makes recommendations for reform but does not condemn states for human rights violations. Finally, the Council has advanced the controversial idea that "defamation of religion" violates human rights.

Both the Commission and the Council are essentially political bodies that do the bidding of the member states. Because the member states need the support of other countries to be elected, the only states that the Commission can directly criticize are those that are internationally isolated—Israel, Sudan,

Myanmar, and a handful of other states. Developing countries with weak human rights records constitute a majority of countries in the world, and therefore they have majority representation on the Council. It is in their interest to protect themselves from official criticism by a UN body. The defamation of religion resolutions emerge from a coalition of Arab, Muslim, developing, and authoritarian states that routinely outvote Western states. Other states have little incentive to employ sanctions to ensure that the Council's judgments are obeyed; even when they agree with the Council, they prefer to free ride.

8

State Responsibility

The notion that a "state" has violated international law masks all sorts of complexities, for the fact is that states do not commit harmful acts—people do. This chapter concerns the core question of which acts are attributed to states for purposes of international law—that is, which acts trigger "state responsibility." For example, if a soldier commits a war crime, then his state—the state of which he is a national—violates international law. But if a tourist commits a murder while in a foreign country, then her state does not violate international law. How are these distinctions drawn and why?

The Analogy to Corporate Liability in Domestic Law

A state's responsibility under international law for certain acts of its citizens may be analogized to corporate liability. Corporate liability involves the imposition of liability on the owners of a corporation for the harmful act of some actual or apparent agent of the corporation. So too, state responsibility under international law involves the imposition of liability on the citizenry of a nation as a whole for the harmful act of individual government agents or citizens. In both cases, individuals with no direct connection to the harmful act, other than their status as part owner of or citizen in the entity to be sanctioned, bear liability. Such liability may be termed *vicarious*, which refers generally in law to the imposition of liability on one party simply because of that party's status in relation to the individual who commits the harmful act.

We suggest that the economic logic of state responsibility under international law is closely akin to the logic behind vicarious liability on corporations. We thus begin this chapter with a quick review of modern economic learning about the rationale for, and appropriate limitations on, corporate liability.

Suppose that an employee of a company commits a harmful act that causes injury to someone unconnected to the company. Perhaps a truck driver for Sears causes an accident with another motorist, for example. Assuming that the driver behaved tortiously, should the driver alone bear responsibility for the accident, or should Sears also bear responsibility?

To answer this question, one must first make some assumptions about what it means for the employer to bear liability. The literature on vicarious liability generally proceeds on the assumption that vicarious liability does not alter the amount of damages that the injured party is allowed to collect. Likewise, it typically assumes that the employee-injurer is subject to personal liability for the harmful act, whether or not the employer bears vicarious liability. These assumptions are accurate most of the time when the issue arises under domestic law.

If vicarious liability simply allows the injured party to sue the employer as well as the employee for the same amount of damages, the first question to ask is, what is the point of vicarious liability? Does it simply add another party to litigation without otherwise affecting what the injured party recovers? In some cases, the answer to this last question is "yes." Indeed, the literature suggests a kind of indifference theorem, specifying circumstances under which vicarious liability is of little or no practical consequence. It may be stated as follows: If (1) employees have the financial resources to pay all judgments against them, (2) employers and employees can reallocate liability by contract costlessly regardless of where the law initially places it, and (3) injured parties can always secure and execute judgments against employee-injurers when the latter alone are liable, then a rule of vicarious liability has no consequences.[1]

Conditions (1)–(3) above need not hold in all cases, however, and a departure from any one of them suggests how a rule of vicarious liability may begin to matter. First, employees often have limited assets that are insufficient to pay for the harms that they cause. Second, the costs of reallocating liability by contract between employers and employees may be significant at times, and the initial allocation of liability under the law may "stick" or may require costly contracts to undo it. Third, cases may arise in which the injured party has difficulty identifying the individual employee responsible for the harmful act or in which judgments against the employee cannot be executed (perhaps the employee has fled the jurisdiction).

The first and third possibilities are widely considered the most important and afford the conventional economic justification for imposing vicarious liability on corporate employers. In both scenarios, businesses will not bear the full costs of the harms that they cause absent vicarious liability (either directly or indirectly through the liability borne by employees and passed along to the corporation via the wage bill). Not only do injured parties go uncompensated, but the corporation's costs of doing business are lower than they should be from a social standpoint, resulting in lower prices and an undue expansion of risky activity. Further, a lack of proper incentive to avoid harm arises because neither corporations nor their employees bear the costs of the harms that they cause. Vicarious liability addresses all of these problems by forcing businesses to bear the full cost of harms caused by employees. Prices will reflect the full costs to society of corporate activity, and corporations will have a proper incentive to do what they can to induce their employees to behave properly.

The extent of the economic gains from vicarious liability depends on the ability of employers to induce employees to take greater precautions against harm—the employers' "monitoring ability." In some cases, employers can do a great deal to monitor employees, and in some cases their ability to do so is extremely limited. When monitoring ability is poor, it is possible that vicarious liability is nevertheless useful because of its effect on prices alone, but such gains may be modest by themselves depending on the circumstances and offset wholly or in part by the fact that vicarious liability may lead to greater litigation costs. Thus, the law routinely looks to monitoring ability as a key factor in deciding whether to impose vicarious liability. The "control test" under the law of agency distinguishes "servants," for which an employer is usually liable, from "independent contractors," for which the employer is usually not liable.

A further limitation on vicarious liability relates to the connection between the employee's wrongful act and the activities of the corporation. For example, suppose that an employee has a fight at a bar after work and incurs tort liability for assault and battery. It would seem odd if the employment relationship led to vicarious liability for such "personal" torts, and indeed it usually does not because they occur outside the "scope of employment." From an economic standpoint, the absence of vicarious liability in such cases has two justifications: (1) the employer's monitoring opportunities are usually rather poor, and (2) the harm is not properly viewed as a cost of the employer's business, because the harm is equally likely to occur, as a first approximation, in the absence of the employment relationship.

In some cases, however, employers may have the ability to monitor employees well even if they are engaged in activities of an essentially "personal" nature. If so, vicarious liability may still be desirable from an economic standpoint. Consider, for example, acts of sexual harassment by employees against coworkers. Even if such behavior is "personal," the employer may nevertheless be able to discourage it effectively by having a strict policy against it, coupled with a procedure under which the targets of harassment can report it to superiors.

How States Differ

State responsibility is a form of vicarious liability, in that some penalty is borne by the citizenry as a whole because of actions taken by their "agents." Many of the basic economic lessons regarding corporate vicarious liability have direct bearing on the economics of state responsibility. First, state responsibility is most often justified because the individual actors whose actions violate international law will not bear the costs—they may be beyond the jurisdiction of any foreign entity with the capacity and authority to sanction them, they may be immune from any personal liability under applicable domestic law, and their personal assets may be far smaller than the harm that they have caused. Second, the benefits of state responsibility will be greater, the greater the capacity (and inclination) of the state to monitor its "agents" and to discourage their harmful acts. Third, state responsibility is generally more useful when the harmful act is "caused" by the activities of the state and less so if the act is of a more "personal" nature on the part of its agents or citizens. If the state is highly effective at monitoring acts in the latter category, however, state responsibility may be appealing nonetheless. Finally, rules of state responsibility must be attentive to the calibration of the remedy—insufficient penalties may lead to inadequate deterrence of harmful acts, while excessive penalties may lead to wasteful monitoring behavior or to the deterrence of socially valuable acts (such as, perhaps, the efficient breach of certain international obligations, a possibility that we discuss in Chapter 9).

But it would be a mistake to suppose that the analysis of corporate liability can be transplanted without modification. States differ from corporations in many ways, and state responsibility under international law differs from the monetary liability of corporations under domestic law in important respects.

First, corporations are generally assumed to act as profit-maximizing entities, at least as a first approximation, an assumption that is important to predictions about how corporations will respond to the incentives created by liability. By contrast, states do not maximize profits, and indeed their "objective functions" are quite unclear. It is also unclear in some cases whether any entity has the capacity to monitor state "agents." Second, the scale of corporate activity is determined in the marketplace, with equilibrium output typically imagined to occur (under competitive conditions) where price equals the marginal cost of production. State activity is not in general "priced," and the determinants of the scale of state activity in equilibrium are much less clear. Third, corporate liability for compensatory damages at least in principle imposes a monetary penalty equal to the value of the harm done. The remedial consequences of state responsibility under international law may be quite different, both in theory and in practice. Finally, international law must attend to the fact that it may overlap with or parallel domestic law. If behavior that violates international law is also a violation of domestic law, the need for a remedy under international law is diminished or even eliminated.

Each of these distinctions has some important implications for the economics of state responsibility. As shall be seen, these implications are not always crisp ones.

Do States Have a "Principal," and How Will It Respond to State Responsibility?

The economic analysis of vicarious liability in the private sector assumes that corporations maximize profits and that shareholders or their managerial agents serve as the "principal" and respond to liability with cost-effective measures to monitor the lower-level "agents" that expose the corporation to liability. How well does this paradigm transfer to states?

Democracies

In democratic states, the analogue to shareholders is voters. When the electorate becomes displeased with the policies of elected officeholders, it can turn them out, but only at specified times (elections). There is no board of directors or large shareholder with the ability to replace officials in between elections and no takeover market. Further, in contrast to the corporation in which the single or primary objective of every shareholder is thought to be the maximization of profit, voters are concerned about a wide array of issues. The consequences for the nation (or for the typical taxpayer) of acts that trigger state responsibility under international law may be far down the list of issues that affect the choices of voters. Except on issues of great national importance, therefore, it seems unlikely that the democratic process will exert much direct discipline over such acts.

Does it follow that state responsibility will have little or no consequence in democratic states? Not necessarily. First, to the degree that state responsibility is accompanied by monetary liability (reparations), some government entity must pay the cost. Even though a bureaucratic entity does not maximize profit, it will often face a budget constraint and will prefer not to waste resources. It has thus been suggested in the literature on governmental tort liability under domestic law that bureaucracies may respond to monetary liability with behavior approximating cost minimization. If that suggestion is right, bureaucracies will respond to monetary liability in much the same way as a profit-maximizing entity, at least to the extent of adopting cost-effective measures to economize on liability. We are unaware, however, of any empirical literature supporting this thesis, and thus it remains for now an optimistic conjecture.

Even if governments will not necessarily respond to monetary liability with cost-effective preventive measures, however, liability will still in all likelihood have political consequences. Governments face budget constraints, and liability inevitably diverts government funds from other things. Political officials will prefer to avoid such diversion because it leaves them with fewer resources to satisfy the demands of domestic constituencies that will reward them for delivering desired projects. The political "opportunity cost" of funds used to pay for governmental liability will be all the greater when funds are disbursed to noncitizens on account of violations of international law. Thus, we suggest that governments will respond to monetary liability with measures to avoid it that are at least "politically cost-effective" and that will discourage acts that trigger state responsibility to some degree.

If state responsibility results in other than monetary penalties, similar forces will often be at work. Suppose, for example, that the consequence of state responsibility is some economic or trade sanction. Such sanctions will damage the economic interests of domestic constituencies. Indeed, foreign governments may select such measures precisely for the purpose of maximizing their political impact in the target country. Those interest groups will have an incentive to mobilize to eliminate the sanctions and to support policies that will avoid them in the future.

Finally, state responsibility can interfere with the international agenda of elected officials in democratic states. Most nations are constantly involved with various diplomatic initiatives, many of which may culminate in international legal agreements. The ability of officials to negotiate credibly on various issues will turn in part on their ability to deliver compliance with prior agreements. Officials thus have an interest in avoiding violations of international law quite apart from their desire to avoid the political costs of formal sanctions and will act to protect that interest.

For these reasons, state responsibility will generally be costly to states that violate international law, at least to an extent. Political officials will respond to state responsibility or to a prospect of it with politically cost-effective measures to address the problem. The relation between political cost-effectiveness and economic cost-effectiveness is unclear, although the mapping may sometimes be reasonably close. In any event, we would expect a positive correlation between them—state responsibility will lead democratic states to reduce violations of international law, much as it leads corporations to curtail the behavior that exposes them to liability.

Nondemocracies

Thus far, we have focused on the consequences of state responsibility for democratic states. To what extent does the analysis apply to other systems of government?

Often, the differences may be minimal. Authoritarian states may have a long-term interest in international cooperation on various fronts, and that interest may be furthered by their demonstrated ability to comply with commitments under other bodies of international law. Indeed, authoritarian states may be even better than democratic states in policing violations of international law by their own officials if senior leaders find it in their interest to do so.

But there is an important class of cases in which we might expect state responsibility per se to have little or no impact on an authoritarian state, owing to the fact that the most senior leaders in such states are often accountable to no one but themselves. If an authoritarian leader is determined to have violated international law (Hitler's invasion of Poland, for example), there may simply be no entity in the polity with the capacity to discourage such behavior. The "agent," in effect, has become the "principal," and one can no longer distinguish the effects of vicarious liability from the effects of personal liability in any coherent way. This does not mean that international law becomes irrelevant in such cases. Perhaps it helps other nations to orchestrate effective opposition to the actions of an authoritarian leader and may well influence the outcome of conflict. The point is simply that any effects of international law operate though their direct impact on the personal interests of the authoritarian leader and not through any monitoring mechanism put in place by his "principal." An obvious problem then arises: because these individual leaders cannot be made to bear the costs of the harms that they cause given their own limited assets and their likely insulation from seizure, and because no superior can restrain their behavior, it is especially difficult for international law to deter their misconduct.

The Scale of Government Activity

As noted, vicarious liability in the private sector forces businesses to internalize the social costs of their operations, which tends not only to promote useful monitoring but also to reduce the scale of risky activity toward its economically desirable level. The latter benefit of cost internalization is less likely to arise with states.

By and large, government services are not priced in the marketplace. And even when they are, prices may or may not be a true reflection of costs. In general, the scale of government activity will be determined by the interplay of interest groups. The resulting political equilibrium may lead to a scale of activity that is too large when measured against some idealized benchmark or to one that it is too small.

The literature on government takings illustrates the point. Proponents of an expansive concept of takings argue that the requirement of just compensation will force government to internalize the costs of taking private property and tend to ensure that property is not taken unless its value in government hands is higher. Critics have responded, however, that the government actors who decide on what property to use for public purposes do not bear the costs of that decision or receive the benefits. It is by no means clear that "cost internalization" by the government will lead to optimal decision making.

The same line of reasoning applies to costs associated with the violation of international law. Consider, for example, violations of the laws of war by soldiers in an army. Will the imposition of state responsibility on the nation that employs the army lead to an "optimal" scale of war? We doubt it. State responsibility will likely lead the army to take the rules of war more seriously and, as we argued earlier, to introduce measures to discourage violations—the monitoring gains from state responsibility. But any effects on the "scale" of war seem far less clear. Realistically, the costs of state responsibility may have little effect on the decision to go to war, how many troops to commit, or other decisions regarding "scale." Wars that many observers deem imprudent will still occur, and wars that might seem socially justified (such as inexpensive humanitarian interventions) will still not occur because the nations that bear the costs do not reap the benefits. To the degree that state responsibility does have an effect on the scale of state activity that causes harm, such as on the number of troops in a war, we cannot in general say whether that effect is favorable or adverse, for we have no basis for saying in general that the scale of activity absent state responsibility is too large or too small. This problem is not unique to military operations but is present with respect to many forms of government activity.

In sum, although state responsibility may promote a kind of cost internalization by governments, the consequences of cost internalization in the public sector are much less clear than they are for the private sector. It is certainly possible that it leads to a useful correction in the scale of government activity some of the time, but one cannot claim that cost internalization will have this effect in general. Hence, the stronger argument for state responsibility rests on its ability to induce monitoring. Where monitoring is unlikely to occur or to be effective, the case for state responsibility is weak unless one can somehow be confident that the scale of government activity is excessive in the absence of state responsibility.

These last observations also suggest caution regarding the gains from state responsibility. Suppose that state responsibility may lead to a scale of government activity in some area that is too small. Even if it also leads to otherwise useful efforts at monitoring government agents to prevent violations of international law, the two effects are offsetting, and the net effect may be ambiguous. As a simple illustration, imagine a humanitarian military intervention that would halt a genocide and that informed observers deem clearly desirable. Suppose further, however, that a nation with the ability to intervene is hesitant to do so because its citizenry will bear the costs but the benefits will flow to others. Conceivably, a prospect of state responsibility for any violations of the laws of war during the intervention could tip the balance against intervention and thus be counterproductive.

The Law

The principles of state responsibility remain controversial and somewhat ill defined, but the rules that do exist broadly correspond with the economic logic above. For illustrative purposes, we will rely on the International Law Commission's draft articles on state responsibility.[2] Although these articles are not formally rules of international law because they have not been ratified by states, many of them are thought to reflect the accepted customary international law principles of state responsibility.

State Officials versus Private Citizens

Acts of state officials implicate state responsibility unless the officials are acting in a personal capacity. International Law Commission (ILC) article 4 provides the following:

1. The conduct of any State organ shall be considered an act of that State under international law, whether the organ exercises legislative, executive, judicial or any other functions, whatever position it holds in the organization of the State, and whatever its character as an organ of the central government or of a territorial unit of the State.

2. An organ includes any person or entity which has that status in accordance with the internal law of the State.

ILC article 5 provides that

The conduct of a person or entity which is not an organ of the State under article 4 but which is empowered by the law of that State to exercise elements of the governmental authority shall be considered an act of the State under international law, provided the person or entity is acting in that capacity in the particular instance.

ILC article 7 provides that

The conduct of an organ of a State or of a person or entity empowered to exercise elements of the governmental authority shall be considered an act of the State under international law if the organ, person or entity acts in that capacity, even if it exceeds its authority or contravenes instructions.

Article 4 establishes that official government acts by "organs" or institutions, such as (to use American examples) Congress, the president, a court, an army, or a state legislature, trigger state responsibility. Article 5 provides that individuals who act in an official capacity but not necessarily in a way that can be attributed to any particular state organ can also trigger state responsibility. Article 7 says that state responsibility occurs as long as the person or entity has official powers. The state does not avoid responsibility if the act was the result of abuse of the official powers, that is, if it was illegal or unconstitutional under domestic law. Numerous reported cases also make clear that ordinary legislative, executive, and judicial acts—statutes, enforcement and military actions, and judicial decisions—are acts of state. Cases also make clear that in federal systems the acts of local units—regional units and cities—are acts of state.

Recall the proposition that state responsibility for the actions of agents is most desirable when (1) individual actors will not bear the costs because they have few assets or are beyond the reach of ordinary domestic judicial process, and (2) the state has the ability to monitor and control the agent. The first condition is typically satisfied for acts by state officials. Such officials are generally beyond the reach of the domestic legal remedies of the victim state. They usually cannot be sued in foreign courts on account of their actions because they are out of the victim state's effective control. Officials on their home territory cannot be seized by the victim state without a military invasion, which is almost always out of the question. And even when officials are on foreign territory, international norms and agreements ensure that the host country has no jurisdiction over them and can only expel them for committing crimes and similar acts. Similarly, official actors are often insulated from suit in their own domestic legal systems by various doctrines of official immunity; so if foreign victims try to obtain a domestic legal remedy, they are likely to fail. Finally, the personal assets of official actors will often be far less than the amount required to compensate the victim state for the harm that they cause even in the rare cases where they can be reached by judicial process under domestic law.

The second condition is also likely to be satisfied. Clearly, states usually have considerable power over their own personnel acting in their official capacities. The internal rules of states determine the powers of officials, provide them with incentives and punishments, determine how they will be selected and trained, and so forth. The typical relationship between a state and its officials is thus essentially an employer-employee relationship, and it comes as no surprise that states bear responsibility for acts of their "employees" within their "scope of employment."

Consistent with this view, state responsibility does not exist when officials act in a purely personal capacity, in ways that are not easily controlled by the state. A government official who runs over an alien while on a private errand is no more easily monitored by the state than a private citizen who runs over an alien while on a private errand. But a government official who, as a police officer, arrests and incarcerates an alien out of personal animus can be controlled by the state. The state can screen out unreliable or malicious people rather than hire them, and it can provide employees who have access to dangerous weapons with suitable training and supervision.

An interesting illustration is the case of Francisco Mallén.[3] An American deputy constable in Texas twice assaulted an official of the Mexican consulate. The first incident occurred when Mallén approached the consul on the street and attacked him. In the second incident, Mallén cornered the consul on a street car, assaulted him, and then arrested him and brought him to jail. A tribunal held that the United States bore direct responsibility for the second act but not the first. The first act was a private act; the second, when the arrest occurred, was an official act.[4] Both acts were motivated by the same private quarrel. The difference is that arrests are public acts that can be monitored and controlled more easily than ordinary assaults. Arrests are recorded and monitored and require the participation of other officials who book and detain the suspect.

Although states are usually not directly responsible for the actions of private citizens, they are obligated to provide access to the domestic tort system to aliens who are victimized by private citizens. This problem preoccupied leaders in the early years of this country. In 1784, the secretary of the French legation was assaulted in Philadelphia by another Frenchman. The weak response by Pennsylvania authorities led to protests by foreign states, but Congress had no power to take action. This caused a national scandal.[5] The first Congress enacted the Alien Tort Statute in order to give federal courts jurisdiction over torts in violation of the law of nations. This ensured that unbiased federal protection of the rights of aliens would be available lest state remedies fail.

State responsibility for not providing effective access to the tort system makes good sense. Although states generally cannot prevent the harms caused by private citizens at reasonable cost because states have relatively little control over private citizens, they can reduce the frequency of these harms by affording aggrieved actors access to a tort system. A state's tort system already exists for the benefit of citizens; having sunk the large fixed costs of setting up and staffing such a system, the state faces low marginal costs from making it available to a small number of aliens. The question, then, is why international law requires only equal access to the tort system (which might be lousy) for aliens rather than a guarantee of an effective remedy. The answer is that the optimal tort system varies from state to state and depends on the particular monitoring technologies of each state, so that it would be impossible for international law to specify the type of tort rules that must be due under international law. When international law compels states to provide equal access to the tort system, it is, in effect, recognizing that the optimal system varies across nations.

Exceptional Cases of Responsibility for Acts of Private Citizens

Acts of private citizens normally do not implicate state responsibility, as noted, but there is an important exception. ILC article 8 provides the following:

> The conduct of a person or group of persons shall be considered an act of a State under international law if the person or group of persons is in fact acting on the instructions of, or under the direction or control of, that State in carrying out the conduct.

Article 8 ensures that states cannot avoid responsibility by contracting out functions. A traditional example is the hiring of mercenaries.

Several cases illustrate the scope of this rule. In the Tehran Hostages case,[6] student militants in Tehran seized the U.S. embassy and held its staff hostage for more than a year. The ICJ held that although Iran was not responsible for the initial breach of diplomatic immunity, it became responsible when the Iranian government announced its approval of the action and took no steps to expel the militants. In the Nicaragua case,[7] the United States trained, funded, and supported insurgents—the Contras—in their conflict against the Nicaraguan government. The ICJ held that the United States was not responsible for internationally wrongful acts committed by the Contras.

What accounts for the different outcomes? The most plausible explanation, albeit open to some question, is that the United States had less control over the Contras than Iran had over the militants. The United States could probably not have prevented the Contras from committing war crimes; even if the United States had cut off funds, the Contras would have continued to fight. By contrast, the Iranian government could have expelled the militants from the embassy. Indeed, evidence suggested that the Iranian government could have caused the militants to leave merely by asking or ordering them to do so.

Acts of Insurgencies

Another important class of cases arises when insurgencies gain control over a portion of a state's territory and commit wrongs on that territory. ILC article 10 provides that

1. The conduct of an insurrectional movement which becomes the new government of a State shall be considered an act of that State under international law.
2. The conduct of a movement, insurrectional or other, which succeeds in establishing a new State in part of the territory of a pre-existing State or in a territory under its administration shall be considered an act of the new State under international law.
3. This article is without prejudice to the attribution to a State of any conduct, however related to that of the movement concerned, which is to be considered an act of that State by virtue of articles 4 to 9.

The insurgency itself can be held responsible for acts that occur on the territory it controls, as though it were a state, even if it is not recognized as one. The legitimate state is not responsible for the acts of the insurgency unless the insurgency eventually obtains control of the state, in which case responsibility attaches.

Once again, these principles accord with economic logic. If the insurgency loses the war, there is no point in holding the government liable for the insurgency's torts against aliens. The government could not have prevented the insurgency from committing those torts because the government had no control over it. If the insurgency wins and starts a new government, holding the state liable for acts of the insurgency creates, ex ante, an incentive for the insurgency to behave more in accordance with international law.

9

Remedies

The topic of remedies is one of the most undeveloped areas of international law. No treaty regime governs remedies. The topic receives no more than a few pages in the standard treatises and texts. Very few international judicial or arbitration opinions outside trade and investment law address remedies, and other authoritative sources are equally scarce.[1] Members of the International Law Commission (ILC) drafted a handful of articles addressing remedies—part of a larger project of describing the customary international law of state responsibility—but states never formally accepted them.[2]

This state of affairs is peculiar. In domestic law, it is a commonplace that one cannot understand a legal right without understanding the remedies for violating that right; a substantial literature on remedies exists, and entire law school courses are devoted to remedies.

In our view, the dearth of attention to remedies reflects the fact that international law is self-enforcing, so that the typical "remedy" historically has been a unilateral retaliatory action that was not subject to legal oversight. Formal rules about remedies were largely lacking or meaningless given the absence of such oversight. But this situation has been changing, in part through the creation of the draft rules of the ILC and in part through the evolution of special remedial principles in areas such as trade and investment. We address the ILC articles in this chapter and the rules in specialized areas later.

A recurring theme in our discussion is the proposition that compliance with international law is not always optimal from an economic perspective. Rather, for reasons that we will elaborate, it is at times desirable (efficient) for states to breach their obligations. The remedial regime needs to take account of this possibility, and indeed, it has done so in various ways. Most important, the rules on remedies for breach of international law tend to emphasize compensatory over punitive remedies, thereby allowing states the flexibility to deviate from international law if they are willing to make other states whole in the process.

Why Compliance with International Law Is Not Always Efficient

As we discussed in Chapter 3, international law may be viewed as a contract among nations, sometimes an explicit contract (as in treaties) and sometimes an implicit contract (as in customary international law). Just as private contracting parties generally benefit from mutual performance of their obligations, nations generally benefit from the performance of obligations under international law. But also as in the case of private contracts, performance of obligations is not always desirable and should not always be required. In domestic contract law, two such cases arise. First, when the promisor commits a "material" or serious breach, the promisee has the right not to perform an obligation that is simultaneously or subsequently due. Second, when contracts fail to address a contingency that increases the cost of performance beyond its value for the other party, the promisor normally has the right to pay damages rather than perform. Both rules have foundations in efficiency. The right not to perform in response to a material breach avoids the dissipation of resources that would otherwise be invested in anticipation of the other party's performance and gives the victim leverage against a judgment-proof promisor, improving the latter's incentive to perform. The right to pay damages rather than perform permits the promisor to avoid inefficient performance.[3] In international law, analogous arguments can be made.[4]

Noncompliance for the Purpose of Retaliation

In the domestic legal system, third-party enforcers exist to compel the performance of legal obligations. If a party to a contract refuses to perform, for example, the other party may bring an action for damages or specific performance depending on the circumstances. If that party is successful, the state can seize the assets of the breaching party to satisfy a damages judgment or to issue an injunction requiring performance backed by a threat of imprisonment should the breaching party ignore the injunction. The economic theory of contracts suggests that contracting parties rationally participate in this system because it makes their contractual promises credible and facilitates greater mutual gains.

In contrast, as we discussed at length in Chapter 3, international law must usually be "self-enforcing," meaning that its enforcement relies on the parties subject to international law rather than on third parties. Further, much of international law exhibits the characteristics of a repeated prisoner's dilemma. Where the function of international law is to orchestrate cooperation in the face of a prisoner's dilemma, it is vital to the preservation of cooperation over time that nations make a credible threat to punish deviation from the rules by other nations. Often, the most plausible threat is reciprocal deviation, and when cooperation fails, threats of reciprocal deviation must sometimes be carried out to maintain credibility.

This observation suggests an important reason for noncompliance with international law—to retaliate for noncompliance by other nations. Indeed, noncompliance for the purpose of retaliation is not only acceptable from an economic perspective but may be essential—without it, the cooperation that international law seeks to achieve may collapse altogether.

To be sure, unilateral retaliation, whether in the form of reciprocal noncompliance with the law or some other punishment, is not a perfect mechanism for encouraging compliance with international law. Retaliation itself may be costly and may consume resources. Further, in the absence of an adjudicative mechanism to rule on the existence of violations, disputes may arise over their existence, and unilateral retaliation may become destabilizing as nations "take the law into their own hands." Likewise, for reasons that we explore further below, it is important to calibrate the punishment for deviation so that it is neither too high nor too low; a system with unilateral retaliation may run the risk that retaliation becomes excessive.

Other Cases of Efficient Breach

In private contracts, a range of contractual clauses excuse performance under contingencies where the costs exceed the benefits—force majeure, acts of war, and the like. Similarly, the law of contract in the United States and other legal systems excuses performance when the costs become prohibitive or the premises that underlie the bargain prove wrong, through doctrines addressing, among other things, mistake, impossibility, and commercial impracticability. But despite the best efforts of contracting parties, courts, and the drafters of statutes, performance will often turn out to cost more than it is worth yet not be excused by any contractual clause or background rule of contract law. Contract scholars thus recognize that opportunities can arise for "efficient breach."

International law must confront the same set of issues. Contingencies may arise in which the costs of compliance to some nations will exceed the benefits of compliance to others. If the law at issue is quite simple and has become inefficient in its entirety, it may suffice for nations simply to withdraw from it—formal "breach" may not be necessary. Often, however, international law is complex and addresses many issues. Much of the law may remain efficient, and only some small part of it may have become inefficient. In such situations, the challenge is to permit deviation from the part that has become inefficient while preserving the gain from cooperation on other issues—efficient breach may be the best option.[5]

A similar situation arises when the circumstances that warrant deviation from the law are temporary. Here, the ideal outcome involves temporary deviation followed by eventual restoration of full cooperation under the original legal rules. Temporary efficient breach may again be the best option.

In yet another class of situations, a body of law may become permanently inefficient, but the mechanism for withdrawal or renegotiation may be quite costly. Here, efficient breach may become the engine of efficient legal evolution.

Finally, scenarios may arise in which international rules require behavior that no other nation cares about. If so, deviation from those rules is again efficient.

To be sure, the identification of circumstances where breach is efficient can be difficult. In the law of private contracts, the problem is addressed in large measure by requiring the breaching promisor to put her money where her mouth is—the promisor must pay expectation damages that in principle make the nonbreaching party whole. The same sort of mechanisms may be employed in international law, as we discuss below.

An alternative to a system designed to permit efficient breach is to require a nation seeking to deviate from international law to secure the permission of affected nations—in effect, a requirement that they renegotiate international law and obtain a modification or waiver. In principle, renegotiation is another mechanism to determine whether a party that wishes to deviate from an agreement can do so and compensate the losers while still remaining better off. Indeed, some critics of the damages remedy in private contract law argue that renegotiation following decrees of specific performance may better identify situations where breach is actually efficient. Whatever the merits of this suggestion for the case of private contracts, however, it is not always plausible in international law. It is most plausible in the case of bilateral treaties covering a narrow range of issues where the transaction costs of renegotiation may be comparatively low. But for complex treaties addressing a wide range of issues affecting many interest groups, and for multilateral treaties involving large numbers of nations, renegotiation can be extremely costly and subject to holdup problems. If so, it may not represent a viable alternative to efficient breach.

Implications for Remedies

The analysis above yields two propositions. First, a credible threat of retaliatory defection from international legal obligations is often necessary to sustain beneficial international cooperation. Second, some instances of deviation from international law are efficient and should not be discouraged.[6] These propositions have important implications for the penalties that states should pay when they fail to comply with international law.

If the relevant international actors can readily distinguish efficient and inefficient breaches, it is sufficient for them to do nothing when an efficient breach occurs and to retaliate when an inefficient breach occurs. In the case of retaliation against inefficient breach, the extent of retaliation can be as high as the victim wants (although the costs of sanctions themselves must be considered). High sanctions will deter inefficient breach, while no sanctions will permit efficient breach—and this is the optimal outcome.

In many instances, however, the relevant set of international actors cannot readily observe whether breach is efficient or not. The benefits of breach to the party that commits a breach and the costs to other states may all be private information. Consider first the possibility that the benefits of breach to the breaching party are private information. Then, as a first approximation, the ideal remedy will force the breaching state to incur a cost equal to the cost that it has inflicted on the victim state. An ideal remedy is monetary reparations, which are analogous to expectation damages: the wrongdoing state simply transfers an amount equal to the loss to the victim state measured against the baseline of full performance. But the wrongdoing state may refuse to pay reparations. In that case, the victim state might retaliate so as to impose the equivalent loss on the wrongdoing state.

Such a system is nevertheless subject to a number of difficulties. Among other things, victims will not always have the proper incentives to retaliate because retaliation may be too tempting or too costly. In the case of a trade treaty, for example, retaliation may be (politically) beneficial and thus quite tempting—it enables political officials in the victim state to secure political gains by supplying protection to import-competing firms. For this reason, the victim may tend to retaliate excessively (unless the rules somehow prevent such behavior). By contrast, in the case of, say, nuclear nonproliferation violations, retaliation may be quite expensive. Perhaps victim states must inflict economic sanctions on wrongdoers, which injure firms in victim states that want to do business with firms in wrongdoer states. The same problem can arise in a trade treaty when the victim of a breach is "small" and lacks the market power to affect the prices received by firms engaged in trade in the violator state—retaliation then passes through in full to the victim state's consumers and can amount to "shooting oneself in the foot." In this second group of cases, retaliation may be insufficient.

Furthermore, when sanctions are costly in themselves and are not simply transfers between countries, the cost of sanctions must be taken into account in designing an optimal remedial system. In particular, the cost of the sanctions mechanism must be factored into any assessment of the costs of breach to decide whether breach is genuinely "efficient."[7] Conceivably, a sanctions system may be so expensive that the ideal remedial system might embody a credible threat of enormous sanctions that will never be used, thus forcing renegotiation as the sole mechanism for adjusting the bargain. It is also possible that sanctions should be set at a level below compensation so that the victim of breach will be less likely to pursue them.

Further complications arise as a result of the dynamic nature of the parties' relationship. Suppose that state X breaches a treaty, and state Y responds with retaliation by imposing economic sanctions as well as suspending its own obligations under the treaty. If X believes that Y's retaliation is excessive, it will treat the retaliation as a breach of international law, warranting a response in kind. If Y believes that Y's retaliation was lawful, it will regard X's retaliation as an independent breach of international law and raise its own level of retaliation. The risk of such escalation helps explain the appeal of neutral adjudicators who can provide impartial judgments about the proper scope of retaliation. It also might suggest that states should not retaliate as aggressively as might otherwise seem justified.

An additional consideration lies in the possibility that some breaches of international law may be difficult to detect. Imagine a fishery treaty that requires a reduction in fishing, for example, and suppose that a party to the treaty regularly cheats on its obligations. It may be difficult to detect illegal fishing in an ocean fishery, however, and many instances of cheating may escape notice. In such cases, and as a first approximation, retaliation must be adjusted upward in accordance with the probability of detection so that the expected cost of deviating from the law is equal to the cost imposed on other states. If cheating is detected only one-third of the time, for example, the appropriate level of retaliation when cheating is detected will be three times the harm done by each instance of cheating.[8]

Finally, we underscore a point that relates to earlier remarks: optimal retaliation may entail more or less than the abandonment of the underlying treaty regime. Suppose, as a benchmark case, that state X and state Y enter a treaty that entails a simultaneous exchange of benefits. Neither party relies on the treaty in the sense of making sunk expenditures. A shock occurs that changes the preferences of state X so that performance of the treaty is no longer worthwhile. Both states can cease performing immediately, and state Y has suffered no loss in reliance on the treaty that requires compensation. Here, the optimal response to changed circumstances is simply for both sides to cease performance, and unless state Y can and will offer some additional inducement for state X to reengage, the treaty efficiently ends.

But one can imagine other possibilities. Suppose state Y makes sunk investments in reliance on the treaty. State X then contemplates breach and may use a threat of breach to extract opportunistic concessions from Y (a type of opportunistic renegotiation). It may be necessary for Y to have the capacity to retaliate more substantially than simply by abandoning its own treaty obligations to avoid such an outcome.

Last, suppose that the treaty spans a wide range of obligations and that some shock occurs to render one of the obligations inefficient while the others remain valuable (consider the WTO, with its thousands of obligations respecting trade in goods, services, and intellectual property). Here, the abandonment of the treaty regime in the face of a breach of one obligation is most undesirable; the challenge is to calibrate the remedy for a deviation from a single obligation to ensure that such deviation is efficient while avoiding instability in the broader regime.

The Law: General Remedial Principles

In the remainder of this chapter, we focus on the generally applicable principles contained in the drafter articles on state responsibility of the International Law Commission. These are (ostensibly) customary international law rules, and they apply to breaches of both customary international law and treaty law (unless the treaty itself provides otherwise). Subsequent chapters (especially those on international trade and investment law) discuss remedies in more specialized settings.

Countermeasures

Draft article 22 recognizes that a state may lawfully engage in an act "not in conformity with an international obligation towards another State" that has engaged in an internationally wrongful act.[9] Such an act is known as a "countermeasure." Thus, the basic idea that noncompliance is permissible to sanction violations of international law is clearly recognized.

The ILC subjects the right to take countermeasures to several restrictions. Most important for our purposes, article 51 provides that "Countermeasures must be commensurate with the injury suffered, taking into account the gravity of the internationally wrongful act and the rights in question."[10] The ILC does not define "commensurate," but the clear focus of article 51 is on the harm done by the violation. A party undertaking a countermeasure must be mindful of the "injury suffered," the "gravity" of the violation, and the importance of the rights at issue. The emphasis on countermeasures "commensurate" with the harm suffered broadly accords with our suggestion that countermeasures should induce violators to internalize the harm done to others and should not in general "punish" them beyond that level.

Of course, the "commensurate" standard is subject to interpretation, and in many scenarios it will be difficult if not impossible to measure precisely the harm done by a violation. We do not wish to overstate our case but merely to make the point that the general standard for countermeasures adopted by the ILC links such measures to the harm done by the violation and does not seek to achieve absolute or maximal deterrence of violations. Although the ILC drafters may not have understood the provision in this fashion, such a standard can help to promote efficient compliance and to permit efficient breach.

Countermeasures are subject to some additional restrictions. For example, a state cannot engage in countermeasures that would violate certain fundamental norms of international law: those in the UN charter, "fundamental human rights," prohibitions on reprisals that violate humanitarian norms, and other peremptory norms.[11] And in the *United States Diplomatic and Consular Staff in Tehran* case,[12] the ICJ said that states may not violate diplomatic immunities even as a countermeasure. These rules may relate to the principle that retaliatory strategies should minimize the collateral or deadweight costs of retaliation conditional on their effectiveness. If a state retaliates against the violation of a treaty by taking the wrongdoing state's ambassador hostage, for example, then communications between the states will break down, interfering with efforts to resolve the dispute and prevent escalation. It would be better if the victim state could find a means to retaliate that has less drastic effects.

Sometimes, however, the only available retaliation may entail substantial collateral costs, yet may be preferable to inaction. To prevent Serbian forces from committing human rights violations, for example, NATO launched a military intervention that violated both the UN charter (it had no Security Council authorization) and arguably some human rights and humanitarian norms (against high-altitude bombing).[13] Yet it is not clear what alternatives there were. Economic sanctions, for example, are frequently ineffective,[14] and can impose their own great hardships on innocent populations. The NATO action may thus have been justified as an "efficient breach" of the usual remedial rules.

A final type of restriction on countermeasures requires states to observe some minimal procedural rules when engaging in them. States must call upon the wrongdoing state to obey the law and must give notice prior to the implementation of countermeasures.[15] These rules seem reasonable to limit the risk of a misunderstanding in which the wrongdoing state interprets a countermeasure as an independent wrong justifying an escalating series of additional countermeasures.

Reparations and Restitution

The ILC draft also requires states to pay reparations or restitution if they violate international law.[16] Restitution means the return of a thing wrongfully taken, such as territory. Reparations are monetary damages. There are limits in both cases. A state is not required to make restitution if the cost to it is out of proportion to the benefit to the victim state.[17] Reparations are supposed to be compensatory, not punitive.[18] Once reparations are paid or restitution is made, countermeasures are no longer appropriate.

Under this system, states have an implicit option to perform or pay reparations, just as contract parties under domestic law have an implicit option to perform or pay expectation damages. The victim state can retaliate with countermeasures only if the wrongdoing state both breaches and fails to pay reparations; if the wrongdoing state breaches but pays reparations, then the victim state has no right to retaliate. If reparations fully compensate the victim state, then the rules governing reparations are broadly consistent with the goal of inducing efficient compliance while allowing efficient breach.

Restitution in its classical sense, however, is potentially in tension with our economic analysis. If a state must make restitution, then it may not obtain any benefit from the breach. Perhaps restitution will be or should be limited to property right–like violations (the seizure of land, ships, equipment, and so forth), where the return of the property approximates compensatory damages (minus, of course, any lost "rental value"). Unfortunately, the law is ambiguous and unsettled.

We are also mindful of the fact that the obligation to pay reparations or restitution coexists with the law on countermeasures. Depending on how the notion of "commensurate" countermeasures is implemented and married with the obligation to make reparations or restitution, the possibility arises that a violator may become subject to an excessive sanction combining, for example, "commensurate" countermeasures with compensatory reparations. Nothing in the draft ILC articles rules out this possibility, and we thus urge that in cases where both countermeasures and reparations are involved, the principles in the draft articles be interpreted with an eye toward ensuring that the combination of remedies does not result in excessive penalties for breach. In this regard, we note again that the optimal aggregate penalties for breach may exceed the harm caused by breach in cases where breach may go undetected.

Reparations and Restitution in Practice

Although the draft ILC articles can be interpreted and implemented in a manner consistent with what economic analysis suggests, it remains to consider how the law operates in practice. Unfortunately, outside the trade and investment areas (which are subject to a *lex specialis* on remedial matters that we discuss later), cases are few and far between.

One case is the Air Service Agreement arbitration.[19] France injured Pan Am's commercial interests by placing certain restrictions on flights from the United States to France.[20] The United States retaliated by suspending Air France flights to Los Angeles.[21] The arbitration panel held that France violated the agreement and that the U.S. response was proportionate,[22] even though it is likely that the harm to Air France's economic interests (a complete ban on flights to Los Angeles) as a result of the U.S. retaliation was considerably greater than the harm to Pan Am's (limited restrictions on the Pan Am flights to Paris).[23] The panel held that a strict comparison of losses was not appropriate given the "importance of the issue" but did not explain further.[24] From an economic perspective, this judgment seems questionable, as it apparently countenances the imposition of a supracompensatory penalty.

Another interesting case, raising the question of whether the international law of remedies should make a distinction between the harm to people caused by a violation of international law and the harm to a state, is the M/V "Saiga" (No. 2) case.[25] The International Tribunal for the Law of the Sea found that Guinea had violated the law of the sea by detaining a vessel registered with Saint Vincent and the Grenadines. In determining damages under general international law principles, the tribunal took into account damage to the vessel itself, the detention of the crew, medical costs, and lost profits but refused to award compensation for violation of the legal rights of Saint Vincent and the Grenadines, concluding instead that the declaration that these rights were violated is adequate "satisfaction."[26] The tribunal also refused to award Saint Vincent and the Grenadines lost registration fees. Presumably, Saint Vincent and the Grenadines believed that vessels would be less likely to register with it after the Guinea attack because the flag did not protect the Saiga from aggression.

Should Saint Vincent and the Grenadines have received compensation for the injury to its "interest" apart from the harm to the owners of the Saiga or for the loss to its honor or dignity? The answer is no. The state's interest is just an abstraction; it is not something that can be injured independently of people or property. The tribunal did not reach the argument about lost registration fees because Saint Vincent and the Grenadines did not provide any proof that it lost registration fees. But the claim is dubious on purely theoretical grounds. If Saint Vincent and the Grenadines wants to protect vessels against predation by other states, it can simply compensate the victims and apply for compensation from the wrongdoing state. If it receives full compensation, it is made whole and will not lose registration fees because vessel owners know that they will be compensated for any harm.

Apportionment

Another pair of rules concerns apportionment of liability. ILC article 39 provides the following:

> In the determination of reparation, account shall be taken of the contribution to the injury by willful or negligent action or omission of the injured State or any person or entity in relation to whom reparation is sought.

Article 47 provides that

1. Where several States are responsible for the same internationally wrongful act, the responsibility of each State may be invoked in relation to that act.
2. Paragraph 1:
   (a) Does not permit any injured State to recover, by way of compensation, more than the damage it has suffered;
   (b) Is without prejudice to any right of recourse against the other responsible.

The notion that an injured state can recover from jointly wrongful states is familiar from domestic tort law, which similarly provides for joint and several liability plus a right of contribution to ensure that no defendant pays more than its share. Although sometimes criticized in the literature,[27] these rules straightforwardly ensure that wrongdoers do not pay more than the harm that they cause, which would result in overdeterrence. At present, these rules must be described as conjectural; we are aware of no examples where they were implemented.

"Serious Breaches"

The original (1996) ILC articles on state responsibility provided for the criminal liability of states. Article 19 provided that a wrongful act is a crime if the international obligation that is violated is "so essential for the protection of fundamental interests of the international community that its breach is recognized as a crime."[28] International obligations that rise to this level include the prohibitions on aggression and genocide.[29] The most recent ILC draft articles avoid the reference to criminal responsibility but do continue to advance the idea of heightened levels of liability:[30]

> Article 40: Application of this chapter
> 1. This chapter applies to the international responsibility which is entailed by a serious breach by a State of an obligation arising under a peremptory norm of general international law.
> 2. A breach of such an obligation is serious if it involves a gross or systematic failure by the responsible State to fulfill the obligation.
>
> Article 41: Particular consequences of a serious breach of an obligation under this chapter
> 1. States shall cooperate to bring to an end through lawful means any serious breach within the meaning of article 40.
> 2. No State shall recognize as lawful a situation created by a serious breach within the meaning of article 40, nor render aid or assistance in maintaining that situation.

These two articles provide that a heightened level of international responsibility occurs when a state commits a serious breach of a peremptory or *jus cogens* norm. A peremptory norm is a norm that binds states regardless of consent; the norms against aggression and genocide are often cited as examples. Unlike the case of a regular violation of international law, where only the victim state may invoke the responsibility of the perpetrator, all states have an obligation to take action against the violator "to bring an end" to the violation.

Do these special rules for "serious breaches" make sense? To answer the question, let us take as our starting point the observation that in domestic law, compensatory remedies are not considered appropriate for a range of activities. A thief cannot escape criminal liability by paying the owner for the goods after being apprehended. The reason is most likely that the opposite rule would cause owners to invest in excessive precautions against theft, and the existing rule forces the thief to prove that she values the goods more in the most effective way—by purchasing them. Another type of activity for which compensatory remedies are considered inadequate is the clearly socially harmful activity, where the wrongdoer's claim that she benefited more than the victim lost is not accepted—for example, murder.

Perhaps the ILC drafters view the violation of peremptory or *jus cogens* norms as the rough equivalent to the latter scenario. Interestingly, the ILC does not adopt the approach that would seem to follow from this notion under domestic civil law, namely, that the violator should pay punitive damages. Instead, it requires other states to intervene. But this approach too may make sense if breach in these cases is presumptively inefficient. Then there is no need for a calibrated remedy to facilitate possibly efficient breach, but instead the goal is to induce the violator to desist, and third-party intervention may in principle serve as an effective device in that regard.

To be sure, third parties may well sit on their hands because of free riding or similar cooperation problems. In general, there is no reason to think that third-party states—when they are not injured by the conduct in question—will systematically intervene in "serious" cases when they bear the costs and the benefits flow to others. But the rule that authorizes such intervention may have sound justification when the conduct in question is clearly undesirable, while a rule discouraging third-party intervention when the conduct may be efficient has some merit. One must be mindful, however, of the possibility that a victim state may be too weak to retaliate at a proper level in some scenarios, in which case there may be value to third-party intervention even if the breach is not "serious."

10

The Intersection between International and Domestic Law

International law and domestic law intersect in various ways. First, although public international law per se is usually binding only on states, it may be incorporated into domestic law either directly or as an aid to interpretation of domestic rules. We thus begin this chapter with a discussion of how international law comes to play a role in domestic legal systems, with particular attention to the distinction between "monist" and "dualist" states.

Second, and related, although states are usually the only parties with standing to invoke public international law in international dispute tribunals, acts that violate international law and/or domestic law may be actionable by private actors in domestic courts. In some cases, only one state may permit such actions; in others, plaintiffs may have a choice among the fora of different states. Accordingly, the second part of the chapter considers the consequences of opening domestic courts to private actions by foreign plaintiffs and the related issues raised by international forum shopping.

Finally, states may seek to apply their own laws in an extraterritorial fashion, often over the objection of other states. The question then arises whether international law places any constraints on such acts. Accordingly, the last part of the chapter considers the possible limits placed by international law on the exercise of extraterritorial jurisdiction.

Incorporating International Law into Domestic Law

To a large extent, states comply with international law as a result of the largely discretionary actions of executive officials. The head of government will direct the navy not to enter the territorial waters of foreign states, for example, or the government will order police to protect a foreign ambassador.

Yet international law is frequently incorporated into domestic law, in which case courts will enforce the law regardless of the wishes of the executive. Suppose, for example, that local police deliberately fail to protect an alien from a mob, in violation of international law. In one scenario, the foreign state protests this failure, and the government of the state that fails to provide protection responds by issuing an apology and sometimes paying reparations. Here, the domestic legal process is not engaged. In the other scenario, the victim brings a lawsuit in the court of the host state and obtains a remedy.

Courts can enforce international law only if they are authorized to do so. Such authority may come from a legislature or from constitutional principles. For example, the U.S. Constitution provides that "The judicial Power shall extend to all Cases, in Law and Equity, arising under this Constitution, the Laws of the United States, and Treaties made, or which shall be made, under their Authority."[1] Thus, at least at first glance (we will qualify this point later), U.S. federal courts may enforce treaties, because the U.S. Constitution tells them that they should.

This section discusses the ways that national legal institutions enforce international law within their jurisdictions. The reader should understand that every country incorporates international law differently, and we will provide some illustrations to indicate this diversity.[2] Because it is most familiar to us, we also focus attention on the United States.

Monism and Dualism

Every international law treatise distinguishes "monist" and "dualist" states. In a monist state, international law has the same status as national law; courts enforce international law just as they enforce domestic law. In a dualist state, international law becomes a part of domestic law only if the government—the legislature, usually—passes a statute that gives a particular treaty or norm of customary international law the force of domestic law. Because international law "automatically" enters domestic law in monist states, enthusiasts for international law tend to applaud monism and criticize dualism.

Great Britain is an example of a dualist state. When Britain enters a treaty, the treaty has no domestic legal effect until an act of Parliament provides that it does. A typical monist country is France. When France enters a treaty, it immediately has domestic legal effect, so French courts will enforce it—unless the French government provides otherwise by law.

States differ in their treatment of international law in another important respect. Some states give international law, or certain types of international law like treaties, the status of "higher law" in their systems. To see what this means, imagine that a legislature passes a statute that conflicts with an earlier treaty. If the statute and treaty have the same status, then under the normal "last-in-time" rule, the statute will prevail over the treaty because it was enacted afterward—just the way earlier statutes always give way to later statutes that repeal or simply conflict with them. But in some states (typically monist), the treaty would prevail because of its higher status.

It is important not to exaggerate the differences between the monist and dualist states. In some dualist states, courts have softened the impact of dualism by adopting interpretive methodologies that give more strength to international law. For example, courts may interpret ambiguous statutes so as to avoid conflicts with existing international law even where such law has not been incorporated into domestic law.[3] If courts apply this interpretive canon aggressively enough, international law may be incorporated into domestic law sub rosa.

Likewise, in some monist states, courts devise ways to refrain from enforcing international law. A common move in this regard is to construe international law as creating no domestically enforceable rights absent further action by the domestic legislature.[4]

Which System Is Better?

Putting aside the fact that differences between monist and dualist states may be exaggerated, which approach is more desirable? Are monist states better international citizens, as the proponents of monism often suggest? Indeed, why not embrace the approach of some monist states in which international law takes precedence over domestic law? Where conflict occurs, international legal norms prevail, even if the domestic law came second. Domestic courts would also defer to the judgments of international tribunals.

Such a system makes a difference only to the extent that governments would not otherwise voluntarily incorporate international law into their legal systems anyway. One possible reason is that executive or legislative discretion over whether to incorporate international law is desirable in some contexts. One potential advantage of discretion is that other states do not always comply with international law, and retaining the power to suspend obligations as a countermeasure therefore has value. That power could be delegated to courts—indeed, it has been in some countries, at least as a matter of formal law—but it is unclear whether courts can evaluate the costs and benefits of countermeasures wisely in many settings. Another benefit of executive and legislative discretion is that it avoids locking in existing norms of international law that may become outmoded and that the executive and legislature may wish to avoid or modify. A third benefit of a dualist approach to international law is that it avoids imposing technical obligations that become enforceable in court but that other states do not really care about. Compliance with international law is not costless, and the dualist approach ensures that private actors need not comply unless their government believes compliance to be important. In turn, governments will tend to push domestic compliance when other states value it significantly. Dualism thus tends to promote compliance where it is valuable but to allow slippage where it may not be.

But there are considerations on the other side. Dualism is costly in that it requires legislative or executive action to implement international law. In small nations and nations with limited resources, therefore, it may be preferable to have a system in which international law has direct or self-executing effect. Dualism also opens the door to a greater degree of opportunistic behavior by national governments that may wish to cheat on international obligations, which may occur in ways that are not entirely transparent and difficult to police. Finally, even if courts in monist states enforce international law more rigorously than courts in dualist states do, one must ask how this difference affects the incentives of governments when they negotiate treaties. Governments of monist states that are wary of judicial enforcement may be more reluctant to enter treaties or might insist on weaker language than they otherwise would.

Thus, it is not obvious on theoretical grounds alone that one system or the other is superior. We are aware of no systematic empirical evidence that sheds additional light on this topic.

Treaties and Judicial Enforcement in the United States

The question of whether U.S. courts will enforce treaties is a question not of international but of domestic law. As noted, the U.S. Constitution provides that treaties are the "law of the land." But the Supreme Court early in its history distinguished "self-executing" and "non-self-executing" treaties; only the former are to be enforced by courts.[5] Non-self-executing treaties can become binding under domestic law only if Congress incorporates them into a statute.

The distinction is nominally based on the intentions of the nations that negotiated the treaty. If the parties did not agree that their domestic courts would enforce the treaty, then domestic courts have no authority to enforce it. In practice, however, explicit statements about judicial enforcement are often absent in treaties. So courts look for other clues, including the general nature of the agreement. Consider a treaty that provides that the United States will reduce its stock of nuclear weapons. Courts are not generally in the business of arms control, and the president and Senate (which jointly make treaties) probably would not want to delegate such a sensitive matter to courts, which do not have any expertise or experience in the area. The tendency will be to conclude that such a treaty is not self-executing (absent contrary treaty text).

Other types of treaties are likely to be seen as self-executing. Such treaties tend to relate to matters that courts are already involved in and to provide definite standards that courts are comfortable enforcing. A typical example is the extradition treaty. Normally, only a court can order that someone be released from prison and handed over to a third party (a foreign power), so the treaty is naturally directed to the court.[6] Extradition treaties, unlike arms control treaties, use the language of courts and so are easily interpreted by them.

This pattern makes broad sense from an economic standpoint, as it reflects underlying considerations of relative institutional competence. There is little reason to think that all treaties should be enforced by courts, and U.S. courts tend to avoid entanglement where they lack comparative advantage.

Customary International Law in the United States

There has been a lively U.S. debate about the status of customary international law in U.S. domestic law. One side argues that customary international law has the status of federal common law—meaning that it has the same status as a statute, superseding previous inconsistent law but overridden by subsequent inconsistent statutes. The other side argues that customary international law can enter domestic law only if incorporated in a statute.[7]

Abstruse doctrinal arguments resting on the intricacies of U.S. domestic law have dominated the debate, but from a policy perspective, the question boils down to how easy it should be for customary international law to enter domestic law. Congress acts only with difficulty, so the practical difference between the two approaches is that the first allows customary international law to have considerably more influence.

The answer to this question depends on how one thinks that domestic law should be made and what one thinks of customary international law. People who think that all law should have a democratic pedigree are uncomfortable if customary international law can easily become domestic law. True, in theory, the elected U.S. executive must consent to a norm becoming customary international law, but the usual rule is that Congress must act to create federal law. In addition, the mushiness of customary international law gives courts an opportunity to err or manipulate the law.

Customary international law itself also has its critics. The positivist conception of customary international law requires the consent of the executive, but if executives err, and Congress is deprived of its say, then courts may end up enforcing customary international law that Congress would reject.

On the other side of the argument, a bona fide international custom may tend to be efficient, or it would never have developed in the first instance. A principle that induces the United States to comply with such customs absent a contrary expression of intent by Congress may then have merit. Once again, theory alone does not make clear which approach is best.

International Forum Shopping: The Alien Tort Statute, Choice of Law, and *Forum Non Conveniens*

We now consider a subject that has become a high-stakes litigation issue in the United States in recent years—efforts by foreign plaintiffs to bring tort and tortlike suits in U.S. courts.[8] A number of these cases allege widespread abuses by U.S. companies, generally in developing countries, including complicity in human rights violations by authoritarian governments or substantial environmental damage. Such cases have been celebrated by human rights lawyers and others for their potential to afford an effective remedy to victims of such acts.

Part of this litigation effort has rested on the U.S. Alien Tort Statute (ATS), which provides in full that "The district courts shall have original jurisdiction of any civil action by an alien for a tort only, committed in violation of the law of nations or a treaty of the United States."[9] The statute not only incorporates international law into U.S. law but affords a private right of action for damages when the violation of international law amounts to a "tort."

Foreign plaintiffs also bring suit under state tort law, arguing that U.S. tort rules should apply to torts committed abroad under the applicable "choice of law" principles. The typical suit involves a U.S. corporation alleged to have some connection to tortious acts abroad. The plaintiff often argues that the application of U.S. law to the foreign tort is appropriate because the defendant is a U.S. company, and the United States has a strong interest in ensuring that U.S. companies adhere to U.S. standards of conduct when operating abroad.

The advantages to the plaintiff of pursuing a lawsuit in the United States are often considerable. On substantive tort issues, U.S. law is frequently more favorable to plaintiffs than foreign tort law. U.S. precedent may impose strict liability or allow for punitive damages when foreign law does not. Compensatory damages awards in the United States may be higher on average, in part because of the jury system. Procedurally, U.S. law may allow plaintiffs greater opportunities to build their case through more liberal discovery rules or may allow the consolidation of claims in class actions that are impermissible abroad. U.S. law also shows no hostility to contingent fee arrangements, while many foreign jurisdictions prohibit them. Finally, U.S. courts may be more efficient, less biased, and better insulated from corruption.

Defendants, of course, resist these lawsuits and often urge the court to send the plaintiffs back to their home country to pursue the available remedies there. Various legal maneuvers can produce this effect. In ATS cases, the defendants urge that the scope of "tort" under international law is narrow and that the alleged conduct does not fall within the statute. They have also argued that corporations are not subject to liability under international law, pointing out that states historically have not imposed such liability,[10] and most recently that the statute should not apply to acts outside U.S. territory and the high seas. In the state law cases, defendants urge that the court should apply the substantive law of the place where the alleged tort occurred—the rule of *lex loci delictus*. They may also argue that the court should send the case back to the courts of the country where the tort occurred because litigation is more appropriate there under the doctrine of *forum non conveniens*.

Economic analysis suggests some important pros and cons to allowing these suits to go forward in the United States. On the one hand, if the remedy available for wrongful acts in the country where they occur is deficient and the U.S. remedy is superior, allowing suit in the United States has the potential in some cases to provide incentives for lawful or careful behavior by U.S. companies (and others subject to jurisdiction in U.S. courts) that would otherwise be lacking.

On the other hand, some scholars question whether the U.S. remedy is necessarily superior. The weaker remedies abroad may reflect different conditions there that justify a lesser degree of investment in measures to avoid tortious conduct.

Another important consideration is the fact that suits in the United States can have the effect of placing American companies, and others subject to jurisdiction in the United States, at a competitive disadvantage. Their foreign competitors, which do not have sufficient contacts with the United States to become subject to U.S. jurisdiction, or which do not have any assets available in the United States to satisfy judgments, will be subject only to weaker foreign remedies. Companies subject to U.S. jurisdiction may then lose out on sales and investment opportunities to foreign companies not subject to suit in the United States. These foreign companies may be less efficient than their U.S. counterparts at producing the goods and services at issue or in performing whatever activity the investment requires, yet may nevertheless outcompete them because of the cost advantage they enjoy due to weaker tort remedies. Indeed, the weaker the remedies abroad, other things being equal, the more likely that foreign competitors will gain a cost advantage that allows them to drive out the U.S. competition. Conceivably, the worst of all worlds will result—efficient companies may be driven from foreign markets, increasing the costs of production in developing countries, while those who actually produce or invest in those markets will be insulated from tort liability and nothing will have been accomplished to promote more lawful or careful behavior. Much the same thing may happen if U.S. companies are induced to spin off their foreign operations into separate companies that cannot be reached in U.S. courts.

In short, economic analysis suggests caution in allowing lawsuits to go forward in U.S. courts for tortious acts that occur abroad, especially if the effect may be to create a discriminatory liability regime that imposes higher costs on U.S. companies and others subject to suit in the United States. But one must also acknowledge that such suits can also promote economic welfare (at least from the global perspective) under certain circumstances.

Indeed, economic distortions can arise when suits proceed in foreign venues as well. Many of the recent lawsuits in the United States are motivated by a belief on the part of plaintiffs that the remedies in their home country are weaker. But home country remedies can also be quite substantial and may be particularly harsh when the defendant is foreign. Many companies doing business abroad have had the experience of being "hometowned" in foreign courts following lawsuits brought by foreign nationals. Thus, the possibility of discrimination against U.S. companies is not necessarily eliminated by sending cases off to the courts where the alleged tort occurred. Likewise, U.S. courts need to exercise some caution in enforcing judgments obtained in foreign courts when a plaintiff comes to the United States seeking to execute a judgment against a U.S. defendant's assets. It is appropriate to ask first whether the foreign proceeding followed acceptable standards of fairness and due process.

Extraterritorial Jurisdiction

Recall that sovereignty refers to the state's control over its internal affairs and correlatively to a prohibition over interference with the affairs of other states. Sovereignty is closely linked to territory. The core notion of sovereignty refers to the state's right to control what happens on its territory (including territorial waters) and to be free from interference of other states. These ideas can also be put in terms of jurisdiction. A state has jurisdiction over its own territory—that is, what happens on its own territory—and not over the territory of other states.

We could imagine a world in which territorial jurisdiction was both a necessary and sufficient basis for all regulation. Suppose that people never left the territory on which they were born and that none of their activities affected the lives of people living in other states. And suppose further that people could never be "between" states (as on the high seas). Such a world would be fully regulated in the sense that everyone everywhere would be subject to the law of some state, and such a world would have no regulatory overlap—no one would be simultaneously subject to possibly conflicting laws of different states. Likewise, if actions in one state had no effect in others, no externalities would arise that might tempt states to regulate in extraterritorial fashion.

Such a world would have many advantages but is not realistic. The real world is different in numerous ways:

- States have agreed to freedom of the seas, which means that no state has jurisdiction over the ocean beyond certain territorial waters. But crimes, torts, and other bad acts can occur on ships and airplanes crossing the oceans. These acts frequently involve people of different nationality. Which state or states should have jurisdiction in these cases?
- People travel a great deal. Tourists, merchants, government officials, and many others leave their states and enter the territory of other states. Suppose they commit, or are the victims of, crimes or torts. Territorial jurisdiction implies that the host state alone has jurisdiction over these people, but states have insisted that in some of these cases a state should have overlapping jurisdiction if its national is a perpetrator or (more controversially) a victim.
- The activities in one state can harm people in another state. State X exports widgets to state Y. State X permits widget producers to form a cartel that fixes prices, hurting Y's consumers. Or factories in state X generate pollution that floats over the territory of state Y. May state Y pass laws that regulate the widget producers or factories of state X on the ground that their activities impinge on Y's internal affairs?
- People leave states and take refuge in other states. The state from which a person leaves might demand him back, claiming that he is an ordinary criminal. The person might claim that he is a victim of political persecution. The host state may believe it proper to grant asylum to this person, but it may anger the other state if it does.
- The Internet is a special case. Web pages designed in a state with lax pornography or libel laws are accessed by people living in states with stricter pornography and libel laws. Can government authorities in the second state regulate the multinational corporation that sponsors or makes available the web page?
- Government officials often authorize controversial actions of questionable international legality. They start wars, order people to be killed or detained, and authorize other abuses. Government officials and their agents must also travel to other states in order to engage in diplomacy. Should foreign states have the right to arrest and try them for violating international law?

As is always the case, we need to distinguish ideal outcomes and realistic outcomes. We might start with the rough proposition that regulatory authority over every act should be allocated to the state that has the best incentives, or is in the best position, to regulate it properly. This principle would avoid regulatory overlap and hence the problem of conflicting rules and the equally problematic outcome where states refrain from regulating in the hope that some other state will do it for them. The latter problem is indeed a problem on the high seas, where piracy can occur in part because states have strong incentives to free ride on other states' enforcement efforts.

Which state has the best incentives or is in the best position to regulate an act? We can start again with the state on whose territory the act occurs. That state has enormous logistical advantages: states construct police stations and courts and the like on their territory, and so they are ordinarily in the best position to regulate what happens on their territory. But not all states regulate their territory very well. Some states are too poor or disorganized. And even when states regulate their territory well, they might have reasons—good or bad—for badly or not-at-all regulating within-territory acts that are mainly consequential for foreign states. A state might not care much about the well-being of a foreign tourist and so might not give him adequate protection if he is a victim of crime or adequate process if he is a suspect. And when local industry conspires to fix prices of export goods or pollute in a way that harms foreigners, then again the state on whose territory that industry is located might have inadequate incentives to regulate it.

As we argued in Chapter 3, these sorts of externality problems are the primary reason for the emergence of international law. In the absence of international law, however, these problems give rise to attempts at extraterritorial regulation. Such regulation typically involves three things: (1) passing laws that apply to conduct abroad; (2) subjecting such conduct and the people who engage in it to actions in a domestic court; and (3) enforcing the judgments of the domestic court, which may require the apprehension of foreign nationals. To pass laws that apply overseas, states assert legislative or prescriptive jurisdiction. To enforce those laws through actions against foreigners in domestic court, states assert judicial or adjudicative jurisdiction. To bring foreign nationals before the court to answer for their behavior, states assert enforcement jurisdiction—though they may well obtain those people with the cooperation of foreign states, for example, through extradition.

Commentators claim that a number of different rules govern these various assertions of jurisdiction. But the rules are sometimes vague and often controversial. Let us start with prescriptive jurisdiction.[11] It is uncontroversial that a state can assert jurisdiction over its own territory—that is the territorial jurisdiction at the heart of sovereignty. It is also often the case that states assert jurisdiction over their nationals operating abroad, so-called nationality jurisdiction.[12] For example, an American travels to France and fails to answer a subpoena requiring him to appear as a witness at a trial in the United States. The French might argue that they should decide whether this person stays or goes because he is on French territory. The U.S. subpoena is valid under international law, however, because the American is a U.S. citizen, an implication of the nationality principle.[13] He is subject to both French and American law.

States also at times try to regulate overseas behavior that simply has an "effect" on their interests, thus going beyond the territoriality and nationality bases for jurisdiction.[14] For example, U.S. antitrust law applies to some conduct overseas under the "effects test." Companies that fix the prices of products exported to the United States, for instance, violate U.S. law. This assertion of jurisdiction sometimes irritates other states, who feel that their ability to regulate behavior on their territory is compromised, and they react in various ways, as by refusing to enforce antitrust judgments issued by U.S. courts or by refusing to cooperate in antitrust investigations. We see here how the interdependence of the world—the fact that goods manufactured in one country may be sold in another country—plays havoc with the simple idea of sovereignty based on territory. The United States does not trust or expect foreign states to prevent price-fixing by their own nationals when it mainly injures Americans and so claims the power to regulate those foreign nationals operating abroad. International law is often said to permit such extraterritorial assertion of jurisdiction on the condition that the overseas activity has a "direct, substantial and reasonably foreseeable effect" on the regulating country.[15]

Of course, it is not enough that a state wishes to engage in extraterritorial regulation; the real problem for states is often enforcement. Legally, a state cannot simply send law enforcement agents to a foreign state and have them arrest a person suspected of violating an extraterritorial law or seize his assets to satisfy a civil judgment. That would be a violation of the foreign state's sovereignty if done without permission of the government of the foreign state. There are also serious practical limits on the ability of states to seize people and assets overseas. Law enforcement agents will not be permitted to enter; military intervention is dangerous and expensive.

It may be, then, that the failure of states to agree on tighter rules governing jurisdiction reflects in part the fact that states often could not enforce their rules, and therefore less was at stake. People who violated foreign law could avoid legal sanctions by staying in their home state, not entering the foreign state, and not holding assets in that foreign state. Likewise, government officials who traveled to other states often received immunity under international law.

But in the modern global economy, things have changed. Multinational corporations are vulnerable to assertions of extraterritorial jurisdiction because of their business contacts with many potential regulating states. Their efforts to do business on a global scale mean that they have assets around the world subject to seizure. Indeed, corporate defendants are the most frequent sources of dispute over these matters.

Consider, then, a case where a foreign corporation violates U.S. antitrust law in a foreign state, by joining in a price-fixing conspiracy with respect to goods exported to the United States. The United States brings a case against the corporation, which has a presence in the United States and assets as well. The United States can thus easily enforce a judgment. The foreign corporation may try to argue that the United States lacks prescriptive or adjudicative jurisdiction because the behavior in question took place on foreign territory.[16] But as noted earlier, U.S. courts will often exercise jurisdiction nevertheless as long as the conduct abroad has substantial adverse effects in the United States.

But because the corporation also does business abroad, it also finds itself subject to laws there. What happens if the laws conflict? This problem has sometimes arisen where a foreign defendant would violate foreign bank secrecy laws (for example) if it revealed information pursuant to a discovery order in the United States. Courts in this situation can invoke the principle of international comity—a doctrine of both domestic and international law—that may excuse defendants from compliance with domestic law in cases of literal conflict with foreign law.[17] In practice, however, literal conflict is infrequent.

International comity also provides a method for courts to sort out who should have jurisdiction when multiple authorities in different countries bring cases (or could bring cases) against the same defendant for the same violations under different laws. For example, an antitrust violation by an exporter in Britain may violate both British and U.S. law, leading to parallel investigations in both states. Courts in each state will often suspend proceedings or dismiss the case when they believe that the court in the other state is in a better position to try the defendant. Comity is likewise invoked as a basis for deferring to regulators abroad when foreign conduct has some domestic effects but most of its effects are in other jurisdictions. The legal basis for declining jurisdiction here is sometimes a "balancing of interests" test or an appeal to the principle (contained, for example, in §403 of the Restatement of Foreign Relations) that states should not exercise jurisdiction when to do so is "unreasonable."

One might ask, why do nations sometimes decline to exercise jurisdiction, in the absence of a clear and explicit international obligation to do so, on grounds of "international comity"? Why offer other nations such "favors"? The answer no doubt lies in part in the belief that comity can promote useful reciprocity—state X will defer to state Y in appropriate cases, in the expectation that state Y will defer to state X in other appropriate cases. As long as states behave in some rough reciprocal fashion, comity principles have the potential to support useful cooperation in the absence of more explicit treaty law on the subject in question. Likewise, if states decline to observe comity in situations where they will benefit slightly while causing significant injury abroad, the potential for conflicting assertions of jurisdiction to cause substantial harm from a global point of view increases considerably. Principles of international comity are thus useful but also seemingly quite fragile ways to promote a mutually beneficial division of regulatory authority.

Indeed, we see many examples in which conflicting assertions of jurisdiction pose problems for international cooperation that have not been solved by appeal to considerations of comity. To return to the antitrust realm for illustration, imagine price-fixing that occurs in state X but that results in high prices in state Y. State X may tolerate or even approve of the price fixing. Under U.S. antitrust law, for example, the Webb-Pomerene Act explicitly allows U.S. firms to participate in cartels that operate exclusively abroad (and thus that only injure foreign consumers).[18] If the company that engages in price-fixing in our example has sufficient contacts with state Y—such as substantial assets there—then that state may also be able to exert control over that company. Otherwise, it cannot. The injury to state Y may well be greater than the benefit to state X, as theory suggests to be the case with price-fixing. If so, an inability of state Y to exert control results in a bad outcome from a global point of view.

In other cases, however, the situation may be reversed. Consider a merger in state X between two companies that will allow the companies to reap massive economies of scale and lower their costs dramatically. But the merger may cause prices to rise slightly in state Y. If state Y can exert control over the parties to the merger, then it may be able to prohibit it, but at the same time it may cause a large economic loss to the two companies in state X, which approves of the policy. This is also a potentially bad outcome from a global point of view.[19] The likely solution, if it is to be found at all, is international cooperation of some sort that goes beyond the rudimentary rules of jurisdiction and principles of comity.

To sum up, a state's power to regulate remains closely tied to its control over its own territory. A state can attempt to regulate conduct abroad but cannot effectively do so unless the regulated entity comes onto its territory or has assets in its territory, or unless the regulating state can induce a foreign state with control over the regulated entity to cooperate in its regulatory efforts. Governments simply have more power over their own territory than over other governments' territories: that is why sovereignty remains closely tied to territory. Nevertheless, in the modern economy, the conditions necessary for extraterritorial regulation to be enforceable often arise, especially with respect to large companies. States can and do assert the power to regulate abroad, basing their assertion of authority on the fact that the regulated entity is one of its nationals or on the proposition that the regulated conduct has substantial effects within its territory. Depending on the circumstances, extraterritorial regulation may be accepted and even welcomed by foreign states, or it may become a source of considerable international tension. Various forms of international cooperation, both explicit (as with treaties) and implicit (as with comity), can ameliorate these tensions, but many of them survive.

III

Traditional Public International Law

11

Treatment of Aliens, Foreign Property, and Foreign Debt

Control over territory is a sovereign prerogative, yet it bumps up against other states' interests in what happens in a foreign state's territory. These interests arise in many ways. Citizens of foreign states—that is, aliens—enter a state's territory, as tourists, temporary employees, merchants, and in other capacities. Foreign states have an interest in the well-being of those aliens. The aliens often bring property when they enter a state or purchase property after they arrive, including immovables such as land. The foreign state has an interest in ensuring that its nationals' property rights are respected. And foreign nationals often lend money to states—they purchase its sovereign bonds—and to people and businesses in those states. Foreign states have an interest in ensuring that the states pay foreign creditors and that debtors in those states pay foreign creditors.

In this chapter, we discuss the ways that international law protects these interests. Speaking loosely, one might say that aliens have certain rights when on foreign soil. They have a right to security of the person. They have property and contract rights. They have the right to access the local law enforcement system. Historically, these rights belonged not to the alien but to his state. If state X injures an alien from state Y, then state Y has a claim against state X. The alien can only plead with his state to demand a remedy and to turn it over to him. Today the alien might have certain other rights under human rights treaties, which he would have directly against the state that harmed him. However, in this chapter we will mostly confine ourselves to the historical rules for protection of aliens. Aside from a brief digression, we will discuss human rights in a later chapter.

Protection of Aliens

The core of sovereignty—control over territory—implies that when foreigners (aliens) enter a state's territory, they lose the protection of their own state and come under the authority of the host state. It would seem to follow that the host state can do whatever it wants to aliens—including kill them or take their property.

But states have agreed not to abuse aliens, for two reasons. First, host states normally benefit from the presence of aliens on their territory. Tourists bring revenues. So do merchants and other business people. Foreign corporations send agents who invest in factories and other infrastructure. And migrants come to work and often to settle permanently. If states abused aliens, then this stream of benefits would cease.

Second, the sending states—the states from which aliens come—take an interest in the well-being of their nationals. These people may vote or have other sources of political influence, after all. When host states abuse aliens or fail to offer them protection, the sending states protest.

This mutual interest in the well-being of aliens has given rise to norms of customary international law, which, however, have also been heavily contested. Let us begin with the standard view—which the United States and Western countries have long held.

On this view, aliens enjoy two sources of protection.[1] First, they must enjoy the same basic legal rights that natives enjoy. Second, these legal rights must be above some minimum standard of treatment.

What are these basic legal rights? A surprising number are excluded. Aliens have no right to work, for example; nor do they have a right to schooling (if they are children), public assistance if they are out of work, or mobility—to live wherever they want. If aliens are prosecuted or sued, they are entitled to the same procedural rights that natives receive (although, unlike natives, they can be deported for committing crimes). They also enjoy the same personal and property rights that natives enjoy: they cannot be arbitrarily killed or deprived of property (though they may not be allowed to purchase homes and other property). In sum, aliens enjoy a limited right to equal treatment.

The legal minimum is more controversial. States have, from time to time, seen fit to expropriate the property of nationals and aliens alike. Pursuant to a policy of redistributing property to the poor (or to politically connected nonpoor), states may also refuse to compensate or fully compensate the owner. The principle of equal treatment is not offended because native and alien receive the same thing—nothing or very little. Western nations have claimed that these policies violate the minimum standard of treatment. The expropriating states—Latin American states in earlier decades, communist states before they collapsed—refused to acknowledge such a rule.

Whatever the resolution of this particular issue, it is clear that states do not always believe that it is in their interest to treat aliens fairly. Indeed, many states have expelled aliens and seized their property. Others heavily tax or regulate them, seeing them as a nonvoting source of revenue. These policies may harm the state in the long run, for the obvious reason that people will stop coming to the country or investing there if they face a serious risk of physical injury or expropriation of their property. Nonetheless, not all governments have the luxury of thinking about the future.

International law protecting aliens can be effective, then, only if the sending states are willing to expend resources to punish states that harm their nationals. And here we see a problem of asymmetry. Western states have little interest in mistreating aliens: they seek tourists, workers, and investors. Thus, even in the absence of international law, they would extend protection to aliens. Poorer states (and, in the past, communist states) therefore did not have to worry about the mistreatment of their nationals abroad (indeed, communist states tried to prevent their nationals from migrating; poorer states, by contrast, welcomed their remittances). They would receive nothing, then, for giving up the power to deal with their own aliens as they wished (at least unless other states extended them some benefit relating to another issue area).

This explains why poorer states have resisted the rule that aliens are entitled to a minimum of rights. But what explains their acquiescence in the equal treatment principle? One answer is that equal treatment provides credibility that a (say) policy of expropriation is in fact in the state's interest. Consider, for example, a poor state with a historically dispossessed population that has fueled a violent insurgency and that can be appeased only through the redistribution of land. The poor state cannot afford to compensate landowners, so it expropriates their land, inadequately compensating them, and redistributes it to people in the dispossessed population. This policy might well be a good one and the only possible remedy to a difficult situation.

Western states might well acquiesce in such a policy, even if it hurts their nationals, if they believe that the only alternative is a civil war that could hurt their nationals even more, for example, by bringing to power a government that is more averse to Western interests. But foreign observers may not be able to distinguish a state facing these circumstances from a more opportunistic state that seeks to take foreign property simply to enrich natives who are not otherwise in a particular bad condition. By expropriating foreign-owned and locally owned property on the same basis—with the same rules of partial compensation, for example—the host state may credibly signal that the policy is a necessary one. The harm to nationals shows that the government is willing to endure the political pain for what it believes is the greater good.

Less dramatic reasons for the equal treatment rule can also be imagined. Some states are too poor to provide civil and criminal process that meet Western standards. Again, the question for the West is whether these states discriminate against aliens or simply are unable to provide them with adequate support. Equal treatment suggests that the weak process is not a method for expropriating from foreigners but is instead a regrettable consequence of the poverty or institutional weakness of the state.

It should be clear, then, why equal treatment is a more sustainable norm than minimum standards. Some states cannot satisfy minimum standards. They lack the capacity, or even if they have the capacity, domestic political considerations cause them to violate these standards. But if states can protect some of the basic rights of natives, they will usually be able to protect the basic rights of aliens as well. This will often be in their interest, and when it is not, the prospect of some form or retaliation on matters of interest to them may be sufficient to keep them in line.

In customary international law, aliens lost the right of protection if the sending and receiving states went to war. The explanation is likely that during wartime, aliens (now "enemy aliens") become a threat rather than a source of revenue. It is interesting to note that an attacking state would give enemy aliens a grace period to leave the country unmolested; defending states would not, at least as a matter of custom.[2] This rule spared receiving states the expense of rounding up enemy aliens while benefiting sending states as well, whose citizens would be able to maintain their freedom.

In the last half century, the customary international law protecting the property of aliens has been partially superseded by treaties, including bilateral investment treaties. We will discuss these treaties in Chapter 19, where we will develop the themes discussed above.

A Note on Human Rights Treaties

For quite a long time, customary international law norms alone protected aliens. In the last half century, a separate but overlapping body of international law has emerged—the law of human rights. Human rights law requires states to give certain protections to all people—aliens as well as their own nationals. However, as we will see in Chapter 14, the theory of human rights law is different from the theory behind the traditional laws governing aliens.

Sovereign Debt

Foreigners also loan money to sovereigns who on occasion refuse to pay back the loan. The strategic and legal issues here are similar to those that arise in connection with expropriation of foreign assets. A state welcomes capital at time 1 but then prefers not to repay at time 2. After all, if the government repays funds to creditors, it does not have those funds for all sorts of pressing needs—aiding the poor, or suppressing an insurgency, or building schools and medical clinics. States usually resist this temptation because if they do not repay loans today, creditors will not lend tomorrow. States that default on loans rarely enjoy prosperity, despite the short-term windfall, for a long time after.

In recent years, however, a number of developing states have argued that they should not be required by international law to repay loans when those loans financed the self-interested activities of authoritarian regimes. Under the so-called odious debt doctrine, a successor regime is not responsible for paying the debts of a prior regime if those debts were incurred by an authoritarian government and used to enrich itself or suppress its citizens rather than to benefit the public.[3] An example of an odious debt would be the foreign loans advanced to the apartheid regime of South Africa, which used many of the funds not for development but to suppress the majority black population. The legal status of the doctrine is controversial, but it has many advocates.[4]

Defenders of the odious debt doctrine often rest their case on the simple and apparently morally compelling claim that an impoverished population that has recently overthrown a dictator should not have to pay sovereign debt incurred by the dictator to pay for personal gain. But the well-being of the postdictatorship population cannot be taken in isolation; one needs to consider the likely impact of the doctrine on the well-being of the population before the dictator is overthrown and on the well-being of populations who are never able to escape a dictatorship. To do this, one needs to take an ex ante perspective, comparing the well-being of affected populations in a world in which the doctrine exists and a world in which it does not.[5]

The conventional ex ante defense of the rule does just this. Suppose creditors know they cannot collect if the money lent to a dictator is used to finance his private consumption. Creditors will respond to the rule by declining to make such loans or by charging a higher interest rate. As a result, dictators will not be able to borrow for private consumption, and more money will be left for future generations of the population. As the dictator is just a single person with a lot of money already, who therefore obtains a small marginal gain from an additional dollar, and as the future public is poor and thus will value an additional dollar a lot, the restriction on lending should, by transferring wealth from the dictator to future public, produce a welfare gain. Of course, not all dictators start off as wealthy people, and some dictators are just figureheads of groups, but the same point holds: the power holders are, in general, wealthier than the public.

Potentially of even greater importance, would-be dictators may be deterred from taking power if they anticipate that they will not be able to borrow for personal gain even though they control the government. If so, the odious debt doctrine will, in the long run, reduce the number of dictatorships and in this way improve the well-being of populations that would be subject to dictatorships but for the deterrent effect of the doctrine. Meanwhile, the loss of the lending opportunity to creditors, most of which are firms with relatively wealthy shareholders, is likely to have a small impact on utility. In the short run, profits might be somewhat smaller, but the international lending market is highly liquid, and investors should be able to find nearly as good opportunities. In the long run, lending opportunities will not be reduced because creditors can lend to the additional states that do not have dictatorships as a result of the odious debt doctrine. This argument in favor of restrictions on lending is no different from an argument in favor of any other kinds of sanction, from economic to military, and thus whether it is valid or not depends on the basic considerations for and against sanctioning.[6]

However, the argument for the odious debt doctrine rests on an implausible assumption. Some of the literature implies that dictators borrow money for the express purpose of building themselves unnecessary palaces. However, dictators generally become wealthy by taking kickbacks on public contracts and through similar forms of corruption. They build roads, airports, power plants, dams, and ports, and although they skim off profits, the resulting infrastructure benefits the public, at least a little. For example, a government might use a loan to build a bridge or some other public project but demand kickbacks from the contractor. If a $10 million loan is used to build a $9 million bridge, with government ministers skimming off the extra $1 million, is this an odious debt? If so, the doctrine discourages an investment that could benefit the public; if not, the doctrine will have little effect on actual behavior. No doubt the dictators prefer this form of corruption because it gives them some political cover, but by the same token, this form of corruption is not as bad as borrowing for personal consumption alone. Although there are well-known cases of prestige projects that yielded no gain to the public, most serious defenders of the odious debt doctrine do not argue that dictatorial governments should be deprived of credit for legitimate projects, even if they turn out to be failures.

During the past half century, numerous dictatorial regimes borrowed money from foreign creditors and made investments in infrastructure and industry, investments that have paid off for future generations. Chile under Augusto Pinochet, South Korea under Park Chung Hee, and Singapore under Lee Kwan Yew are classic development success stories. China's authoritarian regime has borrowed tremendous sums, and currently China is enjoying rapid economic growth. Even the authoritarian regimes that have been less successful in promoting economic growth cannot, in most cases, be accused of using foreign debt for personal consumption. The Latin American dictatorships, for example, did not all squander their loans on consumption; they invested poorly. And even the worst kleptocratic dictators in Africa did not consume all of their loans. They used them mainly to pay off political supporters and to finance the army. All regimes must, to some extent, make transfer payments to keep domestic peace and to finance the army to protect the country from domestic unrest and foreign invasion; these types of payments are quasi-public investments because the public benefits from peace and domestic order.

Even more troublesome, straightforward borrowing for personal consumption is not necessarily harmful to the public. One cannot determine whether a particular debt is odious in isolation. Governments obtain funds from tax receipts and loans. There is no sense in which the two sources can be kept separate from each other. Thus, a dictator can evade the odious debt doctrine by arbitrarily designating bank loans as the source for public projects and tax revenue as the source for the dictator's consumption. The only way that the doctrine could limit borrowing would be if the dictator seeks to spend more money on himself than he could obtain from tax revenues alone. However, in nearly all realistic cases, extremely greedy dictators can satisfy themselves from tax revenues.

The main effect of the odious debt doctrine is to encourage dictators to be shortsighted. If the odious debt doctrine increases the probability of being overthrown by a great enough amount, the dictator will borrow in order to consume rather than to invest, because he will not be in power long enough to reap long-term benefits by choosing the latter option. In the limiting case, he will not invest at all. Although the public does not have to repay the debt for his consumption, it will also suffer from lower economic growth because he did not invest.

If the odious debt doctrine is in place, then creditors will expect not to be repaid if the dictator uses loans for personal projects. If the doctrine is interpreted in a very narrow way, so that repayment is denied only if the loan proceeds are used directly in a personal project, then the doctrine will have little effect on behavior. The dictator will simply reallocate resources, using tax revenues for personal projects and loan proceeds for public or quasi-public projects. If the doctrine is interpreted more broadly, so that, for example, creditors cannot recover loans to dictators who spend a substantial portion of public funds (whether borrowed or obtained through taxes) on personal projects, then creditors will be reluctant to lend. Overall, the doctrine increases the public's utility by (1) decreasing the probability that the dictator will stay in power, (2) decreasing the probability that a would-be dictator will come to power, and (3) either eliminating the negative externality imposed by the dictator's consumption or allowing the public to better enjoy the positive externality from the dictator's quasi-public investment. However, because the dictator is less likely to make the quasi-public investment under the doctrine, the public is less likely to be able to enjoy the fruits of such investment.

12

The Use of Force

War has always been considered the central problem of international relations. It imposes extraordinary hardships on people: killing and maiming soldiers and civilians alike, damaging the environment, wasting resources, and disrupting life in countless ways. Many wars are, of course, relatively small and contained. But some wars spin out of control and cause enormous destruction. In World War I, more than eight million soldiers died in battle, whereas in World War II twice that number died.[1] But even these figures do not fully capture their consequences. During World War I, three empires collapsed: the Russian, Austro-Hungarian, and Ottoman. Subsequently, in Russia, a civil war erupted before a communist dictatorship consolidated power and millions more died. The collapse of the Austro-Hungarian Empire produced instability in the Balkans that has still not receded. The Ottoman Empire left behind weak and unstable states in the Middle East that have continually fought each other or endured civil wars. World War II caused vast suffering to civilians, including the Holocaust, and yielded to the cold war—a fifty-five year period of international paralysis during which the United States and the Soviet Union fought devastating proxy wars in developing countries.

In the nineteenth century, states tolerated war but sought to control it. After World War II, a strong urge to end war came into existence. But war has not ended. Although a world war has since then been avoided, numerous and devastating smaller wars have been fought, including civil wars. which have killed many millions. Tables 12.1 and 12.2 tell the grim story through 2003.

The important thing to understand is that even while states sought to eliminate war, or said that they sought to eliminate war, wars have continued, even if the worst type of conflicts have been avoided. One natural question that arises is about the role of international law in preventing states from going to war. Has it played any role in avoiding war? Why hasn't it been more successful?

Table 12.1. Interstate Wars (1945–2003)

War Name	Dates	Battle Deaths
First Kashmir	1947–1949	3,500
Palestine	1948	8,000
Korean	1950–1953	910,084
China-Taiwan Offshore	1955	2,370
Russo-Hungarian	1956	2,426
Sinai	1956	3,221
Taiwan Strait	1958	1,800
Ifni War	1958	1,122
Assam	1962	1,853
Vietnamese	1965–1975	1,021,442
Second Kashmir	1965	7,061
Six Day	1967	19,600
Second Laotian	1968–1973	N/A
Israeli-Egyptian	1969–1970	5,368
Football	1969	1,900
Communist Coalition	1970	6,525
Bangladesh	1971	11,223
Yom Kippur	1973	14,439
Turco-Cypriot	1974	1,500
Angola	1975–1976	2,700
Vietnamese-Cambodian	1977–1979	8,000
Second Ogaden War	1977–1978	10,500
Ugandan-Tanzanian	1978–1979	3,000
Sino-Vietnamese	1979	21,000
Iran-Iraq	1980–1988	1,250,000
Falklands	1982	1,001
Israel-Syria (Lebanon)	1982	1,655
Aouzou Strip	1986–1987	8,000
Sino-Vietnamese	1987	4,000
Gulf War	1990–1991	41,466
Bosnia Independence	1992	5,240
Azeri-Armenian	1993–1994	14,000
Cenepa Valley	1995	1,500
Badme Border	1998–2000	120,000
Kosovo	1999	5,002
Kargil	1999	1,172
Afghanistan Invasion	2001	4,002
Iraq Invasion	2003	7,173

Source: Meredith Reid Sarkees, *COW Inter-State War Data, 1823–2003* (v4.0), http://www.correlatesofwar.org/COW2%20Data/WarData_NEW/InterStateWarData_v4.0.csv. See also Meredith Reid Sarkees & Frank Wayman, *Resort to War: 1816–2007* (CQ Press 2010).

Table 12.2. Intrastate Wars (1945–2007)

Location	Dates	Battle Deaths of State Participants	Battle Deaths of All Participants
China	1946–1950	327,600	1,200,000
Paraguay	1947	N/A	N/A
China (Taiwanese)	1947	250	1,250
Yemen Arab Republic	1948	N/A	N/A
Costa Rica	1948	1,500	2,000
Colombia	1948–1958	9,800	29,800
Burma	1948–1951	8,000	N/A
Indonesia	1950	N/A	N/A
Philippines	1950–1954	1,600	11,300
Bolivia	1952	N/A	N/A
Indonesia	1953	1,700	2,700
Argentina	1955	N/A	N/A
China (Tibetans)	1956–1959	4,000	16,000
Indonesia	1956–1962	3,700	27,200
Lebanon	1958	N/A	N/A
Cuba	1958–1959	2,000	3,000
Burma	1958–1960	850	3,150
Iraq	1959	N/A	N/A
Republic of Vietnam	1960–1965	23,806	N/A
Zaire vs. Katanga	1960–1965	N/A	N/A
Laos	1960–1962	N/A	N/A
Iraq	1961–1963	500	2,500
Algeria	1962–1962	800	1,500
Yemen Arab Republic	1962–1969	N/A	N/A
Laos	1963–1973	N/A	N/A
Sudan	1963–1972	N/A	N/A
Ethiopia	1963–1964	N/A	N/A
Rwanda	1963–1964	100	1,000
Congo vs	1963–1965	N/A	N/A
Zanzibar	1964	N/A	N/A
Congo	1964–1965	250	4,250
Iraq	1965–1966	500	3,000
Dominican Republic	1965	2,527	N/A
Indonesia	1965–1969	N/A	N/A
Uganda	1966	N/A	N/A
Guatemala	1966–1968	228	N/A
Chad	1966–1971	550	N/A
China	1967–1968	N/A	N/A
Nigeria	1967–1970	N/A	N/A
Burma	1967–1980	6,800	29,200
Iraq	1969–1970	800	4,000
India	1970–1971	100	2,100

(continued)

Table 12.2. (continued)

Location	Dates	Battle Deaths of State Participants	Battle Deaths of All Participants
Jordan	1970	N/A	N/A
Guatemala	1970–1971	50	1,000
Cambodia	1971–1975	45,000	85,000
Pakistan	1971	2,500	N/A
Sri Lanka	1971	53	4,053
Thailand	1972–1973	1,500	2,300
Rhodesia	1972–1979	1,000	11,000
Philippines	1972–1981	10,000	30,000
Burundi	1972	500	2,000
Philippines	1972–1992	9,000	31,000
Oman	1973–1975	505	N/A
Pakistan	1973–1977	3,300	8,600
Chile	1973	400	3,400
Iraq	1974–1975	7,000	20,000
Ethiopia	1975–1975	6,100	12,500
Argentina	1975–1977	250	2,850
Lebanon	1975–1976	N/A	N/A
Angola	1976–1991	N/A	N/A
Indonesia	1976–1978	1,000	1,200
Laos	1976–1979	2,000	N/A
Indonesia	1976–1979	1,800	N/A
Ethiopia	1976–1977 1978–1983	N/A	N/A
Guatemala	1978–1984	1,250	6,000
Afghanistan	1978	1,800	3,000
Afghanistan	1978–1992	N/A	N/A
Iran	1978–1979	100	1,100
Nicaragua	1978–1979	1,000	4,000
Iran	1979–1984	N/A	N/A
El Salvador	1979–1992	N/A	N/A
Mozambique	1979–1992	N/A	N/A
Chad	1980–1988	N/A	N/A
Nigeria	1980–1981	50	1,050
Uganda	1980–1986	40,000	46,000
Syria	1981–1982	1,000	3,000
Peru	1982–1992	4,000	16,000
Nicaragua	1982–1990	7,000	32,200
Ethiopia	1982–1991	10,000	75,000
Zimbabwe	1983–1987	N/A	N/A
Burma	1983–1988	2,800	4,000
Sri Lanka	1983–2002	9,655	N/A
Sudan	1983–1991	N/A	N/A
Turkey	1984–1986	1,500	10,500

Table 12.2. (continued)

Location	Dates	Battle Deaths of State Participants	Battle Deaths of All Participants
India	1984–2005	N/A	N/A
Iraq	1985–1996	N/A	N/A
Uganda	1986–1987	2,000	7,000
Yemen People's Republic	1986	4,200	13,000
Sri Lanka	1987–1989	N/A	N/A
Burma	1988	N/A	N/A
Somalia	1988–1991	N/A	N/A
Chad	1989–1990	3,000	3,800
Colombia	1989	10,480	28,143
Liberia	1989–1990	N/A	N/A
Afghanistan	1989–2001	N/A	N/A
Rumania	1989	300	1,000
Indonesia	1989–1991	N/A	N/A
Cambodia	1989–1991	N/A	N/A
Papua New Guinea	1989–1982	N/A	N/A
Rwanda	1990–1993	N/A	N/A
Sierra Leone	1991–1996	N/A	N/A
Yugoslavia/Serbia	1991–1992	N/A	N/A
Turkey	1991–1999	3,500	16,500
Somalia	1991–1997	N/A	N/A
Moldova	1991–1992	N/A	N/A
Azerbaijan	1991–1994	N/A	N/A
Bosnia/Herzogovina	1992–1994	N/A	N/A
Algeria	1992–1999	N/A	N/A
Tadzhikistan	1992–1997	N/A	N/A
Liberia	1992–1995	N/A	N/A
Angola	1992–1994	N/A	N/A
Georgia	1993–1994	5,000	8,000
Burundi	1993–1998	N/A	N/A
Cambodia	1993–1997	N/A	N/A
Russia	1994–1996	4,000	10,000
Rwanda	1994	N/A	N/A
Yemen	1994	N/A	N/A
Croatia	1995	N/A	N/A
Liberia	1996	N/A	N/A
Congo	1997	N/A	N/A
Rwanda	1997–1998	300	3,300
Congo	1997	N/A	N/A
Yugoslavia	1998–1999	400	1,200
Guinea-Bissau	1998–1999	N/A	N/A
Chad	1998–2000	N/A	N/A
Angola	1998–2002	N/A	N/A

(continued)

Table 12.2. (continued)

Location	Dates	Battle Deaths of State Participants	Battle Deaths of All Participants
Congo	1998–1999	N/A	N/A
Nigeria Christian	1999–2000	N/A	N/A
Indonesia	1999–2002	330	3,830
Ethiopia	1999	200	1,000
Russia	1999–2003	5,000	20,000
Philippines	2000–2001	N/A	N/A
Guinea	2000–2001	N/A	N/A
Burundi	2001–2003	150	3,150
Rwanda	2000–2001	N/A	N/A
Nepal	2001–2003	680	3,780
Liberia	2002–2003	N/A	N/A
Ethiopia Anyuaa	2002–2003	N/A	N/A
Cote de Ivor	2002–2004	N/A	N/A
Philippines	2003	410	1,000
Sudan	2003–2006	N/A	N/A
Indonesia	2003	150	1,550
Nepal	2003–2006	1,260	7,030
Pakistan	2004–2006	1,200	3,000
Nigeria Christian	2004	N/A	N/A
Yemen	2004–2005	900	2,250
Philippines	2005–2006	723	2,823
Chad	2005–2006	100	1,100
Somalia	2006–2008	N/A	N/A
Sri Lanka	2006–2008	N/A	N/A
Yemen	2007	1,500	3,500

Source: Meredith Reid Sarkees, *COW Intra-State War Data, 1818–2007* (v4.1), http://www.correlatesofwar.org/COW2%20Data/WarData_NEW/IntraStateWarData_v4.1.csv. See also Meredith Reid Sarkees & Frank Wayman, *Resort to War: 1816–2007* (CQ Press 2010).

Why Do States Go to War?

This question has occupied scholars for generations, and there is no easy answer.[2] In the spirit of the rationalist approach of this book, we will assume that states go to war because they believe that war serves their interests. Of course, a war will never, or very rarely, serve the interests of both or all the states that take part in it. Usually, one state wins and one loses; if there is a draw, then both suffer losses for no purpose. So it must be the case that when states begin wars, there is uncertainty about the outcome. Each state gambles; only one can win, although both can lose.

Why might a state take this gamble? In fact, gambling is ubiquitous in international relations and in politics generally; it is unavoidable. States face uncertainty when they make decisions, and in this respect the decision to go to war is no more a gamble than the decision to lower trade barriers or to increase the military budget. In the case of war, the leaders of a state know that war can bring either victory or defeat, or numerous shades in between. The probability of victory is a function of numerous highly uncertain variables—including, among others, relative military strength, economic power, morale of the population, the strength of domestic political institutions, and the reaction of foreign states.

Consider state X and state Y. State X is troubled by an insurgency that receives manpower and material support from people living just across the border in state Y. State X believes that state Y should do more to control the border. State Y refuses, perhaps because it would rather spend money on other things, or perhaps because it benefits from seeing its rival, state X, harassed and annoyed. State X threatens to send troops across the border in order to pursue the insurgents' supporters in Y unless state Y uses force against those supporters. What should Y do?

Y has two basic options. It could refuse to change its behavior, thus risking war with X; or it could give in and use force against the supporters of the insurgency. There are intermediate options as well: Y could possibly satisfy X by patrolling the border more strictly, even if some support continues to flow through.

Y would like to avoid war, but yielding to X's threats may be even worse. First, Y must expend resources against its own perceived interest; second, Y might appear weak, inviting further threats from X or from other neighbors.

We can think of this problem more formally by observing that both X and Y have private information about their military power and other things relevant to the probability of success in war—such as the population's loyalty to the government, the stability of the political structure, and the hardships that people are willing to incur to see their interest vindicated. Let us focus on military power. X has better information about the power of its military than Y does; and Y has better information about the power of its military than X does.

Economists and game theorists have spent quite a bit of effort analyzing this strategic situation—where two parties seek a mutually inconsistent outcome while having asymmetric information about each other's relevant characteristics. To understand this problem, let us begin with the full information case— where both sides do, in fact, know the military power of the other and assuming that military power is the sole determinant of who will win the war.

In such a case, X and Y can predict with perfect accuracy the outcome of the war. Suppose that they both know that X has the stronger military but only slightly stronger, so if a war occurs, X will suffer a lot of casualties, as will Y. At the end of the "game," then, X will have achieved its objective—say, destroying the insurgents occupying a portion of Y's territory—but at some cost. Both sides would do better with a settlement, since destruction would be avoided. Thus, X and Y would settle on an outcome that is better for each than the final outcome would be—that is, X would receive a higher payoff than it receives from destroying the insurgency and occupying Y's territory but suffering casualties, and Y would receive a higher payoff than it receives from suffering casualties and losing some territory. One might imagine, for example, that in fact Y incurs the costs of destroying the insurgents, maybe with some financial support from X. Y may suffer casualties but not as many as it would as a result of war; X does not obtain any territory but also does not incur casualties and benefits from the end of the insurgency. In the full information version of the game, war is avoided; the parties costlessly achieve the outcome they would have reached if war had actually occurred.

In the asymmetric information version of the game, the outcome is not as happy. A simple illustration will show why. Suppose that Y alone has private information about its military power; X's military power is known to Y. X must then contemplate two possibilities: that Y is weak and that Y is strong. Suppose that if Y is weak, then X's invasion will be quick, painless, and successful; but that if Y is strong, X's invasion will fail. X assigns a probability of 0.5 to each outcome.

If Y is strong, it will be important for Y to prove that it is strong. To do this, the strong Y will refuse to back down from threats and, more important, fight back rather than surrender. X might then adopt a strategy of invading but immediately pulling back if Y offers any resistance. The problem is that if Y is weak, and it anticipates this strategy, it will also fight back rather than surrender, even though it knows that if X continues to fight, it—weak Y—will be defeated. Weak Y's strategy is to get X to believe that it is strong Y, and it does so by mimicking strong Y's behavior in its initial stages.

Anticipating this strategy by weak Y, X will need to continue the fight until it is clear whether Y is strong or weak. If Y is strong, then X will need to pull back. If Y is weak, then X will at some point learn this, whereupon weak Y will surrender. On this theory, war occurs in the first place only because of asymmetric information; and war itself is essentially a contest of strength, an attempt to reveal one's military power rather than to actually coerce the other side. Once one's superior power is revealed, the other side will surrender without further coercion, and this power disparity will set the trend for future interactions between the two states.

Implications

If this theory of warfare is correct, can international law end war? Can it mitigate war, so that it is less destructive? Consider two approaches.

Under one approach, an institution is set up that has the purpose of conveying information about military strength between the states. The institution could also disclose other types of information that is relevant to whether a state's military threat is credible or not. The institution could be as informal as a mediator, who is trusted by both sides. A mediator could learn from X and from Y what their military strengths really are and then credibly convey this information between the states. More formal, courtlike institutions could also serve this function. In the nineteenth century, people hoped that arbitration would make war unnecessary, and there were cases where arbitration (as well as mediation) did seem to head off war. Needless to say, institutions are not infallible, as we discussed in Chapter 7.

Under the other approach, international law actually forbids war, or certain types of war, or the way that war is conducted. The laws regarding the conduct of war—humanitarian law, *jus in bello*—address the last category. It is possible that if enough deadly weapons and tactics can be regulated, war will become unattractive or not very effective. We discuss these aspects of the laws of war in Chapter 13. Whatever the benefits of these rules, they do not solve the information problem that causes war.

Another body of law pertaining to war—often called the law governing use of force, or *jus ad bellum*—sets down the rules under which states may go to war in the first place. Why not simply outlaw war? If states obey the law, and law forbids war, then maybe states will not go to war. At one time, many people believed just this; today some still do. We will take a brief look at history and then explain why forbidding war has not worked.

Efforts to Regulate War before the UN Charter: The Nineteenth Century

In the nineteenth century, international law did not forbid war. It was understood and accepted that states could go to war for general reasons of politics and statecraft. Wars of conquest still occurred, though most wars had more complicated purposes. Russia used military force to peel off Ottoman territories; Britain and France went to Turkey's aid when Russia's aggression went (in their view) too far. The Crimean War (1853–1856) resulted. Meanwhile, Prussia provoked wars against various European countries—Austria, Denmark, and France—mainly to consolidate German-speaking countries into a single empire. Various wars were fought against nonstate entities—tribes and the like—for purposes of colonization; these wars often entangled other states.

Rules developed that regulated neutrality.[3] Belligerents may impose blockades on each other (subject to certain humanitarian conditions), which affect the ability of neutrals to trade. Neutrals are required to respect a blockade as long as they are effective rather than merely declared. In the absence of blockade, neutrals may trade with belligerents except that they may not sell war materials to them such as military equipment and ammunition. Belligerents may not move troops onto neutral territory; if they do, neutrals are required to intern the troops. There are other rules along these lines, which essentially forbid neutrals to cooperate directly in the war efforts of any belligerent but permit them to cooperate with belligerents in other ways (trade, investment), and require neutrals to treat belligerents equally.

It is easy to see how these rules could have arisen and become self-sustaining. A belligerent that acts aggressively against neutrals risks driving them to enter the war on the other side. Neutrals that supply war materials to a belligerent risk being attacked by the other belligerent. The compromise is that neutrals may trade with belligerents generally but not in such a way that advances the war aims of one or the other. The blockade rule is more puzzling. It may have reflected a simple fact of power: a state powerful enough to maintain a blockade could prevent a neutral from trading with the blockaded state, and in such cases a neutral that sought to run the blockade took the risk of ending up allied with the weaker party. In sum, the rules probably arose as a natural response by neutrals to stay out of wars and by belligerents to prevent neutrals from entering wars on the other side.

Another set of rules governed self-defense. It might seem odd for there to be self-defense rules if war itself was not illegal. But the self-defense rules resembled the neutrality rules inasmuch as they made clear which actions would count as acts of war and which would not. In 1837, some Canadian rebels transported American volunteers and supplies on the U.S. steamer the *Caroline,* from the U.S. bank of the Niagara River to Navy Island, Ontario; the British retaliated by sending troops into the United States, killing some of the American crew, and sending the *Caroline* over the falls.[4] Sending troops into foreign territory could be seen as an act of war, but clearly Britain did not intend to start a war with the United States, and the United States did not seek a war with Britain. At the same time, the United States could not tolerate routine incursions into its territory by British forces in pursuit of insurgents. The U.S. secretary of state, Daniel Webster, and the British privy counselor, Alexander Baring, agreed that certain acts of self-defense would not be considered acts of war—essentially when those acts responded to an immediate or imminent threat. Under the Webster-Ashburton agreement, if insurgents launch an attack across the border, the British could fight back and even bring the fight onto U.S. territory if that was necessary to defeat the foe. But the British could not send forces across the border in order to search out and attack rebel bases without starting a war with the United States.

These and similar rules did not try to prevent war in a robust sense. The most that can be said for them is that they sought to minimize the risk of an inadvertent war, caused by differing perceptions about what types of acts counted as a deliberate initiation of hostilities. In the Hague Peace Conference of 1899 and 1907, a small further step was taken when states agreed that they would try to use arbitration to head off wars. But the rule was only hortatory.

After World War I

This relaxed attitude toward war ended with World War I, which made clear that technology had advanced to the point that mass slaughter of soldiers and civilians alike would replace the less violent wars of the nineteenth century, which killed fewer people and mainly professional soldiers. The Versailles Treaty set up a new League of Nations, the predecessor to today's United Nations, and the Permanent Court of International Justice, the predecessor to today's International Court of Justice. These institutions were supposed to provide places for states to resolve their differences. The League of Nations had the power to impose sanctions on states that threatened the peace. But there was no specific rule against war.

That came in 1928, with the Kellogg-Briand Pact.[5] This was the first international declaration that explicitly stated that states could not use war to resolve their disputes. The treaty came about as a result of diplomatic maneuvers between the United States and France. France sought a mutual defense pact with the United States as protection from German invasion. The United States did not want to be drawn into war and so (cynically?) upped the ante, proposing a ban on all wars between all countries. Whatever the diplomats were thinking, the idea caught on with the general public, and the Kellogg-Briand Pact emerged as a result. The governments hedged their obligations in various diplomatic notes, but all that was lost on the public.

The League of Nations and the Kellogg-Briand Pact failed to stop warfare. A series of smaller wars—including the Italian invasion of Ethiopia and the Japanese invasion of Manchuria—led up to and fed into World War II itself, the most devastating war the world had ever seen. As that war came to an end, diplomats rolled up their sleeves, hoping once again to use international law to prevent war.

The UN Charter

Their efforts produced the UN Charter, which created the United Nations. The UN, like the League of Nations, is an institution devoted to collective security. Unlike the League of Nations charter, the UN charter contains some specific rules governing the use of force.

The UN Charter, article 2(4), provides that

> All Members shall refrain in their international relations from the threat or use of force against the territorial integrity or political independence of any state, or in any other manner inconsistent with the Purposes of the United Nations.

This prohibition on the use of force has two major exceptions. Article 42 provides the following:

> Should the Security Council consider that measures provided for in Article 41 would be inadequate or have proved to be inadequate, it may take such action by air, sea, or land forces as may be necessary to maintain or restore international peace and security. Such action may include demonstrations, blockade, and other operations by air, sea, or land forces of Members of the United Nations.

Article 41 confers on the Security Council the power to order members to impose diplomatic and economic sanctions on states that threaten the peace, breach the peace, or engage in an act of aggression under Article 39. The Security Council is like a police unit that can use force, or authorize the use of force, against states that have acted aggressively or are about to act aggressively.

The other exception is in Article 51:

> Nothing in the present Charter shall impair the inherent right of individual or collective self-defense if an armed attack occurs against a Member of the United Nations, until the Security Council has taken measures necessary to

maintain international peace and security. Measures taken by Members in the exercise of this right of self-defense shall be immediately reported to the Security Council and shall not in any way affect the authority and responsibility of the Security Council under the present Charter to take at any time such action as it deems necessary in order to maintain or restore international peace and security.

States can use force to defend themselves. In sum, then, the UN Charter forbids states to use force, but if they do, victims can use force to repel invaders, and the Security Council can authorize and even order other states to come to the aid of the victims and restore the status quo.

Despite these seemingly straightforward rules, states in practice have had little trouble justifying their use of force—not always convincingly but often enough to overcome whatever political obstacles to war might have otherwise existed. Only three wars since 1945—the U.S.-led response to North Korea's invasion of South Korea in 1950, the U.S.-led response to Iraq's invasion of Kuwait in 1991, and NATO's intervention in Libya in 2011—have received the blessing of the Security Council, yet dozens of wars have occurred since the UN Charter entered into force. Did the Vietnam War violate the Charter? The United States argued that the South Vietnamese government invited U.S. troops to help defend against the North Vietnamese, an exercise of collective self-defense permitted by Article 51. The Soviet Union could say the same thing about its invasion of Afghanistan in 1979 at the invitation of the Soviet-installed and -supported Afghan government. The U.S.-led invasion of Iraq in 2003 also did not receive Security Council authorization, but the United States and the United Kingdom argued that earlier Security Council resolutions had only suspended the hostilities that began in 1991 for as long as Iraq cooperated with weapons inspections. Since cooperation had ceased by 2003, the second invasion was (implicitly) authorized.

Not all of these arguments are equally good, but it is important to see that the UN Charter's rules are not as airtight as they might have seemed when they were drafted. Still, they have some bite. When NATO countries launched an airstrike on Serbia in 1997—to forestall a possible genocide in Kosovo and to punish Serbia for its belligerence—a Charter-based rationale was not plausible. Serbia did not invite NATO to bomb its own cities, and its aggressive behavior took place on its own soil; it did not invade a foreign country. Some NATO countries—Britain in particular—justified the invasion as a "humanitarian intervention," a newfangled concept not in the Charter but allegedly a development of customary international law.

The Presumptive Ban

There is a consensus among respectable opinion that war is in all cases to be avoided if possible and used only as a last resort. It is not our purpose to disturb this consensus, but it is worth pointing out why it is of only recent vintage.

The basic problem with a ban on war is that it freezes the status quo as reflected in the state system. Violence is not the only way to change the status quo—economic sanctions can be used as well, but they too can cause great hardship and are generally effective only if they do—but it is a highly effective way of doing so. If the status quo is unjust or otherwise unacceptable, then war can be justified as a way to change it.

Indeed, that is typically how war has been justified. The old rationales ring less true than they did in the past, but new rationales have taken their place. In the past, states went to war to forge nations from ethnically or linguistically similar groups scattered across borders, to enhance their power and security, to spread the true religion, to force open markets for trade, and to obtain access to raw materials. Wars of independence—civil wars started often by indigenous groups against foreign conquerors—were for a time thought to be just and necessary, despite the violence and destruction. In all of these cases, the war makers clamored against a status quo that they believed or claimed was unjust and hurt their constituencies in various ways. These claims were not always pretexts for power-and-wealth grabs; they were often widely perceived as legitimate.

The status quo presents two types of problems: it can be dangerous, and it can be unjust. If the principle of sovereignty is accepted in all of its rigor, then states can do little against a dangerous, rising power that has shown itself willing to use violence. Today governments sometimes refer to these states as "rogue states," and the specific worry is that they will obtain nuclear weapons, which they will use or sell to terrorist groups. But the concern is not new. In the nineteenth century, Britain's strategy—to some extent shared by other states as well—was to form alliances against rising powers that threatened to become dominant on continental Europe and thus to pose a long-term threat to British power. One of the many lessons of World War II was that the failure to contain a rogue state before it became strong—in this case, Nazi Germany—could be fatal. The UN Charter itself recognizes the importance of this principle, while trying to prevent its abuse by requiring Security Council approval for a preventive war. So, even today, there is agreement that states can justifiably go to war in order to protect themselves from another state that is dangerously aggressive but that has not yet launched an invasion. The major disagreement concerns the conditions under which this type of war is justified.

The status quo also is one in which authoritarian governments can abuse their people. Again, if the principle of sovereignty is accepted in extreme form, then states cannot intervene in another state where the government is committing genocide or other atrocities within its borders. This view was never fully accepted, and in earlier centuries states often did justify their use of military force on humanitarian principles. But today, it is much stronger. There is more agreement today that sovereignty should not be a shield against mass atrocity. World War II once again is the template for understanding this idea. The Holocaust was simply unacceptable, and in retrospect the atrocities committed by the Germans, and to a lesser extent the Japanese, explain why World War II was a "good war" for the allies, at least in popular perception. From a realpolitik view, one might believe that governments that commit atrocities against their own populations are likely to pose dangers to others. For many people, then, war can be justified if its purpose is humanitarian intervention, and lesser forms of pressure have failed.

Self-Defense and Preemptive War

In this section, we limit our treatment of the use of force to cases involving self-defense or defense of others (humanitarian intervention). In particular, we assume that some external actor poses a threat of pure aggression (that is, aggression not motivated by defense of self or others) against a particular state, or against third states that the state we consider may wish to defend. If the aggression occurs, we further assume that it is socially undesirable and will impose net social costs. The threat of aggression is exogenous in that we do not explain why it arises, although we do entertain the question of whether the aggressor can be deterred through various means. It bears emphasis, however, that we rule out by assumption any possibility that the aggressor is engaged in productive activity through aggression or the threat of aggression. The aggressor in our framework is thus much akin to a criminal in the economics of crime literature, in which it is commonly assumed that the criminal's gains from a criminal act are smaller than the social costs of the act, making the act undesirable and posing the problem of how to design an optimal system of deterrence.

We thus analyze only a subset of the situations in which force may be used or contemplated. Historically, many wars or threatened wars have occurred between civilized states that dispute territorial rights, between colonial powers and their colonies seeking independence, and in various other contexts in which it is difficult to analogize any state to a criminal actor engaged in strictly unproductive activity. We do not purport to offer a framework for thinking about all such conflicts and limit ourselves here to the task of addressing what might be termed "rogue" states. We stipulate that what constitutes a "rogue" state is to some degree in the eye of the beholder, but our analysis presupposes that such states can be identified in a principled manner.

Why Use Force against Rogue States?

The analogy between criminals and rogue states affords a useful point of departure for assessing the rules about the use of force.[6] In the economic literature on crime,[7] the use of force plays at most a background role in the design of an optimal deterrence system. The literature emphasizes the virtue of monetary sanctions where they will suffice because of their cheapness and suggests that more costly sanctions such as incarceration should be employed only when monetary sanctions are inadequate for deterrence (because, inter alia, of the insolvency of defendants). The literature on crime is not concerned exclusively with deterrence, of course, but also emphasizes the possible value of incapacitation. Here, too, incarceration is the device generally considered for this purpose. The use of force against criminals (beyond incarceration) is not discussed in most of the literature (aside from that on capital punishment), although it assuredly has an implicit role in providing the state with the ability to coerce criminals to accept sanctions such as fines or imprisonment.[8]

Against this backdrop, consider the problem of how to deter (or incapacitate) a rogue state. The notion in the economic literature on crime that monetary penalties are the preferred line of defense against socially unproductive acts is obviously flawed in this context. Just as with criminals, the rogue state may well lack the assets or will to pay for the harms caused by aggression. And unlike the situation with criminals, the individual actors that lead their state to engage in aggression may bear few if any of the costs of any monetary penalties that might be imposed. Finally, and most fundamental, why would the rogue state pay any such penalties unless a credible threat of force were brought to bear against it? We do see states required to pay reparations at times, but usually only after they have lost a war. Occasional exceptions arise when a rogue state has assets abroad that can be seized, but these cases will be uncommon and even then may have little deterrent value on the leaders of rogue states who do not own the assets personally.

If conventional monetary penalties are not a realistic penalty for most rogue states, however, other forms of international economic sanctions can be employed. Sanctions have been used extensively in the international system, not only against aggressors (such as Iraq after the invasion of Kuwait) but also on humanitarian grounds (South Africa). Their record, however, is mixed at best. Sanctions may cause economic losses for the imposing state, the costs of sanctions are often borne by the citizenry at large rather than by the leaders whose behavior is the source of the problem, and leaders often will not give up power voluntarily or make an important change in their behavior merely to avoid the economic harm that sanctions bring on their economies.[9]

The next line of defense against domestic crime—incarceration and associated incapacitation—is also of limited utility against rogue states. To be sure, the leaders of such states can be and sometimes are incarcerated. But again this outcome usually follows a war or a fortuitous regime change that makes it possible for the leaders of rogue states to be placed under international criminal jurisdiction. Without the use of force or at least a credible threat of it, the leaders of rogue states will usually fear little from the prospect of war crimes trials and related punishment mechanisms.

For these reasons, the use of force, or at least a credible threat of force, will often be essential to deter potential rogue states from unproductive acts or to incapacitate the states that cannot be deterred. The alternative deterrence mechanisms that we take for granted in a domestic criminal justice system simply will not work for the most part in international relations.

To say that force or threat thereof is generally essential, however, says nothing about the timing of force. The current controversy over the rules of *jus ad bellum* centers on the existing constraints on the use of force—the requirement of Security Council authorization or of grounds to invoke the right of self-defense against an actual or imminent attack. Much of our focus in the remaining sections will be on the question of whether force can be justified under other circumstances as well.

The Timing of Force: Preemptive Attack

For the moment, we put aside the role of the Security Council as well as the use of force for humanitarian purposes and focus on the imminence requirement for the use of force in self-defense. The imminence requirement comes from the Webster-Ashburton Treaty,[10] whose definition of self-defense is thought to be retained in UN Charter article 51. Is the right to use force only against actual or imminent attack sufficient for purposes of self-defense against potential rogue states?

One answer is that the target of aggression may be a weak state with insufficient capacity to deter or incapacitate. This problem may be quite real, to be sure, but it does not argue for relaxing the imminence requirement in general.

The state that is weak when attack is imminent will generally be weak at earlier points in time as well. The solution here, if there is one, may be for the weaker state to seek a defense alliance with more powerful states.

If we restrict our attention to potential targets of aggression that have the power to retaliate with enough force to deter or incapacitate aggressors, there are several obvious virtues to a requirement that they wait until an attack is under way or at least imminent before using force in response. Such a rule (if obeyed) ensures that force is used only as a last resort and that all diplomatic means (presumably much less costly) to avoid conflict have been exhausted before force is employed. Likewise, if force is used before an attack is imminent, a significant chance of mistake may arise—perhaps the potential rogue state never would have attacked at all. One must also worry that a right to use force prior to an imminent attack would be invoked opportunistically and become a pretense for aggression instead of a bona fide act of self-defense.

More fundamentally, if the potential victim state has substantial capacity to retaliate against the aggressor, why is it not sufficient for such a state to threaten retaliation against an actual attack at a level that will eliminate any gains to the rogue state and discourage attack altogether? Such a strategy, if feasible and successful, eliminates the need for the use of force altogether. This was the strategy of the United States during the cold war, when "mutually assured destruction" made it difficult to imagine that a rational Soviet leader would launch a nuclear attack.

These considerations have considerable persuasive force and may afford a basis for the imminence requirement across broad classes of self-defense scenarios. We suggest that they are not conclusive in all cases, however, for two reasons.

First, threats of substantial retaliation following an attack may not be credible—the leaders of rogue states may believe (often mistakenly) that the victim state lacks the ability to retaliate. Alternatively, retaliation may kill or injure innocent individuals in the rogue state or neighboring states, and both geopolitical and moral limitations on the acceptable degree of such damage may be present, which may seriously undermine the credibility of the retaliatory threat. Similarly, the behavior that requires deterrence may not be an "attack" per se but a dangerous and threatening policy, such as the development of nuclear weapons by a rogue state. The threat to retaliate against a state that develops such weapons may lack credibility not only because the weapons have not yet been used and political constraints preclude retaliation, but because the costs of conflict with a nuclear state have risen to unacceptable levels. Finally, an attack by a rogue state may not be easily traceable to that state. A rogue state that operates surreptitiously by supplying dangerous weaponry to terrorist agents may have plausible capacity to deny responsibility for an attack and may believe that retaliation is then unlikely given the great collateral damage that it would entail.

Second, even where the threat to retaliate is credible, it may not be effective to deter the leaders of rogue states. Those leaders may care little about their own citizens and may expect to escape the consequences of retaliation themselves. In extreme cases, they may not even care about their own safety. Consider the religious zealots who believe that death during war against enemies will bring them to a blissful existence. Where deterrence is unrealistic for such reasons, the emphasis shifts to incapacitation—to preventing attacks before they occur. Such a policy inevitably requires the use of force before an attack is under way or imminent.

These observations afford some reason to worry that an imminence requirement may not suit all cases terribly well. In the next section, we provide some simple analytic structure to crystallize this concern.

Preemptive Attack in a Two-Period Scenario

Consider a two-period scenario involving two countries, Home and Foreign. In period one, Home is uncertain whether Foreign intends to "attack" in period two. One can think of an "attack" in literal terms or simply as an aggressive strategy by Foreign, such as the development of nuclear weapons.

We further assume that attack by Foreign cannot be deterred by a threat of retaliation after an attack occurs for one of the reasons given above. Consider a scenario where Foreign has private information about its type. The "bad" type of Foreign state is one governed by crusaders, religious zealots, or ideologues that will launch an attack against Home, regardless of whether Home will retaliate. The "good" type of Foreign state will not attack in period 2. Only Foreign knows whether it belongs to the bad or good type, and it cannot credibly reveal its type (bad types are able to "pool" with good types).

Home can attack Foreign preemptively in period one and eliminate the possibility of attack in period two. If Home attacks, each country bears the cost of attack, which will likely differ. Alternatively, Home can wait until period two, when the existence or nonexistence of the threat from Foreign will be revealed. If Foreign does not attack, no losses occur and military action is unnecessary then or in the future—the costs of conflict are zero. If Foreign attacks, however,

Home will incur a variety of possible costs. It may feel obliged to retaliate and may wish to incapacitate Foreign to prevent future attacks. It may also feel obliged to incur sizable defense expenditures to guard against the new threat from Foreign, or it may be forced to transfer resources to Foreign to appease it.

Think of the costs incurred by Foreign from a period 1 attack and a period 2 attack as the welfare costs to Foreign that "count" in a proper social welfare calculus. If we think of states as persons, it might be difficult to understand why these variables should be counted at all in social welfare. In the economic analysis of criminal law, for example, we often do not count the utility of the criminal, only that of the victim, and design the law to deter the criminal rather than to maximize the joint utility of criminal and victim.[11] But in international conflict, much destruction can occur to the life and property of civilians and of soldiers. Without taking any position on which of these costs should "count" and which should not, we assume that some of them may count and include them in our analysis. In the discussion below, the included costs to Foreign are termed the *collateral damage*.

In limiting the game to two periods, we are obviously simplifying the analysis in relation to the open-ended time horizon that nations confront in reality. Indeed, if the world really "ended" in period two, there might well be no reason for Home to incur the costs of responding to an attack by Foreign as there would be no future periods in which to derive any benefit. Our assumption that Home will incur the costs of a response in period two thus is best understood as an abstraction from an environment in which the game does not really end and in which Home's best response after Foreign reveals itself to be aggressive is costly.

Home's Private Calculus

We make the stylized assumption that Home gives no weight to the collateral damage to Foreign (even though in practice such costs may receive some significant weight). Then Home will attack preemptively if the costs to Home of an attack in period one are less than the discounted expected costs of conflict to Home in period two. Trivially, preemptive attack is more likely to be optimal when the costs of preemptive attack are smaller, the probability of the threat materializing in period two is greater, the costs of conflict in period two are greater, and the discount factor is greater.

A further implication is that there can be no gains from preemptive attack unless the costs of conflict are greater if Home waits. Were it otherwise, Home would benefit by deferring the conflict due to the time value of money and to the fact that the probability of actual attack is less than one.

Social Calculus

Preemptive action is socially justified (that is, it lowers the expected social costs of conflict) if the costs of such an attack in period one (including the collateral damage to Foreign) are less than the discounted expected costs of conflict in period two (again including collateral damage to Foreign).

This can be put a different way. Preemptive attack is socially justified if the probability of an attack by Foreign in period two exceeds the ratio of the costs of preemptive conflict in period one to the discounted costs of conflict in period two. As with the private calculus, preemptive attack cannot possibly be justified unless the costs of conflict are growing over time. The rate of growth in these costs required to justify preemptive attack is greater, the smaller is the discount factor and the smaller is the probability of attack. Likewise, preemptive attack is more likely to be justified as the probability of attack rises, a point that loosely provides some basis for the imminence standard (where that probability presumably approaches one). But a probability of attack close to unity is by no means necessary for preemptive attack to be justified in this framework.

Another way to understand these conclusions is to note that delay in the use of force has value as a real option.[12] The option value of delay relates to the time value of money but also to the fact that information becomes better over time. In our simple analysis, Home learns with certainty whether Foreign has aggressive intentions in period two, but our framework is much more general and can accommodate any assumption about the way that information improves over time. In general, preemptive attack will be justified only if the growth in the costs of conflict over time is fast enough that the option value of delay turns negative. Both the private calculus and the social calculus above may be interpreted in this fashion.

Plainly, there is a divergence between the private and social calculations for the optimality of preemptive measures. If Home follows its private calculus, and the losses from a period two attack launched by Foreign are large enough, then Home may launch a preemptive attack that is socially suboptimal. But Home's reliance on its private calculus may also lead it to eschew preemptive attack when it is socially optimal.[13]

As an illustration, suppose that the United States is considering a preemptive attack on Iraq. If the period one cost of attack is very small (the "cakewalk" theory), and the discounted period two benefit is large (the WMD theory), then the United States may launch the attack even if few Iraqi civilians and soldiers would be saved by an early attack, and the attack may fail the social cost-benefit test for that reason. Alternatively, consider again a decision about an invasion of Iraq, but assume now that the period one cost of attack is relatively high (say, $100 billion) and the discounted benefit is low (the probability of WMD is small), so the United States does not launch an attack. But if the first-period harm to Iraq is relatively low (because of precision bombing, few Iraqis are harmed) and the second-period harm is extremely high (if there are WMD, and they are used, the United States would retaliate with a massive nuclear strike), then it may be socially optimal for the United States to attack preemptively. Thus, the divergence between private incentives and social welfare could lead to too many or too few preemptive attacks.[14]

In sum, if one accepts the notion that rogue states are analogous to international criminals, the use of force against them may be unavoidable, and preemptive force may be optimal from a global welfare standpoint. To be sure, there is a divergence between the global calculus and the private calculus when it comes to the decision to use preemptive force. But that divergence is not always in the same direction. A potential victim of aggression, unconstrained by any effective rule of international law, might launch a preemptive attack when it is not globally optimal or fail to launch a preemptive attack when it is.

Preemptive Self-Defense in International Law

The analysis above implies that a state should engage in preemptive war against another state when the costs of waiting for both states is high enough. Under this rule, a state could launch a preemptive war against another state if that other state poses a sufficiently grave threat to the first state's welfare, the joint cost of the war is relatively low, and the welfare loss from the threatened attack would be high for the foreign state as well as for the home state.[15] To a surprising degree, this rule was reflected in the public discussion surrounding the invasion of Iraq by the United States in 2003.

The Bush administration argued that Iraq would eventually either attack its neighbors or support terrorist operations against Americans, in either case necessitating a U.S. military response. The administration further claimed that (1) waiting until this time would cause greater casualties than an immediate attack because in the meantime Saddam Hussein would have improved his WMD capability; (2) waiting would also cause greater civilian casualties in Iraq because a larger response would be necessary; (3) Iraqi civilians would in the interim be killed by Saddam's security forces and the international sanctions; and (4) the probability of eventual Iraqi attack was high.[16] Many critics of the invasion implicitly accepted this normative framework and merely disagreed about the empirics: they thought, correctly as it turned out, that Saddam's WMD capability was low or nil; that sanctions and inspections could prevent Saddam from improving it; that the short-term costs of war would be higher than claimed; and that the probability that Saddam would cause trouble in the future was low.[17]

There were other differences, of course. Many supporters of the invasion emphasized the benefits to Iraqis.[18] Wilsonians and neoconservatives saw long-term gains from spreading democracy in the Middle East.[19] But these differences were more about emphasis than about the appropriate legal rule.

A more important challenge to the implicit rule advanced by the Bush administration came from those who sought UN authorization for the war. These critics argued that the Bush administration should invade Iraq only if it could persuade the Security Council to authorize the invasion.[20]

The critics might have been right that the Bush administration should have obtained UN authorization, or at least the support of other major states, as the U.S. government did for its intervention in Serbia, but the argument begs the (normative) question of what rule should guide the Security Council's decision. Currently, there is no explicit rule governing the circumstances under which the United Nations may authorize the use of force. The standard view is that the United Nations is not constrained at all, although there is some dissent.[21] Whatever the correct view, our argument is that the United Nations should authorize the preemptive use of force only when the costs to the involved states are likely to be less if war occurs sooner rather than later, discounted by the probability of later war and the time value of resources.

The strongest argument for requiring UN authorization of preemptive force is that a rule allowing the unilateral use of preemptive force may be more easily manipulated than the traditional imminence rule. The defenders of the old rule argue that states will use preemptive self-defense as a pretext for launching an invasion for other purposes—territorial expansion, regional dominance, control of natural resources, and the like. Imminent threats, by contrast, are so clear that pretextual invasions will be seen for what they are.

This argument is a kind of rules/standards claim. A rule allowing preemptive self-defense when appropriate is a "standard" in the sense that it allows the decision maker to consider all normatively relevant factors. The imminent self-defense rule is a "rule" in the sense that it bars actions that can at times be justified in order to reduce decision costs or, in this context, the cost incurred by other states in discerning the motives of the decision maker and the costs associated with wars that abuse the standard. The imminent self-defense rule is preferable if the cost of pretextual wars (enabled by the preemptive self-defense rule and barred by the imminent self-defense rule) exceeds the cost of forgone, socially valuable preemptive self-defense (enabled by the preemptive self-defense rule and barred by the imminent self-defense rule). Should the international community be more concerned about aggressors masking their motives behind the pretext of preemptive self-defense,[22] or should their concern focus on rogue states growing in power (as by obtaining WMD) and causing wars in the future?

It is impossible to answer this question with confidence, and we will confine ourselves to the claim that preemptive self-defense has become more attractive over the past fifty years. This is so for three reasons. First, the proliferation of WMD has increased the cost of wars; preemption can now avoid greater losses than it could in the past.[23] Second, decision-making processes in most states are more transparent today than they were during the cold war, when even the Western powers refused to engage in public debate about proposed military interventions. Thus, the pretext problem is somewhat less severe than in the past. Third, although at one time the imminent self-defense rule may have been justified by the Security Council's residual power to authorize preemptive wars, the Security Council system has in the eyes of many proven a failure. It has not authorized a single preemptive war, and if the Security Council cannot be depended on to authorize justified preemptive wars, individual states perhaps ought to have that power.

It is possible that a world hegemon or dominant regional powers could assume some of the functions intended for the United Nations. Some commentators have argued that there is, or could be, a dual system of international law, one in which the United States follows one set of rules and the rest of the world another.[24] The argument is that only the United States can currently serve as an enforcer of international law, because only the United States has the military capacity to do so. Because the United States incurs the costs (or most of them) and takes the risks, it should not be subject to the same rules that apply to other states. This argument lies behind U.S. policy regarding the International Criminal Court and its demand that American soldiers and officials enjoy immunity from the jurisdiction of that court.[25]

Such a system may be superior to the conventional UN system but not necessarily. On the one hand, if the hypothetical system better reflects strategic realities, then compliance is more likely. In addition, as we have seen, the hegemon in some cases has good incentives to enforce international law. On the other hand, there is no reason to believe that the hegemon's incentives are systematically aligned with the social interest: the hegemon will, absent effective Coasean side payments, enforce international law selectively in a way that reflects its interests. And even if side payments occurred, the hegemon will be able to enrich itself at other countries' expense, which may itself be objectionable.

Proportionality

Under the Webster-Ashburton rule of self-defense, the response to any attack must be "proportional." The modern version of this idea is that a state cannot use a minor border incursion or act of violence perpetrated by another state as an excuse for a full-scale war. What is the purpose of the proportionality requirement? It can be understood loosely as an injunction to limit the collateral damage. In our simple two-country framework above, the larger the threat to Home, the larger the collateral damage that can be justified in response. But it remains the case that it should be as small as reasonably possible (implying some tradeoff between the costs to Home and the costs to Foreign in each period that needs to be optimized, a consideration beyond the scope of our earlier discussion). With this interpretation, the proportionality requirement is crudely consistent with the social welfare calculus. Our framework adds only a suggestion that the proportionality requirement might usefully be interpreted to require proportionality not simply to the damage already incurred or imminently threatened but also to the damage that may be avoided by preemptive measures.

Collective Self-Defense

Often the use of force is justified as an act of "collective self-defense": typically, state A attacks state B because B has attacked C. A recent example is the first Gulf War, in which the U.S.-led coalition came to the defense of Kuwait. The U.S.-assisted insurgency against Nicaragua in the 1980s was justified as a defense of El Salvador and other neighboring countries, whose own insurgencies were receiving assistance from the Nicaraguan government.

Collective self-defense is a straightforward extension of individual self-defense. It allows states to pool their resources, increasing the ability of a weak victim to resist a strong attacker. However, it raises the pretext problem in a new form. The problem is that the intervener may use an invasion of a neutral as a pretext for its own aggression. Nicaragua made this argument in an ICJ case it brought against the United States for mining Nicaraguan harbors. The ICJ held against the United States, arguing that El Salvador had failed to notify the United Nations that it sought assistance from the United States. This fact, according to the ICJ, suggested that the United States was using Nicaragua's assistance to the rebels in El Salvador as a pretext for bringing down Nicaragua's communist government.[26]

The ICJ's decision is puzzling. Either the United States was defending El Salvador, or it was invading Nicaragua. This is a purely factual question, although a hard one. The ICJ should have answered the question and ruled for the United States in the first case or for Nicaragua in the second. Requiring notification to the United Nations might have seemed like an attractive way of dealing with the pretext problem, but there is little reason to think that such a rule is sensible. If the United States was looking for a pretext, and El Salvador was compliant, then it would be easy enough for the United States to ask El Salvador to file the notice ahead of the invasion. And where collective self-defense is genuine, the ICJ rule, if obeyed, would prevent nations from obtaining assistance in their self-defense against foreign enemies because of the failure to comply with a formality.[27] This rule is plainly not sustainable, and indeed the United States withdrew in protest from the ICJ's compulsory jurisdiction after the Nicaragua decision was rendered.

Humanitarian Intervention

The use of preemptive force is rarely required or considered in cases of humanitarian intervention—intervention occurs (if at all) only after evidence of an existing humanitarian crisis emerges. One can thus analyze humanitarian intervention as a simple, one-period choice problem. Humanitarian intervention is socially justified if the costs to the intervener of the use of military force plus the collateral damage to the nation where intervention occurs are less than the costs to that nation if no intervention occurs.

Let us refer to the intervener as Home and the target of intervention as Foreign. Home will presumably act in accordance with its private calculus rather than the social calculus. Thus, if Foreign's welfare does not enter Home's welfare function, Home will simply decline to act. Why, then, does humanitarian intervention ever occur? One possibility is that Foreign poses a threat to Home as well as to its own people. The humanitarian benefits of intervention then arise as a by-product of (or perhaps as a political justification for) an action to address a threat to Home.

The other possibility is altruism—Home may experience disutility because the welfare of Foreign does enter its welfare function, and Home may thus be forced to choose between the lesser evils of intervention and nonintervention.

If altruistic humanitarian intervention is possible, how do we explain international resistance to the position that it should be legally permitted? The answer is that humanitarian goals often serve as a pretext for a military intervention undertaken for other reasons (for example, territorial expansion). States rarely act altruistically. States spend little money on foreign aid, so why should we believe them when they claim to invade for the benefit of the citizens of an enemy?

Yet the pretext problem is not special to humanitarian intervention, as noted earlier. Self-defense is also a frequent pretext for aggressive war. Thus, we face a puzzle: if a self-defense exception to the prohibition on war is permitted despite the problem of pretext, why should a humanitarian exception be denied because of concerns about pretext?

A possible answer is that the humanitarian justification for intervention is almost always pretext, whereas the self-defense justification is more often bona fide. Indeed, it is difficult to find a single historical example of a war that was clearly motivated by pure humanitarian concerns. The 1999 intervention in Kosovo is frequently cited, but motives were mixed at best. There was considerable fear in Europe that refugee flows would harm border countries, possibly spreading instability. Similarly, the invasion of Libya in 2011, by NATO and the United States, on the pretext of avoiding a potential humanitarian crisis, has raised speculation that the true motive for intervention was not purely humanitarian but also regime change.[28]

Yet one can certainly find examples of intervention supported by mixed motives, where the humanitarian considerations were arguably present to a degree.[29] And just as other states can decide for themselves whether a self-defense justification is pretextual or real, so too can they decide whether a humanitarian justification is pretextual or real.

As noted earlier, the UN charter does not permit states to use force unilaterally in order to effect a humanitarian intervention. Whether the use of force rules should be altered to permit humanitarian intervention without Security Council authorization depends largely on whether the concern about pretext is serious enough. More precisely, the case for banning humanitarian intervention rests on two assumptions: (1) that genuine humanitarian motives for invasion are rare; and (2) that a state can avoid whatever costs attend a violation of the law of force by advancing humanitarian concerns as a pretext for illegal behavior. The first assumption is probably correct but should not be exaggerated. And even if the first assumption is correct, humanitarian intervention should not be banned unless the second assumption is correct as well. The problem with the second assumption is that there are already plenty of pretexts (for example, self-defense and security) for aggressive attacks; it is not clear that providing aggressive states with a new pretext (humanitarian intervention) would materially increase their propensity to engage in illegal invasions. Accordingly, we question the wisdom of banning humanitarian interventions.

13

The Conduct of War

Laws of war have existed since ancient times. The Greeks recognized a rule prohibiting armies from pursuing defeated enemy armies. Soldiers in the Middle Ages granted quarter to enemy soldiers who threw down their weapons. In the eighteenth century, armies recognized an elaborate code of conduct that determined the rights of soldiers captured after the successful siege of a fortress. Laws of war were, until recently, not formally codified in treaties or conventions but evolved as custom. But by the end of the nineteenth century, the major states agreed that the laws of war that were then recognized ought to be more clearly specified in treaty instruments and that further progress could be made if delegates met and debated the principles of warfare. Conventions were called in The Hague and then in Geneva; these conventions yielded, at intervals, instruments that together record the modern laws of war.[1]

The laws regarding the conduct of war, as they are currently understood, can be divided into general principles and specific rules. The principles hold that soldiers may target only enemy soldiers and other military objectives and not civilians or civilian property; that incidental damage to civilians and their property should not be disproportionate to the value of the military target; and that weapons and tactics used even against military targets should not cause unnecessary suffering.

These principles are reflected in various specific rules. An early rule against the use of dumdum bullets was based on the premise that their military justification—stopping a soldier—could be accomplished with an ordinary bullet, and the dumdum bullet, which expands upon impact, caused unnecessary bodily damage. A similar idea underlies rules against the use of poison gas, blinding laser weapons, and explosives that produce microscopic projectiles that cannot be detected by doctors. Recent efforts to outlaw land mines rest on the argument that these weapons' harm to civilians outweighs their military value. Land mines remain in the ground long after hostilities end and pose hazards for civilians. Rules against the destruction of military hospitals and execution and mistreatment of POWs reflect the principle that suffering should be limited to what is necessary for achieving legitimate military objectives.

The traditional statement in favor of laws of war is that they serve humanitarian principles.[2] Wars are brutal; it would be better to minimize the suffering by requiring soldiers to follow a minimal set of rules. It is better for soldiers to take prisoners than to execute enemies who surrender; it is better to treat POWs well than to starve and torture them; it is better to spare civilians than to kill them.

As attractive as these ideas are, they are vulnerable to diverse criticisms. One problem is that war itself is brutal; and if laws of war are enforceable, why limit them to the scope of the principles described above? Why not outlaw war altogether or limit it to a duel between chosen representatives of each side, as was tried (unsuccessfully) by the Greeks and the Trojans in the *Iliad*? And if this is unrealistic, then why think that the existing laws of war can exert any force in the first place? The implicit assumption of the laws of war is that the evils of war can be lessened but cannot be eliminated. However, the idea of humanitarianism is too vague to provide an explanation for the lines that are drawn.

A second problem with the humanitarian theory is that the laws of war apply equally to both (or all) sides of the dispute and thus indifferently to the aggressor and its victim. In theory, the French should have complied with the laws of war to the same extent as the Nazi invaders, but if aggression was initiated by the Nazis, why shouldn't the prospect of foreign occupation and Nazi tyranny justify the use of all means necessary to resist the invasion, including the mass killing of German civilians? Indeed, by the end of the war, the British and the Americans had concluded that mass killing of enemy civilians was justified for ending the Nazi menace, even if it was formally a violation of the laws of war.[3] This problem was recognized as early as Grotius, who appeared to believe that the belligerent with the just cause was not constrained by the principle of proportionality.[4]

Third, a more humane war may be one that is more likely to occur and more likely to persist once it begins. One argument in favor of area bombing during World War II was that it would demoralize German citizens and end the war earlier. Thus, the short-term costs would be high, but in the long term fewer soldiers and citizens would die than if targeted bombing were used. This was also the justification for dropping atomic bombs on Hiroshima and Nagasaki. And during the cold war, reliance on nuclear weapons was justified for their deterrent value: no war would occur just because the weapons were so inhumane.

These considerations suggest that the humanitarian contribution of the laws of war is ambiguous. The laws may make war more humane by depriving soldiers of destructive weapons and tactics; but they may make war less humane by prolonging it, and they may make the world less secure by making war more attractive. We will put aside these issues and consider the possibility that, given that a war is taking place, laws of war advance the interests of the belligerents.

The Value of Restrictions on Combat Tactics

The laws of war reflect a simple logic that we have seen in other areas of international law. Consider, as an example, the rule that medical care must be given to captured enemy soldiers. For each country, the rule imposes a cost—the cost of caring for enemy soldiers. And for each country, the rule creates a benefit— the saving of lives and improved health of their soldiers after being captured by the enemy. If, for each country, the benefit exceeds the cost, then the rule requiring medical care is desirable.

However, the rule is not necessarily sustainable. The problem has the structure of the prisoner's dilemma. Country X does best by depriving soldiers of country Y of medical care (thus saving costs) and by benefiting from the medical care that country Y gives to X's soldiers. Country Y has symmetrical payoffs. Thus, unless the two countries can cooperate in some way, each will refrain from providing medical care, producing the jointly worst outcome. Fortunately, the game is repeated, so that as long as each country can observe whether the other country deprives POWs of medical care, the victim country can retaliate by doing the same. The threat of retaliation may be able to ensure cooperation. Below we go through this logic in more detail.

Symmetry and Reciprocity

The *symmetry* condition says that a law of war is possible in the first place only if it gives an advantage to neither state in the conflict. It must be neutral as between them.

Consider two examples. Prior to World War II, the Great Powers discussed banning submarine warfare and certain kinds of sea mines. Britain favored such a rule, but other states—including France as well as Germany—opposed it.[5] The Great Powers also discussed banning poison gas, did so, and (for the most part) did not violate the rule. What accounts for this difference?

The best answer is that a ban on submarine warfare and sea mines would have provided an advantage to one state; the ban on poison gas did not. Because every major state had the capacity to manufacture and deploy poison gas, the ban benefited all while not clearly providing an advantage to any state. Thus, a ban was possible and turned out to be self-enforcing during World War II between the major belligerents. By contrast, although both Germany and Britain would have benefited from a ban on submarine warfare because such a ban would have protected their commercial shipping, Britain would have benefited much more than Germany because Britain had a larger navy, and this would have given Britain an advantage over Germany in a war. In the poison gas case, the gains were equal, giving no one a relative gain; in the submarine warfare case, the gains, while positive for both sides, would have been unequal, giving Britain a relative gain vis-à-vis Germany.

These examples are relatively clear, but symmetry is always a matter of context, and often the relative gains of a rule are hard to identify and vary between different pairs of belligerents. Requiring humane treatment of POWs, for example, may seem symmetrical, but in practice it may not be for various reasons. Take the following examples:

- Some states have, for internal reasons, a long history of treating POWs well, so a new rule does not require any changes to practice or culture; other states do not. The rule benefits the first group more than the second.
- Some states turn out to have logistical advantages. If one state captures POWs in its territory, for example, it may be easier to treat them humanely than when a state captures POWs on hostile territory at the end of long supply lines. The rule benefits the first state more than the second.
- Some states may possess resource advantages. A state that has established prison and hospital infrastructure may be able to temporarily house and care for POWs at lower cost than a state that has to arrange alternate facilities for this purpose. The rule benefits the first state more than the second.
- Some states might believe that treating POWs well is a good way to get them to surrender, while other states might believe that treating POWs poorly is a good way to demoralize the belligerent and persuade it to surrender. The rule benefits the first state by not requiring it to act differently from the way it thinks is military appropriate; the rule hurts the second state.[6]

As a result, one finds a complex pattern in the treatment of POWs reflecting all of these factors. We will say more about this in a moment.

Let us turn to the condition for self-enforcing laws of war, which is *reciprocity*. Reciprocity means that if a belligerent violates the laws of war, the opponent has the ability to retaliate by violating the same rule or some other rule. Reciprocity exists only when a war is ongoing, the outcome is unclear, all belligerents share an interest in keeping the war limited, and all belligerents have the ability to constrain those who fight under their flag.

Reciprocity requires that each state maintain an effective military authority that can ensure both that its own soldiers obey the laws of war and that an appropriate response—generally, retaliation—can be made when the other state violates the laws of war. When a war is about to end, and the enemy is in disarray, the other state has less reason to obey the laws of war because the losing state is powerless to retaliate: thus, pillage and looting are more likely to result than otherwise. And when one state violates all the laws of war—if it adopts a scorched-earth policy—then it loses the ability to retaliate against the other state when that state violates the laws of war, as it cannot adopt less restrained tactics than those that it already uses. In a limited war, both states exercise self-restraint so that they have a way of retaliating if the other state fails to follow the rules.

Reciprocity helps to explain the single most ineffective area of the laws of war—the law of occupation. In no case since World War II has a state declared that the laws of occupation are applicable to a particular occupation—the only exception being the U.S. occupation of Iraq beginning in 2003.[7] The reason is that a conquered state has no power to retaliate against the conqueror for violating the laws of war. There is no reciprocity.

Reciprocity is intuitive but frequently misunderstood. One often hears the following complaint about a particular violation of the laws of war—say, the American abuse of detained Iraqis during the recent war in Iraq: "Because the United States has violated the laws of war by torturing POWs and civilians, we can expect that in its next war the United States' enemy will torture American POWs." The logic here is dubious. Suppose that the United States' next war is with North Korea. There is no reason to believe that North Korea will torture American POWs *because* U.S. forces tortured Iraqis. After all, if North Korea tortures American POWs, it can expect the United States to retaliate in some way. North Korea has no interest in vindicating the rights of Iraqis; its interest is in limiting (or not) its war with the United States.

What is true is that if the United States and North Korea are at war, the United States may want to treat North Korean POWs humanely in the hope that North Korea will reciprocate and treat American POWs humanely. This is the true sense in which reciprocity may function to the benefit of both sides.[8]

The symmetry condition and the reciprocity conditions overlap, but they are intended to capture distinct phenomena. The symmetry condition says that the law must give an advantage to no party. The reciprocity condition says that one party must be able to retaliate if the other party violates the law. If it cannot, this is usually because it has already been defeated (as in the case of occupation) or is not a well-organized army (as in the case of civil wars involving guerillas and irregulars, in some instances).

The Laws of War and the War on Terror

There are two polar approaches to the problem of applying the laws of war to international terrorism. One response is that the laws of war apply with full force against terrorists. This view is reflected in the 1977 protocols to the Geneva Convention, which many states, but not the United States, have ratified. Under the 1977 protocols, nearly everyone picked up in a theater of combat is entitled to protection of the laws of war.[9] People guilty of war crimes—including terrorists who blow up civilians—would, under these laws, be entitled to various procedural protections. They could be punished for their crimes but not otherwise treated any differently from regular soldiers.

The opposite response is that no laws of war should apply to a state's military operations against terrorists. Terrorists are just criminals; the laws of war apply to states. However, there are important ways in which terrorist groups are like states. Most terrorist groups have a specific political aim; in the case of al Qaida, this aim is the elimination of U.S. military forces from Arab lands and possibly the elimination of Western influence in the Middle East.[10] This is a coherent political aim, and it could be satisfied if the United States adjusted its strategic priorities. In addition, terrorist groups are able to exercise restraint in the midst of war, just like states. Terrorist groups frequently respect certain rules or enter modi vivendi with particular governments.[11] They grant immunity to message bearers, for example, and restrict their activities to certain targets. Often terrorists seek to force governments into negotiations, and they respect certain ground rules the violation of which would make negotiation impossible.[12] In many cases—including Spain, Italy, Northern Ireland, and South Africa—terrorist organizations ultimately (albeit in some cases only partially) evolved into political organizations that reached a settlement with the government.[13]

Laws of war are possible between states and terrorist organizations for the same reason that they are possible in interstate disputes. Although each side has an interest in defeating the other side, each side also has an interest in minimizing its own losses prior to victory or defeat, as the case may be. When each side can curtail its use of destructive tactics against the other side, can benefit from the other side doing the same, and does not, in doing so, confer a military advantage to the other side, then self-enforcing limitations on conduct are possible.

But there is a difference between saying that the laws of wars can apply to states fighting terrorists and saying that the existing laws of war—those that have evolved to deal with limited wars between roughly equal states—will apply. The premise of acknowledging *a* body of laws of war is that the belligerents have a reason to comply with them; but one expects that the body of laws that two ordinary states would respect would be different from the body of laws that a state and a terrorist organization would respect in their violent dealings with each other.

Indeed, one might argue that the dealings between governments and different terrorist organizations are too heterogeneous to be covered by a single code of law. We might prefer to refer to, and describe, the various conventions that evolve, or should evolve, between one government and one terrorist organization, and another such pair, and so on, rather than a broad code. This is reasonable, but one could say the same thing about the relationships between states that engage in limited war; these are surely just as heterogeneous. What matters is not the label one uses but the substance of the laws, or conventions, or modi vivendi, that arise, or ought to arise, as states and terrorist organizations struggle with each other.

The question is, given that terrorism exists, what rules should govern the military conflict between terrorists and governments?

The first point to recall is the constraint of symmetry. Any rule that provides an advantage to government or terrorist will not be respected. The outlawing of terrorist methods is the extreme example: governments can outlaw terrorism but cannot expect terrorists to pay attention.

As another example, consider the prohibition on coercive interrogation of POWs. This rule has not always been respected during regular wars, but it has been respected sometimes. When each belligerent benefits more from the humane treatment of its soldiers by the enemy than it loses from being deprived of the fruits of interrogation, and—crucially—they can monitor each other's performance either through intermediaries like the Red Cross or through reports from escaped or rescued POWs, then the rule is, in principle, self-enforcing. And even if each state may cheat a little on the margins, it does seem that the laws of war have improved the treatment of POWs during some wars.[14]

But now we must ask ourselves whether the United States could benefit from a similar implicit deal with al Qaida. The answer is probably not. Al Qaida does not currently hold U.S. soldiers as prisoners, and if it ever does, it seems highly unlikely that it would refrain from torturing and killing them, regardless of how the United States treats captured al Qaida members. The problem is that, at the present time, al Qaida would gain less by sparing Americans, if it captured any, than the United States would gain by sparing al Qaida prisoners. The al Qaida–United States conflict is not symmetrical in the way that an ordinary war is: the United States cannot expect to gain any benefits from al Qaida by treating al Qaida prisoners in a humane manner, given al Qaida's demonstrated ferocity in its treatment of enemy civilians.

Thus, the symmetry condition is violated; it may be that the reciprocity condition is violated as well. Suppose that both the United States and al Qaida believed that both would be jointly—and equally—better off if they agreed (implicitly) to treat prisoners humanely. The question now is whether each party can credibly promise to comply with the deal as long as the other party does. We know that the United States could; but we do not know whether al Qaida could. It depends on whether the al Qaida leadership can exercise discipline over all those who see themselves as carrying its banner. On the one hand, some view al Qaida as a relatively coherent organization, and it may be that its leaders can control the activities of its members. If so, reciprocity is met; al Qaida could engage in self-restraint in return for U.S. self-restraint. On the other hand, many people think of Islamic terrorism as a more diffuse phenomenon, and it is doubtful that any one person or organization controls the activities of members. If so, reciprocity is not met. The practical problem is just that al Qaida's leaders would not be able to prevent members from treating prisoners inhumanely; if so, then the United States has no incentive to enter a deal with al Qaida.

This discussion is only illustrative, but one clear implication is that the "laws of war" between states and terrorist organizations are likely to be highly context specific.

14

Human Rights

The principle of sovereignty can be understood as a commitment to mutual indifference about the goings-on in other states. Before that principle developed in the seventeenth century with the peace of Westphalia, states—or the proto-states that then existed—had not made this commitment. States believed that the happenings in other states mattered, down to the religious beliefs and practices of people who lived in them. It was easy to justify war in such circumstances. The Protestant government in one state could argue, plausibly to its people, that the Catholics in another state followed the Antichrist. War, though usually motivated by other goals, could be given an altruistic gloss, and violence based on higher ideals has often proven an irresistible temptation.

The wars that followed, however, convinced people that this temptation had to be resisted. Thereafter, the official doctrine was that states could have no interest in the religious well-being, or any other form of well-being, of the nationals living in other states. The idea of sovereignty was born. At times it has been so heavily entrenched that even an official expression of disapproval of policies or laws in another state could provoke claims that the criticizing government was interfering with the sovereignty of the criticized state. The notion was never pure. The thought lingered that while states could declare an official religion, they could not abuse religious minorities, but it does not seem to have played a major role in international relations.

This idea of sovereignty, with its focus on the right of a state to control the population on its territory without interference, has steadily shrunk ever since. We have seen how states have extended their claims of power over the seas, over their nationals on foreign territory, and over the policies of foreign states that have extraterritorial effect. The last fifty years have also seen a new and dramatic development—the reemergence of the pre-Westphalian belief in the state's right to make claims about how people should lead their lives in other states and about the moral principles that should govern them.

Background Theories of Rights

Rights protect people from the action of others. If one has a right to X, that means that certain specified others cannot deprive one of X. In international law, the starting point is always sovereignty—the state's power to regulate its population and what happens on its territory. Human rights protect people from that power; put differently, the state's sovereignty is qualified by human rights. If people have a right to criminal process, for example, a state may not detain and execute suspected criminals without first giving them fair trials. At one time, a state might respond to criticism about such behavior by claiming sovereign power to do what it wants. Today states instead acknowledge, at least verbally, that they may not invade people's rights.

The philosophical basis of rights is the claim that human beings have inherent dignity that entitles them not to be used as instruments for the advancement of others. A state that sacrifices its citizens (or foreigners) to military glory, or a bloodthirsty god, or even to the well-being of the group as a whole violates people's rights and should be stopped. One is not permitted to plead cultural differences or local traditions; human rights are regarded as universal, as belonging to people simply by virtue of the fact that they are human beings.

Rights are not necessarily absolute. It may well be the case that a person can be killed without a trial, for example. Consider a police shooting to prevent a hostage taker from murdering a hostage. Property rights similarly are not absolute; property can be taxed, and its use can be constrained. Rights generally create rebuttable presumptions that states can overcome if they have a sufficiently good reason—if the safety and security of many others are at stake, for example.

This type of thinking goes back to the Enlightenment. It influenced the U.S. Bill of Rights and the French Declaration of the Rights of Man. The drafters of these documents did not claim to bind foreign states, of course; but they did claim that rights are universal, and thus implicitly, foreign states should respect rights as well. But at that time, most states were authoritarian and believed that populations should simply obey the dictates of the benevolent authorities. It would not be until the end of World War II that a critical mass of states could agree to the concept of universal human rights.

World War II killed off the popularity of nationalism—the idea that a particular group of people, a nation, had some kind of intrinsic value and a divine mission to achieve glory. It left behind two major ideological systems—liberal democracy and communism. Both these systems claimed to be universal, and thus they could agree that human rights were universal. But as we will see, they defined these rights quite differently.

The Birth of Human Rights Law

The modern human rights regime began with the Universal Declaration of Human Rights of 1948. This document incorporated familiar Western negative rights—the right to be free from arbitrary detention, summary execution, and the rest—plus some exotic positive rights, such as the right to education and work.[1] All this was a reaction to the Nazis. The rest of the world could agree on little—and this would become increasingly clear—but they could agree that the Nazis were evil, and thus the Universal Declaration would be everything that the Nazis were not.

But what does that mean? The drafters of the Universal Declaration, led by Eleanor Roosevelt, quickly realized that states could agree only on vague generalities. It could take years to hammer out an agreement on the details. Rather than wait that long, states agreed to issue the Universal Declaration as a "political" rather than "legal document," a statement of aspiration that would have no legally binding effect.

The problem that quickly emerged was that the Western and Eastern blocs had different notions of what it meant not to be a Nazi. The West, led by the United States, promoted liberal democracy—rights of political participation along with negative rights that protect individuals from the power of the state. The East, led by the Soviet Union, promoted socialism—which emphasized positive rights to education and work. Western-style political rights conflicted with the dictatorship of the proletariat, since in practice the proletariat had to delegate power to a small oligarchy, which would run things until conditions were ripe for true democratic socialism.

At the start of the cold war, these differences loomed large. A single treaty that would implement the aspirations of the Universal Declaration seemed impossible, and as we will see, negotiations ultimately proceeded on two tracks.

Negative and Positive Rights

Scholars distinguish negative and positive rights. Negative rights—the right not to be tortured, the right not to be arbitrarily detained—prohibit the government from taking certain actions against people. Positive rights—the right to health care, to a job—require the government to provide people with certain goods or services. Negative rights are associated with small government and the night watchman state: the government does well by doing little. Positive rights are associated with large government and the welfare state: the government has responsibility for the well-being of the public.

It is questionable whether this distinction is philosophically sound, but there is no doubt that it is politically important. During the cold war, negative rights were associated with liberal democracy, and positive rights were associated with communism. The liberal democracies guaranteed "liberty"—freedom from certain type of government restrictions—but not well-being or the components of well-being, such as health and employment. The communist countries guaranteed employment, health care, and the like but not liberty in the Western sense.

These distinctions never held up very well. Many liberal democracies guarantee positive rights; even the United States, in practice, does, with social security (for example), although American positive rights have not (for the most part) been constitutionalized. But there was an important distinction between liberal democracy, on the one hand, and communism, on the other, and a fierce ideological battle raged until the collapse of communism in 1989. Although now over, this ideological battle influenced the development of international human rights law. The Universal Declaration contains both types of rights, but when it came time to put those rights into treaties, the competition between the United States and the Soviet Union overshadowed events. It was agreed that negotiations would proceed on two tracks—one involving positive rights, the other involving negative rights. These sets of negotiations would yield the International Covenant for Economic, Social, and Cultural Rights (ICESCR; positive rights)[2] and the International Covenant on Civil and Political Rights (ICCPR; negative rights).[3] These treaties took decades to negotiate and were adopted by the General Assembly only in 1966 and went into force in 1976. Eventually, nearly all states would ratify both treaties—except for the United States, which ratified only the ICCPR. Most of the Western states had moved toward social democracy, which incorporated positive rights anyway, and the governments of the Eastern states adopted the ICCPR for public relations purposes and did not believe that it would loosen their hold on power.

The collapse of the Soviet Union made clear that communism had no future. Most states—we will see some exceptions—have since opted for liberal democracy with a strong welfare state component, in form if not always in substance. These states endorse both negative (or civil and political) and positive (or economic, social, and cultural) rights. In principle, people have the right to vote, to dissent, and to enjoy various negative freedoms but also to have an education, to receive welfare, and to obtain health care. Of course, there is a tension. If health care is a right, then people's right to vote does not permit them to put into place a government that eliminates health care.

This is the ideological landscape. But states in fact act very differently, and as we will see, it is doubtful that the human rights treaties account for much of their behavior. The treaties are best thought of as a reflection of ideological debate about the best form of government, not as a way for states to constrain themselves.

Why Have States Entered Human Rights Treaties?

Most treaties exist because states use them as tools for cooperation. Each party has some objective—access to markets, cleaner air, protection for fisheries—that it can obtain only with the cooperation of the other party or parties. The treaty sets out a quid pro quo—each party incurs an obligation that benefits the other party—that embodies the cooperative enterprise.

Human rights treaties do not seem to fit this model. When the United States entered the Genocide Convention, did it give up its sovereign right to engage in genocide in order to secure a like commitment from Sweden? That does not seem to describe the situation accurately. A better description of the emergence of the human rights regime starts with the premise that the Western liberal states that set the agenda believed that they would not have to change their behavior. In their view, they already respected human rights. The idea of the treaty regime was to compel other states—authoritarian states, developing states—to do the same. The ICCPR simply set out the rights that liberal democracies already observed. The ICESCR was more ambitious, but the treaty language made clear that states could take their time in complying with those rights;[4] the ICESCR restrictions were just not as tight. The liberal democracies also used reservations, declarations, and understandings to exempt themselves from treaty obligations that they did not agree with. In any event, these addressed relatively minor issues, such as whether juveniles and adults can be held together in prison.

The question then arises why the other states—the authoritarian and developing states—saw any advantage in entering these treaties. They would certainly not gain in the conventional sense, namely, that the liberal democracies' compliance with the treaties would do the authoritarian and developing states any good. There are a number of possible answers. One is that the governments of those states understood that their own populations, or influential segments of them, valued the rights in the treaties and entered the treaties as a kind of public relations gambit[5]—to show that they valued these rights even though they would not actually respect them.[6] Or maybe these governments sought to reassure foreigners that they respected rights; this might reduce foreign criticism and also attract foreign investment, human capital, and trade. Another is simply that the West bribed and threatened states that did not enter the treaties. Why? Maybe because people in the West believed that those poorer states should model themselves on liberal democracies because this system is the best and would advance well-being. Western governments may find it easier to deal with liberal democracies, which are better places to invest in and trade with, and they may have naively thought that these treaties would move authoritarian states in the direction of liberal democracy.

We can think about these problems in more formal terms.[7] Assume that states have preferences over a range of outcomes, which can include altruistic as well as conventionally self-interested outcomes. The preferences of states reflect the preferences of the general population, interest groups, or elites, as they emerge through political institutions. If these groups care about the well-being of people in other countries, then their preferences will be reflected in part in the state's foreign policy. States might also have instrumental reasons for pursuing what otherwise seem like other-regarding goals. For example, states may support human rights in other states because foreign states that respect human rights might be less belligerent and more stable places for trade and investment.

States' other-regarding interests, as we will call them, can differ considerably. One state might care about the health of people living in foreign countries, while another state might care about salvation of their souls. One state might believe that people living in other countries should enjoy the benefits of a market economy, while another state might believe that those people should benefit from education, health care, and social security. A state might be indifferent to the well-being of people in other states as a general matter but draw the line at massacres or genocide. Finally, the intensity of states' other-regarding interests will vary. Many states have highly intense preferences and are willing to back them with substantial resources; other states have weaker preferences.

If, as seems likely, other-regarding preferences overlap, states' efforts to help foreign nationals face a collective action problem. Technically, a state's abuse of its own citizens creates a negative externality that affects all other states, or at least all other states that have other-regarding preferences. These other states all benefit from eliminating the externality, but each foreign state does even better if other foreign states take on the entire burden of doing so. If all states think similarly, it may be that none lifts a finger to help the citizens being abused.

As an example, imagine two states, say, the United States and the European Union (which is not technically a state, of course), which have an interest in improving the well-being of people who live in a third state, say, Zimbabwe. When the well-being of people in Zimbabwe improves, the United States and the European Union are both made better off, in the sense that a "good" for which they have preferences (for which they are willing to pay) has been supplied. But interdependent utility functions of this type lead to strategic dilemmas.

If the United States contributes to Zimbabwe's well-being, the United States also thereby increases the European Union's utility. If the European Union contributes to Zimbabwe's well-being, the European Union increases the United States' utility. But the United States and the European Union have no desire to contribute to each other's well-being. Thus, if they act unilaterally, they will underfund Zimbabwe because they fail to account for this positive externality in their private calculus.[8] They will do better if they can cooperate and agree that both will donate to Zimbabwe.

We have so far spoken in terms of monetary contributions, and the analysis applies straightforwardly to the contribution of financial aid to a poor country. But the analysis can also be applied to more conventional types of human rights enforcement. Suppose that the government of Zimbabwe practices torture. The United States and the European Union incur disutility when Zimbabwe's people are tortured, and so they are willing to contribute to reduce the amount of torture. The United States' and the European Union's contributions now take the form of costly actions—the cutting off of trade, diplomatic pressure, aid for retraining police, and so forth—that will reduce the amount of torture in Zimbabwe. The United States and the European Union face the same strategic dilemma and jointly do best by cooperating.

We now need to examine Zimbabwe's incentives. Zimbabwe's government does not respect human rights, for three possible reasons: (1) doing so interferes with the government's objectives (for example, to stay in power); (2) the government lacks capacity (for example, poorly trained police); and (3) the public does not support the human rights in questions (for example, equality for women in a traditional society). Accordingly, Zimbabwe will not respect human rights unless other countries bribe it to, or other countries threaten to cause harm to it if it does not.

Thus, there are two strands of strategic interaction—one between the United States and the European Union, the other between Zimbabwe and the joint venture of the United States and the European Union, so to speak. A priori, one can imagine multiple outcomes.

In one scenario, Zimbabwe does not respect human rights because the United States and the European Union are not able to cooperate in sanctioning it. In another scenario, Zimbabwe respects human rights because the United States and the European Union cooperate in sanctioning it. One can also imagine alternatives: for example, the United States and the European Union cannot cooperate, but each does discipline Zimbabwe unilaterally if Zimbabwe fails to respect human rights. Their independent efforts will be less than their coordinated efforts, so Zimbabwe's improvement will be less as well.

There are three reasons for being skeptical in practice about the prospects for successful efforts to improve Zimbabwe's human rights behavior. In the real world outside our example, the rich states number in the dozens, and as the number of parties increases, cooperation becomes more difficult. In addition, states frequently disagree about when a human rights violator should be sanctioned, in part because the states have different interests that they balance against the gains from improvement in human rights. During the cold war, the United States refused to sanction human rights violators, such as Guatemala, that were also Western allies. After the cold war, the United States has refused to sanction human rights violators, such as Saudi Arabia and Egypt, that cooperate in the conflict with al Qaida and peace efforts with Israel. Other violators, such as Sudan, receive support from China, which has a strong interest in obtaining reliable suppliers of natural resources.

The basic problem of collective action is aggravated by philosophical and strategic rifts between states otherwise committed to human rights. Europeans condemn the death penalty; Americans do not. Americans insist on stronger protections on freedom of expression. The two sides differ on how much importance should be given to economic and social rights. They have different strategic interests, which they sometimes permit to override their human rights commitments. And then there are other powerful countries like China, Brazil, and Russia, which have different values and interests. The targets of enforcement, countries like Zimbabwe, can exploit these differences and undermine cooperation.

Second, the human rights violator itself may not be able to cooperate with the countries that seek to change its behavior. Recall that cooperation requires a low discount rate. For countries, this means political institutions that place sufficient weight on future payoffs. But many human rights violators have weak institutional capacity. Elected officials face coups; authoritarian leaders act arbitrarily; bureaucracies are corrupt and cannot constrain leaders. In many cases, the government has little power over local officials who commit human rights violations. In extreme cases, such as Somalia, the government collapses and anarchy prevails.

Third, the United States and the European Union can compel Zimbabwe to improve human rights only if they can credibly threaten to sanction Zimbabwe if it fails to do so. However, threats to sanction are not always credible. Sanctions often cost something to the sanctioning state and in the sanctioned state typically harm ordinary people more than they harm leaders; indeed, sanctions work mainly by impelling ordinary people to overthrow the government. Sanctions can do so only by causing pain to ordinary people. However, the humanitarian impulse that causes rich states to pressure poor states to enter human rights treaties also makes it difficult for them to follow through and punish the population, already poor and miserable, if their country does not comply with the treaty. This problem has been dubbed the Samaritan's dilemma.[9]

It should also be kept in mind that liberal countries rarely have a strong interest in improving well-being in other countries. The governments of liberal countries stay in power by providing benefits to voters, not to foreigners. Thus, governments give aid to foreigners only when doing so benefits voters. This can happen for two reasons. First, voters care about the well-being of foreigners. No doubt they do, but it is equally clear that the well-being of foreigners is a low priority for most people. Second, voters care about security and prosperity, and providing help to foreigners may not advance these goals. Although sometimes it does, liberal governments have discovered that they often do better along these dimensions by providing support to illiberal states when the latter are strategically or economically important.

Three Challenges

There have been three challenges to the modern human rights regime. The first arose in the context of the so-called Asian values debates of the 1980s. Certain Asian countries, notably Singapore, which is an authoritarian regime but also one in which citizens are relatively wealthy, claimed that the human rights treaties reflect Western values that do not apply to "Asia," where Confucian and other traditions favor group harmony over individual rights. In these places, individual rights must take second place to order imposed by the government elites. Many Westerners responded that Asian traditions also reflected rights and freedoms, but this response missed the point. These traditions never achieved the dominance that they did in the West, where they were embodied in government policy (in the United States and Britain, among other places) long before states negotiated human rights treaties. In the post-World War II period during which these treaties were negotiated, Asian countries were poor and weak and had little influence over the negotiation process. The genius of this critique was that it blamed the human rights treaties on Western colonialism, an endless source of guilt for Western elites, especially in Europe. The human rights treaties were just another form of colonialism that should be resisted.

The second challenge arose in the 1990s and early 2000s and emanated from certain Islamic countries, which claimed that Western human rights ideas conflict with Islamic values. This challenge was more effective than the Asian values challenge because the Islamic critics did not merely celebrate authoritarianism but proposed certain rights. In particular, Islamic countries have argued for a right against "defamation of religion," which takes place when people fail to show sufficient respect for religious sensitivities—most famously exemplified by the publication of cartoons in Western newspapers that depicted the prophet Mohammed in violation of Islamic strictures. Defamation of religion is deeply in tension with the right to speech and to dissent and also with the secularization of society in Europe. Yet by voting as a bloc, Muslim countries have made headway in placing defamation of religion on the international human rights agenda.

The third challenge is the idea of a right to development, championed by China on behalf of the developing world. The right to development is the right of poor countries to take such actions as they believe necessary to stimulate economic growth, so as to alleviate poverty. Like the religious defamation right, the right to development has not been formally embodied in a treaty, but it can be found in various international documents, and the developing world insists on it. It sounds harmless enough, but it has been used by developing countries to explain why they should not be held up to the human rights standards of the West. If, as seems clear, poverty can be alleviated through economic growth, then human rights standards should not be used to prevent poor countries from adopting necessary growth policies. Indeed, poor countries have cited the right to development to justify excluding them from—or holding them to lower standards in—all sorts of treaties, including climate treaties.

The Empirical Effects of Human Rights Treaties

It has long been understood that states do not necessarily comply with their treaty obligations, but the human rights treaties have had a particularly poor record of compliance. The Soviet Union and its allies, after all, entered the International Covenant for Civil and Political Rights in 1973, but these states did not give their citizens civil and political rights as of the time that they collapsed or underwent regime change in 1989–1991. Nearly all states have entered the Torture Convention, but torture remains common around the world. Even the Genocide Convention did not seem to have an effect. Two genocides occurred in the modern era before the Convention went into force in 1948—the Armenian Genocide and the Holocaust. Since then, genocides or genocide-like mass killings have taken place in Cambodia, Yugoslavia, Rwanda, and Sudan.

In recent years, law professors and political scientists have tried to test more rigorously, using statistical methods, the hypothesis that human rights treaties have affected the behavior of states.[10] Most studies have found no evidence that states that sign human rights treaties improve their human rights records or give more respect to human rights than states that do not sign those treaties. Indeed, a few studies suggest that authoritarian states that enter human rights treaties actually treat people worse—leading to speculation that those states can buy time and breathing space from the West by entering a treaty. For many reasons, these studies should be taken with a grain of salt. It is hard to code the evidence and to control for background conditions. And a few studies have found some improvement in discrete areas, such as the treatment of women, and involving particular states, like those undergoing transitions from authoritarian systems to democracy.[11] But in the end, it is hard to conclude that the human rights treaty regime has greatly affected the way states treat their populations.

Likewise, improvements in human rights over time in some countries may be attributed to other things, such as economic growth.[12] As states become wealthier, they treat their citizens better.[13] It is also the case that democracies treat their citizens better than nondemocracies do. Wealth and democracy also seem to be correlated: poor countries that democratize often suffer from coups that reinstall an authoritarian regime; this does not appear to happen with relatively wealthy countries. It may be that in wealthier societies, people can more easily monitor the government than in poor societies. If the government cracks down on dissent or starts to torture people, then a wealthier public can more easily find out—it has time, the resources, and the ability to read and support newspapers and other media—and put pressure on the government by threatening to strike or in other ways withdraw support.

In sum, there is at best weak evidence that human rights treaties improve human rights. Perhaps human rights regimes have a "demonstration effect" that pulls developing countries toward greater rights over the long run, but if so, the causal pathways are too subtle to show up in empirical research. It is also possible that states can do more to promote human rights in other states by promoting international trade and other forms of international cooperation that lead to growth in poor countries.

15

International Criminal Law

Individuals are generally not liable for violating international law; states are.[1] For example, an individual who commits a tort against an alien is not subject to international liability; the tortfeasor is subject to domestic civil liability, and international law comes into play only if the state in question fails to provide an effective tort law remedy that does not discriminate against aliens. In international law, the victim's state has a claim against the tortfeasor's state for failing to provide a domestic legal remedy. The relevant lawbreaker in international law is the state, not the person.

We explained this general pattern in Chapter 8. Here we discuss an exception. In certain circumstances, individuals may be liable for violating international criminal law. This exception raises several subissues: Why is state responsibility insufficient to achieve the purposes of international law in these cases? Why are the penalties imposed on individuals criminal rather than civil? And why do states create "universal jurisdiction" over certain international crimes?

We will start with some economic background and then consider the paradigmatic international crime of piracy. After examining piracy, we will look at more modern examples.

Background: State Responsibility versus Criminal and Civil Sanctions for Individuals

In domestic legal systems, the main difference between civil and criminal liability turns on the sanction. Incarceration, a criminal penalty, is generally a far more expensive sanction to employ than monetary penalties, and for this reason conventional economic wisdom holds that monetary penalties (often civil) are preferable when they are adequate to the task. But when the assets of individuals who commit harmful acts are too small in relation to the properly calibrated monetary penalty, incarceration may be necessary as a substitute or supplement. Likewise, if individuals have proclivities to commit harm that cannot be deterred, incarceration may be useful to incapacitate such individuals from committing further harm.

The literature on corporate liability also recognizes a potentially useful role for criminal liability at the individual level, even when the corporation is liable for all of the harm caused by an employee's wrongful act.[2] The reason again relates to the limited assets of employees and to the possibility that a threat of incarceration may be needed to deter employees adequately. Corporations are unable to incarcerate employees, and so it may be useful for the state to impose the penalty of incarceration in addition to whatever monitoring and punishment system the employer has put in place. When employees are subject to criminal penalties, however, those penalties become indirect costs of doing business to the employer to the degree that employee wage demands rise to compensate for the danger of incurring the penalties. Unless the liability imposed on the employer is adjusted downward accordingly, the total costs imposed on the employer associated with employee wrongdoing may exceed the harm caused, leading to the problems that result from excessive sanctions.

Criminal penalties for individual actors may also be a useful supplement to state responsibility under international law, albeit for somewhat different reasons. As in the corporate setting, individual actors who cause violations of international law will often lack the assets to pay for the harms that they cause. States may have difficulty imposing "civil" penalties that are large enough to dissuade their officials from committing harmful acts, and sanctions such as incarceration may be a valuable supplement. But in contrast to the corporate setting, states do have the power to incarcerate individuals. Thus, it is not necessary for international law itself, or for international institutions, to impose criminal penalties on individual actors simply because of their limited assets. Properly calibrated sanctions for state responsibility can in principle induce states to incarcerate individual actors under domestic law when such penalties are useful to ensuring compliance with international obligations.

Criminal penalties under international law are necessary, therefore, only when state responsibility alone will not induce states to employ proper deterrence measures, including incarceration if appropriate, against the individual actors whose harmful acts trigger state responsibility. We suggest several reasons why this might be true.

First, consider a situation in which the state agent who violates international law has no "principal" to monitor him. An absolute dictator like Adolf Hitler is a good example. Because no entity exists to monitor the actor at the time that he undertakes to violate international law, a prospect of state responsibility for the violation will have little or no effect on the actor's incentives. A prospect of individual criminal penalties under international law, however, may have some deterrent effect, with its magnitude obviously dependent on the actor's beliefs about his ability to escape punishment.

Second, suppose that the actor who violates international law does so as an official of an exceedingly weak or "failed state." If such a state has few assets with which to pay for the harm it has caused, either monetarily or by incurring some other type of sanction, state responsibility will be ineffective at inducing it to police the behavior of its agents. This case presents a rough analogue to the imposition of vicarious liability on an insolvent corporation. In these cases, penalties imposed directly by international law on actors who cause harm may be necessary if they are to face any prospect of sanction. The criminal penalty of incarceration may again be the best option because of individual actors' limited assets.

Third, and closely related, individual bad actors may have weak connections to states. They often operate internationally, moving around outside the jurisdiction of their home governments. The classic example is the pirate, who moves about on the high seas; the modern example is the terrorist, who moves from state to state. There may be little point in imposing state responsibility on their home governments because those governments have no monitoring capability.

Fourth, imagine that the imposition of sanctions associated with state responsibility is for some reason undesirable or counterproductive. Consider a state that has violated international law and has been defeated in a war, for example; further sanctions might contribute to a humanitarian crisis. If the unwillingness of the international community to impose sanctions is anticipated, it saps the deterrent effect of state responsibility. A prospect of individual criminal penalties can be useful here as well.

Fifth, and also related, circumstances may arise in which states largely disregard the rules of state responsibility. We think this problem may be especially acute when states are at war with each other. International law is effective at disciplining the behavior of states only because violations of international law lead to some adverse consequence for the violator, whether a formal sanction or a reputational penalty. In wartime, however, where belligerents are fighting to destroy or incapacitate each other, each nation may already be inflicting the maximum costs on the other that it is able or willing to inflict. If so, there may be little or no penalty "at the margin" for violations of international law that harm the opposite belligerent. If the violation implicates the interests of third states, some cost to violations may remain, but they may be insufficient in relation to the value of the harm caused by violations. We also doubt that a prospect of reparations after the end of conflict will necessarily discipline states during conflict—reparations tend to run one way, from the loser to the victor. States that expect to prevail in conflict will also expect to avoid reparations. Thus, individual criminal responsibility may become a particularly useful supplement to state responsibility for violations of international law during war.

A final reason for the use of individual criminal penalties under international law is that it can avoid the costs associated with sanctions for state responsibility. International sanctions may take the form of monetary reparations but often involve other measures (trade sanctions, for example) that create substantial deadweight losses. It can also be expensive to calibrate sanctions in accordance with the general international law principle of proportionality. The notion in the economic literature that incarceration is a comparatively expensive sanction, therefore, may simply be incorrect when the alternative sanction associated with state responsibility is also quite costly to administer and enforce.

The question remains, why do states (aside from the United States with its Alien Tort Statute) recognize dual civil and criminal enforcement systems under domestic law, while recognizing only an international system of criminal enforcement for individuals? A possible answer is suggested by the discussion above—that dictators, officials in failed states, soldiers at war, and people in similar positions may lack the assets to pay judgments for their crimes, and/or it may be difficult to find or reach their assets.

With these ideas in mind, we now proceed to consider the evolution of the international criminal regime. An economic issue that we have not yet addressed relates to the phenomenon of universal jurisdiction, which can be understood in part with reference to the historical crime of piracy. As shall be seen, it also remains to consider some possible disadvantages of international criminal liability.

Piracy

During the formative era of modern international law, no state had exclusive jurisdiction over the high seas. If a conflict arose—for example, if a crime occurred on a vessel—the state whose flag was flown by the vessel would have jurisdiction. If vessels flying different flags collided, the states whose flags were flown would have concurrent jurisdiction.[3] Thus, domestic law, including admiralty law, would be brought to bear on the conflict. If sailors aboard a British ship observed a crime occurring on a French ship, the British would have no jurisdiction over the crime and thus no right to board, make arrests, hold trials, and so forth, even if British subjects were perpetrators or victims.

These rules did not apply in the case of piracy. Pirates did not have the protection of the flags that they flew. If the French ship in question was a pirate ship, the British could—without violating international law—board the French vessel, arrest the pirates, and try and punish them, regardless of whether any British subjects were involved. The pirate is "treated as an outlaw, as the enemy of all mankind... whom any nation may in the interest of all capture and punish."[4] Piracy—defined roughly as "robbery on the high seas"—was the single international crime.

The distinctive feature of an international crime was thus that any country could try and punish violators. In modern terms, "universal jurisdiction" existed rather than jurisdiction rooted in the territory or responsibilities of individual nation-states.

Why was piracy an international crime? The answer is that no state could control what happened on the high seas. All states asserted jurisdiction over criminal activity on their own territory and yielded jurisdiction over criminal activity on foreign territory, even when their own citizens were involved. So long as procedural protections were in place (and today they are governed by various treaties), this system made good sense. U.S. authorities had more control over activities on U.S. soil, and German authorities had more control on German soil.

But because no nation has effective control over acts by pirates on the high seas, there would be little point to making states responsible for acts of piracy committed by their citizens or subjects. States cannot effectively deter their own citizens from engaging in piracy, at least not alone. Further, the flag on a pirate vessel is unlikely to be a reliable indicator of the pirates' citizenship in any event. If states were liable for acts of piracy by their putative citizens, therefore, little effective policing of the piracy problem would result. Instead, international law encourages states to fight piracy by giving all states the right to interdict and punish pirates, regardless of their nationality and the flag of their ship.

The fact that states could agree that piracy was undesirable—and could agree on the substantive elements of piracy—was a necessary but not a sufficient condition for making piracy an international crime. States agree that murder is undesirable, but there is no international crime of murder. What distinguishes piracy and murder is that states can enforce laws against murder on their territory; they cannot as easily enforce laws against piracy.

Of course, creating an international crime of piracy does not by itself solve the problem because it does not prevent free riding. When all states are responsible for combating piracy, any one state may nevertheless refrain from using resources against piracy because other states reap many of the benefits. By contrast, a state faces no such temptation when using resources against crime on its territory. The theory must have been that major states deployed navies to patrol the high seas for other purposes—to protect sea lanes, to control colonies, to fight wars—and, as long as those navies patrolled the high seas, they could be used relatively cheaply against pirates that they encountered. The creation of an international crime of piracy removed an obstacle to protection of shipping by permitting navies to investigate suspected sea robbers flying under a foreign flag and thereby facilitated some enforcement activity by patrolling navies, but it did not cure the underincentive for vigorous enforcement.

One must also note that recognition of an international crime carries with it some costs as well as benefits. A court will not necessarily extend standard criminal law procedural protections to foreign citizens. If British territorial courts are biased against French people, then the French can protect themselves by exiting British territory. But if British sailors decide that a French citizen they capture on the high seas is a pirate, the French cannot do much about it. Despite this concern, states compromised and consented to universal jurisdiction over piracy because the alternatives were even worse.

More generally, moving beyond the particular issue of piracy, one must be mindful of the range of costs associated with ceding jurisdiction over one's nationals to foreigners (or international tribunals). Once states agree that war crimes are international crimes, for example, a state must consider the possibility not only that its soldiers will receive an unfair trial before a foreign court or an international tribunal but that it will not be able to issue amnesties to soldiers. It turns out that amnesties and other forms of ex post relief are powerful tools for resolving serious political conflict, and states use these tools a lot. Uganda has found itself in a difficult position because it believes that the best way to end a nasty insurgency is by granting amnesty to rebels, but it has no way to call off the International Criminal Court, which has issued indictments.

We need to keep this tradeoff firmly in mind as we proceed with the discussion. International criminal law is often considered an unproblematic good thing. What could be wrong with subjecting criminals to international criminal liability? The answer is that international criminal law puts stress on the state system. Even when states can agree that certain behavior is unacceptable under all circumstances, they cannot always agree about what should be done about it. States do not always trust each other to prosecute and try criminal suspects fairly, especially when those suspects are foreign nationals. Many states use criminal procedure systematically to punish political dissidents and members of unpopular groups. These states might be tempted to do the same with unpopular or difficult foreigners.

Modern International Criminal Law

Today there are some other international crimes, including war crimes, crimes against humanity, slavery, and genocide. Like pirates, war criminals can be tried and punished by foreign states even if they commit their crimes outside the states' territory (such as on the battlefield in the war criminal's home state). War crimes are embodied in treaty instruments, such as the Geneva Conventions (1949),[5] that reflect the consent of virtually every state; genocide is recognized as an international crime in the Genocide Convention.[6] Virtually all states recognize that these acts are undesirable and ought to be discouraged. Universal jurisdiction exists for these crimes.

What is the rationale for universal jurisdiction? Our discussion of piracy provides an answer.[7] Consider first the case of war crimes by soldiers. One could imagine a system under which states agree that a soldier accused of war crimes would be subject to the jurisdiction of a national court only, and not to the jurisdiction of the enemy's courts or an international court. Armies would have an obligation to try and punish their own soldiers for war crimes; if a suspected war criminal is captured by the enemy, the enemy could hold him for the duration of hostilities, and then return him to his home state for trial after hostilities end. The enemy could not try and punish the foreign soldiers using its own courts.

The problem with this system is that frequently the foreign army that captures an enemy soldier will have the best evidence that the soldier committed a war crime. And nations may have little incentive to punish a national whose misdeeds harmed only foreigners. Punishment deferred may end up being no punishment at all.

The alternative system of universal jurisdiction to prosecute, however, has the problem of bias: what prevents a state from punishing POWs on the pretext that they are war criminals when they are not really? The answer may have to do with the effectiveness of reciprocity in the war setting. If one state punishes POWs for pretextual reasons, then the other state can retaliate by punishing the POWs it holds. By contrast, under the hypothetical system, if one state fails to prosecute its own soldiers for war crimes after the war is ended, it may be that a similar failure by the other state not to prosecute its own soldiers for war crimes would not have a deterrent effect. In fact, states very rarely prosecute their own soldiers for war crimes, so if war crimes are to be punished and deterred, this will happen only if states are permitted to prosecute enemy soldiers. This is the best explanation for universal jurisdiction over war crimes by soldiers.

Universal jurisdiction for genocide and other serious crimes against humanity follows a similar logic. Again, we might ask why states would agree to universal jurisdiction for genocide and mass murder when they do not allow universal jurisdiction for ordinary murder. The answer may be that in any country in which genocide occurs, it most likely occurs with the complicity of the government or powerful interests, and therefore it is quite unlikely that the perpetrators will be prosecuted in domestic courts. States agree that foreign courts have jurisdiction because this enhances the probability of punishment (at a minimum, the perpetrators will be afraid to travel), while the problem of bias may again seem worth tolerating because of the seriousness of the crimes in question.

The Nuremberg defendants were tried for ordinary war crimes, crimes against humanity, and aggressive war. Of these, the war crimes charges were least controversial; war crimes were already recognized as such and had been prosecuted in the past. Crimes against humanity—which encompassed crimes against one's own citizens (unlike war crimes) and crimes committed during peacetime (unlike war crimes, again)—and the crime of aggression were innovations. Crimes against humanity were later recognized in treaty instruments and have provided the basis for subsequent trials, including those stemming from the atrocities in the former Yugoslavia and Rwanda. The crime of aggression initially appeared to have been stillborn; there have been no subsequent prosecutions for commission of this crime. The negotiators of the Rome Statute for the International Criminal Court could not initially agree on a definition of aggression and ended up stipulating that those negotiations would be continued in the future. These negotiations concluded in 2010 when the crime of aggression was finally defined.[8] However, it is not clear how many states will consent to this definition.

Why could states agree that enemy soldiers and leaders can be held guilty for (say) bombing hospitals or killing POWs or massacring their own nationals but not (until recently, with much more dissent) agree that leaders can be held guilty for launching an aggressive war? One reason is that states have different views about when the use of military force may be justified, with some states saying never and some states saying sometimes, for example, to prevent a humanitarian crisis or even to preempt a "rogue state" from obtaining nuclear weapons. Further, no powerful state believes that restrictions on war crimes put it at a disadvantage in war, but such states want to retain a free hand to use military force when it is in their interest to do so. Last, if world opinion, and the threat of state-to-state retaliation, is insufficient to deter states from engaging in improper warfare (however that is defined), the marginal additional deterrence from holding leaders criminally responsible for aggressive war is likely to be low, while the risk of bias—when leaders and former leaders travel to foreign countries and become subject to their courts—is high and likely to interfere with normal diplomatic relations. Instead of individual criminal responsibility for aggression, therefore, international law traditionally makes states responsible for illegal wars under the UN Convention.[9]

Command Responsibility

Under the doctrine of command responsibility, a commander may be responsible for failing to prevent soldiers under his command from committing international crimes. Command responsibility is a species of vicarious liability: the commander is held responsible for the crimes of subordinates. The ordinary rationale for this rule is that the commander has a great deal of control over subordinates, who will usually follow orders; by holding the commander responsible for the crimes of soldiers, the law gives the commander an incentive not to order soldiers to commit war crimes as well as to monitor subordinates who might be inclined to commit such crimes. The monitoring cases present the most difficult issues in practice, when it is alleged that subordinates did not follow orders but engaged in criminal behavior about which the commander knew or should have known.

Consider the important case of General Yamashita of the Japanese Army, who had responsibility for defending the Philippines against U.S. invasion near the end of World War II. During this invasion, Japanese troops committed atrocities on a large scale against U.S. soldiers and Philippine citizens. Yamashita claimed that he did not know about these atrocities because of a breakdown in Japanese communications caused by war conditions, but a military commission found that "the crimes were so extensive and widespread, both as to time and area, that they must have been willfully permitted by the Accused, or secretly ordered by the Accused."[10] Yamashita was found guilty and executed because he failed to exercise "effective control" over his troops.

Command responsibility has recently been extended to civilian officials. Jean-Paul Akayesu was the mayor of Taba, Rwanda, during the massacres that occurred in 1994. The evidence showed that, as mayor, he was responsible for enforcing order in the town and had authority over the police; that he did not try to stop the massacres; that he ordered the police to kill Tutsi; that he was present during acts of violence; and that he encouraged violence against Tutsi. If all of this was true, then Akayesu was correctly found guilty of genocide and related crimes.[11]

Thus, commanders are held responsible for the crimes of soldiers if the commanders ordered the soldiers to commit crimes or, as in the Yamashita and Akayesu cases, the crimes of subordinates occurred on a large scale. They are not responsible for isolated murders. The reason is surely that commanders can, at low cost, prevent soldiers from committing crimes by not ordering them to, or ordering them not to when there is reasonable basis to suppose the commander had notice of their behavior. But small-scale crime is hard to detect. To be sure, one might wonder whether Japanese soldiers would have obeyed if General Yamashita had ordered them not to engage in atrocities. In the chaos of the U.S. invasion, one can plausibly argue that they would not have obeyed and that, in fact, there was nothing General Yamashita could have done to stop the atrocities. If this was the case, then liability was inappropriate.

Superior Orders

A related topic concerns the liability of soldiers who commit war crimes pursuant to an order from a superior officer. Prior to World War II, soldiers could often avoid liability for war crimes if they could show that they were following orders. Nuremberg rejected this defense, and now it is settled that soldiers who obey orders can be held criminally liable. The general rule is that soldiers and other agents may not avoid liability by pleading superior orders unless they can show that they were legally obliged to obey the orders, they did not know that the orders were unlawful, and the orders were not patently unlawful.

The question arises, why the qualification for "patently" illegal orders? Why not hold soldiers liable for all war crimes, given that an employee will be held liable for committing domestic crimes and the fact that although the employer ordered him to commit the crimes, this would be no defense? The answer is probably that states do not want to give soldiers an excuse for insubordination. The rule balances the desire to deter soldiers from engaging in war crimes and the need to maintain discipline on the field.

Extradition Treaties

What marks international criminal law as distinctive is that when a person commits an international crime, any state—at least in principle—can try that person, even if the person has no real contacts with the state in question. The person is not a national of the state; the crime did not occur on that state's territory; the victim is not a national either. An international tribunal such as the ICC can also try that person. As we have seen, states give up their exclusive jurisdictional rights in the hope of maximizing the chance of punishment and deterrence but in the process lose the ability to control outcomes. They lose the ability to ensure that the trial of a national is fair; they also lose the ability to immunize the wrongdoer in situations where this is considered desirable.

In other settings, states are not willing to give up this control. For more "ordinary" criminal violations, states use extradition treaties rather than international criminal law.

The Role of Reciprocity

Suppose that an American named X commits murder in the United States and then escapes to France. The United States does not have the legal right to send police to France to capture X. Short of a full-scale invasion—which would hardly be worth it—the United States has no choice but to ask France politely to capture X and hand him over to American police.

You might think that France would be eager to comply with this request. After all, why would France want a murderer living on its territory? It turns out that things are not so simple. Capturing X takes police resources, and there may be no reason to believe that X will murder again. X's presence on French soil may provide France with some benefit—for example, if X has information or other resources that the French value. And it may turn out that X is innocent. France also objects to the death penalty and has made it clear that it will not send people back to the United States if they will be executed. Finally, imagine that X has fled from China rather than the United States and claims to be a political dissident. China says X is a common murderer. France does not want to return political dissidents to their death. Who should it believe?

Despite these problems, the basic reciprocity of international relations offers a solution. France knows that its own citizens sometimes commit murder and other crimes and flee to the United States. France knows that if it does not return American suspects to the United States, the United States will not return French suspects to France. So there is room for a deal, and the deal will be embodied in an extradition treaty. Note, however, that not all states are able to make such a deal. Extradition treaties are common, but it is not the case that all states have extradition treaties with all other states. The United States, for example, does not have an extradition treaty with China. States must balance the advantage of being able to obtain the return of fugitives against the cost that they will have to return people who they prefer to protect for political or moral reasons.

Political Crimes

One particular category of crime is of special importance for extradition treaties: political crimes. The term is not well defined, but roughly it means acts of political dissent, which in many countries are illegal. A law that criminalizes criticism of the government creates a political crime. Murdering the head of state is also an act of political dissent and so can also be classified as a political crime. But states generally exclude crimes of violence from their understanding of political crimes. Hence, political crimes are essentially peaceful acts of political dissent. Political crimes include, in addition to criticism of the government, such activities as joining illegal political parties, religious organizations, trade unions, and the like.

Extradition treaties typically do not apply to political crimes. The United States will extradite a murderer back to Germany but not someone who has violated German law by joining an illegal political party. (In Germany, unlike the United States, political parties can be banned.) Why? An extradition treaty, like any treaty, must be mutually beneficial. The characteristic distinction between liberal and authoritarian states is that liberal states tolerate political dissent and authoritarian states do not. Accordingly, liberal states would not agree to an extradition treaty that extends to political crimes. True, some liberal states criminalize some limited types of political activity, but these crimes are marginal and the states do not agree on what these crimes should be. In a more Machiavellian vein, states have historically sought to encourage dissent in other states, which can sometimes serve their interests by weakening competitors or influencing policy in a desirable direction. (Germany famously permitted Lenin to reenter Russia to stir up trouble.) In such circumstances, these states will naturally not want to extradite political dissidents who flee persecution.

Dual Criminality

The rules for political crimes are a special case of the dual criminality requirement, which provides that a person can be extradited from state X to state Y only if the crime he is charged with in Y is also a crime in state X. This rule straightforwardly embodies the principle that extradition treaties must serve the interests of both parties. States agree that a range of behavior should be criminalized—murder, robbery, rape. No civilized society tolerates such behavior. Given also the reciprocal nature of extradition, the interest in extraditing such people is strong. But states also disagree about a range of behavior. Political dissent is not the only example. States also disagree about prostitution, drug use, various types of financial crimes, and so forth. The dual criminality requirement ensures that a state does not have to extradite someone to face trial for doing something that it does not deem wrongful.

Tricky problems can arise because of differences in punishment. Many European countries object to the harsh criminal punishments meted out in the

United States. The death penalty is just one example. It is not hard to imagine countries also refusing to extradite to the United States if prison terms are too long or prison conditions too brutal. But if they do this, they could end up losing the cooperation of the United States, which might refuse to extradite to treaty partners who do not reciprocate in kind.

Specialty

Another problem that can arise is that a state seeks extradition to try a national for committing X and then subsequently tries him for Y (instead of, or in addition to, X). Suppose X is a drug crime, while Y is murder with the death penalty attached. Or Y is a political crime. Extradition for X could just be a subterfuge for avoiding conditions in the extradition treaty, such as the ban on political crimes or the double criminality requirement. Extradition treaties therefore include the rule of specialty, which provides that the state can try the extradited person only for X and not for any other crime committed prior to the extradition.

International Criminal Law versus the Extradition Approach

International law might seem wholly unnecessary given the existence of extradition. Or one might make the opposite claim: extradition is unnecessary given international criminal law. Both approaches ensure that punishment is meted out to someone who commits a crime in state X and flees to state Y. Under extradition, the person is sent back from Y to X for prosecution. Under international criminal law, state Y prosecutes the person, or he may be prosecuted by an international tribunal.

What accounts for these different approaches? Extradition is the older and more established tradition. As we saw, states have partially overlapping interests in seeing that criminals are punished. The best way to try and punish those suspected of criminal behavior is to send them back to where they committed crimes, so that they can be tried by their own government (and/or governments with authority over the territory where the crime was committed) and where the evidence is located. But states disagree about many types of crimes. So extradition treaties extend only partway—covering behavior that both states agree is criminal—and are not possible if states distrust each other, distrust each other's courts, or have very different ideas about criminality.

International criminal law requires even closer agreement. All or most states—rather than just pairs of states—must agree that certain behavior is criminal, and their interest in punishing those who engage in that behavior must be strong enough that they are willing to tolerate their own nationals being tried by foreign courts or international tribunals that they do not fully trust.

It has been difficult to reach this level of agreement. There is an old but recurring cliché that one man's terrorist is another man's freedom fighter.[12] Many states, particularly in the West, insist that the use of violence by private individuals against civilians for political purposes is an international crime. But some Muslim and Arab states disagree. The focus of disagreement is whether the various Palestinian terrorist groups are justified by the exigencies of a "war of national liberation." Historical memory plays a role, too. Many states that obtained independence in the last sixty years originated in terrorist movements. Such is the case with South Africa's current multiracial regime as well.

IV The Environment

16

International Environmental Law

Environmental Externalities

Suppose that a factory manufactures goods, producing a benefit for consumers, workers, and shareholders, but in the process causes air pollution that imposes a cost on people who live in the neighborhood. In conventional economic analysis, the factory's production is socially beneficial if and only if the value of production exceeds all of its costs, including the costs of pollution. Ideally, this should be true both in terms of the total value and cost of production but also "at the margin." Thus, if the pollution increases as output increases, the scale of operation should not expand past the point where the value to society of the last unit of output is high enough to cover all of the costs of producing that unit, including the cost of the additional air pollution associated with it. Only then is the level of production "economically efficient." The challenge for the law is to ensure that the factory operates in accordance with these principles, at least as closely as possible.

Many types of law can in principle perform this function. A legislature or agency could determine whether production meets these conditions and order the factory to shut down or reduce production if it does not. Or the legislature might impose a tax on the factory equal to the value of the pollution that it creates, leaving to the factory owners the task of optimizing its scale thereafter, the owners having "internalized the externality" by bearing its costs. Similarly, pollution victims might be given a cause of action against any factory that pollutes. In a strict liability system, the victims would obtain damages equal to the harm suffered, so that the factory will again internalize the externality. In a negligence system, the victims would obtain damages only if the factory's operation was not cost-effective, producing similar incentives (if administered accurately). Or maybe the victims of pollution could obtain an injunction against the operation of the factory, and the factory owners would have to negotiate with them to purchase the right to continue operating, which would be possible only if its benefits exceed its costs. There are other variations—each with its own advantages and disadvantages.

The underlying principle here is that a person or firm should bear the full cost to society of his—or its—conduct. These costs include the harm done to others by externalities such as pollution. Indeed, pollution is the paradigm example of a "nonpecuniary externality," which means that the harmful effects are felt directly (as by breathing in polluted air) rather than through effects on prices. Such externalities, if not corrected, lead to inefficient market outcomes even in perfectly competitive markets. But if some legal mechanism of the sort described above induces agents to internalize these externalities, the market outcome will adjust to something approximating the efficient outcome.[1] Environmental law is the body of law that performs this function.

Externalities are by no means limited to pollution. Consider a lake that is used for various activities—for fishing and swimming, as a source of water, as a place to discharge waste. All of these uses can result in the lake being overexploited in such a way as to lower its value for future users, another kind of nonpecuniary externality. To keep the example simple, imagine that the lake is used only for fishing. As we will discuss in Chapter 17, when private fishermen have unrestricted access to the lake, they will tend to overfish, in the sense that they will deplete the stock of fish excessively because they do not take account of the fact that their fishing activity makes fish more scarce and thereby raises the cost of fishing to others. This class of problems is known as "common pool" problems (no pun) and arises with many types of commonly owned or unowned resources.

Once again, the government can solve the problem in various ways that restrict the amount of fishing. It might be sufficient to prohibit fishing during certain seasons or periods or to restrict the equipment that may be used to catch fish (poles, not drift nets). Or the government can require licenses and charge a price for them that reduces fishing to an appropriate level.

Application to States

A state with an adequate government may solve externalities and common pool problems within its borders, but may be unable or unwilling to address such problems when they cross borders. If, as seems plausible most of the time, governments act in the interests of their own populations (or subsets, such as elites) but do not care much about foreigners who have no vote or other source of local political influence, then they will permit domestic factories and other polluters to impose externalities on people living in other states. This behavior can occur in many ways. Factories placed on the border may spew pollutants into the air that will be inhaled by people on the other side of the border. Factories may dump waste into a river that flows across a border, contaminating the water supply of foreigners. Trawlers may overfish in the territorial sea or on the high seas, depleting a fishery that extends into the territorial sea of another state.

These problems are not always as serious as they might seem. States that care about the health of their own citizens will not want factories on the border to pollute the air if the wind can shift and send the pollution back. Some rivers wind back across the border at some other point. Interestingly, major international disputes about environmental pollution were rare before the twentieth century. The Trail Smelter case of 1941 was the first environmental pollution case ever to reach international arbitration.[2] But with the advance of technology and the spread of industrialization, cross-border pollution has become more severe and more detectable. Likewise, as incomes have risen, tolerance for pollution has declined and people are willing to spend more resources to abate it. States have responded by entering new treaties to control pollution.

Sic Utere Tuo

Let us begin, however, with customary international law on the environment. The maxim of *sic utere tuo ut alienum non laedas* ("use your own property so as not to injure another's") is a long-standing norm, or maybe just slogan, of customary international law. It seems to follow from the nature of sovereignty. If states have the right to control their own territory, and therefore not the territory of other states, then pollution-generating activities that affect people in a foreign state ought to be prohibited as violations of sovereignty. The principle was endorsed in bold form by an arbitral panel in the Trail Smelter case of 1941:

> no state has the right to use or permit the use of its territory in such a manner as to cause injury by fumes in or to the territory of another or the properties of persons therein, when the case is of serious consequence and the injury is established by clear and convincing evidence.[3]

The arbitration involved a Canadian plant that emitted pollution that crossed into the United States. The United States objected, and the two countries agreed to arbitrate. Trail Smelter seems to lay down a broad prohibition on activity that causes transboundary harms. But its holding has generated little enthusiasm among states—so little, in fact, that no further such arbitrations have occurred since then.

The problem with the sic utero rule, as reflected in the Trail Smelter holding, is that the state on which, say, a factory is located is regulating its own territory and not purporting to regulate the territory of another state. The polluting state could just as well regard the victim state's insistence that the polluting state shut down the factory as a violation of its—the polluting state's—sovereignty. The factory produces some benefit, B, for the polluting state and some cost, C, for the victim state. Why should the polluting state give up B in order to eliminate C? Here we see again the tension contained in the concept of sovereignty, a tension that arises whenever activity in one state affects people in another state. Sovereignty implies both that the first state has the legal right to engage in such activity and that the second state has the legal right to be free from its effects.

Indeed, the Stockholm Declaration on the Human Environment of 1972 endorses both the sic utero rule (states must ensure "that activities within their jurisdiction and control do not cause damage to the environment of other States") and its opposite (states have the right "to exploit their own resources pursuant to their own environmental policies").[4]

The tension is easy to understand. A rule that banned all cross-border pollution would not be socially optimal because some activities that create cross-border pollution nevertheless have benefits that exceed the costs in a global sense. An efficient rule would permit pollution to that extent. Thus, a ban on all pollution would be a mistake, whereas a rule requiring compensatory damages might make sense.

Such a rule does not yet exist in customary international law. The International Law Commission made an effort to develop a general rule that would be acceptable to states. Article 3 of the Draft Articles on the Prevention of Transboundary Harm from Hazardous Activities provides,[5] not very helpfully, the following:

> The State of origin shall take all appropriate measures to prevent significant transboundary harm or at any event to minimize the risk thereof.

The wiggle words here—"appropriate," "significant," "minimize"—leave plenty of room for disagreement. One could certainly read into these words a cost-benefit analysis. Measures are "appropriate" if the costs are less than the loss discounted by the risk of loss (and Article 2(a) suggests that such an expected-harm approach is correct). But the language admits of other interpretations, and the states said "thanks but no thanks" rather than adopting the draft articles.

In lieu of adopting such a general rule of international environmental law, states have instead negotiated hundreds of treaties governing different aspects of the environment. One example is the multilateral Convention on Long-Range Transboundary Air Pollution,[6] which has fifty-one parties. The treaty itself mainly provides for information sharing and erects a number of procedural mechanisms for cooperation; its substance is largely hortatory. Its eight protocols, however, are more substantive; the 1985 Helsinki Protocol provides that

> The Parties shall reduce their national annual sulphur emissions or their transboundary fluxes by at least 30 per cent as soon as possible and at the latest by 1993, using 1980 levels as the basis for calculation of reductions.[7]

One imagines that this rule resulted from a rough cost-benefit analysis. We conjecture that all the states believed that they were made better off by such a reduction but would not be by a greater reduction—presumably because, for one or more states, the costs of a greater reduction would exceed the benefits, and (possibly) side payments were not possible.

Plainly, this rule and other real-world rules do not endorse the type of absolute prohibition in the Trail Smelter case. One question is why states cannot agree to a more general treaty term that prohibits cost-unjustified pollution while permitting cost-justified pollution. A possible answer is that such a rule would require a dispute resolution system to administer it, and perhaps states cannot conceive of an international mechanism that would operate acceptably in this regard, free of bias and excessive error. States instead prefer to negotiate specific targets or limits on the basis of the costs and benefits and then monitor each other for violations.

Montreal Protocol

The most important and successful environmental treaty is the Montreal Protocol on Substances That Deplete the Ozone Layer.[8] In the early 1970s, scientists discovered that chlorofluorocarbons, compounds used in aerosols, refrigerators, and other common products, leak into the air and damage the stratospheric ozone layer, which protects people from some of the harmful effects of the sun. Subsequently, scientists discovered an ozone "hole" over Antarctica and neighboring regions, including a portion of southern Chile. These events galvanized public opinion in the United States, and domestic regulation of chlorofluorocarbons was implemented. But restrictions on the use of chlorofluorocarbons in the United States alone could not stop destruction of stratospheric ozone. The ozone layer is a commons, and if the United States alone restricted use, the essential problem would remain because emissions in other countries would continue to deplete the commons. Under U.S. leadership, countries agreed to the Montreal Protocol, which instituted strict limits on the use of chlorofluorocarbons and related ozone-damaging gases.

Although ozone destruction presents what looks like a classic collective action problem, several factors proved auspicious for the production of a treaty.[9] First, the United States conducted a cost-benefit analysis and discovered that Americans would benefit even from unilateral action. Industry was able quickly to invent cheap substitutes for chlorofluorocarbons, so the cost of regulation was low. The benefits—mainly in the form of avoided skin cancers, which can be lethal—were high. Although the benefits would be even higher if other states joined in, unilateral action was in American self-interest.

Second, as noted, the costs of restriction for other countries were relatively low as well. Most countries did not produce or use chlorofluorocarbons in any significant quantity. The European countries did, and they were initially reluctant to join a treaty but were later persuaded. Accordingly, negotiations involved a relatively small number of countries with a history of cooperating with each other. Developing countries could be paid off at low cost—they were promised technical assistance or access to technologies that did not produce or use chlorofluorocarbons.[10]

Climate Treaties

The most significant environmental challenge of our time is posed by the gradual warming of the earth's atmosphere, which most climate scientists believe to be the result of the emission of carbon dioxide and other greenhouse gases into the atmosphere. Temperature and other features of the global climate reflect complicated interactions between energy coming from the sun, elements of the atmosphere, and the oceans and other parts of the earth. You can think of the atmosphere as a commons that absorbs carbon (as well as the other gases). Like a fishery, the commons can be overexploited. That is what the climate science community believes has happened. Industrial pollution has overwhelmed the atmosphere's (and the oceans' and forests') capacity to absorb carbon, with the result that now temperatures are rising. As they rise, glaciers and Arctic ice melt, oceans rise, and weather patterns change. Flooding and other hazards have already killed people and destroyed property; as these hazards worsen, nations will need to invest enormous resources to build sea walls, relocate towns, absorb migrations, and so forth.

The erosion of the atmospheric commons poses a classic collective action problem for states. Lax regulation that permits citizens of a particular state to burn fossil fuels in excessive quantities causes harm to citizens in other nations as a result of the accumulation of greenhouse gases. All nations would be better off if they curtailed greenhouse gas emissions; but because each nation internalizes only some of the benefits of emission reduction, it is insufficiently motivated to regulate. To solve the collective action problem, states need to agree to a treaty that obliges states to cut back on emissions and restrict land use.

States recognized this problem and in 1992 agreed to the United Nations Framework Convention on Climate Change (UNFCC),[11] which set the stage for the Kyoto Protocol,[12] which went into force in 2005. The UNFCC set up some institutions for gathering and disseminating information about climate change and established a scaffolding for negotiations on the climate problem itself. These negotiations proved to be extremely difficult. The Kyoto Protocol finally put limits on emissions and other activities with adverse climate effects, but it excluded developing nations from these limits even though several of them were on the verge of becoming top emitters (indeed, China's emissions now exceed those of any other country), the United States refused to ratify it, and many parties to the Protocol have not lived up to their obligations. Negotiations continued, and in a convention at Copenhagen in 2009, most major emitters agreed to place undefined limits on their emissions in a nonbinding agreement that had no legal effect. Negotiations continue but in an atmosphere of increasing gloom. At the latest 2010 UN Climate Summit, Japan, Russia, and Canada were particularly reluctant to accept any future cuts in carbon emissions.[13]

Why has it been so difficult to negotiate a satisfactory climate treaty? What makes this type of treaty so much more difficult to negotiate than the Montreal Protocol? There are several answers to these questions.

First, although something approaching a scientific consensus exists to the effect that human activity has caused global warming, there is a great deal of uncertainty about the details—precisely how high temperatures will rise, and how rapidly, and to what extent people will be able to adjust to the changed climate. It is also quite unclear how much any given reduction in carbon emissions will affect the time path of temperatures. Some commentators also argue that various geoengineering options that inject sun-reflecting material into the atmosphere may be cheaper than emissions abatement. These details matter for states, which must decide how much they are willing to incur in the form of higher energy costs today in order to avoid future losses that are to some extent speculative. Many developing states simply see current needs—to address poverty, crime, and disorder—as more urgent than the climate.

Second, it has become increasingly clear that climate change will hurt some nations more than others. It is even possible that some nations (such as Russia) will gain. Climate change hurts poor southern states more than wealthier northern states because in the north the climate will become more temperate, whereas in the south it will become more extreme. Richer states can also adjust more easily to climate change than poor states. Relocating people, building sea walls, and converting agricultural land requires money, which the north has and the south lacks. The differential impact of climate change can make bargaining more difficult. States are unlikely to agree to uniform obligations; a better approach would be to vary obligations from state to state, or side payments will need to be arranged, so that all states believe that a treaty is in their interest.[14]

Third, a great deal of ill feeling has arisen over this topic. The developing world blames the developed world for climate change, and it is true that the stock of greenhouse gases in the atmosphere comes mostly from the developed world. Partly for this reason, and partly based on "ability to pay," the developing world believes that richer nations should bear more of the cost of abatement. But the developed world has never been particularly generous with foreign aid and rightly points to the fact that developing nations such as China and India are major greenhouse gas emitters. Without serious participation by the developing world, cutbacks in the developed world may be ineffective.

Finally, difficult technical problems will need to be solved. It is not clear that greenhouse gas emissions can be reliably monitored and controlled (or that countries like China will agree to monitoring) or that the elaborate cap-and-trade schemes that have been proposed can work as intended (European experience with such a scheme suggests pessimism on this score, as does recent work suggesting that the Kyoto Clean Development Mechanism has been "gamed" by nations claiming saleable credits for abatements that are phony).[15] Never before in human history have governments been able to cooperate successfully in such a complex and uncertain scheme that will require constant and swift modification as science progresses and experience accumulates to reveal unforeseen problems. Perhaps some dramatic events (like the Ganges running dry for a season) will galvanize public opinion and global action, but at this writing there is not a lot of basis for optimism.

17

The Law of the Sea

The law of the sea derives from an array of treaties and customary norms dating back centuries.[1] The United Nations Convention on the Law of the Sea (UNCLOS) represents an effort to codify and to some extent reform the law of the sea for the modern era.[2] UNCLOS has been ratified by most major nations, but the United States remains a holdout.

UNCLOS is among the most significant developments in international law of the last half-century. States traditionally sought to maintain international order by dividing the world and assigning exclusive or quasi-exclusive regulatory authority over areas to the states with the power to control them. States were given authority over their territory and internal waters and a small band of territorial sea. The large tracts of ocean over which no state could assert control were for the most part not subject to the jurisdiction of any particular state. Each state had the right to use the seas and to exercise jurisdiction over ships of its flag and the duty to ensure that its freedoms were exercised with reasonable regard for the exercise of high seas freedoms by other states. The resulting regime of open access to natural resources was tolerable as long as the oceans were effectively an inexhaustible resource. But population growth, technological change, and economic development have increased demand for the ocean's resources to the extent that overexploitation and congestion have become serious problems; in the meantime, advances in marine technology have made control over larger portions of the ocean possible. States have responded by extending authority over larger portions of the waters and seabed and subsoil, albeit subject to certain rights of other states, and by trying to create international mechanisms for the regulation of areas and activities beyond the control of individual states, an effort that has had notable achievements with respect to safety of navigation and overflight.

This chapter examines the most important features of UNCLOS.[3] In brief, we argue that UNCLOS represents a broadly sensible response to a wide range of externality problems that arise when nations engage in activities at sea. Regulatory jurisdiction is for the most part allocated to nations that value it the most or can exercise it most cheaply. Constraints on jurisdiction respond to externalities that arise when regulators tend to ignore the welfare of other nations. International cooperation on regulatory matters is encouraged and facilitated where national regulation alone is inadequate.

The Economic Rationale for an International Law of the Sea

International externalities are a commonplace with activities at sea. The sea contains a wealth of valuable resources, including food, minerals, energy, and materials for bioresearch. To the degree that such resources are unowned until some actor asserts dominion over them, they are "common pool resources."

The exploitation of common pool resources can create some important and familiar negative externalities. First, assume that resources in a common pool are available to any actor who can capture them and that no actor can secure control of the entire common pool. Put differently, users can lay claim to a "flow" of resources from the pool but not to the pool itself (to the "stock" of resources). For example, a fishing enterprise may take ownership of any fish that it can catch in a setting where no one owns the fishery as a whole. Yet the consumption of the resource by one actor raises the cost to other actors of obtaining the resource. To use the fishing example once again, fishing by one enterprise will generally reduce the stock of fish and thus make it more costly for another enterprise to secure a catch of given size. The effect on the costs of other enterprises is an externality. Users of a common pool resource will maximize their own returns from exploiting the resource without regard to the increased costs imposed on others. The result is overexploitation of the resource—the marginal private benefit of consuming the resource will be equal to the marginal private cost of capturing it, which is below the marginal social cost.

A second and closely analogous problem with common pool resources goes under the rubric of "excessive search." The externality that leads to overexploitation of a resource arises when multiple enterprises compete for the flow of resources from a common pool. It would not arise if the common pool had a single owner—that is, it does not arise when a single entity has the right to the entire "stock" of the resource contained in the common pool. But an equivalent externality problem does arise when multiple enterprises compete for the right to become the single owner. In particular, when ownership of a common pool is given to the enterprise that is first to discover it, the result will often be overinvestment in search for common pool resources. In general, enterprises will invest in search up to the point where the marginal cost of additional search is equal to the marginal expected return. Suppose in this regard that the number of enterprises is so large that marginal returns to search and the average returns appear to converge. Suppose further that each relatively small enterprise can purchase inputs into the search process at a fixed price. Each enterprise will then expand its search for new resources to the point where the costs of exploration are equal to the average expected return. As in the classic common pool situation, the value of the resource is fully dissipated—the expected returns from search (in expectation) are equal to the value of the resources expended on search.[4] As we will see, this problem applies straightforwardly to undersea resources such as minerals in the seabed.

The sea is also a means of transportation, which can become subject to congestion and navigational hazards. In addition, various activities that endanger life or property, or that undermine government efforts to regulate on land or to protect territory, occur at sea. These activities include shipboard crimes, piracy, smuggling, and espionage. The sea is also the locus of important military activity. With some of these activities, externalities arise because the activities of one government interfere with those of another. In other cases, the dilemma lies with a kind of "free rider" problem and an attendant lack of incentive on the part of governments to control the harmful acts of individuals. Again, international cooperation is required to address such issues.

Implications: The Role of Government and International Cooperation

The simple economic points developed above assume that rational private actors pursue their own economic interests without regard to the interests of other actors. Conceivably, as highlighted in the work of Elinor Ostrom, private actors may overcome the resulting externality issues through voluntary cooperation.[5] Perhaps the fishing enterprises that exploit a particular fishery will voluntarily agree to limit fishing, for example. But in many cases, voluntary private cooperation will be too difficult to orchestrate or enforce, and a role for government arises.

In cases where private actors compete for the flow of resources from a common pool, governments may be able to increase the value of the resource by restricting the rate at which the resource can be consumed. Governments may restrict fishing hours or the volume of the catch in a fishery, restrict the rate at which oil can be withdrawn from an oilfield, and the like. Similarly, with respect to marine pollution, governments may restrict or prohibit polluting activity.

Governments may also devise a single owner solution in some cases, as by auctioning off the mineral rights for an entire oil or gas field on public lands to the highest bidder. As noted, a single owner structure will generally lead private actors to maximize the value of a known common pool resource.

Analogous possible solutions exist for the problem where multiple enterprises compete for ownership of undiscovered resources and as a result overinvest in search. Governments may restrict the right to search to only a few enterprises or a single enterprise, perhaps by administering an area of potential discoveries as public lands.

Of course, any government solution to these problems is costly. The costs of creating and enforcing the regime must be considered, as must the costs of resources that may be dissipated by private enterprises that lobby to affect the regime. In some cases, government intervention may be more costly than it is worth.

More important for our purposes, however, the difficult tradeoffs that must be confronted in the management of common pool resources will often be a purely domestic affair. Perhaps overfishing in Lake Okeechobee is a problem, for example, but it is unlikely to materially affect the welfare of nations other than the United States, and we would not expect international law to address it, apart perhaps from more general environmental concerns such as protection of endangered species.[6] When the geographic scope of a common pool resource is confined to the territory of a single nation, international externalities often do not arise.

Resources at sea, however, are by definition outside the land territory of any individual nation. This observation suggests an immediate rationale for international cooperation on two margins.

First, nations (and their citizens) may assert competing claims to the common pool resources of the sea. The United States may claim the right to all oil and gas discovered within x miles of the U.S. coastline, for example, and other nations may dispute that claim. International cooperation is thus valuable to resolve competing claims over resources. Absent a resolution of these claims, costly international conflicts can arise, and the costs of private exploitation may increase as well due to uncertainty about the locus of regulatory authority. And even if conflict does not result, unresolved competing claims are themselves manifestations of the common pool problem. Each actor will seek to maximize the value of the resource to itself, without regard to the costs imposed on other parties with competing claims. Overexploitation of the resource will follow, under circumstances in which no government has the generally recognized authority to abate it.

Second, circumstances will arise in which no government can or will claim appropriate jurisdiction over the entire common pool. This situation may arise because the resource lies in an area over which no nation wishes to claim jurisdiction, or because the resource is mobile across geographic areas under the jurisdiction claimed by different nations. In either instance, the fundamental common pool problem reemerges.

In the first case, where no government claims jurisdiction over a resource, private actors may overexploit the resource as they compete for the flow of returns or may invest excessive amounts in search for a resource over which they can assert dominion privately. In some instances, the global costs of abating these problems may exceed the benefits. But in other cases, global gains from controlling the rate of exploitation or search may be possible, yet no nation undertakes the task because of a free-rider problem—the nation that regulates the resource will bear the costs of regulating, but the benefits will flow in part to others. Here international cooperation can enable nations to share the costs of regulation appropriately, or can create an international regulatory authority, to abate the free-rider issue.

Now consider the second case, where a resource is mobile across the jurisdiction of different countries. Such mobility is characteristic of much marine life and of the sea itself. Here a common pool problem arises for a somewhat different reason. Each nation will tend to maximize the value of the resource to itself without regard to the adverse effects on other nations who wish to exploit the same resource. If salmon migrate between the waters of the United States and Canada, for example, and even if both nations undertake self-interested fishery regulation with respect to salmon, regulators may tend to ignore the fact that local salmon fishing (say, in Canada) increases the costs of salmon fishing elsewhere (say, in the United States). Again, the tendency will be toward overfishing, and cooperation between the two nations can usefully address the problem. As another example, if marine pollution in waters under the jurisdiction of the United States travels north to Canada, the United States may tend to underregulate pollution in the waters that it controls. Again, international cooperation to establish higher pollution standards may be warranted.

Proximity as a Basis for Resolving Competing Claims: The Territorial Seas

To recapitulate, common pool issues of one sort or another arise with respect to all of the valuable resources of the sea—fisheries, undersea oil and gas, seabed minerals, and the sea itself. As indicated, the potential role for international cooperation (and for UNCLOS) in relation to these issues is threefold: to minimize and resolve competing claims between states (and their nationals) over resources; to encourage and facilitate international cooperation when governments decline to engage in optimal regulation because of free-rider problems; and to improve the quality of regulation when common pool resources are mobile across jurisdictions. Of course, it remains to be seen how well UNCLOS succeeds at these tasks.

With respect to the first of them—the avoidance and resolution of competing claims—we shall see that the most important guiding principle in UNCLOS is the proximity of the resource to the claimant. The approach of UNCLOS to the natural resources of territorial seas, in particular, is to award regulatory control to the coastal state (including the power to create private property rights). The logic is straightforward. Territorial seas are close and easier to patrol, and at least their living resources are comparatively cheap to exploit for nearby actors. As a rule of thumb, the state in closest proximity to the resources will have a cost advantage in exploiting the resources and in regulating to prevent overexploitation or excessive search. Coastal states thus have strong incentives to make rules for them and to enforce those rules.

Not only is an allocation of authority to the coastal states likely to be the most efficient option, it is also likely essential if international cooperation regarding the allocation of jurisdiction is to be stable. In general, cooperation will not arise unless nations gain more from cooperation than from opting out of it. For the reasons just given, if nations were denied authority over resources proximate to their coast (over which they could probably exert physical control anyway) under any proposed international arrangement, they would likely conclude that participation in the international arrangement was unattractive.[7]

Of course, proximity cannot be the sole consideration in the choices that must be made by a treaty like UNCLOS. In some instances, resources may be located close to the coasts of multiple nations. Some reasonable basis for dividing them must be fashioned that will be acceptable to all participants. Similarly, common pool resources may straddle the resulting dividing lines, necessitating further cooperation.[8]

One must also ask, "how close is close?" Beyond a certain distance, proximity to the coast may become a poor proxy for which nation can regulate most cheaply. Moreover, it would be a mistake to suppose that the proper geographic scope of regulatory jurisdiction is the same for all resources. The capacity to monitor activities and enforce regulations may vary considerably according to the nature of the resource—it may be far easier to detect and prevent unacceptable offshore drilling at long distances, for example, than to detect and prevent unauthorized fishing at such distances. As shall be seen, these considerations come into play in various aspects of UNCLOS.

Distant Resources and the High Seas

As noted, the approach taken by UNCLOS to the territorial seas is akin to the assignment of private property rights in land. An alternative approach to regulation, however, is analogous to open access regimes that are subject to a set of rules that all actors must obey. For example, a government might allow anyone to enter a lake and catch fish but subject them to regulations governing how many fish they catch, the equipment they use, and so forth. UNCLOS takes this general approach to the resources of the high seas. The resources of the high seas are generally subject to open access, yet states must obey certain rules in the navigation of the high seas[9] and the exploitation of its resources.[10]

Why does UNCLOS create an open access regime (subject to regulation) for the high seas while creating a limited-access regime for territorial seas? There are several possible reasons. First, the cost of patrolling across vast distances is surely a factor, even if satellite technology and other advances are reducing this cost. States may be reluctant to expend the resources necessary to exert jurisdiction over the high seas unless the gains are very high. Second, until recently, seabed resources at great depths and distances from shore could not be exploited profitably; this has been changing, and many such resources now fall within coastal state jurisdiction pursuant to the expansive definition of the continental shelf in UNCLOS as extending either to 200 miles or to the edge of the continental margin, whichever is farther seaward. Third, the environmental costs of activities farther out to sea are not (yet) perceived to be as serious as those that occur close to shore. Fourth, in the case of safety of navigation on the high seas, regulation is generally self-enforcing because all parties have a mutual interest in avoiding collisions, and rules for identifying ships and other rules that facilitate navigation do not pose difficult distributional problems.

Of course, the result will be highly imperfect. While UNCLOS requires conservation of high seas resources, and while that obligation is subject to compulsory arbitration or adjudication, it cannot in itself solve some of the thorniest common pool problems like overfishing, discussed below; this requires precisely targeted regulation, careful monitoring, and effective enforcement by governments.

Other Externality Issues

The law of the sea must confront a variety of additional issues that go beyond conventional common pool problems but that nevertheless involve situations in which the actions of one nation can have an adverse impact (create negative externalities) for others. One can again divide cases into situations in which the activities of nations at sea conflict in some way and cases in which problems arise at sea that no nation has adequate incentive to address acting unilaterally.

The clearest example of the first type of situation is the conflict between international navigation and the desire of nations to protect themselves against activities that infringe their resource rights or territorial integrity. Such activities include smuggling, illegal immigration, and poaching of resources. As we suggested above, it is natural to allocate jurisdiction over such matters closely proximate to a coastline to the coastal state. But the coastal state might respond by prohibiting foreign vessels from passing near its coast or near an area containing resources that it controls. Such policies can increase the costs of navigation considerably, and some mechanism must be devised to accommodate this tension.

Accordingly, regulatory rights in territorial seas are not absolute. States have general discretion to regulate natural resources but cannot, for example, deny certain navigation rights and freedoms to other states. This pattern has a simple explanation. We have already suggested why every state likely values the resources of its territorial sea more than any other state. But states also value freedom of navigation, which reduces the costs of commercial activity at sea and is also important to a variety of military and security objectives. As long as vessels in transit take measures to avoid the creation of congestion hazards and harms such as pollution, freedom of navigation imposes few costs on coastal states while conferring substantial benefits and is thus efficient. Yet if coastal states were allowed to regulate without any restriction, they might restrict navigation by foreign ships extensively or even prohibit it, perhaps out of stated concerns for security, pollution, and so forth. International cooperation to prevent the imposition of such externalities, while attending to the legitimate concerns of coastal states, is valuable.

Crimes at sea offer examples of situations that straddle the two classes of problems delineated above—sometimes multiple nations will wish to exercise jurisdiction over the purported criminal, and in other instances no nation may have an adequate incentive to act against the criminal. A shipboard homicide is a possible example of the first situation, in which multiple nations may claim an interest based on the nationalities of the ship, criminal, and victim and the geographic location of the crime. Other crimes such as piracy in the open ocean may attract no government action—the nation from which the offending ship emanates may have little interest in punishing a crime that benefits its nationals, and those harmed by such crimes may face a substantial free-rider problem in patrolling the oceans to prevent incidents of piracy. In both types of situations, it is in the interest of the international community to allocate jurisdiction over the criminal act to the nation that can most cheaply take cost-effective steps to deter crime,[11] and if necessary to provide an incentive for that nation to exercise its jurisdiction. It may also behoove nations to encourage cooperative efforts to overcome the free-rider problem. It remains to be seen how effective UNCLOS may be in addressing such potential problems of underenforcement.[12]

The UN Convention on the Law of the Sea

UNCLOS divides the seas into zones over which states have greater or lesser authority. At one extreme are lakes and rivers, over which a state has exclusive control, just as it does over its landmass. At the other extreme are high seas, over which no state may claim sovereignty. In between, as we will see, a state's right to control activities on or under water decreases as distance from the coast increases. There are certain bodies of water close to the coast over which the coastal state has sovereignty, such as bays, which are treated as internal waters like lakes and rivers, and the territorial sea, which forms a belt that projects up to twelve nautical miles from the coast or coastal baselines. In the territorial sea, there is a right of innocent passage for all ships and a more liberal right of transit passage for all ships and aircraft where the territorial sea overlaps a strait used for international navigation. Beyond the territorial sea, the coastal state may exercise more limited authority in the contiguous sea, which may extend another twelve miles; in the exclusive economic zone (EEZ), which may extend up to 200 miles from the coastal baselines (approximately 188 miles from the twelve-mile limit of the territorial sea); and in the continental shelf, which may extend to the outer edge of the continental margin or at least to 200 miles from the coastal baselines.

The High Seas

The starting point for our discussion is the high seas. Under UNCLOS the entire regime of the high seas applies to those portions of sea that are not included in the EEZ, the territorial and inland waters, and archipelagic waters.[13] The high seas are governed by the classic principle of freedom of the seas, which goes back to the seventeenth century. UNCLOS specifies that the freedom of the high seas includes, inter alia,

(a) freedom of navigation;
(b) freedom of overflight;
(c) freedom to lay submarine cables and pipelines, subject to Part VI;
(d) freedom to construct artificial islands and other installations permitted under international law, subject to Part VI;
(e) freedom of fishing, subject to the conditions laid down in section 2;[14]
(f) freedom of scientific research, subject to Parts VI and XIII.[15]

The freedom of the seas establishes an open access regime. It therefore raises a puzzle. If open access regimes are overexploited, why would international law create one?

To resolve this puzzle, we need to consider the alternatives. The principle of freedom of the seas arose as a reaction to attempts by powerful states to claim exclusive control over vast swaths of the oceans. One alternative, then, would be to carve up the oceans among all states in the same way that (almost) all territory has been carved up and assigned to states. Such a regime would surely produce constant conflict as some states would be tempted to sends ships across and exploit resources in areas over which other states have jurisdiction but no real control. Another alternative would be to subject the oceans to the jurisdiction of some kind of international authority. A final alternative would be to give states overlapping jurisdiction over activities on the high seas.

Freedom of the seas might best be understood as reflecting the assumption that no country has an interest in attempting exclusive control of the oceans except along the coasts. The cost of enforcing assertions of jurisdiction over foreign ships in remote ocean spaces is just too high. Originally, freedom of the seas reflected both a preoccupation with navigation access and a judgment that states either do not have the capability or would prefer to avoid expending the resources necessary to secure global lines of trade and communication against interference from other states. Mutual agreement not to engage in such interference therefore served the interest of global cooperation. The logic can be extended to protection of fishing and other forms of resource extraction. There may be some limits to this proposition as we will see, but in general it seems correct.

In addition, freedom of the seas originally may have reflected the view that overexploitation of portions of the oceans remote from the coasts is not a serious problem. Given the vastness of the areas and their resources, congestion and overexploitation are at most limited problems, and laws are of limited utility. Moreover, states would have weak incentives to enact and enforce any desirable laws, so that states with exclusive jurisdiction would often fail to act.

Rather than assign jurisdiction over portions of the high seas to states, UNCLOS lays down a set of basic rules that reduce the risk of conflict that might occur on the high seas. It imposes a general duty to have due regard to the interests of other states and some more particular rules that, among other things, require ships to send signals that identify their locations and take other steps to minimize the risk of collision.[16] These rules are essentially self-enforcing for the reasons discussed in Chapter 3. A ship from state X benefits by making itself visible to a ship from state Y, because both the ship from state X and the one from state Y would be harmed by a collision. Where the means of making oneself visible to others involves a choice among technologies (such as radio bands), it is in everyone's interest to use whatever technology everyone else uses, and the relevant actors can coordinate on a standard. Thus, enforcement of the rules of the road on the high seas is not a serious challenge.

A more ambitious set of rules for the high seas—for example, rules that protect fisheries against possible overfishing—poses a more significant challenge because it would require states to expend resources with the expectation that other states do the same. But if it is extremely costly to monitor and patrol the high seas, as we have suggested, it will also be difficult for states to prevent free riding and defections from any rule-based regime. We will say more about these issues in connection with fisheries (and whaleries) below.

UNCLOS does grant states the authority to regulate ships that fly their flags and the conduct of those on board. This rule can be given two justifications. First, to the extent that the ship has connections with the state whose flag it flies (for example, if the crew and passengers are nationals of that state, or the ship's home port lies on the coast of that state), the state has both an interest in regulating the ship and the capacity to enforce regulations (inasmuch as relevant people and assets are likely to be located on the state's territory when not on the ship). Second, to the extent that states make their flags available to ships owned and operated by foreigners, the rule still makes clear which state is responsible for order on the ship without regard to the nationality of those on board. Those at risk of being harmed know which state to ask for help. When ships collide, the flag states and states of which the accused officers or crew members are nationals have overlapping jurisdiction, which enables them to work out a solution without interference from other states.[17]

Other activities that take place on the high seas are of broader concern to a number of different states. These include slave trading, piracy, drug smuggling, and unlicensed broadcasting. UNCLOS regulates or prohibits these activities and gives warships from any country the right to stop and inspect ships suspected of engaging in piracy and the slave trade.[18] Here UNCLOS gives states overlapping enforcement authority but not unilateral legislative authority—the substantive rules that may be enforced by states other than the flag state are limited to those that states have agreed to in UNCLOS. This overlapping enforcement authority contrasts with the regime for run-of-the-mill criminal activity that occurs on ships, where flag states have legislative jurisdiction and exclusive authority over boarding and detention while the ship is on the high seas.

The differences in approaches to these subjects reflect a basic tradeoff discussed in Chapter 15. When states have exclusive legislative and enforcement authority, the risk of inconsistent policies is minimized, but states may also have an incentive to legislate and enforce in a way that is biased against other states. This risk is tolerable with respect to crimes that may occur on board; after all, foreign passengers and crew can avoid ships that fly the flags of states that they do not trust. In the case of an activity such as piracy, by contrast, the activity affects the interests of many states simultaneously, and here the limits of unilateral enforcement come into play—any state with exclusive jurisdiction over a particular act of piracy, say, may have inadequate incentive to expend the costs necessary to address it. Overlapping jurisdiction can enhance the chances that some state will be moved to act, though, to be sure, overlapping jurisdiction would not solve the collective action problem, because states may still have inadequate incentives to take account of the interests of other states. For piracy, the risk of inconsistent policies or parochial bias is limited inasmuch as the basic substantive rules have been hammered out in the treaty. Some risk may remain at the enforcement level, but it is tolerated because of the importance of increasing the chances that some state will find it in its interest to act against piracy.

Inland Waters, the Territorial Sea, the Contiguous Zone: Baselines, Straits, and Archipelagic Waters

The territorial sea is the band of water, now up to twelve nautical miles wide, that lies off the coast of the state.[19] The territorial sea, unlike the high seas, is a zone of exclusive control of the state—in this way, identical to the treatment of the state's landmass—with one important exception. All other states have the right of innocent passage. This right includes the right to enter and navigate through the territorial seas, whether to traverse them or to reach a port of call; it extends to all ships, including commercial and military ships. States can regulate passage, for example, by designating sea lanes; but they cannot prohibit it unless the passage is not innocent, meaning that the ship engages in specified activities such as espionage, weapons exercises, smuggling, fishing, willful pollution, and the like.[20]

This treatment of territorial waters is consistent with our framework. Areas of the sea near the coast have high value to the coastal state—much higher than that of the high seas. Because the cost of transportation to the territorial sea is low, the value of fishing, research, mining, and similar activities is correspondingly high.[21] Similarly, coastal states can also easily patrol their territorial waters, enforce the law, and guard against foreign threats. Airplanes and helicopters can reach them from bases on the land; shore batteries can stand guard; the coast guard can operate from nearby ports.

Yet the right of innocent passage is clearly of great value to foreign states. Without an opportunity for innocent passage, ships would spend extra time and fuel circumnavigating large swaths of the sea as they travel from one place to another. At the same time, innocent passage imposes relatively limited costs on the coastal state: congestion (but limited because the ships may not dawdle) and the attendant risks of accident. Of course, if the right of innocent passage did not exist under international law, the attendant inefficiencies might be eliminated through bargaining—coastal states might charge tolls for entering their waters. But this solution is inferior—it would involve transaction costs and presumably would also be affected by inefficiencies associated with states' "market power" over the relevant area of the ocean. Such inefficiencies would arise whenever the fee charged for passage by a state exceeded the marginal cost to that state of permitting passage, which we have suggested is very low, and when ships responded to such fees by circumnavigating the area covered by the fee, thereby increasing the cost of navigation. A right of innocent passage reflects, in effect, a deal under which states give up their right to charge such fees in return for being spared having to pay the fees of other states, either directly or in terms of higher costs for movement of trade.

One might ask, why does international law recognize a right of innocent passage for territorial seas but not for land? After all, the two areas are otherwise subject to the same rules. The answer is surely that innocent passage could be much more easily abused, and pose greater burdens on the territorial state, if it were applied to the land. This is evident in the complex provisions of the Law of the Sea Convention regarding landlocked states' right of access to the sea.

Some of the most difficult questions that arise in connection with territorial seas concern the baselines for defining them. Coasts are not straight lines. They have indentations and projections; small and large islands are nearby; so are reefs; the tide ebbs and flows; rivers open out on them. UNCLOS contains a number of rules that stipulate the baseline in areas of ambiguity. Consider, for example, a convexity in the coastline. If it is relatively deep, it might be considered a bay. If the convexity is shallow, however, so that it offers nothing of value for shipping (protection from the weather on open seas) and is unlikely to be used for a port, it is unlikely to be considered a bay.

Bays and similar formations, like river mouths, are considered internal waters, and thus not even the right of innocent passage applies to them. The reason is plain. Foreign states do not need to traverse these areas in order to go from one place to another (except to ports in the bay or on the rivers, where entry can be denied anyway), so the value of such a right is low for foreign states. At the same time, these are sensitive and congested areas and thus suitable for maximum control by the coastal state. Interestingly, states generally permit foreign sovereigns to regulate the "internal economy" of ships at port (for example, employer-worker relations) and claim jurisdiction only when activities on the ship disturb the peace or in some other way cause harm to the state's interest (for example, smuggling and serious crimes).[22] In addition, where foreign states do have a strong interest in entering the waters in close proximity to a state's territory, the law provides for rights of innocent or transit passage. This comes up, for example, where a generalized system of straight baselines drawn to and between islands along coasts are used to enclose internal waters and similarly in the case of archipelagic waters. In the latter cases, in addition to innocent passage, the right of transit passage or of archipelagic sea lanes passage ensures that coastal states cannot block important types of navigation by claiming that islands enclose internal waters.[23]

Because the UNCLOS rules treat bays as part of internal waters, UNCLOS provides additional rules so that states do not opportunistically claim enormous portions of the oceans as bays.[24] A straight line is drawn across the bay; the territorial sea begins only at that point. Similar rules are used to handle reefs and the other geographic formations noted above.[25]

States' near-exclusive control over their internal waters and territorial seas has created special problems where these areas are unusually important for transit by other nations. This arises in two situations: straits and archipelagos. Straits are narrow passages that connect large bodies of water that contain areas where there is freedom of navigation and overflight, be they classic high seas or exclusive economic zones. Because the passages are narrow—they lie between bodies of land only a few miles apart—they are part of the territorial seas or internal waters of the state or states that control those bodies of land.

During the UNCLOS negotiations, naval and other maritime powers insisted that straits be subject to "the right to transit passage," rather than the right to innocent passage, in response to the extension of the territorial sea from three miles to twelve miles, which would enclose a number of existing straits. Innocent passage does not apply to aircraft and requires that submarines surface. It has an ambiguous history with respect to warships and is subject to unilateral regulation by the coastal state. This regime was not liberal enough to satisfy the naval powers and other maritime states. Accordingly, states agreed to transit passage, which means "navigation and overflight solely for the purpose of continuous and expeditious transit of the strait between one part of the high seas or an exclusive economic zone and another part of the high seas or an exclusive economic zone."[26]

A great deal can turn on whether a waterway is classified as a strait or not. The United States and Canada have long disputed whether the Northwest Passage, a route through Canada's northern archipelago that connects the Atlantic and Pacific oceans, constitutes a "strait used for international navigation." Canada argues that no legal strait exists; it claims that the waters constitute its historic internal waters through which there is no right of passage and, in any event, that the Northwest Passage was not traditionally used for international navigation. In its view, foreign vessels may traverse the Northwest Passage only with Canadian permission. The United States and other countries contest Canada's internal waters claim and argue that in any event the use of the strait for purposes of international navigation renders it a strait in which there is a right of transit passage through that strait. If a legal strait does exist, foreign vessels may travel through the Northwest Passage without Canadian permission, though they would be subject to unilateral Canadian pollution control regulations under a special provision regarding ice-covered areas that was negotiated with the Arctic specifically in mind.[27]

Until recently, the dispute was largely academic. The Northwest Passage was almost always frozen, so surface ships rarely used it. However, in recent years it has become clear that the ice will eventually retreat, and at that time the waterway will be navigable during substantial portions of the year. Canada has recently announced plans to patrol the Northwest Passage and to build a deepwater port, while the United States has said that it will continue to regard it as a strait.

We now consider the rules relating to the contiguous zone. The contiguous zone, aptly named, is a zone of water contiguous to the territorial sea. Like the territorial sea, its width is twelve nautical miles. In the contiguous zone, the coastal state may exercise the control necessary to

(a) prevent infringement of its customs, fiscal, immigration, or sanitary laws and regulations within its territory or territorial sea;
(b) punish infringement of the above laws and regulations committed within its territory or territorial sea.[28]

The coastal state's power over the contiguous zone is thus more limited than its power over its territorial seas. It has no power to legislate in that zone. But it does have the power to enforce. This arrangement is sensible. All states have a greater interest in freedom of navigation and overflight in the area. At the same time, coastal states have a weaker interest in regulating behavior in the contiguous zone than in the territorial seas because there is less congestion, and ships in that location pose less danger to the mainland. But in the absence of a contiguous zone, a state's coast guard would be powerless, for example, to intercept a suspected smuggler just outside the territorial sea absent agreement with the flag state.

Continental Shelf and Exclusive Economic Zone

Two further sets of rules extend coastal states' jurisdiction. First, article 77 gives coastal states exclusive rights to exploit the minerals and other natural resources in the continental shelf. The continental shelf comprises the

> seabed and subsoil of the submarine areas that extend beyond its territorial sea throughout the natural prolongation of its land territory to the outer edge of the continental margin, or to a distance of 200 nautical miles from the baselines from which the breadth of the territorial sea is measured where the outer edge of the continental margin does not extend up to that distance.[29]

The continental margin typically ends in a slope that reaches (and at times a rise formed by sedimentary rock that overlays) the deep seabed, which is thousands of feet deep. Beyond that point, underwater mountains, ridges, and other protuberances are not considered part of the continental margin. Numerous ambiguities arise because portions of a shelf might continue as a ridge that extends to the shelves of other coastlines, as in the case of the Lomonosov Ridge, which extends from Russia to Canada and Greenland.[30]

Jurisdiction over the continental shelf is defined functionally, unlike jurisdiction over the territorial sea: the state has exclusive control only for limited purposes, notably exploration and exploitation of natural resources of the seabed and subsoil. It has no control over the waters above the continental shelf unless they fall in some other designated zone. What distinguishes the continental shelf from the deep sea is that most exploitable deposits of hydrocarbons are likely to be found within the limits of the continental shelf as defined in UNCLOS. This creates the problem of potentially inefficient races to control those resources. Exclusive jurisdiction helps mitigate this problem.

Second, article 56(1) confers on coastal states similar exclusive rights for the EEZ, including

> rights for the purpose of exploring and exploiting, conserving and managing natural resources, whether living or non-living, of the waters superjacent to the seabed and of the seabed and subsoil, and with regard to other activities for the economic exploitation and exploration of the zone, such as the production of energy from the water, current and winds.[31]

The EEZ extends 200 miles from the baseline used to measure the territorial sea. All states continue to enjoy the high seas freedoms of navigation, overflight, and laying and maintenance of submarine cables and pipelines, and related uses, in the EEZ.

In addition to seabed resources, which are in any event covered by the continental shelf regime, the EEZ regime establishes coastal state exclusive jurisdiction over natural resources in the water column, notably fisheries. Coastal states have a stronger interest in these fisheries than foreign states do as well as a better capacity to regulate them—in both cases because coastal states have the advantage of proximity.

In the years following World War II, states made claims over the continental shelf, which were generally accepted,[32] and over the water column for fisheries or other purposes, which were often resisted. The famous "cod war" between Britain and Iceland erupted when Iceland claimed exclusive jurisdiction over fisheries twelve miles from shore. Eventually Britain accepted Iceland's claim, and gradually other states accepted fisheries' and EEZ claims that were not too aggressive.[33] These developments, later refined in UNCLOS, reflect the strong economic logic of giving states exclusive jurisdiction over resources in areas where states can control their use rather than treating these as open access resources.[34]

The melting of the Arctic Ocean has given rise to a similar set of developments. Growing access makes the resources both more valuable and easier to regulate. On August 2, 2007, a Russian minisub deposited a Russian flag on the seabed of the North Pole. The apparent purpose of this gesture was to dramatize a Russian claim to control of mineral resources over a large portion of the Arctic Ocean, extending from the north coast of Russia to the North Pole. Russia had submitted this claim to the Commission on the Limits of the Continental

Shelf created by UNCLOS, basing it on the theory that the Lomonosov Ridge, an underwater mountain range that extends from the Russian coast northward, was part of Russia's continental shelf. The Commission has made recommendations, but Russia need not accept them and can make a new submission. If Russia, or any other coastal state party to the Convention, ultimately does establish the limits of its continental margin on the basis of the Commission's recommendations, UNCLOS provides that the limits are final and binding to the extent that they determine that the area is continental shelf extending from the coast.[35] But that does not resolve the question of which parts are Russia's continental shelf rather than that of some other Arctic coastal state. If the Lomonosov Ridge is properly understood to be continental shelf, then Canada and Denmark (through Greenland) may have claims to part of it, and the coastal states concerned would have to agree on its delimitation pursuant to article 83 of UNCLOS.[36]

Critics argue that Russia's flag-dropping gesture was an anachronistic appeal to nineteenth-century norms of territorial conquest, and it is clear that the flag planting gives them no rights under international law. Others note that Russia has conformed to UNCLOS procedures for asserting claims to its portion of the seabed.[37] Whatever the true motivations of the Russians, parceling out ocean resources to coastal nations that can actually control them makes a great deal of sense, and Russia was essentially demonstrating that it had an interest in mining the resources under Arctic waters and the capacity to control those waters.

Division and the Equidistance Rule

A recurrent problem that extends across many of these different topics is that of dividing areas to which states have overlapping claims. If a body of water less than twenty-four miles wide divides two states, then their territorial seas overlap. Similar conflicts can arise over the EEZ and continental shelf and even inland waters—as when states share a bay. In all these cases, the states must divide jurisdiction over the resource.

Many states have used a simple equidistance rule to resolve these disagreements. The equidistance rule draws a line across the area in question, so that any point that is closer to one coastal state is deemed to be subject to that state's jurisdiction and control. The rule is not expressly mentioned in UNCLOS except with respect to the territorial sea, but it is popular as a matter of state practice and is increasingly used in judicial and arbitral decisions with respect to delimitation of the EEZ and the continental shelf under UNCLOS.[38]

There is nothing particularly fair about the equidistance rule, which does indeed favor states with convex coasts or small islands and disfavor states with concave coasts. The ICJ stressed this point in its first case delimiting the continental shelf.[39] But the same point can be made about virtually all the rules of the law of the sea, which make states' rights dependent on arbitrary features of their coastline such as its length; why is curvature more arbitrary than length?[40] Indeed, dozens of landlocked states have virtually no rights to the sea's vast coastal resources.[41] Accordingly, fairness does not provide much guidance here.[42] By contrast, the equidistance rule does have a good efficiency justification. Its location is easily determined. States that are closer to a portion of the sea are often in a better position to control it. By granting the closer state jurisdiction, the equidistance rule on average favors the state that can more cheaply regulate.

Deep Seabed

The deep seabed contains extensive hard mineral deposits. Although at present they are not exploited economically, and many of the same resources can be found on land and within EEZs, states have long believed that technology would eventually develop to the point that deep seabed exploitation would be economically advantageous. Since the 1970s, the developing states have tried to establish a principle that the deep seabed is the "common heritage of mankind" and therefore that the economic value of resources in the seabed should be shared among nations. Although industrial nations were prepared to accept the term *common heritage* and to share revenues, they objected to discretionary control by multilateral voting majorities.[43]

During the negotiations that led up to UNCLOS, an initial compromise provided for the creation of an international agency (the ominously named "Authority") and an international corporation (the "Enterprise") that would license and regulate exploration and exploitation of deep seabed minerals that lie beyond the broad limits of the continental shelf. Developing nations would receive royalties and technology transfers. After the United States balked, a new "Implementing Agreement," in effect an amending agreement, weakened the Authority (and strengthened influence of developed nations over it), eliminated advantages given to the Enterprise and perhaps in practice the Enterprise itself as originally conceived, and enlarged the freedom of private corporations to engage in mineral extraction without international interference.

The current regime, which was agreed to in 1994, can be described, briefly, as follows.[44] While both scientific research and prospecting are largely free of restrictions, private mining enterprises must obtain a license from the Authority before exploring and exploiting a particular area of the deep seabed, the portion of the seabed that lies outside of the jurisdiction of states under the other provisions of UNCLOS, namely, beyond the continental shelf. In order to obtain a license, the mining enterprises must be sponsored by a member state and show that they meet certain standards of technological and financial capacity. The original treaty required mining companies to transfer technology to the Enterprise and developing states. The 1994 revision eliminated this requirement but permits the Authority to "request" mining companies and their sponsoring States "to cooperate with it in facilitating the acquisition of deep seabed mining technology by . . . developing States on fair and reasonable commercial terms and conditions, consistent with the effective protection of intellectual property rights."[45] Some commentators have argued that this provision could conceivably be read to require some kind of forced albeit compensated transfer—with the amount of compensation to be determined by the Authority itself or by other relevant institutions and states.[46] However, there is no clear textual support for this position.[47]

When private mining enterprises seek the approval of the Authority for a plan of work, their application must identify two mining sites. The applicant would have the right to exploit the first; the second would be reserved for the Enterprise or developing states. (Initially, the Enterprise would be required to act through joint ventures; later it would operate as a stand-alone mining company, albeit subject to a prior right to a joint venture enjoyed by the applicant.[48]) The Authority may turn down applications for the following reasons: (1) the area has already been claimed by or assigned to another applicant; (2) the mining activities would cause significant harm to the marine environment; and (3) the applicant is sponsored by a state that has sponsored an excessive amount of mining activity. This last so-called antimonopoly clause relies on two alternative tests: the applicant's state sponsors activities covering 30 percent of a 400,000 square kilometer circle surrounding either of the two sites in the application, or those activities cover (roughly) 2 percent of the deep seabed area subject to the mining regime.[49]

Mining companies that are approved would be required to provide significant operational information to the Authority, so that it could ensure that they comply with the terms of their contract and do not violate regulations. The mining companies would have to pay an initial application fee and then annual royalties, which would be set by the Authority. Surplus revenues of the Authority and the Enterprise would be distributed to states on an "equitable" basis, with preference for developing states whose commodity exports compete with the products of seabed mining.

Overall, the deep seabed regime has three features that trouble its critics.[50] First, it provides for redistribution of wealth (arguably including intellectual property) to developing nations and others—as compared with a baseline where states (or their mining companies) kept whatever they exploited. Second, it imposes a number of restrictions on the free exercise of the market. Here the baseline would be a system in which the Authority merely recorded and enforced claims on a first-in-time basis, so as to prevent conflicting and overlapping claims. Technology transfer, antimonopoly rules, and the Enterprise would be unnecessary. Third, it creates an international bureaucracy dominated by developing countries, which would further strengthen the redistributive and regulatory themes of the UNCLOS by interpreting vague terms to promote those goals.

The interpretations of the text proffered by these critics are not accepted by most industrial states and experts in the field, notably on the grounds that the substantive and decision-making provisions of the 1994 Implementing Agreement largely eliminated the textual basis for such concerns. Thus, although economic analysis would support at least the second and third concerns in theory, the extent to which there is reason to fear that the Convention as modified by the 1994 Agreement could or would be interpreted and applied in a manner giving rise to such concerns is a different matter. Economic analysis can tell us that major producers and consumers of deep seabed minerals, as well as those benefiting from transfer payments in respect of deep seabed mining, have an interest in maximizing the efficiency of the system; but it can also tell us that land-based competitors do not share that interest, that the interest of beneficiaries of transfer payments may be too contingent and diffuse to have a significant impact on their policy preferences, and that states whose coasts and EEZs are exposed to potential environmental risks from deep seabed mining have an interest in imposing rules to minimize those risks.

As to the first concern, economic analysis usually puts questions of distribution to one side; there is no distinctive economic perspective on optimal distribution. From the perspective of general utilitarian ethics, as well as certain approaches to fairness, poor people should receive transfers of wealth from richer people, and it would seem to follow that poorer countries should receiver transfers from richer countries. Royalties and taxes are typically paid by mining companies to the states in whose territory and on whose continental shelf they operate. For these reasons, some form of redistribution may be defended.

Economic analysis can, however, distinguish better and worse forms of redistribution. Poorer states should prefer cash transfers to in-kind transfers, such as technology transfers and subsidization of the Enterprise. The reason is that poor countries can always use cash transfers to purchase intellectual property if that is in their interest; if it is not, they can put cash transfers to their best use, for example, to build medical clinics or schools. Moreover, expenditure and distribution of cash payments to the Authority by miners are subject to an effective veto by each of the principal industrial states on the Council of the Seabed Authority, which could mean that the funds are more likely to be used for widely supported aid purposes.[51] Most experts are of the view that the 1994 Implementing Agreement effectively eliminates mandatory technology transfer and subsidization of the Enterprise. The critics remain concerned with the potential for mischief in the persistence of references to technology transfer and the Enterprise.

There is no dispute that applicants must discover and transfer a second mining site. This is another inefficient form of taxation. This rule raises the applicants' prospecting costs without necessarily providing a benefit to anyone—it may turn out that the second site cannot be economically exploited once output from the first site enters the market.[52] If the second site can be economically exploited, it may turn out that the transferee is simply not an efficient mining company. To be sure, the text gives priority to the mining company that originally contributed the site, and the transferee could otherwise sell the site to an efficient mining company, but the extra transaction would itself be costly. If the purpose of the rule is to subsidize the Enterprise or redistribute wealth to developing nations, and this purpose is appropriate, then a cash tax would be a more efficient device.

As for the Enterprise, we cannot think of an efficiency justification for its creation. If the Enterprise competed with private mining firms on an equal basis, creating it would do no harm. In the unlikely event that it operated more efficiently than private firms, consumers would gain. In the more likely event that it operated less efficiently than private firms, it would be driven from the market and the only loss would be the costs of setting up the institution in the first place. However, it is possible that the Enterprise would not compete with private mining firms on an equal basis. If so, the Enterprise could survive in the market even if it is operated less efficiently than the private firms. This may be the source of the critics' concern that some kind of implicit (and inefficient) redistribution might take place; as noted before, there is no explicit textual support for this concern under the regime as modified in 1994.

The antimonopoly rule tries to prevent any single state (or a small group of states) from dominating the deep sea mining industry. From an economic perspective, a possible objection to this rule is that neither states nor miners would be given monopoly power in the economic sense because the types of commodities likely to be mined exist in international markets with multiple sources of supply. Commodities must be sold on the world market at market prices regardless of source. It also follows that the antimonopoly rule will not redistribute wealth to smaller states. In addition, to the extent that a few states develop special bureaucratic or legal expertise with respect to deep seabed mining so that they can effectively carry out their obligations under UNCLOS, it would be better to ensure that those states sponsor miners even at risk of "monopoly." However, none of this is to deny that there may be important symbolic and political purposes in ensuring that a few powerful states do not end up with excessive influence over the seabed; our limited point is that the economic benefits of the antimonopoly rule are hard to discern.

What remains of the technology transfer provisions is at best hortatory and unnecessary and at worst an invitation to impose another inefficient tax. If technology transfer takes place only at market prices, then a rule is not necessary—the transaction would occur without the rule. Unlike the original text, the Implementing Agreement does not impose a technology transfer obligation directly on private mining firms. But if, as some fear, technology transfer nevertheless could be forced, this would mean that the market price would not be paid. Private mining firms would underinvest in research and development if they must share the proceeds with others.

This brings us to the third set of concerns involving the institutional dimension of the seabed regime. Because no state has the power to control the deep seabed effectively given current technology, UNCLOS does not assign jurisdiction to states. In this sense, the seabed is like the open water subject to the freedom of the high seas, with the mining company's "sponsoring state" performing functions analogous to those of the flag state of a ship. But because exploitation is potentially economical down the road, there remains a potential problem of overuse—here, technically, the problem of excessive investment in search. Because no nation is the cheapest regulator of the deep seabed, an international authority, supported by all states, suggests itself as a natural alternative. An additional reason for such an authority is that states cannot agree on all rules for the exploitation of seabed minerals because of conflicting interests. Many issues are thus left to the international agency to resolve at a later date. The Authority established by UNCLOS has the power to determine the rules.

The problem with this approach is that there is no guarantee that the international agency will in the long run act in the interest of states in general. Treaty designers thus face some familiar tradeoffs. States will submit to an international agency's jurisdiction only if they expect the gains to be greater than their returns to opting out and enjoying the benefits of the pre-UNCLOS regime. For most states, the implicit "reservation price" is low or zero because they have no capacity to exploit underwater resources in the high seas—or it is highly uncertain, to the extent they envision rapid development or the possibility that they could attract mining companies as potential "flags of convenience." But for the United States, at least, the price is relatively high because it expects that its firms will eventually be able to exploit deep-sea resources. Accordingly, the United States and countries in its position need a guarantee that the Authority will not act against its interests. Only a unanimity rule or a veto right for the United States and similarly situated countries can provide clear assurance in this regard, but a unanimity rule would make decision making too difficult, and a veto right would enable the United States to demand an excessive share of the rents created by the legal regime. However, if other nations have veto rights, they can prevent mineral exploitation by Americans unless the United States makes concessions to them. The current compromise features a complex power-sharing arrangement. The Authority consists of an Assembly, where every state has one vote and a qualified majority rule prevails, although consensus is preferred; and a more powerful Council, which has thirty-six members, including representatives of the major interests in seabed mining. The Council, unlike the Assembly, must (generally) act by consensus.[53] This protects all major states but creates a risk of holdups and gridlock. Only time will tell whether the Council will promote economically justified or economically dubious applications of the regime.[54]

The three concerns articulated by the critics emphasize the risks of the latter outcome. However, it would be a mistake to conclude that the seabed regime of UNCLOS is necessarily a bad one on balance. On the benefit side, the seabed regime can clearly perform an important function by enabling mining firms to stake claims and thus obtain property rights in minerals in the deep seabed. Firms would do less in the way of duplicative search and exploitation efforts; this would both encourage research and avoid overexploitation of discovered resources. Many of the other rules, such as those that restrict damage to the marine environment, are also important.

In an ideal world, we might advocate a further revision of the rules to eliminate the inefficiencies noted above. A better approach would simply allow mining operations to establish clear property rights over exploitable seabed resources, much as governments have awarded rights to prospectors on land. Property rights over discrete areas of the seabed, awarded at a point in time before companies make excessive sunk investments in search, seem like the best way to provide proper incentives for exploitation.[55] To the degree that such a system would award excessive rents to developed countries from a distributive standpoint, some system for redistributing cash compensation to developing countries might be devised.

At this stage, however, we suspect that political realities preclude such a renegotiation. The various market restrictions and technology-transfer requirements have bought the assent of developing nations, and the mining authority has the ability to create property rights and regulate against abuses in a manner that improves on the potential chaos of a pure open access system. Despite its imperfections, it is important to recognize that the UNCLOS regime may be significantly better than none at all.

Likewise, we are skeptical of proposals for countries like the United States to enter a stripped-down seabed treaty with the handful of developed states that have firms capable of deep seabed mineral exploitation. To be sure, such an arrangement would cut out the developing countries and avoid any need to make transfers to them. Even if such an approach could be defended from a distributive standpoint, it would sacrifice the other benefits of UNCLOS and would be beset with its own economic weaknesses. Among other things, international capital is mobile, and mining companies could simply relocate to nonmember states if they wished to avoid the regulatory regime (much as shipping companies have at times avoided regulation by registering their ships with developing countries and flying their flags). Any regime that permitted such de facto "opt out" choices might accomplish little.

Fisheries

Fisheries (and whaleries) vary in their characteristics. Some fish occupy a relatively stable and confined area in the sea. Other fish migrate great distances. Certain species spawn in rivers and then head out to sea; other species go in the reverse direction. Some types of sea life are sedentary (like oysters) or crawl along the seabed (like lobsters).

UNCLOS handles some of the attendant issues in a straightforward fashion. Fisheries that fall entirely within the EEZ, territorial seas, or inland waters of a single state are subject exclusively to the regulation of that state. At least in theory, it should have the correct incentives to regulate the fishery. The UNCLOS regime does not mandate efficient regulation, of course, but simply empowers the single regulator to do what is necessary and trusts it to proceed appropriately.

The biggest problems concern fisheries in the high seas and those that cross the EEZs of different states or that straddle an EEZ and the high seas. Various species fit this description and have become subject to significant overexploitation, including certain whales and bluefin tuna. The states that share in the fishery (or whalery) have an incentive to overexploit the resource for the reasons we described earlier.

UNCLOS addresses such problems to a limited degree, relying largely on various regional and sectoral arrangements that are encouraged by (and to some degree enforceable under) UNCLOS. For example, article 63 requires nations confronting a situation where fish stocks straddle their EEZs "to agree upon the measures necessary to coordinate and ensure the conservation and development of such stocks." Article 64 imposes a similar requirement with respect to "highly migratory species."[56] Articles 118–119 impose an obligation on states to cooperate to preserve the living resources of the high seas and offer some general principles to that end. A 1995 supplemental agreement on highly migratory species and straddling stocks has also been negotiated. UNCLOS permits states to take other states to arbitration if they violate the rules negotiated in regional or sectoral agreements. To date, however, the general results of this system have been disappointing. The failure of fishery and whalery regimes is a case study of the collective action problem. States can agree, but they cannot enforce.

The Distribution of Sea Resources

UNCLOS reflects a large number of distributive choices that could have been otherwise. Consider, for example, the concept of the exclusive economic zone. Although distribution of area and distribution of valuable natural resources are not necessarily the same thing, at least with respect to area this concept favors countries with long coasts facing the open sea. One could imagine alternative concepts that would have different distributive effects. For example, all states (including landlocked states) could be given control over natural resources in identically sized portions of the seas, whether or not those areas are next to their coasts (if they have coasts). Or states could be given control over natural resources in proportion to the size of their population or in proportion to need. Such distributive principles can be found elsewhere in international law. Indeed, the provisions for sharing revenues from seabed mining appear to reflect such principles, as does the norm of common but differentiated responsibilities, which holds that poorer nations ought to be given less burdensome obligations than rich nations in trade and environmental treaties.

As we noted above, economic principles do not shed light on distributive issues other than recommending that redistribution should occur through taxes and transfers rather than through distortion of rules. This idea suggests some puzzles about UNCLOS. For example, UNCLOS distributes EEZs of equal breadth to all coastal nations, even weak nations that cannot control them. Our analysis suggests that this is a mistake: if a nation is too weak to control its coastal waters, it should not be granted that control. Indeed, our analysis suggests that more powerful states should have broader jurisdictional limits than weak states have. How can we account for these anomalies?

We suggest a partial answer. It may well be that proximity gives all states a significant advantage in controlling the sea, just because of the high cost of sending patrol ships and aircraft over great distances. In addition, states have relatively similar interests in the regulation of coastal waters—to prevent congestion, to enable the exploitation of resources, and so on, so that it is rarely worthwhile for one nation to try to wrest control of them from another nation. Further, it is valuable to have a relatively simple and uniform system of regulation. Finally, the de facto regime may well give larger fishing nations access to larger areas of the ocean—because weaker states do not have the naval resources to keep the fishing trawlers of foreign states out of their EEZs, nor do they have greater incentives to permit foreign access. Accidents of geography may have similar effects. Under the Convention, the United States has the largest EEZ in the world.

Other factors may also be in play. Bargaining over the law of the sea no doubt required some focal points for agreement, and norms of equal treatment may have pushed the negotiators toward uniformity in the rules (such as the rules that extend the EEZ 200 miles for all nations with a seacoast). As we indicated earlier, we do not claim that every detail of UNCLOS has an efficiency justification.

V | International Economic Law

18

International Trade

International trade law is by far the most elaborate and detailed body of international law in existence, consisting of dozens of bilateral, regional, and multilateral treaties. The largest multilateral arrangement—the World Trade Organization (WTO), successor to the General Agreement on Tariffs and Trade (GATT)—now has over 150 members as well as the most extensively developed dispute resolution system of any body of international law. International trade law also happens to be the area of law that has received by far the most attention from economists. Accordingly, this chapter is rather longer than a number of others.[1]

The Case for "Free Trade" and the Political Economy of Trade Protection

Neoclassical economic theory suggests that government intervention in trade flows generally reduces aggregate, global economic welfare—a proposition on which most economists will agree and which affords the traditional case for "free trade." Formal treatments of this proposition abound, but the basic reason why free trade increases economic welfare is easy to grasp in words. Consider a market in some country protected by a tariff (that is, a border tax on imported goods), and imagine what happens when the tariff falls. Goods in the market become cheaper for consumers, who earn extra consumer surplus as prices fall.[2] Of course, domestic producers of the goods in that market are hurt by those falling prices, as their producer surplus declines.[3] Thus, to some degree, the increased consumer surplus is a "transfer" from domestic producers of the goods in question, but not all of it. Some of the increased consumer surplus results from additional, cheaper imports. Likewise, domestic producers can economize on their loss of surplus by shifting resources into the production of other things. For this reason, the gains to consumers exceed the losses to producers.

The reverse argument applies to export markets. When tariffs come down abroad, demand for exports rises, which causes the price of exported goods to rise. Domestic producers of those goods benefit, while consumers are hurt. But some of the additional producer surplus on exports comes from sales abroad; it is not all at the expense of domestic consumers. Likewise, consumers can reduce their losses by shifting purchases to other things that they value more highly given the increase in prices of the goods that they purchased before. So the gain to domestic producers of exports exceeds the losses to domestic consumers of those goods. Finally, because these net gains hold for every country that trades, they must hold for the world as a whole.

Notwithstanding this fact, government intervention to restrict trade has nevertheless been extensive throughout modern history, raising a puzzle as to why and motivating a vast economic literature on the positive economics of national trade policies. Early work focused on the incentives facing "large" countries that seek to maximize national economic welfare, understanding "large" to mean simply that the nations are not price takers on international markets—their trade policies have the potential to affect the prices received by foreign exporters and importers. Such countries have monopoly power over their exports (collectively, their exporters face a downward sloping demand curve), and monopsony power over their imports (collectively, their import consumers face an upward sloping supply curve). Although individual firms and consumers may be unable to act collectively to exploit that power, the government can exploit it through taxation. At appropriate import and export tax rates, national welfare will increase because some of the tax revenue is extracted from foreign exporters and consumers. Tariffs set on this basis are sometimes termed *optimal tariffs,* and their contribution to national welfare arises through their effects on the "terms of trade"—the ratio of the price of a nation's exports to the price of its imports. Optimal export taxes improve the terms of trade by increasing export prices (inclusive of tax revenues) relative to import prices; optimal tariffs improve the terms of trade by lowering import prices (net of tariffs) relative to export prices.[4]

Economists quickly realized that these simple models of national income maximization did not explain the pattern of trade intervention very well in practice. Among other things, the pattern of tariffs across industries did not seem tightly related to the market power of the importing nation (although modern empirical research has indeed detected a correlation). And on the export side, nations seemed more likely to engage in policies such as export subsidization than export taxation, a behavior that cannot reflect national welfare maximization in competitive markets.[5] Economists began to examine different models of what governments maximize, generally drawing on ideas from the contemporaneously burgeoning literature on public choice. A wide range of modeling strategies was employed, all capturing in one way or another the idea that governments behave as though they care about the distribution of national income as well as its magnitude, usually because some interest groups are better organized than others and will reward their leaders more generously for pursuing policies that benefit them. The best known work along these lines is by the economists Gene Grossman and Elhanan Helpman.[6] They posit that some domestic industries are organized and some not and that the organized industries commit to schedules of campaign contributions, which are a function of trade policy choices by their government. The government maximizes a weighted average of campaign contributions and per capita economic welfare. Their analysis has a wide range of implications. For example, when governments choose policy in "Nash equilibrium" (taking the policies abroad as fixed), equilibrium trade policy involves higher tariffs for well-organized import competing industries than national income maximization would predict. It also involves lower export taxes on organized export industries, even to the point that export subsidies may arise.

These analyses also suggest why nations cooperate on trade policy through trade agreements. The primary reason goes back to the fact that countries are often "large" in the sense of possessing monopsony power over the price of their imports (again, an upward sloping import supply curve). Thus, tariffs on imports will not pass through in full to domestic consumers but will to some degree induce foreign exporters to cut their prices to remain more competitive. When trade policy is set unilaterally (Nash equilibrium again), governments will tend to ignore the harm that higher tariffs impose on foreign exporters—the adverse effects on the foreigners' "terms of trade." This negative externality leads to tariffs that are too high from a global point of view, a proposition that underlies the "terms of trade theory" of trade agreements,[7] which holds that the primary role of international trade agreements is to overcome this externality problem.[8]

Having identified a likely source of externalities, the next question is how trade agreements will address them. If governments were national welfare maximizers, then an optimal trade agreement should maximize global welfare conventionally defined. Under competitive conditions, free trade will do so (although some large countries might lose out from free trade by foregoing their optimal tariffs, and hence some side payment mechanism might be necessary to achieve free trade). Actual trade agreements do not come close to completely free trade, however, perhaps in part because of the difficulty of fashioning a side payment mechanism but, more important, because governments are not national welfare maximizers. Even after the international externalities are taken into account through international negotiation, governments still have preferences over distribution that lead them to retain significant pockets of protection.

The Legal Architecture of World Trade

Formal trade agreements arose in the nineteenth century, and in more recent times an enormous number of preferential trading arrangements (NAFTA, the EU, and Mercosur, for example) have come into being. We focus here, however, on the modern WTO/GATT system.[9]

GATT began in 1947 and was limited to trade in goods. The centerpiece of the GATT was its reciprocal commitments to lower tariffs embodied in article II, along with a general commitment to nondiscrimination among trading partners contained in article I. The remainder of GATT served three primary functions: it constrained policy instruments that were substitutes for tariffs; it provided for various adjustments to the bargain, including tariff renegotiation, amendments, waiver, accessions, and preferential trade exemptions to the most favored nation (MFN) obligation; and it provided a dispute resolution system.

GATT subsequently evolved through a series of negotiating "rounds," which initially involved little more than further reciprocal tariff reductions. By the time of the Tokyo Round in the 1970s, however, GATT signatories had become increasingly concerned about the growth of various nontariff barriers that were inadequately disciplined by the original GATT. The result was several plurilateral "codes" on such matters as subsidies, antidumping measures, product standards, and government procurement. The next major stage in the evolution of GATT came in the Uruguay Round, which led to the creation of the WTO in 1995. The WTO replaced the GATT (although its treaty text was incorporated into WTO law). The WTO elaborated and tightened obligations with respect to nontariff barriers and made them binding on all members; it created the General Agreement on Trade in Services (GATS), for the first time bringing services trade under multilateral discipline; it created the Agreement on Trade Related Aspects of Intellectual Property Rights, which required all members to create and enforce intellectual property rights in a number of areas; and it overhauled the dispute resolution system with a new Dispute Settlement Understanding (DSU).

Conventional wisdom holds that the WTO/GATT system has been quite successful at liberalizing trade.[10] Developed country tariffs have declined steadily, from an average rate of around 40 percent when GATT was founded to an average rate of about 4 percent presently. And although the history of the WTO/GATT system is not free of tension, it has so far avoided the problem of large-scale trade wars that plagued the global economy before it, such as the widespread tariff increases during the 1930s initiated by the Smoot-Hawley tariff in the United States.

"Tariffication" and the Broad Reach of WTO/GATT Commitments

GATT arose for the purpose of memorializing reciprocal commitments to reduce tariffs. It does not prohibit tariffs but allows them to be negotiated downward subject to negotiated ceilings on their magnitude, termed "bindings." Since tariffs are different on different goods, and there are thousands of goods, it is immediately apparent that a trade agreement such as GATT may become voluminous quite quickly.

But the obligations of the WTO/GATT system reach far beyond tariff reduction commitments, for the simple reason that many other policy instruments may be substituted to achieve trade protection. Quantitative restrictions (such as quotas) on imports are an obvious alternative to tariffs, and other available devices include discriminatory domestic taxation, subsidies, regulatory policies that burden imports disproportionately, state-franchised monopolies that disfavor imports in their purchasing decisions, and discriminatory government procurement policies. Effective agreements to reduce trade protection must attend to this array of protectionist options. The challenge of formulating appropriate constraints on all of these instruments is complicated by the fact that many of them also address "legitimate," nonprotectionist objectives. Subsidies may correct other externality problems; regulations may address important issues of safety and quality; procurement choices may affect national security; and so on.

These observations suggest that an agreement such as WTO/GATT must pursue a number of related objectives concurrently. First, signatories must ensure that commitments to reduce protection associated with one policy instrument are not undermined by the substitution of protection using some alternative instrument. Second, and closely related, signatories must manage the challenge of negotiating reductions in protection given all of the available instruments of protection and will benefit from strategies that reduce the costs of negotiation. Third, to the extent that some instruments of protection produce greater economic costs than others, signatories will benefit if they can channel whatever protection remains under their agreement into the instruments that do the least damage. Finally, signatories must design agreements that constrain trade protection appropriately on the one hand, while leaving themselves free to pursue their domestic regulatory agendas on the other.

Regarding the first three of these objectives, the central strategy of WTO/GATT is a process of "tariffication"—the conversion of most protectionist measures into tariffs. This process is accomplished through a number of legal measures, such as the general prohibition on quantitative restrictions, import licensing schemes, and the like in article XI of GATT.

Tariffication lowers the transactions costs of reciprocal trade negotiations directly by reducing the number of protectionist instruments that are part of the negotiation. It may afford additional benefits by reducing uncertainty about the degree of market access that trade concessions afford, an important consideration if trade negotiators are risk averse. Tariffs also have the virtue that when applied in nondiscriminatory fashion, they avoid the loss of joint surplus that results from trade diversion (discussed further below). Other instruments, such as quotas, may result in greater trade diversion depending on how they are administered or in other kinds of deadweight loss (see the discussion of regulatory protection below). Finally, because tariffs tend to be more transparent, cheating on tariff commitments is easier to detect than cheating with respect to commitments on other protectionist instruments. As long as the general commitment to tariffication is itself enforceable, therefore, tariffication discourages cheating and facilitates cooperation.

Multilateralism, Bilateralism, Regionalism, and Trade Discrimination

An important feature of the international trade law is its long-standing emphasis (since 1947 anyway) on multilateral agreement. Prior to 1947, however, trade agreements tended to be bilateral in nature. Why the shift toward multilateralism?

An advantage of bilateral agreements is that cooperation is generally easier to orchestrate because the number of parties to negotiations is two rather than many. This factor alone would seem to favor a bilateral approach. But bilateral agreements create important externalities. Imagine three countries, A, B, and C, each of which trades with the others. Imagine further that tariffs on imports into each country are initially nondiscriminatory. Suppose that A and B contemplate a trade agreement in which each lowers its tariffs on imports from the other, and suppose for concreteness that A lowers its tariff on imports of grain from B. The effect on C will depend on whether it is an importer or exporter of grain. If C initially exports grain to A, then the tariff reduction on A's imports from B will cause imports into A from B to rise at the expense of imports from C. The weakening in demand for C's exports causes C's terms of trade to worsen. And to the degree that the tariff preference for B causes consumers in A to shift purchases from C to B, the phenomenon of *trade diversion* arises. In general, trade diversion occurs whenever discriminatory trade policies cause consumers in an importing nation to make purchases from abroad that would not be made but for the discrimination. It yields a loss in global welfare, *ceteris paribus,* because imports do not originate from the lowest cost supplier.

Another type of externality arises if C is instead an importer of grain. The preference for grain imports into A from B will then tend to increase the cost of grain to C. C's terms of trade worsen because the price of its imports increases.

Of course, an agreement to liberalize trade within a subset of trading nations also has its benefits. Most important, if an agreement leads to an expansion of trade between nations that are efficient suppliers to each others' markets, the phenomenon of *trade creation* arises. It is entirely possible that the benefits of trade creation will exceed the losses from trade diversion, so that a bilateral (or regional) agreement can on balance enhance global economic welfare and can assuredly enhance the welfare of its members.

Because of the terms of trade externalities for nonmembers, however, any agreement involving only a subset of trading nations has the potential to injure nonparties to the agreement. One thus wonders whether a prohibition on discrimination may be valuable. Precisely such a general prohibition is contained in articles I and XIII of GATT, which prohibit discriminatory tariffs and quota regimes (when quotas are allowable at all). This obligation is termed the *most favored nation* (MFN) obligation. By joining a multilateral agreement such as GATT and committing themselves to respect the MFN obligation (subject to a very important exception to be discussed in a moment), signatories avoid the loss of joint surplus associated with trade diversion that could arise in a smaller agreement.

In addition to ensuring that goods are imported from the lowest cost foreign supplier, the MFN obligation may facilitate trade negotiations in an important way. Imagine once again a trading system consisting of countries A, B, and C, and suppose that A and B contemplate a trade agreement with each other. Negotiators for A and B may worry that after concluding an agreement, their partner may later negotiate an agreement with C, offering C a more attractive arrangement. Whatever benefits they expect to get from the agreement may be undermined, and they may be reluctant to conclude any agreement at all. But if they mutually promise each other that no third nation will be offered better terms later through an MFN commitment, such worries can be put to rest.

To be sure, the MFN obligation may also carry a cost. If benefits extended by A to B must be extended automatically to C because C is entitled to MFN treatment, then C may become a free rider on trade negotiations between A and B. To solve the free rider problem, it may be necessary for A and B to draw C into the negotiations. And as the number of countries drawn into negotiations rises, the costs of negotiation rise and the problem of holdouts surfaces.

Thus, the role of the MFN obligation in trade agreements raises crosscutting and complex issues. A considerable literature now exists on the subject, which confirms that the welfare implications of the MFN obligation are complicated, to say the least.[11]

The reader may note, however, that even if an MFN obligation is on balance desirable in the trading system, that observation by itself does not necessitate multilateral agreements. One could imagine in the abstract a web of bilateral agreements, each containing an MFN clause. We then return to the question posed at the outset: what is the value of multilateral agreements in this context?

A trivial answer is that economies of scale may exist to the degree that the optimal bilateral agreements would all contain many of the same terms. It may then be easier to write a single multilateral agreement. Further, given the free-rider problem that arises if bilateral agreements contain an MFN obligation, it may make sense for all trading nations to meet and negotiate at once, each holding off any final deals until all offers are on the table. Finally, even when an MFN obligation precludes the possibility of discriminatory tariffs, bilateral negotiations nevertheless create terms of trade externalities for third countries. For example, if nation A offers a tariff concession on some product to nation B and extends it to all other exporters of the product pursuant to an MFN obligation, a worsening of the terms of trade will still occur for any third nation that imports the product. Such externalities provide further justification for multilateral negotiations.

Multilateral cooperation may also be useful to enforcement. Imagine three countries once again, A, B, and C, and suppose further that A runs a large trade surplus with B, B runs a large surplus with C, and C runs a large surplus with A (although aggregate trade for each country is balanced). In this scenario, an imbalance of power may be said to exist in each bilateral relationship. Because of that imbalance, the amount of self-enforcing cooperation that is sustainable in bilateral tariff agreements is limited—if B defects from an agreement with A, for example, A loses much more than B loses if A defects from the agreement. This scenario suggests a role for an agreement with a multilateral enforcement mechanism, whereby defection by any party can be punished by all of the others.[12] Interestingly, however, the extent to which such coordinated enforcement occurs in practice within the WTO is quite limited.

If trade discrimination is often problematic, and if important externalities argue for multilateral trade negotiations, an important puzzle remains. GATT article XXIV permits signatories to form customs unions and free trade areas (the latter differing from a customs union in that the members do not harmonize their external tariffs). Both customs unions and free trade areas permit member nations to deviate from the MFN obligation, as long as they eliminate barriers on "substantially all" trade between them. Why should GATT include this gaping exception to the MFN obligation, allowing discrimination as long as it occurs on a grand scale ("substantially all trade")? Related, is the proliferation of preferential trading arrangements, such as the EU, NAFTA, and Mercosur, a positive or unfortunate development for the international trading system?[13]

Note that nothing in article XXIV ensures compensation to nations that are injured in their terms of trade by the formation of a preferential trading arrangement.[14] For this reason, an enormous theoretical and empirical literature has developed on preferential trading arrangements. In general, theoretical work tends to be skeptical of preferential trade for the reasons suggested by the discussion above, while empirical work tends to be more agnostic, with some support for the idea that the beneficial trade creation under existing agreements may exceed the harmful trade diversion. But on the ultimate question of whether preferential arrangements are "building blocks" or "stumbling blocks" to multilateral cooperation, the issue remains unsettled.

Adjusting the Bargain over Time

Like most long-term agreements, WTO/GATT commitments have been negotiated under conditions of considerable uncertainty about the future. The treaty text thus contains many provisions for adjusting the bargain over time. Here we emphasize two features that have received attention from economists: provisions for renegotiation and the GATT "escape clause."

In the WTO, as in many commercial contexts, it is no doubt too costly to write a complete contingent contract. Commitments entered at one point in time may thus prove undesirable (at least from the political standpoint of government officials) at some future time. One solution, of course, is simply to renegotiate when circumstances change, recognizing that renegotiation is a potential double-edged sword if sunk costs can be exploited.

Ordinarily, agreements do not require express provisions providing for renegotiation, inasmuch as renegotiation is always a possibility without them. But GATT included a provision for the renegotiation of tariff commitments, article XXVIII, in its original 1947 text. Article XXVIII provides that a nation wishing to withdraw a tariff concession should attempt to obtain the permission of affected nations by offering to substitute some other concession. If such negotiations fail to reach agreement, however, a nation can unilaterally withdraw its tariff concession. Affected nations may then retaliate by withdrawing "substantially equivalent" concessions of their own. This structure can be seen as maintaining the balance of concessions. Roughly speaking, a nation that proposes to withdraw a concession must restore the terms of trade for affected nations, either by substituting an alternative concession or by accepting a withdrawal of comparable concessions on its exports. The question of what is "comparable" is now a proper subject for the dispute process.

But why is it necessary to memorialize this mechanism in article XXVIII, instead of simply recognizing that GATT members can renegotiate the agreement when they wish? One reason is that the members desired to make clear that tariff concessions could be withdrawn if necessary without securing the permission of affected nations beforehand. In a rough sense, they wished to create what economists term a *liability rule* rather than a *property rule*.[15] The reason for preferring a liability rule here is the holdout problem. If the permission of all affected GATT members had to be obtained before a politically uncomfortable concession could be modified, the negotiation process could drag on indefinitely and the opportunity to adjust the bargain to changing circumstances would be diminished.

Of course, renegotiation is but one option for avoiding the performance of obligations that become inefficient due to changing circumstances. In commercial contracts, for example, we often see provisions that excuse performance under various contingencies—force majeure and Act of God clauses are illustrative. In the WTO/GATT system, a similar state-contingent device for excusing performance is the GATT article XIX "escape clause." It provides for the temporary suspension of tariff concessions when, due to unforeseen developments, increased quantities of imports cause or threaten to cause "serious injury" to an import-competing industry. The escape clause thus permits temporary tariff increases, under specified conditions, in response to import surges.

Economic analyses of the escape clause offer a number of related explanations for its presence in GATT. One possibility is that import surges risk destabilizing cooperation because they enhance the incentive to cheat, either to earn greater tariff revenue or to respond to pleas for protection from an import-competing industry that is well organized. To avoid unraveling of the agreement that might occur if tariff increases under these circumstances were defined as cheating (so that nations respond by reverting to their Nash equilibrium policies), the GATT may instead allow temporary tariff increases during the import surge to preserve long-term cooperation.[16]

A slightly different take on the escape clause suggests that it permits GATT members to withdraw a tariff concession when it is no longer jointly optimal for the concession to be honored—essentially, when the cost of performance to one party exceeds the benefit to the other party (in political terms). Such a rule increases the expected utility of trade concessions and thereby allows more concessions to be negotiated in the first instance. This explanation focuses not on the temptation to cheat but on the stylized fact that troubled industries seem to lobby harder for protection than successful industries, perhaps because they are more likely to garner public sympathy and secure protection if they have many unemployed workers, or perhaps because any protection they receive will not raise investment returns above a competitive level and thus will not attract new entry that dissipates those returns. Because the escape clause has a tendency to allow troubled industries to receive protection at the expense of prosperous exporting industries abroad, it may yield protection in precisely the cases where the import-competing industry is likely to lobby hard for protection, while the exporting industry does not resist it too much because it expects competitive entry to dissipate its profits anyway.[17]

Constraints on Domestic Regulation

We noted earlier that the WTO/GATT system encourages tariffication and the elimination of substitute forms of protection. To say that it is valuable to channel protection into tariffs, however, begs the question of what measures constitute protection. Nowhere is this problem more acute than in the case of domestic regulatory policies. For example, one quite famous and thorny WTO dispute has centered on the question of whether a European prohibition on hormone-raised beef imports, ostensibly for health reasons, is really a pretense for measures to protect the European beef industry.

The tension between international trade liberalization on the one hand and domestic regulation on the other is among the greatest sources of political tension in the WTO system. Critics of the WTO often urge that it treads on national sovereignty and elevates the value of open trade above other values such as health, safety, and environmental protection.[18] Defenders insist that the system merely seeks to ferret out protectionist capture of domestic regulatory processes. The task of accommodating these tensions is a considerable one.

One possible solution to such problems, at least in principle, is based on the familiar idea that international law should induce nations to "internalize the externality." The externality in the trade area arises, as noted, because choices by individual governments affect the prices confronting foreign buyers and sellers on world markets. If nations commit through trade agreements to maintain a particular level of market access—particular terms of trade with other nations—they can then be allowed freedom to vary their domestic regulatory policies as they wish as long as any effects on the terms of trade are offset by countervailing changes in their tariff and subsidy policies. Through such a mechanism, other nations would be insulated from the terms of trade consequences of domestic regulatory policies, the externality would be "internalized," and nations would then behave efficiently in relation to their internal welfare judgments.

In practice, however, trade agreements do not undertake to specify the terms of trade. Such undertakings are probably unrealistic in an environment of volatile exchange rates and innumerable other macro- and microeconomic shocks to world prices. Instead, the key strategy of the WTO/GATT system has been to constrain protection per se, while leaving signatories free to pursue nonprotectionist objectives, such as health and safety regulation, environmental protection, and national security. But this strategy requires an additional set of rules to distinguish protectionist measures from nonprotectionist measures.[19]

The initial strategy of GATT in this respect was to prohibit discriminatory regulations through a "national treatment" obligation in article III. No regulatory burden could be imposed on imports unless it was also imposed on domestic producers of "like products." GATT also provided a number of exceptions to this principle in articles XX and XXI, which covers things such as measures "necessary" to protect the environment or measures "considered essential" to national security.

To the degree that the national treatment obligation was limited to facially discriminatory regulations, however, it soon proved inadequate. Consider a "nondiscriminatory" regulation that requires all products to embody a certain design or technology, when domestic producers have a cost advantage in producing or obtaining that design or technology, and when some other design or technology available more cheaply abroad will achieve the nonprotectionist regulatory goal just as effectively. The cost difference between the two technologies then represents pure regulatory protection.

The need for additional disciplines to deal with related issues culminated in two important new agreements during the Uruguay Round, the Agreement on Technical Barriers to Trade and the Agreement on the Application of Sanitary and Phytosanitary Measures (pertaining mainly to pests, disease-causing organisms, and contaminants in foodstuffs). These agreements impose numerous additional constraints on domestic regulators, such as general least restrictive means requirements and a requirement that product regulations specify performance goals rather than design limitations. Somewhat more controversially, they also introduce requirements that certain health and safety regulations have adequate scientific basis. To return to the example of the European prohibition on hormone-fed beef imports, that regulation was found to violate WTO law because it lacked adequate scientific foundation.

Where domestic regulations appear to have bona fide, nonprotectionist goals, however, the primary constraint on them remains a simple national treatment requirement. Such a rule tolerates changes in domestic regulatory policy even if they have significant trade externalities, but it is not clear that any alternative rule is better.

Subsidies

Another important body of WTO law concerns the use of subsidies. Most of the work that has been done on this subject is normative, asking whether WTO rules on subsidies promote global economic welfare conventionally defined. Early writers observed that subsidies to domestic industries can protect them just as effectively as tariffs, yet subsidies may also be justified for reasons other than protectionism. A question then arises as to whether rules can be developed to distinguish "good" subsidies from "bad" subsidies, avoiding the welfare loss from the former while preserving the welfare gains from the latter. There are reasons to be skeptical of this enterprise—simple rules for the identification of welfare-reducing subsidies may not be easy to construct, particularly if one allows that "legitimate" subsidies may include those where the citizenry is willing to pay to preserve certain forms of inefficient enterprise (such as cultural industries or family farms).[20]

Nevertheless, the WTO system has evolved increasingly detailed rules governing subsidies. In goods markets, the governing principles are three: (1) new and unanticipated subsidy programs that upset market access expectations are potentially illegal, even if they do not violate any provision of the treaty text, under the rubric of "nonviolation nullification or impairment"; (2) export subsidies (subsidies that favor exportation over domestic production) are illegal (putting aside some exceptions in the agriculture sector); and (3) domestic subsidies, which are identified by the criterion that they must be targeted to a single industry or narrow group of industries, may be illegal if they cause "injury" to foreign exporters or import competing industries and may also be a basis for unilateral countervailing duties (duties to offset the value of the subsidy) by importing nations whose industries are injured by subsidized imports.

Putting aside the difficult question of what constitutes a "subsidy," the first principle is arguably defensible as a way to protect the value of the bargain associated with tariff concessions against opportunistic erosion. Absent this rule, trade negotiators would fear that tariff concessions might be undermined by future subsidies and thus negotiate fewer of them.

The second principle may also make sense from the perspective of traditional welfare economics, as it is difficult to imagine any constructive role for export subsidies as a first-best policy. Yet it is important to note that export subsidies arise in practice under "second-best" circumstances. Against a backdrop of trade protection that survives in many markets, export subsidies expand trade and may move the world toward the welfare-maximizing "free trade" ideal. Accordingly, it is not obvious that export subsidies are always undesirable.[21]

The third principle is also somewhat questionable in that it defines "subsidies" by using a dubious criterion—the targeting criterion may well condemn useful subsidies (like a targeted subsidy for research and development in an industry where the returns to innovation are hard to appropriate) and is quite underinclusive as to economically wasteful subsidies or as to subsidies that may have harmful external effects (such as broadly available subsidies in the agricultural sector). Further, regardless of the degree of targeting, it is not clear that coherent criteria can be developed for determining the existence of domestic subsidies at all given the vast range of tax/subsidy and regulatory policies that affect the competitive position of firms—WTO rules view each government program in isolation and make no effort to assess the net impact of government as a whole on the competitive position of firms.[22]

Finally, the unilateral use of countervailing duties by importing nations to counteract subsidized imports is difficult to defend if the policy objective is to maximize either national or global economic welfare (conventionally defined). Countervailing duties almost always will lower the welfare of nations that use them, unless by coincidence they are applied in a manner that exploits the monopsony power of the importing nation (recall the "optimal tariff") or are applied in industries where domestic firms generate positive externalities (offering a rationale for "strategic trade policy"). From the global perspective, the uncoordinated use of countervailing duties by individual trading nations is unlikely to do much to discourage wasteful subsidy practices, especially since the criteria for identifying and measuring countervailable subsidies suffer from the deficiencies noted above.[23]

Antidumping Policy

"Dumping" refers to certain pricing practices by private firms engaged in international trade. Although its precise meaning has changed through the years, dumping occurs under modern trade laws when an exporting firm's prices satisfy (roughly) one of three conditions: (a) its free on board (FOB) price to the complaining export market is below its FOB price to its home market for the same goods (or for similar goods adjusted for cost and quality differences); (b) in the absence of substantial home market sales of identical or similar goods, its FOB price to the complaining export market is below the FOB export price to some third country market; or (c) its FOB price to the complaining export market is below the fully allocated cost of production for the good in question (including an allocation of fixed costs, general selling and administrative expenses, and so on).

GATT article VI provides that dumping "is to be condemned" but does not prohibit it or impose any obligation on WTO members to prevent or punish it. Instead, importing nations are permitted to take countermeasures against dumping, in the form of an "antidumping duty" that may not exceed the "margin" of dumping found to exist on the goods in question. That margin is equal to the difference between the "fair value" of the goods computed by using one of the three benchmarks above and the FOB export price to the country imposing the duty. For example, under the first criterion for dumping, the margin would be computed as the FOB price to the home market minus the FOB price to the export market. GATT does not permit antidumping duties in all instances of dumping, however, but limits them to cases in which the dumping is causing or threatening to cause "material injury" to the import-competing industry, a requirement known as the "injury test." These requirements were elaborated, along with the procedures for the conduct of antidumping investigations, in the WTO Antidumping Agreement, the successor to the Tokyo Round Antidumping Code.

Antidumping laws first emerged in Canada in the early 1900s and quickly spread to the United States. Their proponents put them forward as an adjunct to antitrust statutes, plugging a purported "loophole" that would otherwise allow foreign firms to engage in monopolization through aggressive pricing. A moment's reflection on the standards for dumping described above, however, suggests that they are radically different from the variable cost-based standards for predatory pricing that have evolved under modern antitrust law. Price discrimination dumping, reflected in possibilities (a) and (b) above, can assuredly occur at prices above variable cost. And possibility (c) involves not a comparison between price and some measure of variable cost but a comparison between price and (roughly) a measure of long-run average cost. Further, although the material injury test requires that some harm befall import-competing firms as a prerequisite to antidumping duties, it falls far short of a structural analysis of the industry to determine whether monopolization is a plausible outcome, and antidumping duties are routinely observed in industries producing such items as steel products, potatoes, textiles, and footwear—all industries that are highly unconcentrated on a global level and where a danger of monopolization is utterly implausible. The connection between antidumping policy and sensible antitrust policy is thus a tenuous one at best.[24] Not surprisingly, therefore, modern economic commentators generally question the wisdom of antidumping policy.[25]

But if antidumping policy is so foolish, why is it also so durable, particularly in the WTO environment where nations have mutually agreed to forego economically foolish policies on some other fronts? There is little systematic work on this question. One conjecture is that the political support for antidumping is akin to that for some form of escape clause and relates back to the fact that troubled industries are particularly efficacious in lobbying for protection (and securing antidumping protection). Likewise, the popular misconception of antidumping policy as some variant of a sensible antimonopoly policy may help its proponents to resist reform.

Trade in Services

As noted, the advent of the WTO produced multilateral rules for the liberalization of international trade in services in the form of the General Agreement on Trade in Services (GATS). The inclusion of services within the WTO is one of the great steps forward over the old GATT system.[26]

Conceptually, the international externality in the services area that motivates a trade agreement is the same as in the goods area—national restrictions on services imports can adversely affect the prices received by foreign service providers. The mechanism that gives rise to this externality will often be different in the services area, however, as will be the approach to ameliorating it. The reason lies in the fact that tariffs are generally not used in services trade because services imports rarely cross the border in a manner that allows them to be taxed. Instead, most of the market access impediments in the services area involve various barriers to efforts by foreign service providers—banks, insurance companies, law firms—to establish a physical presence in the importing nation. These barriers are generally regulatory, in the form of licensing requirements, prudential requirements, residency requirements, immigration restrictions, and the like. Some such regulations are applied in a facially discriminatory fashion, and in other instances regulation simply imposes a disproportionate burden on foreign service suppliers.

The liberalization of trade in services thus poses difficult new challenges that the multilateral system has only begun to tackle. The process of "tariffication" that characterizes the approach of GATT to goods markets simply cannot work here. Moreover, tight nondiscrimination requirements such as those seen in GATT might eliminate the ability of GATS signatories to protect their service industries at all, a result that is unlikely to be politically palatable. Hence, the strategy of GATS is to allow discriminatory policies to be "scheduled" (along with certain other types of market access restrictions). In each service sector, signatories make a determination of whether to afford national treatment to foreign service providers. If they do so, they can nevertheless reserve the right to discriminate in particular ways by listing the discriminatory policy in their schedule of service commitments. Thus, for example, a member might agree to afford national treatment to foreign accounting firms but retain a discriminatory requirement for them to carry liability insurance that domestic firms need not purchase, or require foreign accountants to pass an examination that domestic accountants need not take. This approach enables nations to retain all of the regulatory measures that they regard as essential and makes their trade barriers more transparent but also allows the protectionist effects of certain types of regulation to persist for the time being.

Because so much in the services area turns on negotiations to reduce "discrimination," the challenges of defining discrimination become particularly acute in the services realm. For example, is it "discrimination" to require that a foreign attorney seeking to practice domestic law must obtain a degree from a domestic law school, even if that attorney can pass the bar exam with flying colors without such a degree? Plainly, such a requirement can have a profound impact in discouraging foreign lawyers from entering the domestic market, but it may nevertheless be deemed to satisfy a "national treatment" rule if it is applied uniformly to all foreign and domestic attorneys. The general lesson is that eliminating formally discriminatory measures alone may not liberalize services trade as much as some observers might wish, and negotiations may ultimately need to go beyond the national treatment principle.

Immigration issues are also prominent in the services area. If a foreign lawyer wishes to practice law in the domestic market, she must have the ability to meet with clients in person, appear in court, and so on. Even if she has the right to do so under the rules governing the domestic practice of law, it is of little value if she cannot obtain a visa to enter the country. In this respect, services liberalization touches importantly on immigration law, raising issues that have proven particularly thorny in various service sector negotiations to date.

Trade-Related Aspects of Intellectual Property

The WTO also created a new agreement on Trade Related Aspects of Intellectual Property Rights (TRIPs), which requires all WTO members to afford a range of intellectual property rights on a nondiscriminatory basis to domestic and foreign nationals, including patent, copyright, and trademark protection. Subject to a few exceptions and to some transition provisions for developing countries, it harmonizes national intellectual property law to a considerable degree on issues such as what is patentable or copyrightable and the duration of patent protection.

Much of the early writing on the TRIPs proposal focused on the welfare economics of globalizing intellectual property rights, particularly in the patent arena. The literature posed two central questions: does the globalization of intellectual property protection enhance global welfare, and does it enhance the welfare of developing countries? The answers depend importantly on what one assumes to be the set of available policy instruments for inducing the production of intellectual property. It is well known, for example, that patent protection involves an economic tradeoff between the costs of (transitory) monopolization of patented products and the incentives to innovate. In theory, public subsidies to innovation might achieve an optimal rate of technical progress without the monopoly distortion of patent protection, although in practice the subsidization of invention is quite limited, perhaps for good reasons related to the capacity of governments to direct subsidies appropriately or to the costs of such a process. Assuming that public subsidies are infeasible, intellectual property protection has appeal in the abstract, but harmonizing the law globally may not be appealing, depending on one's perspective. Suppose that the "North" is wealthy and that most innovation occurs there. The "South" is poor and incapable of doing much innovation. If so, requiring the South to embrace intellectual property rights may have little impact on innovation incentives (because its markets are so small) but may transfer significant rents to the North and thus from poor to rich.[27]

The issue is not quite so simple, of course, because intellectual property protection can affect welfare in other ways besides simply the monopoly/innovation tradeoff. It is conceivable, for example, that greater patent protection facilitates technology transfer from North to South, which in turn may facilitate the growth of industries in the South. The ultimate question as to how an agreement like TRIPs affects economic development is thus a complicated empirical one. The notion that TRIPs is likely injurious to developing countries, however, has been widely credited.

Why did the WTO membership nevertheless agree to TRIPs? Clearly, intellectual property policies chosen in Nash equilibrium will have externalities. Nations will not take account of the benefits to foreign innovators of intellectual property, for example, or the benefits to foreign consumers of innovation that lowers prices to them in one manner or another. Given all of the possible externalities, it would be a surprise if Nash policies were the best that the world could achieve, and so some role for cooperation seems clear. It is much less clear, however, that optimal cooperation involves global harmonization.

In addition, given the disparate effects of intellectual property harmonization on the welfare of different countries, any agreement almost certainly needed to be linked to other issues. This observation offers a key insight into the origin of TRIPs,[28] which was accepted by all WTO member states, including less innovative states that are unlikely to be net beneficiaries of TRIPs standing alone, at least in the short term. Many developing countries, which perceive themselves in large measure as consumers rather than producers of intellectual property, were opposed to the idea of TRIPs during much of the Uruguay Round negotiations. Intellectual property interest groups in the developed countries, representing such industries as pharmaceuticals, sound recording, and filmmaking, were the principal proponents of TRIPs. The ultimate willingness of developing nations to accept TRIPs was a consequence in large part of their ability to obtain market access concessions on other sectoral issues, such as textiles and agriculture. Their acquiescence suggests that as a whole, developing countries believed that they gained more from accepting TRIPs and its quid pro quo than by rejecting it. This observation calls into question some of the criticism of TRIPs from the development perspective—its impact cannot be assessed in isolation but must be considered in relation to the trade concessions that developing countries received in exchange for it.

Dispute Resolution

The WTO Dispute Settlement Understanding (DSU) applies to disputes of all sorts in the WTO. It is the most elaborate and detailed dispute settlement mechanism in international law.

We begin with a bit of history. Shortly after GATT was formed in 1947, the organization gravitated toward a "consensus" rule for many decisions. Under the consensus rule, an investigation into an alleged violation of the agreement (originally undertaken by a "working party" and later by a dispute "panel") could be authorized only by consensus (unanimity). Even if the dispute panel was constituted and ruled in favor of the complaining nation, the ruling still had no force of law unless it was "adopted" by the membership, again requiring consensus. Finally, sanctions for violations following the adoption of a ruling could be authorized only by consensus. Thus, the violator nation could always block the process at any one of three stages—investigation, adoption of the dispute ruling, and sanctions. Nations often allowed investigations to go forward nevertheless and also in many cases permitted adverse rulings to be adopted. But sanctions were authorized only once during the history of GATT (prior to the creation of the WTO).

Under this system, cheating or alleged cheating could be punished only through unilateral "self-help." Nations such as the United States would bring cases to the GATT and retaliate unilaterally if the target country refused to comply with an adverse ruling or blocked the process from going forward. Studies of the efficacy of unilateral retaliation during this phase of GATT indicate that its results were mixed, although retaliation often induced nations to alter their policies, and many nations were observed to comply with adverse panel rulings without the need for any retaliation.[29]

In 1989, GATT signatories agreed to end the ability of accused nations to block an investigation, although they could still block the adoption of panel reports and block sanctions. Finally, with the creation of the WTO in 1995, the system put an end to blocking altogether.

The new approach to dispute resolution was laid out in the DSU. Under the DSU, nations claiming a violation by another must first seek "consultations" with that nation, ideally leading to a mutually satisfactory settlement. Such settlements are, in fact, fairly common. Failing settlement, a complaining nation (only member nations have standing to bring cases) now has the right to a "panel," composed of three trade law experts from countries other than the disputants. They are chosen by the disputants if possible or by the WTO director general if the disputants do not agree on a panel. The panel receives briefs, hears oral arguments, and can seek outside expertise on relevant issues. It decides issues of fact and law and issues a decision, confidentially at first to the parties and later publically after the parties' comments have been addressed.

The losing party has a right to appeal to the Appellate Body, which will afford a panel of three judges chosen from the seven permanent Appellate Body members (who serve for six-year terms). Informally, major players such as the

United States have had a "seat" on the Appellate Body, but the U.S. judge will not hear cases involving the United States (the same applies to other judges not hearing disputes involving their own countries). The Appellate Body reviews issues of law de novo but defers heavily to panels on findings of fact.

Rulings by a dispute panel, as modified in the course of any appeal, are automatically adopted unless a consensus among WTO members exists against adoption (the winning litigant would have to join that consensus). Thus, adoption is effectively automatic. Following the adoption of a ruling that finds a violation, the violator has a "reasonable period of time" to cure its behavior. This length of time is itself subject to arbitration if the disputants do not agree on it. At the expiration of that period, if the violator remains out of compliance, the original complaining nation is entitled to impose sanctions against the violator (after appropriate findings by a "compliance panel"). But in addition to some other limitations, sanctions are limited to the withdrawal of "substantially equivalent" trade concessions (equivalent to the harm done by the violation), and the level of retaliation under this criterion is subject to arbitration. Only the nations that brought the case can retaliate; there is no collective punishment mechanism.

The system seems in many ways quite successful. Out of hundreds of formal disputes, many are settled before dispute reports are issued. Others reach a satisfactory conclusion after the dispute process concludes, and nations very often comply with rulings. Actual retaliation is fairly rare, in only a dozen or so cases to date. Noncompliance is a bit more common. Nations sometimes forego their right of retaliation if they have no effective way to do so (usually because they are so small, although even a small nation may now be able to retaliate by obtaining authorization to suspend intellectual property rights under TRIPs) or if they have other diplomatic reasons for acquiescing in a violation.

The system has one particularly unusual feature. If a nation violates WTO law, it is not sanctioned for the violation per se. Rather, as noted, a sanction is permissible only after the nation in question has been adjudicated to be in violation and has been given a "reasonable period of time" to comply with the adverse ruling. A nation that complies within a "reasonable period of time" thus faces no sanction at all. Further, although the treaty text is not entirely clear on the matter, the general view is that any sanctions should be "substantially equivalent" to the prospective harm from the refusal of the violator nation to comply after the reasonable time to comply expires—there is no sanction for the trade injury that was caused by the violation up until that date. Because cases take a good while to litigate, the seeming implication is that a violator can cheat for some time, get caught, drag out litigation, slowly correct its behavior, and ultimately pay no price. This element of the system has been somewhat cynically characterized as the "three-year free pass."

How can we explain this history and evolution of WTO/GATT dispute resolution? Economic models of trade agreements suggest that such agreements are self-enforcing, with cooperation supported by mutual threats of defection. The work of economists Kyle Bagwell and Robert Staiger is illustrative of the mainstream work on these questions.[30] They imagine that two nations agree to cut tariffs in an infinitely repeated game. Each nation is reasonably patient and plays the "grim" strategy—if either nation cheats in one period, the other reverts to its Nash equilibrium tariff choice in the next and all future periods. Recurring cooperation is then a (subgame perfect) equilibrium as long as the cooperative tariff does not create too much incentive to cheat in the short term. This latter requirement places a limit on the amount of tariff cooperation that is self-enforcing, and it is possible that the politically first-best tariff level is unsustainable.

Trade retaliation in this framework (as distinguished from compensation for an adjustment to the bargain, discussed earlier) is generally an out-of-equilibrium behavior that will not be observed in practice (although retaliation may be observed in a suboptimal equilibrium of an infinitely repeated game). There is also no role for a formal dispute resolution system. Despite its rigor, therefore, the simple self-enforcement framework offers quite an incomplete account of WTO/GATT enforcement, where retaliation is in fact observed at times, is transitory in almost all cases, and is now (generally) seen only after an adverse ruling by a formal dispute settlement proceeding.

Some features of the system may be explained by other considerations. The formal dispute resolution system, for example, serves in part as an information revelation mechanism. WTO members may be unable to discern on their own whether another member has cheated, and a formal investigation may be helpful to identify cheaters and trigger sanctions. In addition, the dispute resolution system may be useful as a source of "gap filler" rules for an incomplete bargain, approximating what WTO members would have negotiated had they been able to address all possible contingencies explicitly in the treaty text.[31]

A particularly interesting question concerns why the old GATT system with "blocking" under the consensus rule was replaced by the new WTO system with automatic sanctions. Some commentators suggest that the new system was designed to toughen sanctions and discourage cheating. One can argue, however, that the new system was designed to reduce rather than increase the penalty for cheating. The penalty for cheating in both the old and the new systems is essentially the same—aggrieved nations retaliate with their own trade sanctions. One thing that has changed, however, is that the aggrieved nations can no longer set the level of sanction themselves without central oversight. Instead, all sanctions are subject to arbitration to determine whether they are "substantially equivalent" to the harm caused by the ongoing violation. The new system thus reins in the magnitude of unilateral retaliation. Indeed, in the cases that have gone so far as to produce retaliation, violators routinely argue to the arbitrators that the proposed sanctions are excessive, and arbitrators typically cut them back. This is valuable if excessive retaliation can destabilize the system by triggering a trade war or if it is important to calibrate retaliation to facilitate "efficient breach" (discussed further below).

We know of no entirely satisfactory explanation for the fact that sanctions are prospective only and limited to situations in which violator nations refuse to comply with rulings after a "reasonable time." Perhaps litigation in the WTO has large positive externalities in clarifying the terms of the bargain, and the delay of sanctions encourages disputants to litigate to conclusion. Or perhaps informal sanctions alone are enough to discourage most blatant cheating, so that the bulk of cases are expected to involve good faith disputes over legal obligations. Because trade sanctions are costly (creating deadweight costs and perhaps political costs as well), the membership may not wish to sanction behavior that arises in good faith. Sanctions may then be used only as a last resort against recalcitrant cheaters. These suggestions are little more than conjectures, however, and a fully convincing explanation remains to be developed.

Another issue concerns the choice of sanctions within the system. If it is indeed the case that trade sanctions are costly because they create their own deadweight losses, why does the WTO not embrace an alternative sanctions regime, such as a regime involving money damages that are a "pure transfer" in the language of economists? One possible answer is that money damages are not really a "pure transfer" given the deadweight costs of taxation, the potential for the availability of money damages to increase litigation costs (both because they are hard to measure and because litigants may spend more money to obtain them), and the challenges that many developing countries would face in raising the funds to pay money damages. In addition, what would happen if a nation refused to pay money damages? Perhaps trade sanctions would have to remain in the background as the ultimate sanction. And given that fact, nothing prevents nations from settling disputes today with money to avoid trade sanctions under current law (indeed, we have seen such behavior on occasion, as when the United States set up a fund to aid Brazilian farmers after Brazil prevailed in the recent Upland Cotton dispute over U.S. agricultural subsidies).

Yet another question relates to standing: why is standing to bring cases in the WTO limited to WTO member nations, even though violations of WTO law plainly impose substantial costs on private firms and other powerful interest groups? One possible answer is that a decision by private actors to bring a dispute case may itself have various externalities, such as the possibility of an unfavorable impact on other aspects of international relations. Likewise, if we conceptualize trade agreements as bargains between political officials designed to maximize the welfare of those officials, it is possible that political officials collectively prefer not to enforce all of the rules all of the time. Cases that benefit poorly organized or out-of-favor industries at the expense of a well-organized and politically connected industry, for example, may be on balance undesirable, and political officials may prefer a standing mechanism that allows them to be avoided—all officials can benefit on average from such a mechanism over time. The denial of private standing means that cases will be brought only on behalf of industries that governments find it in their interest to help, which goes at least partway toward ensuring that cases are not brought on behalf of politically weak or out-of-favor exporters.[32]

Further, what explains the standard for calibrating trade sanctions—the "substantial equivalence" standard for retaliation under the DSU? A possible answer, although it has sparked some controversy in the literature, is that this standard bears a very rough similarity to the rule of "expectation damages" in contract law, which requires a party who breaches a contract to compensate the other for its losses and thus induces the breaching party to internalize the joint costs of breach and thus to breach only when it is "efficient." By allowing aggrieved parties to withdraw "substantially equivalent" concessions and subjecting retaliatory withdrawals to arbitration under this criterion, the WTO may accomplish something quite similar, making a violator pay a measured price for the violation while allowing aggrieved nations to bestow politically valuable trade protection on well-organized industries as a form of rough "compensation." The opportunity for signatories to "buy out" their obligations under this rule is particularly valuable in circumstances where the other options for adjusting the bargain, such as tariff renegotiations and the escape clause, do not address the underlying political problem.[33]

The beef hormone controversy between the United States (and Canada) and Europe, noted earlier in this chapter, is again illustrative. If one assumes that European officials are under intense pressure to prohibit hormone-raised beef from entering the domestic market, they cannot achieve this limited goal by adjusting MFN tariffs applicable to all beef in an article XXVIII renegotiation or by invoking article XIX on temporary import surges. As a result, they may have no option but to breach the relevant agreement (here the Agreement on Sanitary and Phytosanitary Measures) if they are to achieve their political objective. Moreover, it is possible that the political gain to European officials exceeds the political cost of breach to officials in beef-exporting countries, so that breach is in this sense "efficient." The substantial equivalence standard may allow this efficient breach to occur, and indeed for many years Europe simply refused to comply with the dispute settlement ruling and suffered retaliation as a consequence. The dispute appears at long last to be settling after an offer by Europe to afford increased market access to U.S. exporters of hormone-free beef, but Europe will still retain the prohibition on hormone-raised beef.

Finally, many commentators have raised the question of whether developing countries receive a fair shake from the WTO dispute system. The basis for concern is obvious—developing countries, particularly those with smaller economies, have limited capacity to retaliate because access to their markets may be relatively unimportant to trading partners. The empirical evidence suggests that developing countries fare better than one might expect on this basis, however, and that they may be hampered more by their lack of legal capacity to pursue their rights than by lack of retaliatory capacity.

19

International Investment, Antitrust, and Monetary Law

We conclude with three areas of international economic law that have received less attention from scholars but that nevertheless raise a range of fascinating questions. Because the literature on these subjects is scant, our treatment of each will be fairly brief.

International Investment Law

Foreign investors are vulnerable to actions by host governments that diminish the value of their investments. Once an investor builds a factory, for example, the costs are largely "sunk," in the language of economics—that is, an investor cannot recoup costs by dismantling the factory and leaving but must be allowed to operate to earn a reasonable return. Without legal protections for the investor, the host country can thus take advantage of the investor in many ways (by expropriating the factory, taxing away all of its economic profit, imposing heavy regulatory burdens, and so on). To be sure, governments can take advantage of their domestic investors in such ways as well, but foreign investors may be particularly vulnerable due to a lack of local political influence.

Investors are not ignorant of these risks and consider them in deciding whether, when, where, and how much to invest. They may refuse to invest at all in particularly risky environments, and in less risky settings they may require a significant "risk premium" as part of their expected rate of return before they can be enticed to invest.

From the host country perspective, an investor risk premium is detrimental ex ante, as it effectively raises the price of imported capital. The quantity of foreign investment declines (because fewer investments yield the necessary expected return), and a greater share of the returns to investments that are undertaken must be promised to foreign investors. After sunk investments are in place, however, the government's temptation to take advantage of them may nevertheless be great. The government thus faces what economists term a time consistency problem—ex post, they are tempted to exploit foreign owners of sunk investments, but this situation harms the government ex ante because it increases investor risk premiums.

This analysis suggests a role for legal devices that commit host governments not to exploit foreign investors after investments are sunk. If such devices are credible, investors will reduce their risk premiums, and the host country will benefit from a cheaper supply of imported capital.

Legal protections for foreign investors may of course be embodied in the domestic law of the host country. The "takings clause" in the Fifth Amendment to the U.S. Constitution, for example, applies to any private property taken for public use, regardless of whether the owner is a citizen. Such commitments under domestic law may not be terribly credible in some countries, however, because investors may fear that the government will change the law or that domestic courts will not enforce it faithfully on behalf of foreigners. These concerns may be particularly prominent in developing countries, where government can be unstable or corrupt and the "rule of law" may not be well established.

International investment law can help to overcome these problems. Depending on the circumstances, investor protections under international law may be more difficult for a host country to alter after investments are undertaken. And if investor protections are enforceable in impartial international tribunals, investors need not worry that they will be "hometowned" in the courts of the host country.

Yet it is also important for host governments to retain policy flexibility to deal with legitimate changes in circumstances. Perhaps the government needs to construct a railroad or highway and needs to take property owned by foreign investors. Or perhaps new information comes to light about some safety or environmental problem that requires new regulation that may reduce the returns to foreign investors. A blanket commitment against any policy changes that might affect foreign investors adversely thus seems undesirable, and it is accordingly necessary to balance the virtues of investor protection rules against any constraints that they may place on policy adaptation.

As a final note, contrast the rationale for investment agreements with the rationale for trade agreements. In the trade area, as we explained in Chapter 18, the primary externality arises because "large" countries (countries with some market power over their terms of trade) will adversely affect the prices received by foreign exporters when they engage in protectionist policies. "Small" countries whose policies do not affect foreign exporters do not create any externality, and hence their participation in trade agreements must have some other explanation. Here, by contrast, a country need not be "large" in relation to world capital markets for it to benefit from policies that reduce investor risk premiums. Even if investors have equally good (risk-adjusted) investment opportunities elsewhere, a reduction in the risk that investors face from an investment in a small country will lower the price of imported capital in that country and thus comport with the rationale for an investment agreement as put forward above.

History

In the main, international investment law evolved in relation to disputes between investors from developed, capital-exporting countries and the governments of developing, capital-importing nations. The law began as customary international law but in modern times has moved heavily toward treaty-based law. This evolution is due to a number of perceived weaknesses in the customary regime.

Early customary law concerning the treatment of foreign investors rested on the proposition that host states owed certain minimum obligations to aliens and their property.[1] One possible rule was that host states owed foreign investors treatment equal to that afforded to domestic investors—in essence, a national treatment obligation. Yet some states treated their own investors quite badly, which led many international law commentators to urge that host states must meet a certain "minimum standard" for the treatment of aliens, no matter how badly they may treat their own nationals. The precise contours of this minimum standard, however, were unclear. Indeed, some nations denied that international law provided any investor protection. The "Calvo Doctrine," named for a nineteenth-century Argentine foreign minister, asserted that alien investors were limited to whatever local remedies were afforded them by host state law.

Although the substantive protections under customary law were in dispute, it was clear that any customary norm was enforceable only by governments. Investors had no private right of action under international law (unless a host state chose to create one in its domestic courts).

These limits of customary law were less significant in colonial times. Much of the foreign investment that took place arose within colonial empires, and the colonial powers used force to protect their interests. With the erosion of colonial empires in the twentieth century, however, tensions began to rise. One of the more significant disputes from a legal perspective involved a taking of U.S.-owned agricultural lands by the Mexican government. Mexico insisted that it was entitled to take the property and had no obligation to afford compensation, citing the Calvo Doctrine. In response, U.S. Secretary of State Cordell Hull insisted that minimum international standards for the treatment of aliens included a requirement for "prompt, adequate and effective compensation," a phrasing that became known as the Hull formula. Various Latin American countries nonetheless incorporated "Calvo clauses" into their constitutions, denying any international legal remedy and rejecting the Hull formula. They also inserted Calvo clauses in their contracts with foreign investors.

The fractious state of customary law continued after World War II, as developed countries increasingly sought to broaden the protections for their investors, while developing countries sought to limit or eliminate their obligations under international law. The matter became a focus of attention at the United Nations, where the developing countries sponsored and passed various General Assembly resolutions on the subject. Among the most significant were Resolution 3171 in 1973 and Resolution 3281 in 1974. These resolutions essentially provided that, in the event of a nationalization of foreign-owned property, compensation would be paid in accordance with the laws of the nationalizing state, unless agreed otherwise. Thus, developing nations sought to preserve an option to expropriate property with minimal compensation if their domestic laws so allowed.

The weaknesses of international customary law led investors to seek greater protection through treaty law. One can find elements of treaty protection for investors as early as the Byzantine Empire, where the emperors granted Venetian merchants various rights to trade without customs duties and rights to establish dwelling and trading houses on Byzantine territory. In more modern times, the United States negotiated treaties of "friendship, commerce, and navigation" (FCN) as early as the late eighteenth century. The earliest FCN treaties focused mainly on international trade issues, but over time they increasingly included protections for investors. Their terms included provisions guaranteeing investors access to domestic courts, precluding discrimination between domestic and foreign investors, ensuring a minimum standard of treatment for U.S. investors and requiring "sufficient" or "just" compensation for any taking of property.

Beginning in the 1960s, European nations, led by Germany, began to negotiate bilateral investment treaties (BITs) with (primarily) developing countries. The United States initiated its own BIT program in 1981, and many countries followed suit. Today BITs number in the thousands. Typical BITs provide investors with a right to prompt compensation in the event of expropriation and require national treatment toward foreign investors of the other party. They may also grant investors certain rights to transfer earnings freely out of the host country. Most BITs also provide that disputes may be referred to neutral international arbitration and that arbitration may be initiated by private investors.

WTO law does not contain investor protection rules save for some provisions respecting policies that negatively impact trade in goods and a few investment-related rules in services sectors, but a number of modern preferential trade agreements do include investor rights provisions. Chapter Eleven of NAFTA, for example, includes nondiscrimination rules (most favored nation and national treatment), a "minimum standard of treatment" principle, and assurances against expropriation without compensation. It also provides investors with a private right of action for money damages before international arbitrators.

Recent years have witnessed rapid growth in private litigation under BITs and similar treaty arrangements such as NAFTA. According to a 2010 report from the United Nations Conference on Trade and Development, the total number of known treaty-based arbitration cases had risen to 357 by the end of 2009. Of those, 57 percent had been initiated since 2005. With respect to venue, 225 cases were filed with the International Centre for Settlement of Investment Disputes (ICSID), an arm of the World Bank, or under the ICSID Additional Facility; 91 under the United Nations Commission on International Trade Law rules; 19 with the Stockholm Chamber of Commerce; 8 were administered by the Permanent Court of Arbitration in the Hague; 5 with the International Chamber of Commerce; and 4 were ad hoc cases.[2]

Do Investment Treaties Benefit Developing Countries?

Developing countries are voluntary parties to BITs and similar treaties with investor protection provisions. One might thus assume that these treaty commitments are in the best interests of the developing countries that accede to them. Nevertheless, questions have been raised about the benefits of investor protection treaties to the host countries. Some of these concerns relate to the interpretation of particular treaty provisions, as shall be seen in a moment. Other concerns are broader.

In particular, an interesting puzzle arises from the fact that just as developing countries were pushing for weaker investor protection under customary law in the UN General Assembly during the 1970s, developing countries were also beginning to sign BITs in increasing numbers. What explains this seeming contradiction in their position? One possibility is that developing countries were better off as a group by resisting stronger investor protections, thus explaining their collective behavior in the United Nations. Yet, acting individually, perhaps developing countries believed that they could benefit by being the first to sign onto BITs with major investor countries, thereby diverting investment to themselves and away from their developing country competitors that had not yet signed BITs. Put slightly differently, the developing countries faced a prisoner's dilemma—maybe it was in their collective interest to refuse to grant greater investor protections, yet when confronted with the individual option to accept or reject BITs, they acceded to them because they reaped individual benefits at the expense of other developing nations.[3]

This hypothesis is intriguing but difficult to assess. The benefits to developing countries from signing BITs are not limited to the diversion of investments from nonsignatories. For reasons given earlier, BITs can reduce investor risk and lead to an overall net increase in global investment, not merely a transfer from one host country to another. The benefits of cheaper imported capital to the developing world may outweigh any loss of wealth due to the subsequent costs of investor protection rules—the balance of costs and benefits cannot be signed as a theoretical matter but is instead an empirical question.

It is also possible that the resistance of the developing world to the Hull formula in the United Nations can be reconciled with the proposition that BITs yield net benefits to developing countries. Note that the battle within the United Nations was about the rules of customary law, which applied in the event of any expropriation of an existing investment prior to the creation of a BIT. Thus, developing countries may have pursued a strategy of exploiting existing sunk investments for a period of time, relying on the weak protections of customary law. But they may have realized that the opportunities for such behavior would diminish after sunk investments were expropriated or otherwise depreciated, and it may then have been in their best interest to sign BITs to attract more investment going forward.[4]

Indeed, if it had been in the collective interest of developing countries to reject BITs, why did they not use some forum like the General Assembly to communicate with each other and agree to eschew them? After all, the essence of a prisoner's dilemma is that the players lack the ability to make commitments to each other before deciding how to behave, but the developing countries were already in close communication on these issues.

We note finally that a considerable empirical literature exists on the question of whether BITs in fact lead to greater investment in developing countries. The studies exhibit wide variation—some find little effect, some find significant positive effects, and a few even suggest adverse effects. The differences result from different samples of countries, different time periods, and different statistical methods. We will not try to arbitrate the debate; suffice it to say that consensus on the matter does not yet exist.[5]

The Logic of Investor-State Dispute Settlement

Private rights of action for money damages are available under many investment treaties but are clearly an anomaly in international law. Generally speaking, only states have standing to bring claims under international law (except to the degree that domestic legal systems incorporate international law into domestic private rights of action, as under the U.S. Alien Tort Statute). Even in other areas of international economic law—such as international trade—private rights of action do not arise. Private parties cannot bring claims to the WTO, for example, as we noted in Chapter 18. NAFTA affords a particularly crisp example of the distinction as well. Violations of NAFTA relating to trade in goods and services, as well as intellectual property rights, are actionable only by member governments, but violations of the investor rights provisions are actionable by the investors themselves.

What explains the widespread availability of private rights of action in investment treaties? Recall our discussion of the rationale for investor protection. Host governments wish to assure foreign investors that they will not be expropriated or otherwise exploited. Such assurances benefit the host country by lowering the cost of imported capital. Imagine, however, that an aggrieved investor had no standing to bring a claim and no right to a monetary remedy but instead had to rely on its home government to bring a complaint and provide an eventual remedy. The investor would then face the risk that its home government would lack the resources to pursue the case or that it would choose not to do so for political reasons. And even if its home government brought a claim, the investor might not receive much of a remedy—perhaps the matter would be "settled" with a promise by the host country to behave better in the future. In short, if investment treaties could be enforced only by states, private investors would face substantial risk to their investments even if treaties provided for investor protection. Investor risk premiums would incorporate these risks, and capital-importing states would face a higher cost of capital, other things being equal.

Private rights of action for money damages alleviate these problems. Investors can bring claims on their own behalf without having to persuade their home governments to act, and money damages can compensate the investors for their losses. Risk premiums decline and capital-importing states have cheaper access to foreign capital.[6]

Of course, private rights of action alone do not guarantee that investors will feel secure. If any action had to be brought in the host country's courts, and those courts could not be trusted, much risk would remain for the investors. Accordingly, investment treaties not only afford private rights of action but allow them to be brought in reliable and neutral forums. The most popular forum is ICSID, as noted. Various other international arbitral facilities are also used. These arbitrations typically proceed much like domestic arbitrations, with each side selecting one arbitrator and those arbitrators then selecting a third, "neutral," arbitrator.

Further issues arise with respect to the enforceability of awards. States subject to legal action in foreign countries may be protected by sovereign immunity; even when not, they can take the simple expedient of not storing seizable assets abroad. Investors who attempt to enforce judgments against assets on the state's home territory must go through the same courts that could not be trusted for ordinary litigation. Although international conventions exist that are aimed at enhancing enforceability, significant problems may arise in practice.

Controversies in Substantive Law

Investment treaties raise innumerable intriguing and difficult legal questions. What is an "investor"? What is an "investment"? What is "expropriation"? What is "fair and equitable treatment" under international law? What defenses are available to a government that violates a treaty commitment (e.g., "necessity")? A glance at an investment law treatise will confirm that these and numerous other questions are central to modern investor-state litigation.[7]

Scholarly writing on such matters is thin and generally quite doctrinal. Economic analysis is even more scant. We cannot hope to address the lacuna here and will simply mention one area of recent controversy for purposes of illustration.

The *Metalclad* case[8] involved a dispute over the construction of a hazardous waste landfill in Mexico. Metalclad, a U.S. investor, incurred substantial costs in building the new landfill. Before the landfill opened, it became embroiled in environmental protests and subsequent disputes with local authorities over environmental permits. Eventually its operating permit was denied, despite initial assurances from Mexican federal officials that the permits would eventually be forthcoming. Ultimately, the area was designated a cactus preserve and the landfill was abandoned.

Metalclad brought claims under two investor rights provisions of NAFTA. Article 1105(1) states that "[e]ach Party shall accord to investments of another

Party treatment in accordance with international law, including fair and equitable treatment and full protection and security." Article 1110(1) further states that "[n]o Party may directly or indirectly nationalize an investment of an investor of another Party in its territory or take a measure tantamount to nationalization or expropriation of such an investment . . . except . . . on payment of compensation. . . ." The arbitrators found that Mexico had violated both provisions and entered a substantial award for Metalclad. They held that Mexico had failed to provide a "transparent and predictable framework for Metalclad's business planning and investment." The result was a denial of "fair and equitable" treatment, which amounted to an "indirect expropriation."

Critics of the decision argue that the arbitrators went beyond international law under section 1105, effectively creating an open-ended obligation of "fair and equitable treatment" that had no precedent in customary law. Likewise, they argue that the "indirect expropriation" finding effectively opens the door to claims of expropriation anytime that changes in regulatory policy impair the value of an investment. A requirement that governments compensate for such "regulatory takings," urge the critics, may chill the regulatory process even when it involves desirable policies. And to the degree that the compensation requirement under international law is more generous than under domestic law, it may advantage foreign investors relative to domestic investors and distort the pattern of investment.[9] Compensation requirements may also induce firms to invest excessively, or unwisely accelerate the pace of investment, when regulatory uncertainty exists about the desirability or permissibility of the investment.

More broadly, cases like *Metalclad* are often cited as evidence that investment treaties unduly impinge on the sovereignty of host countries. It is often suggested that they elevate commercial values above other, more important, values relating to health and the environment. Such arguments were central to the debate over a proposed multilateral agreement on investment, an Organisation for Economic Co-operation and Development (OECD) initiative that failed in the mid-1990s.

The critics make useful points, but there are important considerations on the other side. Host governments often have better information about the course of their future policies than foreign investors. If a host government can dither around and even mislead foreign investors about the likely course of regulation, as arguably happened in *Metalclad,* investors may be led to make wasteful expenditures. The danger may be particularly acute with foreign investors, who may lack efficacy in the host country's political system and thus be particularly unsuccessful at protecting themselves through local political participation. When investors are aware of this problem ex ante, risk premiums may rise uneconomically. To the degree that *Metalclad* can be read not as a general requirement of compensation for any regulatory taking, therefore, but as a requirement that host governments behave in good faith and with due care in advising foreign investors about likely regulatory policies and decisions, it may well make sense.

More broadly, *Metalclad* illustrates a fundamental tension between the importance of protecting investors against uneconomical risk that raises the cost of imported capital on the one hand and the importance of preserving policy flexibility in host countries on the other. It is no doubt unwise to require that investors be compensated for any change in government policy that reduces investment returns, yet it is also unwise to afford host countries unfettered discretion to act in careless or arbitrary fashion in the name of regulatory sovereignty. Some sort of intermediate position is needed. In that regard, the vague and open-ended notion of "fair and equitable treatment" offers little help, as does the notion of "indirect" expropriation or "measures tantamount" to expropriation. One of the future tasks of investment arbitration is to refine these concepts to produce a more tailored body of doctrine.

International Antitrust Law

We have already touched on some of the externalities that arise in the antitrust area during our earlier discussion of prescriptive jurisdiction under international law in Chapter 10. One fundamental problem is that antitrust policy decisions in one state affect firms and consumers in other states, in ways that may lead governments to behave inefficiently from a global perspective because they care about their own firms and consumers but not about foreign firms and consumers. An export cartel may benefit firms in the exporting state and thus be tolerated by that state, for example, yet it will hurt consumers abroad and reduce global economic welfare for the same reasons that domestic cartels tend to reduce domestic economic welfare. A merger between two firms in state A may enhance global economic welfare by producing cost-saving efficiencies, yet the increase in market concentration may lead to slightly higher prices for consumers in state B. State B's antitrust authorities may thus try to block the merger even though it is efficient. Likewise, a dominant firm in state A may engage in various practices that reduce costs to consumers and have efficiency justifications, yet that may make it harder for rivals in state B to compete successfully. Antitrust authorities in state B may thus attack such practices as anticompetitive and impose large fines on the dominant firm, despite the efficiency of its practices. Innumerable other examples might be offered.

A related set of concerns pertains to the existence of overlapping jurisdiction and potentially inconsistent regulation affecting multinational firms. Consider a multinational firm that does business in many countries and that wishes to employ a certain type of intellectual property cross-licensing arrangement of the sort that is occasionally condemned by antitrust authorities as a cartel-facilitating device. The question for antitrust purposes is whether the benefits of cross-licensing, which broadens access to useful technology and quiets the threat of intellectual property litigation, are greater than the potential costs of a cross-licensing arrangement that might serve as cover for price fixing, market division, or other objectionable practices. Antitrust authorities in each jurisdiction where the multinational proposes to use a cross-license may investigate and make their own judgment about this question. Even if the authorities are well intentioned and do not take parochial considerations into account (no doubt an unrealistic assumption), the multinational firm will nevertheless face the task of persuading all of the national authorities to allow the cross-licensing. If only one national regulator balks, the ability of the cross-licensing arrangement to afford multinationals worldwide access to essential technology without threat of litigation may be lost or greatly diminished. An arrangement that has been judged to be efficient and desirable by multiple regulators around the world may become infeasible because one outlier regulator disagrees.

Finally, to the degree that national regulators share similar policies and agendas, their work may have a great deal of overlap. Regulators investigating a suspected international cartel in some industry, for example, may all be after essentially the same information and evidence. The costs of gathering information may be reduced considerably if they can cooperate and share what they find.

Because of these and other issues, the possible benefits of international cooperation are readily apparent. At a minimum, regulators can benefit from the exchange of information and analysis that each regulator would otherwise have to generate independently. At a deeper level, all states would benefit from a credible commitment by each national regulator to pursue globally efficient antitrust policy and not to sacrifice global efficiency for parochial national interest. One might even imagine that the plethora of national regulators creates much redundancy and that national regulation might usefully be replaced with a global competition authority.

The literature on the possibility of international cooperation is thus extensive, and proposals from the commentators range from the modest to the ambitious to the skeptical.[10] Various national governments and international institutions have become involved as well. The OECD, for example, has pushed for international convergence on certain substantive principles, especially "hard core cartel practices." The most ambitious initiative involved the WTO and a 2001 Doha Round negotiating agenda item that included a push for a global competition policy agreement.

To date, however, international agreements have been few and more or less limited to modest bilateral commitments. The WTO initiative foundered. We will take a brief look at some of the more significant bilateral agreements and then consider why broader and deeper international cooperation has failed.

Bilateral Agreements

Numerous (mainly developed) countries have negotiated bilateral agreements requiring cooperation on certain antitrust matters, and a few regional trade arrangements such as NAFTA and Mercosur also include cooperation provisions. By and large, the scope of required cooperation is quite limited, and much of the language imposes rather weak obligations (e.g., one party must "consider" the interests of another). To give a flavor of such agreements, we consider here two agreements between the United States and the European Union—an "Agreement . . . Regarding the Application of Their Competition Laws" from 1991 and a 1998 "Agreement . . . on the Application of Positive Comity Principles."

The 1991 agreement begins with a "notification" requirement, compelling the authorities to notify each other whenever "enforcement activities may affect important interests of the other party." Examples of situations requiring notification include situations in which enforcement activities bear on the other party's enforcement activity, involve anticompetitive activity in the other party's territory, relate to a merger involving a company from the other party, or involve remedies that would affect conduct in the other party's territory. The agreement also requires the parties to meet regularly to exchange relevant information and to otherwise exchange information when requested (subject to confidentiality restrictions). A section on positive comity permits one party to ask the other to initiate enforcement activity against conduct in its territory that adversely affects the interests of the requesting party. A section on "avoidance of conflicts" essentially requires each party to "consider" the interests of the other party in pursuing its own enforcement actions.

The 1998 agreement elaborates the positive comity obligation somewhat, providing that parties may request the other to take action when they believe that conduct occurring in the territory of the other violates that party's antitrust laws. It further suggests that the requesting party suspend its own enforcement activities, inter alia, if action by the country in which the conduct is occurring is likely to provide a sufficient remedy to the party requesting enforcement.

Plainly, the obligations in these agreements are quite limited. They oblige some notification and information exchange (subject to confidentiality issues) and suggest that each party must weigh the interests of the other in deciding whether and how to enforce its laws. But each enforcement authority remains essentially free to pursue its own agenda in the end. There is no tight obligation to forgo parochial behavior, only an obligation to "consider" the interests of the other party. Likewise, there is no dispute resolution system or enforcement mechanism. If one party makes a parochial decision favoring its own interests over those of the other party or the global interest, there is little that the other can do except to voice its concern. Likewise, if the parties disagree about some substantive question, such as whether to permit a merger, to go after some practice by a dominant firm, or to exercise extraterritorial jurisdiction over conduct abroad, each authority remains free to take enforcement action in accordance with its own judgment. Not surprisingly, therefore, conflicts between the United States and Europe continue to arise, and suspicions of parochialism have not been put to rest.

In short, the existing cooperation agreements (and the others in place among various countries) have some capacity to reduce redundant investigative activities, and provide a formal mechanism for an exchange of views on matters of mutual interest, but do nothing to resolve significant disagreements about appropriate antitrust policy. Whether those disagreements result from the pursuit of parochial interests at the expense of outsiders or simply from good-faith differences of opinion about the economic consequences of conduct under investigation, enforcement authorities remain largely free to go their own way. Some additional restraint may flow from the customary international rules on jurisdiction and comity discussed in Chapter 10, but much room remains for policy disagreements that may undermine global efficiency.

The Failure of Global Cooperation

Why has international cooperation on antitrust matters been so limited? As noted, commentators have certainly called for broader measures, and multilateral initiatives were undertaken at the WTO. These initiatives failed, however, and at this writing there is no serious prospect of greater cooperation. Why the lack of success?

There is no one answer to this question, but we note a few factors. Most important, it is not clear that all nations would gain politically from a competition policy agreement that imposed sound principles of antitrust policy. Developing countries in particular showed a lack of enthusiasm for the competition policy initiative at the WTO. Some may be net beneficiaries of a system that allows the persistence of export cartels. Others may be home to firms that benefit from lax antitrust enforcement and that are quite powerful politically, in comparison to consumer interests that may be particularly weak politically.

In addition, international consensus does not exist on many of the substantive issues of antitrust law. The compromises necessary to reach an international agreement on key principles, therefore, might undermine core judgments of some national antitrust enforcers. Comparing Europe and the United States, for example, Europe is far more likely to go after single firm conduct under its "abuse of dominance" jurisprudence, condemning practices that American regulators would likely deem efficient and permissible. U.S. regulators were, accordingly, rather unenthusiastic about the WTO initiative.

The lack of consensus on some antitrust principles, particularly relating to single firm conduct, has led to proposals for more modest agreements, perhaps imposing a basic national treatment obligation (an obligation to treat foreign firms no less favorably than domestic firms), and an agreement to prohibit certain hard-core cartel practices. The OECD in particular has focused on encouraging all nations to address the problem of cartels. But even these limited initiatives are not without problems. Consider first a national treatment obligation. Antitrust enforcement often involves difficult and rather subjective judgments—will a merger lead to substantial efficiencies, and will the increase in concentration cause prices to rise importantly? If national authorities were accused of shading these judgments to favor their domestic firms over foreign interests in violation of a national treatment obligation, for example, it is not at all clear how a dispute process could confidently determine the truth of the allegation.

Even cartel practices raise challenging issues. Although a consensus may exist that hard-core cartel practices such as price fixing are undesirable, disagreement may well arise over the question of when price fixing is present. The long-standing controversy in the United States over the line between price fixing and mere "conscious parallelism," and the "plus factors" that are required to prove the former, illustrates the problem.

National regulators may be particularly reluctant to agree to any arrangement that entrusts these difficult questions to international arbitrators. WTO adjudicators are not competition policy experts historically, for example, and it is unclear whether participants in any international dispute process would have both the skills and the incentives for a proper evaluation of the subtle antitrust issues that national regulators often confront.

Of course, some of the same concerns about difficult and subtle policy issues, and about the skills and incentives of international arbitrators, might be raised about trade agreements and their dispute resolution processes, yet the world has made great strides in multilateral cooperation on trade matters. But perhaps trade agreements differ at least in degree. Although we cannot quantify or prove this claim in a precise way, it does seem that many trade obligations are relatively crisp and straightforward. (Is the tariff commitment being observed? Is there an impermissible quota? Is there reasonable scientific support for this regulation? Has the antidumping duty calculation ignored some substantive or procedural rule? And so on.) In antitrust, by contrast, the questions can be much harder to answer with confidence. (Is this merger likely to raise prices a lot? Does bundling a browser with an operating system somehow foreclose competition in some software market?) The uncertainties and potential error costs associated with entrusting such matters to international arbitration may simply be too great, or may at least be perceived to be too great. The specter of problematic international decisions also affords entrenched domestic bureaucrats an opportunity to argue against international cooperation that might undermine their authority.

In sum, although cooperation on international competition policy is quite restricted, one cannot exclude the possibility that the absence of greater cooperation is efficient—the costs may simply exceed the benefits. In any case, the politics of international antitrust suggest that deeper cooperation is unlikely to arise anytime soon.

International Monetary Law

International monetary law[11] refers principally to the Articles of the International Monetary Fund (IMF) and to a few miscellaneous matters elsewhere to which we will allude briefly. Informal cooperation on international monetary matters among leading finance ministers (soft law) is also an important part of the regime, although we will have little to say about it.

International monetary cooperation spans a number of issues. The first is currency convertibility, which is essential to the facilitation of international trade in goods and services. A second, and much more problematic area, has involved cooperation on exchange rate policies. We discuss each in turn after providing some background on international monetary economics.

Background on Exchange Rates and the Balance of Payments

"Exchange rates" are the prices at which currencies are bought and sold on world currency markets. If the Euro-dollar exchange rate is 1.30, for example, then one Euro costs $1.30 in U.S. dollars. The price of dollars in Euros (the dollar-Euro exchange rate) is simply the reciprocal (1/1.30) or approximately €0.77, meaning that a dollar can be purchased for about 0.77 Euros.

Exchange rates and foreign exchange play a seminal role in international commerce. People buy and sell goods and services on an everyday basis in their local currencies, and they wish to be paid in their local currency when they collect a paycheck or make a sale. When transactions cross borders, the seller ultimately wishes to be paid in his local currency, but the buyer initially has only her own local currency. The foreign exchange market solves this problem by allowing the buyer, the seller, or more frequently some sort of middleman like a bank or credit card company to exchange the buyer's currency for the seller's currency at the prevailing exchange rate.

Movements in the exchange rate can make international commerce more or less profitable, holding other things equal. Consider transactions between the United States and Europe. When the Euro-dollar exchange rate increases, U.S. exports to Europe become cheaper for Europeans (again holding other things equal) because Euros buy more dollars, a fact that will tend to increase U.S. exports to Europe unless prices in dollars adjust upward to offset the higher exchange rate (as they will tend to do over time). Likewise, when the Euro-dollar exchange rate increases, European exports become more expensive to Americans and will tend to decline unless prices in Euros adjust downward to offset the higher exchange rate.

In the simplest economic models without government intervention into exchange markets, the exchange rate reaches its "equilibrium" value when trade is balanced—when imports equal exports (in value terms) for all countries. If the United States were importing more from Europe than it was exporting to Europe in such a model, for example, the U.S. demand for Euros would exceed the European demand for dollars at the initial exchange rate. This excess demand for Euros would cause the Euro to appreciate, making imports from Europe more expensive in the United States and exports from the United States cheaper in Europe. U.S. imports would decline and U.S. exports would increase until balanced trade was attained, at which point the exchange rate would be in equilibrium.

Balanced trade does not always occur in practice, however, and indeed one frequently reads about national "trade deficits" and "trade surpluses." A trade deficit arises when a nation imports more goods and services than it exports over some period of time; a surplus exists when the opposite is true. Using the simple model of equilibrium exchange rates that balance trade, a nation with a trade deficit should expect its currency to depreciate, while a nation with a surplus should expect its currency to appreciate. Such exchange rate movements do not necessarily occur, however, for two reasons that the simplest exchange rate models do not capture.

First, governments may intervene in the market to prevent depreciation or appreciation. A nation that wishes to avoid depreciation will buy its own currency to prop up the price, using its foreign exchange "reserves" of other currencies (or, in the old days, gold). A nation that wishes to avert appreciation can sell its own currency to drive down the price and will accumulate foreign currency reserves in exchange. In modern times, for example, China has accumulated over U.S.$3 trillion in foreign exchange reserves as it has sold the Chinese yuan to prevent its appreciation.

Second, even without government intervention, trade deficits and surpluses do not necessarily produce the exchange rate movements predicted by the simple balanced trade models. The reason is that the balanced trade models ignore the role of capital flows and the possibility that trade deficits and surpluses create no pressure on exchange rates when trading partners are content to buy or sell offsetting amounts of capital assets.

Consider, for concreteness, a transaction in which an American buys an automobile from Europe using Euros purchased with dollars in the foreign exchange market. The foreign holder of those dollars may have no interest in buying American goods with them. Yet she may be quite content to put them into U.S. treasury bonds, a U.S. savings account, the New York Stock Exchange, or real estate in the United States. If so, the transaction contributes to a trade deficit in the sense that U.S. exports are less than imports, but there is an offsetting transaction that involves the "export" of a U.S. capital asset (the sale of such an asset to a foreigner).

National income accounting accordingly makes a distinction between "current account transactions" and "capital account" transactions.[12] Current account transactions include all imports and exports of goods and services (plus gifts, usually minor). Capital account transactions include all other transactions in the private sector (bank deposits, stock purchases, real estate purchases, and so on) as well as government sales and acquisitions of foreign assets. The net sum of current account and capital account transactions (plus, in practice, a statistical discrepancy) is zero—an accounting identity ensured by double-entry bookkeeping.

The sum of the current account and capital account is sometimes termed the "balance of payments," and the fact that the sum is identically zero is the basis for statements that one may hear to the effect that "the balance of payments is always in balance." Sometimes the term balance of payments is used differently, however, to refer to the sum of the current account plus the private transactions in the capital account. The "balance of payments" then captures the net change in government-held assets that is necessary to balance the capital account against the current account.[13]

References in the press to trade deficits are invariably to the current account. The trade deficit or balance is discussed in two ways in popular discourse. The "merchandise trade balance" refers to current account transactions involving imports and exports of goods only. The "overall" or "current account" trade balance captures transactions in both goods and services.

Why does popular writing about "trade deficits" so often present them as a worrisome problem? One take on this question presupposes that a current account deficit arises when a nation is spending beyond its means and is effectively borrowing from abroad to finance positive net imports of goods and services. At some point the bills come due, and the nation in question may have difficulty repaying its debts. The problem may be particularly acute if the nation in question has obligations to its creditors denominated in another nation's currency. Borrower nations in the developing world, for example, are often unable to borrow in their own currencies because lenders do not have confidence that the currency will maintain a stable value. When obligations must be repaid in foreign currency, and foreigners are not willing to accept the domestic currency in exchange for it, the borrower can meet its obligations only by exporting goods and services for currency that lenders will accept. Various debt crises and sovereign defaults through the years in developing countries have arisen when their ability to export became inadequate to pay their debts denominated in foreign currencies.

The situation is somewhat different for a nation like the United States that is able (at least for now) to borrow in its own currency. Such a borrower does not face the same problem of running short on the foreign exchange needed to repay the debt but may nevertheless find itself with obligations that exceed what it can comfortably repay out of its tax revenues. At that point, the borrower may be tempted to print money to pay its debts, causing inflation and a fall in the value of its currency. Just the fear of such behavior may lead holders of debt obligations to try and sell them and to switch their holdings into assets denominated in another currency. The price of the other currencies rises and the value of the borrower's currency falls. In addition, "capital flight" occurs as foreigners try to liquidate their assets in the borrower's country—its real estate and stock markets might collapse, for example. The net effect may be significant economic disruption in the economy as a whole, although export industries and import-competing industries can benefit from the currency depreciation. This last point hints at one reason why nations may not always be upset about a drop in the price of their currency, as there are industrial beneficiaries who may be politically powerful and welcome it.

In short, there are important scenarios in which serious current account deficits may portend future economic problems. But as the discussion above suggests, there are also benign scenarios associated with a current account deficit. Nations have different savings rates for reasons that are not fully understood but that no doubt relate to the nature and generosity of their entitlement and safety net programs, among other things. Imagine a nation with a low savings rate, and imagine further that this nation is a particularly attractive place for new investment. Suppose, for example, that it has a highly productive and creative work force and a tax regime that is generally favorable to new businesses. Assume that the amount of saving generated domestically is inadequate to take advantage of all the attractive investment opportunities. Foreign investors will gladly step in to fill the gap and happily purchase capital assets on which they expect to make a nice return. If a net capital inflow is to occur in this scenario, the nation must run a current account deficit (again the capital account and the current account must sum to zero). The current account deficit is simply the way that foreigners are able to generate the additional revenues in the currency of the capital-importing country to finance the capital investments that the foreigners desire to make there. This situation can persist in principle for many years, and the capital-importing country is in no danger of becoming strapped to repay its debts—the earnings on investments made by foreigners cover the debt service.

Currency Convertibility

For a variety of reasons relating to exchange rate policies and macroeconomic stabilization policies, some of which are discussed below, governments often restrict the free market exchange of currencies. Such restrictions can become quite problematic for international trade. Suppose, for example, that a U.S. exporter of automobiles wishes to sell its products in Mexico. The U.S. exporter must meet its expenses in dollars and will ultimately wish to obtain dollars for its exports. The Mexican buyers, however, may have only pesos. If the transaction is to occur, some mechanism must exist whereby Mexican buyers can exchange pesos for dollars to make the purchase or whereby the U.S. exporter can accept pesos and later exchange them for dollars. If governments restrict the ability of their citizens to purchase foreign currency, however, and if governments restrict the ability of their citizens to exchange foreign currency for domestic currency, the necessary foreign exchange transactions will not occur.

To avoid such difficulties, the Articles of the International Monetary Fund (article VIII) require members (subject to some exceptions) to permit their currencies to be freely converted into other currencies for purposes of current account transactions. Absent an applicable exception, members cannot restrict the ability of private actors to exchange domestic and foreign currencies to finance current account transactions, and members must agree to buy their own currency from foreign central banks if that currency has been accumulated through current account transactions or if foreign exchange is needed for such transactions. These rules ensure what economists term "currency convertibility." Because the U.S. dollar was convertible after World War II and many other currencies were not, the U.S. dollar became an international medium of exchange. Many trade transactions were invoiced in dollars, and central banks held dollars as reserves. The dollar remains the central reserve currency in the international monetary system, although recent concerns about its long-term stability have led some commentators to question whether it can retain this status.

Note that the convertibility obligations of article VIII do not extend to capital account transactions. Governments may restrict the sale of their currency to foreign purchasers who wish to use it to buy domestic capital assets, for example, and need not buy back their currency if it has been used to make capital purchases abroad. Such restrictions are known as "capital controls" and remain fairly common. The Chinese yuan, for example, is freely convertible for purposes of current account transactions but not when foreigners wish to buy Chinese capital assets (or wish to accumulate yuan for speculative purposes). To be sure, the distinct rules for current and capital account transactions are not always easy to enforce, and actors seeking to engage in capital transactions may at times disguise them as current account transactions. An importer of goods from China, for example, might represent that it needs to buy yuan to finance imports of goods but buy more than is needed immediately.

The IMF rules on current account convertibility have been successful, by and large. Although some deviation from them is allowed in times of balance-of-payments difficulties, nations generally recognize that convertibility is essential for mutually beneficial trade to occur. In that respect, they are self-enforcing and few problems have arisen.

Modern History of Exchange Rate Management by Governments

We now turn to the history of international cooperation on exchange rate policies. Here cooperation has proven much more difficult and unstable.

In principle, exchange rates might be left entirely to the market. Governments could ignore exchange rate movements, and no international cooperation on monetary issues would occur. In such a setting, there would be no role for international monetary law.

For a variety of reasons that will become clear as we proceed, however, governments have never been content to leave exchange rates entirely to market forces in modern times. Before considering the reasons why, let us briefly describe the different ways that governments have managed exchange rates through the years.

The Gold Standard

For a period of time in the late nineteenth and early twentieth centuries, a number of nations (including the United States and Great Britain) adhered to the "gold standard." This policy was not required by any "international law" but was unilaterally followed in accordance with domestic legislation, perhaps accompanied by informal agreement among some finance ministers. The details of its operation were complicated and variable, but roughly speaking the policy involved a commitment to convert national currency into a fixed amount of gold. Of course, if dollars could be converted to gold at a fixed rate, if pounds sterling could be converted to gold at a fixed rate, and if gold was always worth the same in the United States and Great Britain because of free international trade in gold (which there was, more or less), then the value of the pound sterling was also fixed relative to the dollar.

The gold standard regime was thus also a regime of "fixed exchange rates." With fixed exchange rates, anyone engaged in international commerce has some confidence that foreign currency will have a predictable value in terms of domestic currency. The predictability of the relationship between currencies reduces the riskiness of foreign transactions that require currency conversion at some point—so-called exchange risk—and makes such transactions more attractive to risk-averse actors. The ability of fixed exchange rates to reduce exchange risk is often touted as an important virtue of fixed rates (and also affords an argument for currency unions, such as the creation of the Euro). The argument is not a terribly strong one, however, for a variety of reasons. Fixed exchange rate systems have not been terribly stable, as shall be seen, and a sudden, large devaluation over a weekend (as has sometimes occurred historically) can impose a big loss on commercial actors. It is also possible to lay off exchange risk in a forward market. Studies of the impact of exchange rate volatility on trade flows have tended to find little impact, perhaps for this reason.

The gold standard also placed constraints on national monetary (and indirectly fiscal) policies, some useful and some not so useful. To maintain a stable rate of convertibility between currency and gold, nations could not print too much money either to pay for government purchases or to pay off government debt. Excessive increases in the money supply lead to inflation, including inflation in the market price of gold. Once the market price of gold exceeds the implicit value of gold set by the government through currency conversion, holders of currency will all want to convert their currency to gold and the government will quickly run out of gold. Proponents of the gold standard thus argued that it encouraged responsible monetary policy, discouraging inflation and promoting a stable price level.

This purported virtue of the gold standard was somewhat illusory, however, because nations could (and at times did) "devalue" their currency by unilaterally reducing the amount of gold that could be obtained for a unit of currency. Also, the effectiveness of the system in checking inflation depended importantly on a stable relationship between the price of gold and other things. Conceivably, for example, the price of gold might fall on world markets in relation to the price of (say) wheat and oil. There might be no inflation in the price of gold, but the prices of other things could still climb. Indeed, the historical evidence indicates that price levels were much less stable than one might have imagined under the gold standard, apparently because of fluctuations in the supply of gold and thus in the price of gold relative to other things.[14]

Another possible difficulty with a gold standard is that governments may become unable to use monetary policy for economic stabilization purposes. During a recession, for example, the government might wish to lower interest rates to stimulate economic activity. It can do so, for example, by purchasing government securities, which provides money to private actors who deposit it in banks, which then have more money to loan out and reduce interest rates accordingly. But such a policy expands the money supply, leads to inflation in the price of gold and to a run on gold reserves. For believers in the efficacy of monetary policy as a stabilization measure, therefore, the gold standard can become problematic.

Whatever its advantages and disadvantages, the gold standard fell apart around the beginning of World War I. Its demise followed periods when various gold standard nations ran short of gold and devalued their currencies.

Between the end of World War I and the late 1920s, nations experimented with a variety of exchange rate policies. A number of countries had nevertheless returned to the gold standard by 1929, when the United States was engaged in a period of monetary contraction (thus putting downward pressure on the price of gold in terms of dollars). The holders of gold thus wished to exchange gold for dollars at the fixed rate, and other countries began to run short of gold reserves as the United States accumulated reserves. To protect their dwindling gold reserves, other countries were forced into their own contractionary monetary policies to raise the value of their currencies. They also became reluctant to lend money to banks threatened with insolvency during the early days of the Depression, fearing that the holders of the additional money would try to convert it to gold. A number of economists have thus argued that the gold standard contributed importantly to the depth of the Depression in the 1930s.[15]

Bretton Woods, the IMF, and the Revival of Fixed Exchange Rates

The ups and downs of the international monetary system prior to World War II were widely believed to have contributed to economic distress and to the conditions that led to war. Germany in particular was beset with a legendary period of hyperinflation when it started to print money to pay the substantial reparations that were asked of it after World War I. The resulting economic conditions likely contributed to the rise of fascism and Germany's renewed aggressive posture.

Toward the end of the war, therefore, the allies began to plan for the creation of a more stable international monetary system. A meeting was held in Bretton Woods, New Hampshire, in 1944, at which the Articles of the International Monetary Fund were drafted. The IMF was conceived as a part of the broader United Nations system, and the Articles of Agreement were an ambitious effort at multilateral treaty-based cooperation on monetary affairs.[16]

The initial approach of the IMF was a return to a variant of the gold standard. The United States agreed to maintain a stable relationship between the dollar and the price of gold ($35 an ounce). This commitment was to be made credible by a promise to redeem dollars for gold on demand. Other nations, in turn, were obliged to maintain a roughly fixed relationship between their own currencies and the dollar—termed the "par value." Thus, the dollar became the international "reserve currency." Nations other than the United States needed dollar reserves so that, in the event of a depreciation of their currency relative to the dollar, they could use dollars to buy their own currency, bid up its value, and maintain the par value (within small allowed margins of deviation). The United States, by contrast, needed gold reserves to back up its promise to convert dollars to gold.

The legal commitment to a particular par value was not necessarily permanent. Par values were to be set initially in negotiations between each member and the IMF. Thereafter members were not to change them absent "fundamental disequilibrium" in their balance-of-payments situations. The question of who should decide whether such disequilibrium existed was a subject of intense negotiations,[17] and the eventual compromise essentially provided that members could deviate without prior IMF approval but that in certain circumstances they would forfeit access to the resources of the IMF.

But what exactly were those resources? Why did the world need an international monetary "fund" under this plan? The answer relates back to prior experience with the gold standard and the perceived problems that arose when nations devalued their currencies. If the new regime was to be effective at maintaining fixed exchange rates, it was important that nations not run out of reserves—they would then be forced to devalue just as they did when they ran out of gold in earlier times.

The basic design of the fund was that each member contributed both gold and its own currency up front based on the size of its economy—a contribution equal to its assigned "quota." A member could borrow an amount equal to its gold contribution without any ado. Additional borrowings were subject to increasingly stringent restrictions, known as "IMF conditionality." These restrictions might relate to the future monetary and fiscal policies of the debtor, its trade policies, or other relevant issues. All of these rules were embodied in the Articles of Agreement, as amended and interpreted from time to time. Of course, in addition to policy conditionality, borrowers from the fund had to repay the loans eventually, with interest.

The legal details need not detain us, however, for the system gradually fell apart. Among other things, the United States engaged in a period of monetary expansion during the 1950s and 1960s and at times ran significant current account deficits. Inflation in the United States increased. Not surprisingly, the holders of U.S. currency became interested in converting it to gold. Although the U.S. commitment to convert currency to gold was limited to foreign official institutions (U.S. citizens could not convert currency, and gold ownership was restricted), the United States found that its gold reserves were declining rapidly by the early 1960s. At times the world market price of gold climbed well above the "official" price of $35 an ounce. Eventually, the international community came to accept the existence of a two-tiered gold market, and central banks agreed to stay out of the commercial market and continue to trade gold at the official price. The position of the United States was perilous, however, as the value of its gold holdings (at $35 an ounce) fell well below the foreign holdings of dollars. The United States thus depended on the forbearance of other countries from demanding gold at various times when they could have arbitraged it into the commercial market for a tidy profit.

The international community became concerned about the potential lack of reserves in the system and in 1968 embarked on a rather creative move to establish a new kind of international reserve—the "special drawing right" (SDR). The SDR was just an accounting unit, backed by nothing. But if central banks agreed to accept SDRs just as they would gold or dollars, nations running short of reserves could use them to maintain the value of their currencies.

The SDR experiment did not solve the problems in the system, however, especially for the United States. By 1970, external holdings of dollars by official institutions were more than four times the value of U.S. gold reserves. Other nations, most notably Great Britain, had devalued their currencies by lowering their par values, and the United States wished to reduce the value of its currency as well to encourage exports and curtail its current account deficit. Further, nations continued to demand gold from the United States. Finally, on August 15, 1971, President Nixon "closed the gold window." That is, Nixon announced that the United States would no longer convert dollars to gold. The United States also had no capacity to convert dollars into other foreign currencies at the official rates.

Thereafter, a negotiation occurred at which the nominally fixed exchange rates were adjusted, including a 7.89 percent devaluation of the U.S. dollar. Nations agreed to intervene in exchange markets to maintain the newly established rates within a few percentage points. The United States did not agree to reopen the gold window.

The new system did not last long. Continued weakness of the dollar in foreign exchange markets meant that governments would need to intervene substantially to prevent other currencies from appreciating. The United States made clear that it would not intervene given its weak reserve position, and eventually other nations refused to intervene as well. (Note that such countries would have had to sell their own currencies and buy dollars, which would increase their money supply and promote inflation.) One by one, major players in Europe along with Japan and others announced that they would allow their currencies to float (upward) against the dollar—that is, they would allow exchange rates to be set by market forces and would no longer seek to maintain any announced parity relationship. The Bretton Woods system of fixed exchange rates thus came to an end.

The International Monetary System Today

The international monetary system since the demise of fixed rates under the IMF has become a mixed system. Article IV of the IMF Articles of Agreement has been amended to permit members to maintain a value of its currency in relation to the SDR or "another denominator, other than gold," to enter cooperative arrangements to maintain the value of their currencies in relation to other currencies, or to engage in "other exchange arrangements of a member's choice." The latter option permits members to let the value of their currencies float in the market.

Most of the larger developed economies allow their currencies to float. In principle, a nation that allows its currency to float does not need foreign exchange reserves, since it does not intervene in exchange markets. But in actuality, most nations still tend to intervene at times if movements in exchange rates become too large from their perspective, and thus their policy might be characterized as a "managed float." Intervention is justified on various theories. Large movements in exchange rates magnify exchange risk and may dampen international commerce. An argument can also be made that market movements in exchange rates may at times induce them to move away from their "true" or long-term values, perhaps due to excessive speculation. When that happens, price signals can become distorted—international trade or investment may then flow to or from the wrong countries. If one assumes that governments can recognize such situations accurately, which is perhaps a bold assumption but conceivably plausible if governments have private information about factors that will affect future exchange rates, intervention might be justified to correct the distortion.

To be sure, the rationale for intervention may at times be grounded more in politics than in sound economics. A currency appreciation injures exporters and threatens import-competing firms, which may collectively form an effective coalition for intervention to prevent appreciation, whatever its economic merits.

Although a float is now a viable option under IMF law, many countries still prefer a formal commitment to maintain the value of their currencies in relation to others. The most important such country at the moment is China, which has "pegged" the yuan to the dollar (or at times to a basket of currencies) for many years, although it has at times adjusted the peg upward somewhat under pressure from abroad. Various economists argue that an exchange rate peg can be useful, particularly for developing countries, which might not otherwise have the discipline to pursue responsible monetary policies.[18] A country that pegs to the dollar, for example, cannot long tolerate a rate of inflation above that in the United States lest it be forced to expend massive amounts of its foreign exchange reserves to support the price of its currency.

The decision within the IMF to permit a mixed system and to allow members to choose their approach to exchange rate management was accompanied by fear that members might abuse this greater freedom. Article IV thus also provides that "each member shall . . . avoid manipulating exchange rates or the international monetary system in order to prevent effective balance of payments adjustment or to gain an unfair competitive advantage over other members." Later it provides that the fund "shall exercise firm surveillance over the exchange rate policies of members." This "surveillance" work occupies a considerable portion of the time and resources of the IMF staff today. Staff members consult with members on their international monetary policies and regularly offer advice on policy matters that affect the international monetary system, including monetary and fiscal policies, trade policies, capital inflow and outflow restrictions, and so forth.

Assessment: The Checkered History of International Monetary Cooperation

Our account of international monetary cooperation reveals considerable instability in both the approach to cooperation and its durability. The gold standard came and went. A modified gold standard with fixed exchange rates was created by multilateral treaty and later collapsed. Today we see a hodgepodge of national exchange rate policies, chosen more or less unilaterally and subject to a few general oversight principles married with IMF staff "surveillance." What explains this checkered history?

To facilitate analysis, it is important to specify what cooperation means. One alternative to cooperation is simply the free market—letting exchange rates be determined by market forces. Floating currencies with occasional unilateral intervention is also an option. Cooperation, in turn, amounts to some kind of arrangement that commits nations to engage in a form of intervention into the market that they would not choose unilaterally. These arrangements can include a gold standard, or some other approach to fixed rates, or some form of cooperatively "managed float" where exchange rate swings are kept within an agreed range or market volatility is somehow dampened in accord with mutually agreeable rules. To keep the discussion simple, however, we will consider the choice between market-determined rates (no cooperation) and a fixed-rate system (cooperation). As shall be seen, it is by no means clear which choice is best.

A recurring theme in this book is that international law emerges mainly to address international externality problems. To understand the utility of cooperation on monetary matters as we have defined it, therefore, it is useful to take a step back and identify the pertinent externality problems that cooperation might address.

One externality relates to exchange risk, which we discussed earlier. If nations alter their exchange rates regularly in accordance with unilateral intervention or simply allow them to fluctuate too much in the market, risk-averse commercial actors may find international commerce less attractive and engage is less of it. Because some of these actors are foreigners, nations may have too little incentive to maintain exchange rate stability. Fixed exchange rates ameliorate this problem if they are stable and credible. But given the availability of a forward market in which exchange risk can be laid off, as we noted earlier, it is questionable whether exchange risk offers much of an argument for fixed rates.

More important externalities probably arise with respect to the effect of exchange rate policy on the prices paid by and received by trading partners. There are various possibilities that one might consider, but in the interest of brevity we mention only one. Suppose that all buyers and sellers set prices in their own local currencies. A currency devaluation (at least if it is not anticipated by the market and incorporated into prices already) makes a nation's exports cheaper for foreign buyers, at least until such time as export prices adjust upward to offset the devaluation. Likewise, devaluation makes a nation's imports more expensive from the perspective of domestic buyers. The net external effect on trading partners is not immediately obvious, but note that if we take the ratio of the price of the nation's imports to the price of its exports, that ratio has risen. Of course, as discussed in Chapter 18, the ratio of import prices to export prices is the nation's terms of trade. An unexpected devaluation thus worsens the terms of trade for the nation that devalues under our local currency pricing assumption and concomitantly improves the terms of trade for trading partners—a positive externality from their perspective. Of course, an upward revaluation of the currency would have the opposite result.

The general point is that from the perspective of trading partners, exchange rate movements create both positive and negative terms of trade externalities. There is no simple result suggesting that exchange rate movements are necessarily harmful. Indeed, the practice that brought forth the greatest number of complaints historically—devaluation—may actually confer a positive terms of trade externality in many cases for the reason just noted. It is thus hardly obvious that fixed exchange rate systems have any advantage over allowing rates to be determined in the market if one focuses on the externality that flows through the terms of trade.

Another set of externalities relates to macroeconomic policies. These too can be complicated, and so we simply provide a flavor of the issues. Imagine a fixed exchange rate system, and let one major country pursue an inflationary monetary policy. The result will be downward pressure on the value of its currency, while other currencies tend to appreciate. To prevent appreciation and maintain the fixed rate, other nations must intervene by selling their currencies and buying the currency of the inflating country. Such intervention increases the money supply of the other currencies and thus precipitates inflation elsewhere. Thus, inflationary policy can be "exported" under a fixed rate system to nations that do not wish to have inflation.

Conversely, imagine that a major country pursues a contractionary monetary policy. Other countries must now buy their currencies to avoid depreciation and maintain the fixed rate. This policy reduces their money supply, raises interest rates, and may tend to cause contraction in their economies. In this sense, contractionary policies initiated in one country may lead to undesired economic contraction in others. Recall the research noted earlier arguing that precisely this phenomenon may have contributed to a worsening of the Great Depression.

The key point is that fixed exchange rates, if they are taken seriously, link together the monetary policies of the nations that employ them. This linkage can be valuable if one country would otherwise behave irresponsibly, as by promoting unacceptably high levels of domestic inflation. Linkage then becomes a potentially useful hands-tying device. But linkage may also force countries to allow increases or decreases in their money supply that they do not desire and that clash with important macroeconomic objectives.

To be sure, macroeconomic policy externalities can arise under floating exchange rates as well. Suppose, for example, that some nation wishes to reduce its inflation rate. It adopts a contractionary monetary policy that reduces its money supply, increases interest rates, and causes domestic economic activity to contract, thereby dampening upward pressure on prices. But this policy will also cause its currency to appreciate and contribute to the reduction of inflation in another way by making its imports cheaper in the short term. Of course, the logical consequence is that the currency of other nations depreciates in relative terms, and those nations will then find some of their imports to be more expensive. The anti-inflation policy of the first nation thus produces a potentially negative externality for other nations in the form of increased import prices. Yet it is hardly clear that this externality is worse than the externality noted above that would arise with a fixed exchange rate (economic contraction in other countries).

Now suppose that a nation seeks to use low interest rates to stimulate its economy (as the United States is trying to do at the time of this writing). Low asset returns in such a country may lead investors to wish to buy capital assets elsewhere (economists sometimes say that "hot money" will flow into other countries in search of better investment returns or in anticipation of exchange rate appreciation). The demand for assets rises abroad, inflating their prices and the value of the currency needed to buy them. Countries experiencing this phenomenon will find their exports becoming more expensive on world markets (thus tending to decline) and may fear asset bubbles as well due to the (potentially temporary) increase in demand for their capital assets.

In sum, if we pose the choice as a simple one between floating and fixed rates, it is by no means obvious that the fixed-rate regime dominates. The instability of cooperation under the old gold standard and under the modified gold standard of the early IMF seems much less of a mystery once one recognizes that fixed rates are not necessarily better for the international community.

Another recurring theme of this book is that international law must usually be self-enforcing. Cooperation requires nations to do things that they would not otherwise do, and it can be sustained only if the penalty for deviation from the rules is sufficiently high. But no army exists to enforce the rules, and to a great extent reciprocal deviation is the implicit sanction that sustains cooperation (absent effective issue linkage to some other form of sanction). If we assume, perhaps counterfactually, that a fixed exchange rate system is superior to floating rates, is it possible for a fixed exchange rate system to be self-enforcing?

Recall that historically such systems tended to break down when some nations began to run short of reserves and devalued their currencies. The point of the international monetary "fund" was to backstop national reserves to avoid this scenario. But the existence of a fund did not solve the problem of nations running low on reserves. At that point, they could borrow reserves from the IMF but would have to repay the loans with interest and perhaps accept some onerous "conditionality" as well. The alternative was simply to devalue, perhaps claiming "fundamental disequilibrium" in the balance of payments, and that of course is what happened with a number of countries despite the existence of the IMF (culminating, of course, with the decision by the United States to close the gold window and devalue).

In principle, the IMF might have adjudicated some such countries to be in violation of the rules and denied them future access to IMF resources. But it was not clear that such a threat would have much impact—IMF members facing reserve shortages may simply have preferred to devalue without regard to any legal constraints. To be sure, if enough members behaved in this fashion, the system might break down (as it did), and any benefits of cooperation would be lost. But the short-term incentives to deviate may have been too great for cooperation to be sustainable.

The Mission of the IMF, Yesterday and Today

The Nobel laureate economist Milton Friedman once remarked, "few things are so permanent as government agencies, including international agencies."[19] Our short history of the international monetary system makes clear that the core mission of the IMF, as originally conceived, has largely evaporated. The purpose of the IMF was to oversee the operation of a system of fixed exchange rates, under which nations had a legal obligation to maintain the par values of their currencies (absent "fundamental disequilibrium," as noted earlier). The reserves of the IMF were established to assist nations running short of reserves to meet this legal obligation.

The legal obligation to maintain par values no longer exists. Nations that allow their currencies to float need not intervene at all in exchange markets, and if they do not then they have no need for foreign exchange reserves. To be sure, nations that seek to maintain a target exchange rate may need reserves if their currency would otherwise depreciate, but if they run short they can always abandon their target.

So why is the IMF still around, and what does it do besides traveling the globe and kibitzing on national policy matters in the name of "surveillance?" The answer is that the IMF uses its reserves to lend money to nations in financial trouble. Typically, such nations have run up debts, often denominated in foreign currencies, that they lack the capacity to repay. Fears arise that the government will print money to pay its local obligations and cause rapid inflation. Default fears make the countries unattractive for new investors, and existing investors may rush to sell their local assets to withdraw their capital before defaults occur and while local currency is still worth something. Asset markets can collapse, and economic activity can decline rapidly.

The IMF will loan money to these countries. Major IMF bailouts have involved various developing nations such as Mexico, Russia, Indonesia, Thailand, and Argentina. More recently, the IMF has become involved with European nations such as Greece and Ireland. To be sure, the loans come with conditions under IMF "conditionality" authority. These conditions often entail tough austerity measures to rein in government spending, tighten monetary policy, and so on, with the goal of making the borrower governments creditworthy down the road.

But how does making new loans to overindebted countries solve their problem? There are various possible answers. The loans are made at below-market rates (otherwise why would the borrowers want them in the first place?). Subsidized credit can allow a borrower to repay a high-interest loan with one at a lower interest rate, for example. The terms of the loans may also be longer, allowing the borrower to extend the repayment schedule. In addition, conditionality perhaps coerces the borrower toward more responsible public policies that place them on a sounder footing.

Thus, although borrowers rarely express gratitude for IMF conditionality, it is easy to understand why they are nevertheless willing to accept IMF loans. The much harder question is whether the loans make economic sense from a global perspective.

To this question, one can raise some doubts. First, it is not obvious as an economic matter why the international community should provide subsidized loans to debtor nations. The usual economic rationale for a subsidy is the notion that a market failure exists—here, the notion would be that the borrower country is actually a good place to invest, but global capital markets fail to recognize its attractiveness and charge too much for loans to the borrower. Such a capital market failure might arise with imperfect information. If the IMF could overcome this problem and identify attractive investment opportunities that the capital markets are missing, it might make sense for the IMF to lend at below market rates. Yet is this story plausible?

Absent an economic basis for believing that market loans are overpriced, subsidized IMF loans are essentially just foreign aid. One might argue for aid on humanitarian grounds, and indeed the ordinary citizens of debtor nations often face bleak economic prospects. But do the IMF loans really help them? Various commentators have made the point that bailout loans are largely used to pay off foreign creditors such as multinational banks. Concurrently, the austerity measures required by IMF conditionality often make life quite miserable for ordinary citizens, and the standard of living in the countries bailed out by the IMF is often considerably lower after the bailout than before.[20] It is not clear that the lives of ordinary citizens would end up much worse if the borrower country simply defaulted on its obligations or renegotiated them in the shadow of possible default.

The fact that much of the money goes to pay off foreign creditors raises suspicions that the system is a cleaver mechanism devised primarily to transfer money from taxpayers (whose governments pony up the money for IMF reserves) to international lending institutions that have made poor lending decisions. It is easy to see where the political constituency for such a system may be found but harder to justify it on principle.

Also, as many commentators note, a system that bails out creditors creates significant moral hazard. If lenders know that the IMF will come to the rescue in the event that a borrower country finds itself in serious financial trouble, lenders become more willing to make loans to questionable borrowers (at lower rates) than otherwise. The effect of IMF bailouts ex post may be to induce more imprudent loans ex ante.

Commentators also regularly question the soundness of the policy changes that the IMF imposes under the rubric of conditionality. Among other things, critics argue that austerity measures often lead to a greater contraction of economic activity than is necessary. They argue that formal default—or debt renegotiation in the shadow of prospective default—might well leave the borrower nations better off in the long run than following the IMF's policy advice.

Accordingly, many commentators in recent years question the modern mission of the IMF and even argue for its abolition. Prominent economists calling for abolition of the institution have included Robert Barro, Milton Friedman, and George Schultz. Jeffrey Sachs has advocated radical reform that would turn the IMF into less of a lender and more of a bankruptcy court.[21]

But the modern IMF also has its defenders, including Lawrence Summers and Paul Krugman.[22] These commentators argue that the value of the IMF in its modern role is much like the value of the Federal Reserve during a banking crisis—to serve as a lender of last resort that prevents a crisis of confidence from spiraling out of control.

Summers and Krugman suggest that without the prospect of IMF bailouts, financial trouble in one country will spook investors in similar countries into selling their capital assets due to fears of future inflation and default. Asset markets in those other countries will crash, as will their currencies as speculators drive down their prices. Economic activity will contract in such countries, and exporters who supply them will suffer a sizeable drop in sales. Foreign lending institutions that hold their debt obligations will see the market value of those obligations plummet and may themselves be imperiled. Summers and Krugman thus suggest that when one country develops financial trouble, it may initiate a contagion that brings down the economies of other countries. They credit IMF bailouts with helping to contain the damage from the Latin American debt crisis of the 1980s and the Asian financial crisis of the 1990s. In the more recent European crisis, it has similarly been suggested that a default by, say, Greece, may trigger bank failures in, say France, that will have negative repercussions for the international economy.

Even if these concerns are right, one must still ask whether bailouts are the best policy instrument to address the problem. In principle, other options might include standstill rules on debt obligations that allow debtors a period to negotiate with and reassure lenders—an international bankruptcy process akin to that advocated by Jeffrey Sachs. Capital controls are another possibility, as investors cannot race to pull their assets out of a country if they are prohibited from repatriating the returns to asset sales. Such options raise their own problems, to be sure, and we are in no position to offer definitive recommendations. We simply note that the core activity of the IMF today is dramatically different from the tasks it was conceived to perform and that the value of its current mission is a subject of debate.

Currency Manipulation

The role of the IMF today is not entirely limited to its lending and surveillance operations.[23] A controversy of recent note, about which IMF law has something to say, concerns the allegation that certain nations—especially China—may be "manipulating" their currencies to gain an unfair advantage in international trade. The criticism of China rests on the fact that it has now accumulated about U.S.$3 trillion in foreign exchange reserves, which it has obtained by selling yuan in exchange markets to maintain a rough "peg" to the dollar. It has concurrently run large current account surpluses. Critics allege that China's policy is the economic equivalent of a tariff on imports and a subsidy on exports, both of which would violate WTO law if done explicitly.

The economic soundness of this claim is open to some question. Among other things, China's policies have not produced an unexpected devaluation but have instead maintained a fairly stable value of the yuan relative to the dollar for many years. In such an environment, other prices have time to adjust, and the possibility arises that China's domestic prices have changed to offset the effects of a weaker yuan. In fact, labor costs in China are known to have been rising significantly. Economic analysis indeed suggests that changes in other prices will tend to offset the effects of exchange rate movements on economic activity over time. If the value of a currency declines below its equilibrium market value due to government intervention, for example, export prices denominated in that currency will be bid up over time and import prices will tend to fall to restore the equilibrium balance of trade.

In addition, some economists believe that China's accumulation of reserves, and its current account surplus, is an inevitable consequence of a high Chinese savings rate coupled with low savings rates in countries like the United States, where investment is attractive. China then runs a capital account deficit (it is importing capital assets), which has to be offset by a current account surplus. These economists question whether an upward revaluation of the yuan will actually reduce China's trade surplus. The argument is that an upward revaluation may discourage investment in China, which in turn reduces the demand for imports in China. They point to the Japanese experience a few decades earlier, where a dramatic appreciation of the yen did not eliminate the Japanese trade surplus.[24]

Whether or not China's currency policies may be benign, it is instructive to consider what IMF law has to say about them.[25] As noted earlier, article IV of the IMF Articles of Agreement prohibits members from "manipulating exchange rates . . . to prevent effective balance of payments adjustment or to gain an unfair competitive advantage over other members." The Articles do not define the terms "manipulating" or "unfair competitive advantage," but a June 2007 decision of the IMF Executive Board defines manipulation as "policies that are targeted at—and actually affect—the level of an exchange rate." Moreover, manipulation may "cause the exchange rate to move or may prevent such movement." Regarding the concept of unfair advantage, the decision goes on to state that

[a] member will only be considered to be manipulating exchange rates in order to gain an unfair advantage over other members if the Fund determines both that:

(A) the member is engaged in these policies for the purpose of securing fundamental exchange rate misalignment in the form of an undervalued exchange rate and (B) the purpose of securing such misalignment is to increase net exports. Thus, a touchstone for manipulation is an effort to influence the balance of trade. A determination whether such an effort has been undertaken is to be based on an objective assessment . . . based on all available evidence, including consultation with the member concerned. Any representation made by the member regarding the purpose of its policies will be given the benefit of any reasonable doubt.

How do China's policies fare in relation to this interpretation of IMF rules? On the question of fundamental misalignment, China's critics will point to its large current account surplus and to its accumulation of over $3 trillion in foreign exchange reserves. Further, the potential problem of misalignment has apparently been the subject of staff discussion with China within the IMF already, although the details are not public. Let us assume *arguendo,* then, that a fundamental misalignment could be found.

The more difficult hurdle concerns the purpose of China's policies. Chinese officials, of course, deny that they are manipulating the exchange rate to increase net exports. They can offer alternative accounts of their motivations, which are entitled to the benefit of any reasonable doubt, as noted above. Some are supported by the work of prominent academics, who have argued that the peg between the yuan and the dollar creates an anchor for China's monetary policy that has controlled inflation and created a favorable environment for steady economic growth or that China's current account surplus is inevitable given the imbalance between domestic savings and investment opportunities. It would be difficult to reject such arguments under the reasonable doubt standard.

It is also clear that the IMF is ill equipped as a practical matter to pressure China to change its conduct. The basic enforcement mechanism is "surveillance," through which the staff offers advice on member policies. The history of surveillance suggests a strong emphasis in the IMF on the avoidance of confrontation. A former staffer reports that the number of surveillance consultations pursuant to article IV is in excess of 40,000, yet in none of these consultations has the IMF ever concluded that a member was out of compliance with its obligations regarding its exchange rate policies or any other matter.

Finally, even if the IMF were to make an exception for China and declare it to be in violation of the rules, it has little practical leverage over China. The available sanction would be to curtail China's access to the resources of the IMF. A country such as China, however, with trillions of dollars in foreign exchange reserves has no need to borrow from the IMF and no serious prospect of such a need in the foreseeable future. Thus, if one were to believe that "currency manipulation" by China is an important contemporary problem, the IMF seems an unlikely solution.[26]

The problem once again illustrates the limits of self-enforcing cooperation in international law. Currency manipulation is defined as an effort to distort exchange markets through government intervention for the purpose of increasing net exports. The essential nature of such conduct is that it drives down the price of the intervening nation's currency to make its exports cheaper and its imports more expensive. Manipulation thus entails selling the domestic currency and buying foreign currency, with the result that the manipulator inevitably accumulates foreign exchange reserves in the process. It is perhaps folly to expect that an institution formed for the purpose of lending reserves to nations in need of them will be able to enforce a rule against the accumulation of reserves by threatening to cut off access to reserves.

European Monetary Integration and the Eurozone Debt Crisis

In the Maastricht treaty of 1992, the EU agreed to take a major step toward integration by adopting a common currency, which became known as the euro. Adoption of the euro was not obligatory for members, and others have not satisfied the criteria for joining the eurozone, so currently only seventeen of the twenty-seven EU members belong to the eurozone. Most of the current members had adopted the euro by 2001, and for the next decade, monetary integration seemed to be a resounding success. European economies grew over those years, and Europeans as well as foreigners avoided the trouble and expense of purchasing foreign exchange as they moved from one euro country to another.

The entire system was called into doubt in 2009 when it became clear that Greece could not pay its debts. It soon became clear that other countries in the eurozone periphery—including Portugal, Spain, and Ireland—may not be able to pay their debts either. The crisis remains unresolved as of this writing.

The eurozone crisis holds important lessons for international law. There were two reasons for monetary integration. The first was political: European leaders believed that the forward momentum of political integration needed to be maintained. Either Europe would continue forward and culminate in a state, or it would fall apart. Because national currencies created a sense of separateness, they were an appropriate target for pro-integration forces. The logistical difficulties of switching back to a national currency would also discourage separation.

The second reason was economic: significant gains, it was thought, could be obtained from monetary integration. Individuals and business would no longer be required to buy foreign currencies and take out costly hedges against currency fluctuations. And by anchoring European monetary policy in the core economies, especially Germany, it was thought that monetary policy for the continent as a whole would be more responsible.

The economic rationale for currency union clearly fits within the externalities framework that has been the central theme of this book. States issue currencies that are used by individuals in other states, creating transaction costs and financial risk due to exchange rate fluctuations. Further, states may manipulate their currencies or their money supplies without regard to the impact on foreigners. The political rationale is also about a species of externality. Those who advanced it implicitly relied on a psychological theory, namely, that Europeans would be more willing to support an EU state if their national currencies did not remind them of everything that separated them. On the premise that unification produced joint benefits, the maintenance of separate currencies thus created a negative psychological externality that would be ameliorated by monetary unification.

The harder question is whether these two strands of argument for unification were sound. The political rationale is difficult to evaluate. Although plausible, it is also possible that squabbles over common monetary policy and the current need for bailouts will in the end drive European countries further apart rather than closer.

The economic rationale, too, has difficulties, which were recognized at the beginning of the process by economists. The relevant framework is optimal currency theory,[27] which recognizes that the benefits of monetary integration must be weighed against certain costs. The most important of these costs is that if there is a single currency, then there must be a single monetary policy applied to all the states that join the currency union. A single monetary policy is potentially problematic because states often experience economic booms and busts at different times. For those who believe in the efficacy of countercyclical monetary policy, monetary unification prevents the constituent states from pursuing individual monetary policies that respond to their immediate needs. To be sure, it is possible that the states will experience macroeconomic shocks at the same time or that other factors will mitigate the differential effects of shocks (labor mobility, easy migration, common fiscal policy, and so forth). That is why monetary integration is commonly appropriate at the nation state level. But many economists did not believe that this was the case for Europe.[28]

The last few years suggest that they were right. Greece suffered an economic downturn that was aggravated by its questionable fiscal policies. Various Greek governments borrowed far more than the country could pay back. What was worse for Greece is that the European Central Bank would not pursue an expansionary monetary policy to help Greece out of its slump (or inflate away its debt) because Germany and other eurozone countries were experiencing economic growth. In years past, Greece might have tried to stimulate its economy by devaluing its currency, but that route was also cut off because Greece no longer had its own currency. Likewise, because Greece's debts are denominated in euros—a currency that Greece cannot print unilaterally—it cannot address its debt problems by printing money. Finally, fiscal stimulation was impossible because Greece could borrow no more money, and the EU (or eurozone institutions) had no authority to engage in fiscal transfers from places like Germany to Greece.

Meanwhile, the crisis spread because banks in other European countries held vast quantities of Greek debt. If Greece defaulted, the solvency of those banks could be called into question; in the worst case, depositors might initiate a run on the banks, causing a new financial crisis akin to that of 2008 when the value of mortgage-backed securities collapsed. As it became clear that the other eurozone countries would not bail out Greece, at least not as generously as Greece hoped, creditors began to wonder whether other governments with weak economies (Portugal, Spain, Ireland, even Italy) might default on their loans. Creditors began demanding higher interest rates to protect themselves from default, which increased financing costs for those countries, which in turn increased the risk of default, contagion, and economic collapse.

We do not know how the crisis will be resolved. Some commentators predict that Greece and possibly other countries will exit the eurozone, while others believe that further integration must take place. One possibility in the latter respect is fiscal integration, whereby all borrowing is undertaken by a single European authority rather than by individual national governments. Short of that, the EU might engage in a greater degree of direct fiscal transfers to member nations in financial distress. But such policies are intensely unpopular among Germans and others in the wealthier, better managed economies, who believe that fiscal integration will just cause a permanent leakage of wealth from the richer countries to the poorer countries, while rewarding governments in those poorer countries for their irresponsibility. Yet dissolution of the eurozone would create enormous short-term economic problems, including, as noted, possible financial panic and government default.

The eurozone crisis illustrates the complexity of international cooperation in cases where countries seek the benefits of cooperation but want to avoid losing too much control over their affairs. It may turn out that Europeans must choose either currency union accompanied by fiscal integration or no currency union at all. In the first case, they obtain the benefits of a common currency but take the risk that European institutions will transfer wealth from rich countries to poor countries or in other ways that citizens do not support. In the second case, countries maintain fiscal autonomy but do not gain the benefits of currency union. The crisis illustrates the limits of cooperation at the international level. Beyond a certain point, countries must either integrate or forgo some of the benefits of cooperation. If integration is impossible as a result of nationalism and other forms of heterogeneity, international law alone may simply not be up to the task of securing cooperative gains.

ial Law (2005); Joel P. Trachtman, *The Economic Structure of International Law* (2008); Andrew T. Guzman, *How International Law Works: A Rational Choice Theory* (2008); Robert E. Scott & Paul B. Stephan, *The Limits of Leviathan: Contract Theory and the Enforcement of International Law* (2006); Joost Pauwelyn, *Optimal Protection of International Law: Navigating between European Absolutism and American Voluntarism* (2008); and Eric A. Posner, *The Perils of Global Legalism* (2009). For criticisms and responses, see *Symposium: The Limits of International Law*, 34 Ga. J. Comp. & Inter'l L. 253 (2006); and *Public International Law and Economics*, 2008 U. Ill. L. Rev. 1 (Christoph Engel, Anne van Aaken, & Tom Ginsburg eds.). For an earlier discussion, see Jeffrey L. Dunoff & Joel P. Trachtman, *Economic Analysis of International Law*, 24 Yale J. Int'l L. 1 (1999).
2. See, e.g., Robert O. Keohane, *After Hegemony: Cooperation and Discord in the World Political Economy* (2d ed. 2005); David Lake, *Entangling Relations: American Foreign Policy in Its Century* (1999); *Cooperation under Anarchy* (Kenneth A. Oye ed., 1986); *Strategic Choice and International Relations* (David A. Lake & Robert Powell eds., 1999).
3. *Legalization and World Politics* (Judith L. Goldstein et al. eds., 2001); Barbara Koremenos, Charles Lipson, & Duncan Snidal, *The Rational Design of International Institutions*, 55 Int'l Org. 761 (2001).
4. See, e.g., Peter Malanczuk, *Akehurst's Modern Introduction to International Law* (8th rev. ed. 2002); *Oppenheim's International Law* (Robert Jennings & Arthur Watts eds., 9th ed. 1992); Mark W. Janis, *International Law* (2008).

2. Fundamentals of International Law

1. Restatement (Third) of Foreign Relations Law of the United States § 201 (1987).
2. Restatement (Third) of Foreign Relations Law of the United States § 102 (1987).

3. Economic Analysis of International Law

1. See generally Louis Kaplow & Steven Shavell, *Fairness versus Welfare* (2002).
2. As advocated by Bruno S. Frey, *Functional, Overlapping, Competing Jurisdictions: Redrawing the Geographic Borders of Administration*, 5 Eur. J. L. Reform 543 (2005).
3. We draw here on the argument of Alberto Alesina & Enrico Spolaore, *The Size of Nations* (2003).

4. As noted, a "public good" is commonly defined as a good for which the consumption by one individual has no effect on the ability of other individuals to consume the good or the value of such consumption ("nonrivalrous consumption"). In reality, virtually everything produced by government is subject to some consumption rivalry—roads and parks become congested, an army deployed to the south leaves the north more vulnerable, and so on.
5. The distinction is important in economics because pecuniary externalities do not lead to economic inefficiency in competitive market settings but may if conditions are not competitive. Nonpecuniary externalities lead to inefficiency in all market settings.
6. Economic welfare is conventionally defined as the sum of producer and consumer surplus, or sometimes as aggregate national income.
7. Imagine two states, denoted A and B, each of which has control over a vector of policy instruments, α and β, respectively. [Nothing important changes (beyond the algebra) if the analysis is generalized to N states.] The respective welfare functions for the two states are $W^A(\alpha, \beta)$ and $W^B(\alpha, \beta)$. Assume that each state's welfare is increasing and concave in its own policy choices. The vectors α and β can represent a myriad of policy areas—tariffs, tax rates and rules, immigration restrictions, emissions controls, and so on. In the absence of communication and agreement, each state maximizes its welfare by taking the actions of the other as given, selecting α and β such that

$$\partial W^A(\alpha, \beta)/\partial \alpha = 0 \text{ and } \partial W^B(\alpha, \beta)/\partial \beta = 0.$$

Noncooperative equilibrium (Nash) arises when both conditions hold, given the other state's choice of policies. Will the equilibrium be (first-best) efficient? The answer is plainly no in general: a point on the Pareto frontier may be derived by choosing α and β simultaneously to maximize the welfare of one state, subject to the constraint that the welfare of the other achieve some fixed, attainable value (a standard technique for deriving conditions for any optimal contract). The first order conditions for Pareto optimality thus require that

$$\partial W^A(\alpha, \beta)/\partial \alpha + \lambda \partial W^B(\alpha, \beta)/\partial \alpha = 0 \text{ and } \lambda \partial W^B(\alpha, \beta)/\partial \beta + \partial W^A(\alpha, \beta)/\partial \beta = 0,$$

where λ is a Lagrange multiplier.

With the welfare constraint binding and thus $\lambda > 0$, it is clear that the conditions for Pareto optimality cannot correspond to the earlier conditions for Nash equilibrium unless

$$\partial W^B(\alpha, \beta)/\partial \alpha = 0 \text{ and } \partial W^A(\alpha, \beta)/\partial \beta = 0.$$

In words, the equilibrium without international cooperation will achieve the Pareto frontier only in the absence of externalities, and the function of international agreements in the presence of externalities is to enable states to commit to behavior that will move them closer to the Pareto frontier.
8. Andrew Moravcsik, *The Origins of Human Rights Regimes: Democratic Delegation in Postwar Europe,* 54 Int'l Org. 217 (2000).
9. Ronald Coase, *The Problem of Social Cost,* 3 J.L. & Econ. 1 (1960).
10. The economic costs of monopoly arise because a monopolist elevates price above marginal production cost, thereby pricing some consumers out of the market who would be willing

to pay the marginal cost of what the monopolist makes. In addition, because monopoly can be highly profitable, resources may be wasted in pursuit of monopoly or to protect it.
11. See Ian Ayres & Robert Gertner, Filling Gaps in Incomplete Contracts: An Economic Theory of Default Rules, 99 *Yale L.J.* 87 (1989).
12. See Barbara Koremenos, *Contracting around International Uncertainty,* 99 Am. Pol. Sci. Rev. 549 (2005).
13. See Laurence R. Helfer, *Exiting Treaties,* 91 Va. L. Rev. 1579 (2005).
14. Legal rights are protected by a property rule if they cannot be infringed without the rightholder's permission. They are protected by a liability rule if a party may infringe them and simply pay damages.
15. Cf. George W. Downs, David M. Rocke, & Peter N. Barsoom, *Is the Good News about Compliance Good News about Cooperation?,* 50 Int. Org. 379 (1996).
16. See, e.g., James D. Fearon, *Domestic Political Audiences and the Escalation of International Disputes,* 88 Am. Pol. Sci. Rev. 577 (1994).
17. See Lester G. Telser, *A Theory of Self-Enforcing Agreements,* 53 J. Bus. 27 (1980).
18. Numerous basic texts on game theory are available: e.g., Eric Rasmusen, *Games and Information* (4th ed. 2004). For applications to political theory, see James Morrow, *Game Theory and Political Theory* (1994); for applications to international relations, see Robert Keohane, *After Hegemony* (1984); David Lake, *Entangling Relations: American Foreign Policy in Its Century* (1999); for applications to international law, see Jack L. Goldsmith & Eric A. Posner, *The Limits of International Law* (2005). For recognition of the role of repetition in explaining the enforcement of international law, see John K. Setear, *An Iterative Perspective on Treaties: A Synthesis of International Relations Theory and International Law,* 37 Harv. Int'l L.J. 139 (1996).
19. Robert Axelrod, *The Evolution of Cooperation* (1984).
20. Jonathan Eaton & Michael Engers, *Sanctions,* 100 J. Pol. Econ. 899 (1992). See also Jonathan Eaton & Alan O. Sykes, *International Sanctions,* in 2 *The New Palgrave Dictionary of Economics and the Law* (Peter Newman ed., 1998).
21. Gary C. Hufbauer, John J. Schott, Kimberley A. Elliott, & Barabara Oegg, *Economic Sanctions Reconsidered: History and Current Policy* (3d ed. 2007). See also Glen Biglaiser & David Lektzian, *The Effect of Sanctions on U.S. Foreign Direct Investment,* 65 Int'l Org. 531 (2011).
22. See Howard F. Chang, *An Economic Analysis of Trade Measures to Protect the Global Environment,* 83 Geo. L.J. 2131 (1995).
23. Andrew T. Guzman, *How International Law Works: A Rational Choice Theory* (2008).
24. See Douglas G. Baird, Robert H. Gertner, & Randal C. Picker, *Game Theory and the Law* (1994).
25. See, e.g., James H. Lebovic & Erik Voeten, *The Politics of Shame: The Condemnation of Country Human Rights Practices in the UNCHR,* 50 Int'l Stud. Q. 861 (2006).
26. For further critical discussion regarding the role of reputation in international law, see Rachel Brewster, *The Limits of Reputation on Compliance,* 1 Int'l Theory 323 (2009); Rachel Brewster, *Unpacking the State's Reputation,* 50 Harv. Int'l L.J. 231 (2009).
27. We will ignore the mixed strategy equilibrium.
28. Stephen D. Krasner, *Global Communications and National Power: Life on the Pareto Frontier,* 43 World Pol. 336 (1991).

29. See Alan O. Sykes, *Product Standards for Internationally Integrated Goods Markets* (1995).

4. Sovereignty and Attributes of Statehood

1. Restatement (Third) of Foreign Relations Law of the United States § 201 (1987).
2. Restatement (Third) of Foreign Relations Law of the United States §§ 201–202 (1987).
3. See Restatement (Third) of Foreign Relations Law of the United States §§ 202 cmt. b, d (1987).
4. See Lassa Oppenheim, 1 *International Law: A Treatise* 136 (1921).
5. *CIA—The World Factbook, Country Comparison,* https://www.cia.gov/library/publications/the-world-factbook/geos/tv.html (accessed June 22, 2011).
6. Barry E. Carter, Phillip R. Trimble, & Allen S. Weiner, *International Law* 451 (5th ed. 2007).
7. See Mingtai Fire & Marine Ins. Co. v. United Parcel Service, 177 F.3d 1142, 1145–1147 (9th Cir. 1999) (holding that UPS's liability for a lost package from Taiwan was limited to $100 released value on an airway bill because Taiwan is not bound by China's adherence to an international convention standardizing international transportation by air and is not a signatory state to the convention itself—a conclusion supported by the United States as amicus).
8. See, e.g., Charter of the Organization of American States art. 9, as amended, Feb. 27, 1967 (enabling member nations to suspend membership and enact sanctions against governments that replaced the prior government through unconstitutional means such as a coup d'état).
9. Kosovo declared independence in 2008. Although some other states have recognized its independence, not all have.
10. Vienna Convention on the Succession of States in Respect of Treaties art. 16, Aug. 23, 1978, 1946 U.N.T.S. 3.

5. Customary International Law

1. Restatement (Third) of Foreign Relations Law of the United States § 102(2) (1987).
2. Restatement (Third) of Foreign Relations Law of the United States § 712(1) (1987).
3. We discuss this theory more formally in Chapter 3. For discussions of customary international law from this perspective, see, e.g., Jack L. Goldsmith & Eric A. Posner, *The Limits of International Law* (2005); George Norman & Joel P. Trachtman, *The Customary International Law Game,* 99 Am. J. Int'l L. 541 (2005). For a theory of customary international law that relies on economic conceptions of reputation rather than retaliation, see Andrew T. Guzman, *Saving Customary International Law,* 27 Mich. J. Int'l L. 115 (2005).
4. Cf. Eugene Kontorovich, *Inefficient Customs in International Law,* 48 Wm. & Mary L. Rev. 859 (2006). Kontorovich's skepticism is related to the view that customs are likely to be efficient in small groups, where members can monitor each other and enforce the norms, conditions that may not obtain for the world as a whole. But this suggests that customary international law is weak, not that it is inefficient where it has come into existence.

5. Restatement (Third) of Foreign Relations Law of the United States § 102(2) (1987).
6. The Paquete Habana, 175 U.S. 677 (1900).
7. *Id.* at 719–720 (Fuller, C. J., dissenting). The majority noted that there may have been a distinction between comity and law initially but that the practice had become "a settled rule of international law" in the hundred years since. *Id.* at 694–695.
8. But see Curtis A. Bradley & G. Mitu Gulati, *Withdrawing from International Custom*, 120 Yale L.J. 202 (2010) (arguing that states are free to withdraw from customary international law).
9. Restatement (Third) of Foreign Relations Law of the United States § 331(2) & cmt. e.
10. Vienna Convention on the Law of Treaties art. 53, May 23, 1969, 1155 U.N.T.S. 331.
11. Convention against Torture and Other Cruel, Inhuman or Degrading Treatment or Punishment, Dec. 10, 1984, 1465 U.N.T.S. 85.
12. Case Concerning Right of Passage over Indian Territory (Port. v. India), 1960 I.C.J. 6 (Apr. 12).
13. Proclamation No. 2667, 10 Fed. Reg. 12,303 (Sept. 28, 1945).
14. R. R. Churchill & A. V. Lowe, *The Law of the Sea* 144 (3d ed. 1999).
15. For further discussion, see Vincy Fon & Francesco Parisi, *Stability and Change in International Customary Law,* 17 Sup. Ct. Econ. Rev. 279 (2009); Vincy Fon & Francesco Parisi, *International Customary Law and Articulation Theories: An Economic Analysis*, 2 B.Y.U. Int'l L. & Mgmt. Rev. 201 (2006).

6. Treaties

1. The Paquete Habana, 175 U.S. 677 (1900).
2. Laurence R. Helfer, *Exiting Treaties,* 91 Va. L. Rev. 1579 (2005).
3. For a discussion of some of the problems that arise in connection with multilateral treaties, see Vincy Fon & Francesco Parisi, *The Formation of International Treaties,* 3 Rev. L. & Econ. 37 (2007).
4. See Edward T. Swaine, *Reserving,* 31 Yale J. Int'l L. 307 (2006).
5. See Chapter 14.
6. Vienna Convention on the Law of Treaties, May 23, 1969, 1155 U.N.T.S. 331.
7. *Id.* art. 18.
8. Richard Boucher, *International Criminal Court: Letter to UN Secretary General Kofi Annan (May 6, 2002),* http://2001-2009.state.gov/r/pa/prs/ps/2002/9968.htm.
9. Helfer, *supra* note 2.
10. Vienna Convention on the Law of Treaties, *supra* note 6, art. 56.
11. Convention on the Prohibition of Military or Any Other Hostile Use of Environmental Modification Techniques, May 18, 1977, 31 U.S.T. 333, 1108 U.N.T.S. 152.
12. See Swaine, *supra* note 4.
13. United Nations Convention on the Law of the Sea, Dec. 10, 1982, 1833 U.N.T.S. 397.
14. Vienna Convention on the Law of Treaties, *supra* note 6, art. 19, 21.
15. For analysis, see Vincy Fon & Francesco Parisi, *The Economics of Treaty Ratification,* 5 J.L. Econ. & Pol'y 209 (2009).
16. Montreal Protocol on Substances That Deplete the Ozone Layer, Sept. 16, 1987, 30 I.L.M. 537.

17. Rome Statute of the International Criminal Court art. 120, July 17, 1998, 2187 U.N.T.S. 90.
18. International Convention on Civil and Political Rights, Dec. 16, 1966, 999 U.N.T.S. 171.
19. Vienna Convention on the Law of Treaties, *supra* note 6, art. 19(c).
20. Convention on the Punishment and Prevention of the Crime of Genocide, Dec. 9, 1948, Status, http://treaties.un.org/pages/ViewDetails.aspx?src=TREATY&mtdsg_no=IV-1&chapter=4&lang=en (accessed June 7, 2011).
21. *Id.* (see Netherlands reservation, Feb. 23, 1996).
22. See Fon & Parisi, *supra* note 15, at 212–219.
23. See Kenneth W. Abbott & Duncan Snidal, *Hard and Soft Law in International Governance*, 54 Int'l Org. 421 (2000).
24. See Jacob E. Gersen & Eric A. Posner, *Soft Law: Lessons from Congressional Practice*, 61 Stan. L. Rev. 573 (2008).

7. International Institutions

1. A conference volume of *Law & Contemporary Problems* contains a number of useful articles on this topic; see, e.g., Curtis A. Bradley & Judith G. Kelley, *The Concept of International Delegation*, 71 Law & Contemp. Probs. 1 (2008); David Epstein & Sharyn O'Halloran, *Sovereignty and Delegation in International Organizations*, 71 Law & Contemp. Probs. 77 (2008). See also Kenneth W. Abbott & Duncan Snidal, *Why States Act through Formal International Organizations*, 42 J. Conflict Resol. 3 (1998).
2. For more on the IMF, see Chapter 19.
3. Sanchez-Llamas v. Oregon, 548 U.S. 331, 355 (2006).
4. This has been frequently discussed, mainly in the context of international adjudication. See Paul B. Stephan, *Courts, Tribunals and Legal Unification—The Agency Problem*, 3 Chi. J. Int'l L. 333 (2002); Eric A. Posner & John C. Yoo, *A Theory of International Adjudication*, 93 Cal. L. Rev. 1 (2005); Andrew T. Guzman, *International Tribunals: A Rational Choice Analysis*, 157 U. Pa. L. Rev. 171 (2008).
5. For an explanation for why states are reluctant to delegate authority to international dispute resolution bodies, see Andrew T. Guzman, *The Cost of Credibility: Explaining Resistance to Interstate Dispute Resolution Mechanisms*, 31 J. Leg. Stud. 303 (2002).
6. The least populous UN member nation is Tuvalu, with 10,544 people. *CIA—The World Factbook—Country Comparison: Population*, https://www.cia.gov/library/publications/the-world-factbook/geos/tv.html (accessed June 6, 2011).
7. We focus on the European Union here; we address the European human rights system in Chapter 14 and European monetary institutions in Chapter 19.
8. See George Tsebelis & Geoffrey Garrett, *The Institutional Foundations of Intergovernmentalism and Supranationalism in the European Union*, 55 Int'l Org. 357, 359 (2001).
9. We qualify this claim in Chapter 19 in connection with our discussion of the eurozone crisis.
10. We refer to international arbitration between states, not international arbitration between individuals or firms that are located in different countries (or between individuals and states, as under a Bilateral Investment Treaty). The latter type of arbitration is governed by the New York Convention on the Enforcement of Foreign Arbitral

Awards, under which national courts are required to enforce valid international arbitration awards. There is no similar treaty for state-to-state arbitration.
11. For details, see Eric A. Posner, *The Perils of Global Legalism* 137–143 (2009).
12. Leslie Benson, *Yugoslavia: A Concise History* (rev. and updated ed. 2004).
13. ICTR—Statute of the Tribunal, S.C. Res. 955, app., U.N. Doc. S/RES/955 (1994), http://www.un.org/ictr/statute.html.
14. In 2006–2007, the joint budget for the ICTY and ICTR was $545 million. See David Wippman, *The Cost of International Justice,* 100 Am. J. Int'l L. 861 (2006).
15. On the ICTY, see James Meernik, *Victor's Justice or the Law? Judging and Punishing at the International Criminal Tribunal for the Former Yugoslavia,* 47 J. Conflict Resol. 140 (2003).
16. For an argument that states joined the ICC as a commitment device, as a way of reducing violence, see Beth A. Simmons & Allison Danner, *Credible Commitments and the International Criminal Court,* 64 Int'l Org. 225 (2010). However, it is not clear what prevents states from leaving the court if they choose to do so.
17. *Sudan Leader Al-Bashir to Skip Malaysia Forum,* Associated Press, June 16, 2011, http://abcnews.go.com/International/wireStory?id=13851947.
18. *Delayed Sudan Leader Omar Al-Bashir Arrives in China,* BBC News, June 27, 2011, http://www.bbc.co.uk/news/world-africa-13929867.
19. *European Court of Human Rights, FAQ—The Court's Activity,* http://www.echr.coe.int/NR/rdonlyres/5C53ADA4-80F8-42CB-B8BD-CBBB781F42C8/0/FAQ_ENG_A4.pdf (accessed June 7, 2011).
20. The first quantitative study is Laurence R. Helfer & Erik Voeten, *Do European Court of Human Rights Judgments Promote Legal and Policy Change?,* http://papers.ssrn.com/sol3/papers.cfm?abstract_id=1850526 (accessed June 7, 2011). The authors find some evidence of influence.

8. State Responsibility

1. The proof of this proposition rests on very simple intuition. Imagine first that the employee alone is liable for harm and that an optimal allocation of that liability exists between employer and employee that takes account of their attitudes toward risk bearing and the employee's incentives to avoid causing harm. Perhaps the employee should bear all of the liability to motivate him to be careful, or perhaps the employer should assume some of the liability because of the employee's aversion to risk. Whatever the optimal allocation, assume that the employer and the employee enter a contract to achieve it. Now imagine that a rule of vicarious liability is imposed on the employer and that injured parties choose to collect their judgments from the employer rather than the employee. Whatever allocation of liability was optimal before will still be optimal, because the amount of liability has not changed. Accordingly, on the assumption that the employer and the employee can costlessly reconstruct that allocation by contract, they will do so. It follows that vicarious liability will have no effect on the amount that the injured party collects or how the burden of liability is distributed between the employer and the employee. Likewise, the allocation of risk between employer and employee will remain the same, as will the employee's incentives to avoid harm. See Alan O. Sykes, *The Economics of Vicarious Liability,* 93 Yale L.J. 1231 (1984).

2. Report of the International Law Commission on the Work of Its Fifty-Third Session, 53(2) Y.B. Int'l L. Comm'n 26, U.N. Doc. A/CN.4/SER.A/2001/Add.1 (Part 2).
3. Case of Francisco Mallén (Mex. v. U.S.), 4 R. Int'l Arb. Awards 173 (Perm. Ct. Arb. 1927).
4. *Id.* at 175, 177.
5. William R. Casto, *The Federal Courts' Protection Jurisdiction over Torts Committed in Violation of the Law of Nations,* 3 Conn. L. Rev. 467 (1986).
6. United States Diplomatic and Consular Staff in Tehran Case (U.S. v. Iran), 1980 I.C.J. 3 (May 24).
7. Military and Paramilitary Activities in and against Nicaragua (Nicar. v. U.S.), 1986 I.C.J. 14 (June 27).

9. Remedies

1. There are two previous sources of which we are aware that address remedies in general international law (as opposed to trade law) from an economic perspective. In Joost Pauwelyn, *Optimal Protection of International Law* (2008), the author argues that the default remedy for violation of international law should be a property rule, by which he means that a state may not acquire another state's legal entitlement without the consent of the latter state. *Id.* at 45. As will become clear, we take a somewhat contrary view. In John K. Setear, *Responses to Breach of a Treaty and Rationalist International Relations Theory: The Rules of Release and Remediation in the Law of Treaties and the Law of State Responsibility,* 83 Va. L. Rev. 1 (1997), the author provides a framework similar to ours.
2. Responsibility of States for Internationally Wrongful Acts, G.A. Res. 56/83, U.N. Doc. A/RES/56/83 (Jan. 28, 2002) [hereinafter ILC Draft], http://untreaty.un.org/ilc/texts/instruments/english/draft%20articles/9_6_2001.pdf. For commentaries on the draft articles, see Rep. of the Int'l Law Comm'n, 53d Sess., Apr. 23–June 1, July 2–Aug. 10, 2001, U.N. Doc. A/56/10; GAOR, 56th Sess., Supp. No. 10 (2001) [hereinafter ILC Commentaries], http://untreaty.un.org/ilc/texts/instruments/english/commentaries/9_6_2001.pdf.
3. See Steven Shavell, *Damage Measures for Breach of Contract,* 11 Bell J. Econ. 466 (1980). Of course, renegotiation is a possible option in this regard as well, as we subsequently discuss.
4. We should clear up a possible misunderstanding about nomenclature. In international law (as in domestic contract law), "noncompliance" is not the same as illegality. If a party injured by a breach of international law thereafter itself "breaches" as a form of justified retaliation, the "breach" should not be viewed as a violation of the law (although commentators may at times so characterize it). Similar terminological confusion arises with the concept of efficient breach. In domestic contract law, an efficient breach may be viewed as a breach of contract and a violation of the law. Yet some scholars also believe that contract law gives the promisor the option to perform or pay damages and that one does not violate the law by "breaching" and paying damages. In international law, one could similarly say that efficient breach of a treaty, when one thereafter accepts the agreed consequences of the violation, is either noncompliance or compliance with the law. In the case of WTO law, for example, a lively debate exists over whether a state that violates WTO rules and

thereafter accepts authorized retaliation is in violation of international law or not. See Alan O. Sykes, *The Dispute Resolution Mechanism: Ensuring Compliance?*, in *Oxford Handbook of the WTO* (Amrita Narlikar et al., eds., forthcoming). Nothing of substance turns on this terminological distinction in our view.

5. As argued in Setear, *supra* note 1; Joel Trachtman, *The Economic Structure of International Law* 142–145 (2008).
6. See Setear, *supra* note 1.
7. See A. Mitchell Polinsky & Daniel L. Rubinfeld, *The Welfare Implications of Costly Litigation for the Level of Liability*, 17 J. Legal Stud. 151 (1988).
8. Such adjustments are familiar in other contexts. For example, the possibility that a tortfeasor may commit a tort without detection offers a standard economic justification for increasing the level of damages and has been suggested as a basis for punitive damages in some cases. See A. Mitchell Polinsky & Steven Shavell, *Punitive Damages: An Economic Analysis*, 111 Harv. L. Rev. 869, 873–874 (1998).
9. ILC Draft, art. 22; see also *id.* art. 49 (establishing the object and limits of countermeasures).
10. *Id.* art. 51.
11. *Id.* art. 50, ¶ 1.
12. United States Diplomatic and Consular Staff in Tehran (U.S. v. Iran), 1980 I.C.J. 3, ¶ 86 (May 24).
13. See Jonathan Charney, *Anticipatory Humanitarian Intervention in Kosovo*, 93 Am. J. Int'l L. 841 (1999) (noting violation of UN charter); William Joseph Buckley, *The Strength of an Argument: A Response to General Clark's Essay*, in *Kosovo: Contending Voices on Balkan Interventions* 256 (William Joseph Buckley ed., 2000) (discussing high-altitude bombing).
14. See Gary Clyde Hufbauer et al., *Economic Sanctions Reconsidered* 158–160 (3d ed. 2007) (concluding that economic sanctions failed to achieve their goals in a large majority of 204 cases studied).
15. ILC Draft, art. 52. But see Anthony Aust, *Modern Treaty Law and Practice* 304 (2000) (denying that this rule has entered customary international law).
16. ILC Draft, arts. 31, 34. The principle was first recognized by an international court in Factory at Chorzów (Ger. v. Pol.), 1928 P.C.I.J. (ser. A) No. 17, at 29 (Sept. 13) (holding that "any breach of an engagement involves an obligation to make reparation" as part of determining whether Poland owed reparations to Germany for seizing a German factory); Factory at Chorzów (Ger. v. Pol.), 1927 P.C.I.J. (ser. A) No. 9, at 21 (July 26) ("It is a principle of international law that the breach of an engagement involves an obligation to make reparation in an adequate form").
17. ILC Draft, art. 35.
18. *Id.* art. 36.
19. Air Service Agreement of 27 March 1946 between the United States of America and France, 18 R.I.A.A. 417 (Perm. Ct. Arb. 1978). This is discussed in ILC Commentaries, at 134.
20. *Id.* ¶ 2.
21. *Id.* ¶ 17.
22. *Id.* ¶ 99.

23. In any event, the tribunal did not attempt to determine the relevant costs.
24. ILC Commentaries, ¶ 99.
25. The M/V "Saiga" (No. 2) Case (St. Vincent v. Guinea), 38 I.L.M 1323 (ITLOS July 1, 1999).
26. *Id.* ¶¶ 175–176.
27. William M. Landes & Richard A. Posner, *Economic Structure of Tort Law* (1987).
28. Rep. of the Int'l Law Comm'n, 48th Sess., May 6–July 26, 1996, art. 19, U.N. Doc. A/51/10; GAOR 51st Sess., Supp. No. 10 (1996).
29. *Id.*
30. Rep. of the Int'l Law Comm'n, 53rd Sess., Apr. 23–June 1, July 2–Aug. 10, 2001, U.N. Doc. A/5610; GAOR, 56th Sess., Supp. No. 10 (2001), reprinted in 53(2) Y.B. Int'l L. Comm'n 26, U.N. Doc. A/CN.4/SER.A/2001/Add.1 (Part 2).

10. The Intersection between International Law and Domestic Law

1. U.S. Const. art. III, § 2, cl. 1.
2. See *The Role of Domestic Courts in Treaty Enforcement—A Comparative Study* (David Sloss ed., 2009).
3. In the United States, this is known as the Charming Betsy Canon, derived from Murray v. Schooner Charming Betsy, 6 U.S. 64 (1804).
4. See Richard Carver, *A New Answer to an Old Question: National Human Rights Institutions and the Domestication of International Law,* 10 Hum. Rts. L. Rev. 1, 9–10 (2010) (describing two recent decisions in monist states that held that international law did not apply because the treaties themselves required separate legislative action).
5. See Medellin v. Texas, 552 U.S. 491, 504–506 (2008).
6. There are exceptions—for example, extraordinary rendition.
7. Curtis A. Bradley & Jack L. Goldsmith, *Customary International Law as Federal Common Law: A Critique of the Modern Position,* 110 Harv. L. Rev. 815 (1997).
8. This section draws on the analysis in Jack Goldsmith & Alan O. Sykes, *Lex Loci Delictus and Global Economic Welfare: Spinozzi v. ITT Sheraton Corp.,* 120 Harv. L. Rev. 1137 (2007); and Alan O. Sykes, *Transnational Forum Shopping as a Trade and Investment Issue,* 37 J. Legal Stud. 339 (2008).
9. 28 U.S.C. § 1350.
10. This argument was accepted in Kiobel v. Royal Dutch Petroleum, 621 F.3d 111 (2d Cir. 2010), but rejected in Flomo v. Firestone Nat. Rubber Co., 643 F.3d 1013 (7th Cir. 2011). The issues of corporate liability and extraterritorial application of the ATS are before the Supreme Court at this writing.
11. Restatement (Third) of Foreign Relations Law of the United States §§ 401(a), 402 (1987).
12. *Id.* § 402(2).
13. See Blackmer v. United States, 284 U.S. 421 (1932).
14. Restatement, *supra* note 11, § 402(1)(c).
15. *Id.* § 415.
16. On adjudicative jurisdiction, see the discussion that follows.
17. Restatement, *supra* note 11, §§ 403(3), 441–442.

18. Export Trade Act (Webb-Pomerene Act), ch. 50, 40 Stat. 516 (1918) (codified at 15 U.S.C. §§ 61–66).
19. Alan O. Sykes, *Externalities in Open Economy Antitrust and Their Implications for International Competition Policy,* 23 Harv. J.L. & Pub. Pol'y 89 (1999).

11. Treatment of Aliens, Foreign Property, and Foreign Debt

1. Restatement (Third) of Foreign Relations Law of the United States § 721–722 (1987).
2. See Emerich de Vattel, *Law of Nations* 318 (AMS Press 1982) (1863), discussed in Philip Hamburger, *Beyond Protection,* 109 Colum. L. Rev. 1823, 1864–1869 (2009).
3. For recent discussions of the doctrine and its history, see, e.g., Lee C. Buchheit, G. Mitu Gulati, & Robert B. Thompson, *The Dilemma of Odious Debts,* 56 Duke L.J. 1201 (2007).
4. See, e.g., Patricia Adams, *Odious Debts: Loose Lending, Corruption, and the Third World's Environmental Legacy* (1991); Seema Jayachandran & Michael Kremer, *Odious Debt,* 96 Am. Econ. Rev. 82 (2006) (arguing that loan sanctions would be more effective than trade sanctions). The major source for the odious debt doctrine is the Tinoco Case (Gr. Brit. v. Costa Rica), 1 R. Int'l Arb. Awards 369, 375–385 (1923), available at 18 Am. J. Int'l L.. 147 (1924).
5. For a formal model, see Albert Choi & Eric A. Posner, *A Critique of the Odious Debt Doctrine,* 70 Law & Contemp. Probs. 33 (2007).
6. This point is obvious but is mentioned because some commentators might be read to say otherwise. See, e.g., Jayachandran & Kremer, *supra* note 4, at 88 ("[L]oan sanctions make the population better off in future periods [than trade sanctions do] since it has no debt repayment to make"). However, Jayachandran and Kremer acknowledge in a footnote that this is false if the dictator can trade nonrenewable resources (*id.* at 88 n.7), which in our view is fatal to their claim.

12. The Use of Force

1. Meredith Reid Sarkees, *COW Intra-State War Data, 1816–1997* (v3.0), http://www.cor relatesofwar.org/cow2%20data/WarData/IntraState/Intra-State%20War%20Format %20(V%203–0).htm. See also Meredith Reid Sarkees & Phil Schafer, *The Correlates of War Data on War: An Update to 1997,* 18 Conflict Mgmt. and Peace Sci. 123 (2000).
2. See, e.g., James D. Fearon, *Rationalist Explanations for War,* 49 Int'l Org. 379 (1995).
3. The rules can be found in the fifth and thirteenth articles of the 1907 Hague Convention and the influential *San Remo Manual on International Law Applicable to Armed Conflicts at Sea,* as well as various sources of customary international law. See Convention Respecting the Rights and Duties of Neutral Powers and Persons in Case of War on Land, Oct. 18, 1907, 36 Stat. 2310 [hereinafter Hague V]; Convention Concerning the Rights and Duties of Neutral Powers in Naval War, Oct. 18, 1907, 36 Stat. 2415 [hereinafter Hague XIII]; *San Remo Manual on International Law Applicable to Armed Conflicts at Sea,* 89 Am. J. Int'l. L. 192 (1995).
4. The Caroline (exchange of diplomatic notes between Great Britain and the United States, 1842), 2 J. Moore, *Digest of Int. L.* 409, 412 (1906).

5. General Treaty of Renunciation of War as an Instrument of National Policy (Kellogg-Briand Pact or Pact of Paris), Aug. 27, 1928, 46 Stat. 2343, 94 L.N.T.S. 57.
6. The remainder of this chapter is a revised version of Eric A. Posner & Alan O. Sykes, *Optimal War and Jus Ad Bellum*, 93 Geo. L.J. 993 (2005).
7. See Gary S. Becker, *Crime and Punishment: An Economic Approach*, 76 J. Pol. Econ. 169 (1968).
8. See Steven Levitt, *Incentive Compatibility Constraints as an Explanation for the Use of Prison Sentences Instead of Fines*, 17 Int'l Rev. L. & Econ. 170 (1997).
9. A classic study of the efficacy of economic sanctions is Gary C. Hufbauer, John J. Schott, Kimberley Ann Elliott, & Barbara Oegg, *Economic Sanctions Reconsidered: History and Current Policy* (3d ed. 2007). The theoretical and empirical literature on sanctions is also surveyed in Jonathan Eaton & Alan O. Sykes, *International Sanctions*, in *The New Palgrave Dictionary of Economics and the Law*, vol. 2 (Peter Newman ed., 1998).
10. Treaty on Boundary, Slave Trade, and Extradition (Webster-Ashburton Treaty), U.S.--U.K., Aug. 9, 1842, 8 Stat. 572.
11. See generally Steven Shavell, *Foundations of Economic Analysis of Law*, 245, 540–568 (2004). The notion that utility may be illicit and should not count in the social welfare calculus may also be found in the literature on punitive damages. See Robert Cooter, *Economic Analysis of Punitive Damages*, 56 So. Cal. L. Rev. 79 (1982).
12. The literature on real options theory is vast. A thoughtful introduction to much of it may be found in Avinash K. Dixit & Robert S. Pindyck, *Investment under Uncertainty* (1994).
13. A further source of potential distortion outside the model relates to the fact that Home may not even pursue its own interest systematically. There is perhaps no more reason to suppose that governments maximize national welfare in the pursuit of their security policies than in other policy spheres (such as international trade), where it is well known that policy decisions routinely diverge from the national welfare optimum. Eisenhower's famous warning about the "military-industrial complex" can be taken as a suggestion that interest groups favoring more militaristic policies may be particularly well organized and may thus lead states to devote more resources to defense activities than may be justified on national welfare grounds.
14. We take no position on the actual values of these variables and on whether the U.S.-led invasion of Iraq was either privately or socially beneficial. We do note, however, that an important caveat to our analytic discussion arises if one assumes that an attack on Foreign confers net benefits on it (as by eliminating a repressive regime). Then one must ask whether attack is justified from a social standpoint even if Foreign turns out not to be aggressive. That is, one must modify the social calculus to consider the costs of not attacking Foreign in either period.
15. This is similar to Yoo's argument that the old "imminent" self-defense rule fails to take into account the magnitude of the risk and harm of war. John Yoo, *Using Force*, 71 U. Chi. L. Rev. 729 (2004). However, although Yoo argues (as we do) that a state should take account of the expected harm from waiting, he does not say what this expected harm should be compared with. Here is an excerpt from his discussion:

> International law should allow states to use force in their self-defense, rather than pursuing diplomatic means or waiting for the UN to solve the problem, when the expected harm of a potential attack reaches a certain level. Admit-

tedly, the Hand formula does not inform us where that line should be, but it does allow us to see that use of force should move away from pure temporal imminence—which was just a proxy for a high level of probability—to include probability and magnitude of harm. (*Id.* at 757)

By contrast, we argue that the expected harm from an attack should be compared with something: with the costs (both to Home and Foreign) from initiating a war earlier rather than later.

16. See President George W. Bush, *Remarks before the United Nations General Assembly (Sept. 12, 2002)*, available at http://www.un.org/webcast/ga/57/statements/020912usaE.htm. All of these factors were touched on in the *National Security Strategy of the United States (Sept. 2002)*, available at http://georgewbush-whitehouse.archives.gov/nsc/nss/2002/.
17. Various views can be found in Hearings to Examine Threats, Responses, and Regional Considerations Surrounding Iraq: Hearings before S. Comm. on Foreign Relations, 107th Cong. 2 (July 31 & Aug. 1, 2002).
18. See, e.g., Kenneth M. Pollack, *The Threatening Storm: The Case for Invading Iraq* (2002).
19. See, e.g., William Kristol & Lawrence F. Kaplan, *The War over Iraq: Saddam's Tyranny and America's Mission* (2003).
20. The Bush administration claimed that earlier UN resolutions authorized the invasion. For the arguments pro and con, compare John Yoo, *International Law and the War in Iraq*, 97 Am. J. Int'l L. 563 (2003), and Thomas M. Franck, *The United Nations after Iraq*, 97 Am. J. Int'l L. 607 (2003).
21. One view is that the United Nations may authorize force only for purposes identified in the UN Charter, such as protection of the territorial integrity of members; another view is that the UN could not authorize force in violation of jus cogens norms, e.g., to commit genocide.
22. Note that we are talking about the margin: aggressors can already use ordinary self-defense as a pretext.
23. Yoo, *supra* note 17.
24. For various perspectives on this issue, see the essays collected in *United States Hegemony and the Foundations of International Law* (Michael Byers & Georg Nolte eds., 2003).
25. See John R. Bolton, *Under Sec'y for Arms Control and Int'l Sec., Remarks to the Federalist Society: The United States and the International Criminal Court (Nov. 14, 2002)*, available at http://stage.amicc.org/docs/Bolton11_14_02.pdf.
26. Military and Paramilitary Activities in and against Nicaragua (Nicar. v. U.S.), 1986 I.C.J. 14 (June 27).
27. Cf. Yoram Dinstein, *War, Aggression, and Self-Defense* 240 (3rd ed. 2001).
28. See, e.g., Stephen M. Walt, *Why Obama's Libya Speech Didn't Matter*, Foreign Policy (Mar. 29, 2011), http://walt.foreignpolicy.com/posts/2011/03/29/why_obamas_libya_speech_didnt_matter.
29. Compare the discussions in Fernando R. Tesón, *The Liberal Case for Humanitarian Intervention*, in *Humanitarian Intervention: Ethical, Legal, and Political Dilemmas* 93 (J. L. Holzgrefe & Robert O. Keohane eds., 2003); Thomas A. Franck, *Recourse to Force: State Action against Threats and Armed Attacks* (2002); and Michael J. Glennon, *Limits of Law, Prerogatives of Power: Interventionism after Kosovo* (2001).

13. The Conduct of War

1. On the history, see generally Geoffrey *Best, War and Law since 1945 (1994); Geoffrey Best, Humanity in Warfare* (1980); and the essays in *The Laws of War: Constraints on Warfare in the Western World* (Michael Howard, George J. Andreopoulos, & Mark R. Shulman eds., 1994).
2. See Christopher Greenwood, *The Law of Weaponry at the Start of the New Millennium,* in *The Law of Armed Conflict: Into the Next Millennium* 185 (Michael N. Schmitt & Leslie C. Green eds., 1998).
3. The issue arose again during the Kosovo intervention, when human rights groups complained that NATO's use of high-altitude bombing protected pilots at unreasonable expense to civilians who were killed or injured by errant bombs. See, e.g., Amnesty International, *"Collateral Damage" or Unlawful Killings? Violations of the Laws of War by NATO during Operation Allied Force 13–16* (June 2000), available at http://www.amnesty.org/en/library/info/EUR70/018/2000. The relevant question is, if you think that the Kosovo intervention was justified on humanitarian or security grounds but think that American public opinion would not have tolerated an air campaign that resulted in nontrivial casualties to American pilots, should the U.S. government have chosen not to intervene in order to avoid violating international humanitarian law?
4. See Judith Gail Gardam, *Proportionality and Force in International Law,* 87 Am. J. Int'l L. 391, 396 (1993).
5. See Jeffrey W. Legro, *Cooperation under Fire: Anglo-German Restraint during World War II* 37 (1995).
6. For a discussion of these and related factors, see James D. Morrow, *The Institutional Features of the Prisoners of War Treaties,* 55 Int'l Org. 971 (2001).
7. See Eyal Benvenisti, *The International Law of Occupation* (1993).
8. Note that there will often be divergence between the formal laws of war agreed to in advance of war and the "law in action," as the war progresses. This happens because during wars, weapons and tactics evolve quickly and unpredictably, rendering earlier judgments irrelevant. For example, during World War I, when the British imprisoned German U-boat crews for war crimes, Germans responded by imprisoning a group of British officers. Eventually, the British gave in: they could not deter the Germans from their U-boat tactics because they valued humane treatment of their captured soldiers more than any gains from imprisoning U-boat crews. Gary Jonathan Bass, *Stay the Hand of Vengeance: The Politics of War Crimes Tribunals* 61–62 (2000).
9. Protocol Additional to the Geneva Conventions of Aug. 12, 1949, and Relating to the Protection of Victims of International Armed Conflicts art. 48, Dec. 12, 1977, 1125 U.N.T.S. 3.
10. See Stephen Strasser, *The 9/11 Investigations* (2004).
11. Religious terrorists may be undeterrable because motivated by religious duties. See Bruce Hoffman, *Inside Terrorism* 168 (1998). They are also more violent. *Id.* at 93. But they have aims that they pursue via rational means, and this is true for terrorists generally. *Id.* at 183.
12. Hoffman provides some examples. Israel and the Palestinian Liberation Organization exchange prisoners (*id.* at 67); so have other states and terrorist organizations (*id.* at

133–135); and terrorist organizations sometimes try to avoid targeting civilians, focusing on soldiers and officials instead (*id.* at 164).
13. See Michael van Tangen Page, *Prisons, Peace, and Terrorism* 164–168 (1998).
14. See Morrow, *supra* note 6.

14. Human Rights

1. Universal Declaration of Human Rights, G.A. Res. 217A (III), U.N. GAOR, 3d Sess., U.N. Doc. A/810, at 71 (Dec. 10, 1948) (enumerated rights include "the right to life, liberty and security of person" in art. 3, "the right to work" in art. 23, and "the right to education" in art. 26).
2. International Covenant for Economic, Social, and Cultural Rights, Dec. 16, 1966, 993 U.N.T.S. 3.
3. International Covenant for Civil and Political Rights, Dec. 16, 1966, S. Exec. Doc. E, 95-2, 999 U.N.T.S. 171.
4. U.N. Econ. & Soc. Council, Comm. on Econ., Soc., & Cultural Rights, The Nature of States Parties Obligations, General Comment No. 3, U.N. Doc. E/1991/23 (Dec. 14, 1990), available at http://www.unhchr.ch/tbs/doc.nsf/0/94bdbaf59b43a424c12563ed0052b664?Opendocument.
5. See, e.g., Oona Hathaway, *Why Do Countries Commit to Human Rights Treaties?*, 51 J. Conflict Res. 588 (2007); Emilie M. Hafner-Burton & Kiyoteru Tsutsui, *Justice Lost! The Failure of International Human Rights Law to Matter Where It's Needed Most*, 44 J. Peace Research 407 (2007).
6. A more sophisticated signaling explanation asserts that authoritarian governments enter human rights treaties in order to signal to domestic opposition groups their *willingness* to engage in repression. If they face sanctions from foreign countries for using repression, and then they torture political opponents, they will be less likely to leave power voluntarily. See James R. Hollyer & B. Peter Rosendorff, *Why Do Authoritarian Regimes Sign the Convention against Torture? Signaling, Domestic Politics and Non-Compliance*, 6 Quarterly Journal of Political Science 275 (2011).
7. Taken from Eric A. Posner, *Human Rights, the Laws of War, and Reciprocity* (2010) (unpublished manuscript).
8. Of course, they will typically do too little even in the absence of this externality if they do not fully value the benefits to Zimbabwe.
9. James M. Buchanan, *The Samaritan's Dilemma*, in *Altruism, Morality and Economic Theory* 71 (Edmund S. Phelps ed., 1975).
10. See, e.g., Oona A. Hathaway, *Do Human Rights Treaties Make a Difference?*, 111 Yale L.J. 1935 (2002).
11. Beth A. Simmons, *Mobilizing for Human Rights* (2009).
12. Alan O. Sykes, *International Trade and Human Rights: An Economic Perspective*, in *Trade and Human Rights: Foundations and Conceptual Issues* (Fredereick M. Abbott, Christine Breining-Kaufmann, & Thomas Cottier eds., 2006).
13. See Steven C. Poe & C. Neal Tate, *Repression of Human Rights to Personal Integrity in the 1980s: A Global Analysis*, 88 Am. Pol. Sci. Rev. 853 (1994); Steven C. Poe, C. Neal Tate, & Linda Camp Keith, *Repression of the Human Right to Personal Integrity*

Revisited: A Global Cross-National Study Covering the Years 1976–1993, 43 Int'l Stud. Q. 291 (1999).

15. International Criminal Law

1. Up until the discussion on extradition treaties, portions of this chapter are taken from Eric A. Posner & Alan O. Sykes, *An Economic Analysis of State and Individual Responsibility under International Law,* 9 Am. L. & Econ. Rev. 72 (2007).
2. A. Mitchell Polinsky & Steven Shavell, *Should Employees Be Subject to Fines and Imprisonment Given the Existence of Corporate Liability?,* 13 Int'l Rev. of L. & Econ. 239 (1993).
3. S. S. Lotus (Fr. v. Turk.), 1927 P.C.I.J. (ser. A) No. 10 (Sept. 7).
4. *Id.* at 62.
5. There were a number of Geneva Conventions beginning in 1864 and extending through a series of protocols, the last of which was adopted in 2005. The 1949 treaties are the most broadly accepted.
6. International Convention on the Prevention and Punishment of the Crime of Genocide, Dec. 9, 1948, 102 Stat. 3045, 78 U.N.T.S. 277.
7. But see Eugene Kontorovich, *The Piracy Analogy: Modern Universal Jurisdiction's Hollow Foundation,* 45 Harv. Int'l L.J. 183 (2004), who argues that piracy does not provide a relevant analogy for modern universal jurisdiction.
8. *After Years of Debate, ICC Member States agree on definition of aggression,* UN News Service, June 14, 2010, http://www.un.org/apps/news/story.asp?NewsID=35018&Cr=international+criminal+court&Cr1.
9. But as we have seen, the ICC has moved toward recognizing individual criminal responsibility for aggressive war.
10. Leon Friedman, *The Law of War: A Documentary History* 1596 (1972) (quoting the Yamashita Commission).
11. Prosecutor v. Akayesu, Case No. ICTR-96-4-T, Judgment (Int'l Crim. Trib. for Rwanda, Sept. 2, 1998); Prosecutor v. Akayesu, Case No. ICTR-96-4-A, Appeal (Int'l Crim. Trib. for Rwanda, June 1, 2001).
12. Cited in Tel-Oren v. Libyan Arab Republic, 726 F.2d 774, 807 (D.C. Cir. 1984).

16. International Environmental Law

1. Actually, the discussion in the text is overly simple, because all corrective mechanisms are costly and potentially make errors. An ideal system will factor these issues into the efficiency calculus as well.
2. Trail Smelter (U.S. v. Can.), 3 Int'l Arb. Awards 1938 (1941) (final decision).
3. *Id.* at 1965.
4. Declaration of the United Nations Conference on the Human Environment, Principle 21, U.N. Doc. A/CONF.48/14/Rev.1 (June 16, 1972).
5. Draft Articles on the Prevention of Transboundary Harm from Hazardous Activities, Rep. of the Int'l Law Comm'n, 53d Sess., Apr. 23–June 1, July 2–Aug. 10, U.N. Doc. A/56/10; GAOR, 56th Sess., Supp. No. 10 (Aug. 10, 2001).
6. Convention on Long-Range Transboundary Air Pollution, Nov. 13, 1979, T.I.A.S. No. 10,541, 18 I.L.M. 1442.

7. Protocol to the 1979 Convention on Long-Range Transboundary Air Pollution on the Reduction of Sulphur Emissions or Their Transboundary Fluxes by at Least 30 Percent, July 8, 1985, 27 I.L.M. 698, 707 (entered into force Sept. 2, 1987).
8. Montreal Protocol on Substances That Deplete the Ozone Layer, Sept. 16, 1987, S. Treaty Doc. No. 100-10, 1522 U.N.T.S. 3.
9. See Cass R. Sunstein, *Of Montreal and Kyoto: A Tale of Two Protocols,* 31 Harv. Envtl. L. Rev. 1 (2007); James Murdoch & Todd Sandler, *The Voluntary Provision of a Pure Public Good: The Case of Reduced CFC Emissions and the Montreal Protocol,* 63 J. Pub. Econ. 331 (1997).
10. Murdoch & Sandler, *supra* note 9, at 334.
11. United Nations Framework Convention on Climate Change, May 9, 1992, S. Treaty Doc. No. 102-38, 1771 U.N.T.S. 164.
12. Kyoto Protocol to the United Nations Framework Convention on Climate Change, Dec. 10, 1997, 37 I.L.M. 22.
13. *Japan Targeted on Kyoto Climate Stance at Cancun Summit,* BBC News, Dec. 10, 2010, http://www.bbc.co.uk/news/science-environment-11966710.
14. See Eric A. Posner & David Weisbach, *Climate Change Justice* (2010).
15. See Michael Wara, *Is the Global Carbon Market Working?,* Nature, Feb. 2007, at 595.

17. The Law of the Sea

1. The material in this chapter is a revised version of Eric A. Posner & Alan O. Sykes, *Economic Foundations of the Law of the Sea,* 104 Am. J. Int'l L. 569 (2010).
2. United Nations Convention on the Law of the Sea, Dec. 10, 1982, 1833 U.N.T.S. 397 [hereinafter UNCLOS]. For a short, lucid history, see David Anderson, *Modern Law of the Sea* 1–22 (2008).
3. The most thorough economic treatment of issues within the scope of UNCLOS that we have encountered is that of Ross D. Eckert, *The Enclosure of Ocean Resources* (1979), which was written before UNCLOS was finalized. Of course, the general economic problem that justifies some kind of international regulation of the oceans—namely, the tragedy of the commons—has been widely recognized. See, e.g., Robert L. Friedheim, *A Proper Order for the Oceans: An Agenda for the New Century,* in *Order for the Oceans at the Turn of the Century* 537, 539 (Davor Vidas & Willy Østreng eds., 1999); Richard James Sweeney, Robert D. Tollison, & Thomas D. Willett, *Market Failure, the Common-Pool Problem, and Ocean Resource Exploitation,* 17 J.L. & Econ. 179 (1974). Our analysis also relates closely to theories regarding the emergence of property rights. See Harold Demsetz, *Some Aspects of Property Rights,* 9 J.L. & Econ. 61 (1966). Eyal Benvenisti briefly touches on some issues of the efficiency of the law of the sea in the course of an article focused on international courts; see Eyal Benvenisti, *Customary International Law as a Judicial Tool for Promoting Efficiency,* in *The Impact of International Law on International Cooperation* 85 (Eyal Benvenisti & Moshe Hirsch eds., 2004).
4. See generally Thrainn Eggertsson, *Economic Behavior and Institutions* (1990); Dean Lueck & Thomas Miceli, *Property Law,* in *Handbook of Law and Economics* (A. M. Polinsky & S. Shavell eds., 2007).

5. See, e.g., Elinor Ostrom, *Governing the Commons: The Evolution of Institutions for Collective Action* (1990). Ostrom's work is in part a response to more pessimistic analyses, such as Garrett Hardin, *The Tragedy of the Commons,* 162 Science 1243 (1968).
6. Domestic pollution, by contrast, may have international consequences if it later becomes pollution of the oceans. Sovereignty over internal bodies of water is, to this degree, not unlimited, as we note below. See also UNCLOS, arts. 193, 194(2).
7. This observation may help to explain some aspects of UNCLOS that are sometimes viewed as inequitable, such as the fact that landlocked states do not receive any exclusive allocation of ocean resources. See generally Bernard H. Oxman, The *Territorial Temptation: A Siren Song at Sea,* 100 Am. J. Int'l L. 830 (2006).
8. This problem is particularly likely in the case of fisheries, discussed later in the chapter.
9. Some such rules are found outside of UNCLOS. Rules regarding such matters as maritime safety and prevention of pollution are contained in conventions developed under the auspices of the International Maritime Organization. UNCLOS encourages the development of such rules and promotes their universal application. See UNCLOS, arts. 39(2),(3), 94, 210, 211(1),(2), 217.
10. The limits on open access include those concerning seabed minerals; requirements concerning pollution by ocean-going vessels, such as those in UNCLOS, arts. 211(2), 217(1); and various limits established in accordance with the UNCLOS framework but in complementary agreements, such as the obligation to cooperate in the conservation of highly migratory species.
11. The first type of situation, illustrated by the shipboard homicide, may also raise difficult conflict-of-law issues relating to the substantive elements of the crime or the attendant penalty.
12. See J. Ashley Roach, *Agora: Piracy Prosecutions; Countering Piracy off Somalia: International Law and International Institutions,* 104 Am. J. Int'l L. 397 (2010).
13. UNCLOS, art. 86. Most of the high seas provisions, other than those concerning living resources, also apply within the EEZ pursuant to art. 58(2).
14. With due regard to the interests of other states. *Id.* art. 87(2).
15. *Id.* art. 87(1).
16. *Id.* art. 94(3).
17. *Id.* art. 97.
18. *Id.* arts. 109–110; other illegal activities are addressed in other international agreements.
19. *Id.* arts. 2, 3.
20. *Id.* arts. 17–19.
21. These resource justifications are, to be sure, no longer specific to the territorial sea, as coastal states now have control over resources extending well beyond the territorial sea through the continental shelf and EEZ.
22. Robin Rolf Churchill & Alan Vaughan Lowe, *The Law of the Sea* 56–67 (3d ed. 1999).
23. See UNCLOS, arts. 8(1), 35(c), 49, 52–54.
24. "For the purposes of this Convention, a bay is a well-marked indentation whose penetration is in such proportion to the width of its mouth as to contain land-locked waters and constitute more than a mere curvature of the coast. An indentation shall not, how-

ever, be regarded as a bay unless its area is as large as, or larger than, that of the semicircle whose diameter is a line drawn across the mouth of that indentation." *Id.* art 10(2).

25. For a discussion of the problem of opportunistic baseline drawing and possible solutions, see Tullio Scovazzi, *The Establishment of Straight Baselines Systems: The Rules and the Practice,* in *Order for the Oceans at the Turn of the Century,* at 445.
26. UNCLOS, art. 38(2).
27. See *id.* art. 234.
28. *Id.* art. 33(1).
29. *Id.* art. 76.
30. *Id.* art. 76(8) contains a provision by which a coastal state, if it agrees with the recommendation of a commission established by UNCLOS, may establish "final and binding" limits.
31. *Id.* art. 56(1)(a).
32. The scramble for claims was initiated by President Truman in 1945.
33. Churchill & Lowe, *supra* note 22.
34. See Benvenisti, *supra* note 3.
35. UNCLOS, art. 76(8).
36. To be sure, development of the law, including through the ICJ and arbitral tribunals, has helped resolve some of the ambiguity.
37. See Betsy Baker, *Law, Science and the Continental Shelf: The Russian Federation and the Promise of Arctic Cooperation,* 25 Am. J. Int'l L. Rev. 251 (2010).
38. See Maritime Delimitation in the Black Sea (Rom. v. Ukr.), 2009 I.C.J. 9 (Feb. 3).
39. North Sea Continental Shelf Cases (F.R.G./Den.; F.R.G./Neth.), 1969 I.C.J. 3 (Feb. 20).
40. See Wolfgang Friedmann, *The North Sea Continental Shelf Case—A Critique,* 64 Am. J. Int'l L. 229, 236–240 (1970).
41. See Churchill & Lowe, *supra* note 22, for the limited exceptions.
42. For additional criticisms of the "proportionality" criterion, as it is sometimes called, see Malcolm D. Evans, *Maritime Boundary Delimitation: Where Do We Go from Here?* in *The Law of the Sea: Progress and Prospects* 137, 154–156 (David Freestone, Richard Barnes, & David Ong eds., 2006).
43. For a discussion, see Bernard H. Oxman, *The 1994 Agreement Relating to the Implementation of Part XI of the UN Convention on the Law of the Sea,* in *Order for the Oceans at the Turn of the Century,* at 15.
44. We follow the discussion in Churchill & Lowe, *supra* note 22, at 248–253.
45. Agreement Relating to the Implementation of Part XI of the United Nations Convention on the Law of the Sea of 10 December 1982 §5-1, July 28, 1994, 1836 U.N.T.S. 42, reprinted in 33 I.L.M. 1309 (1994).
46. Doug Bandow, *Don't Resurrect the Law of the Sea Treaty,* Policy Analysis, Oct. 13, 2005, at 8, 9.
47. See Bernard H. Oxman, *Law of the Sea Forum: The 1994 Agreement on Implementation of the Seabed Provisions of the Convention on the Law of the Sea: The 1994 Agreement and the Convention,* 88 Am. J. Int'l L. 687, 691 (1994), and for a more detailed discussion, Oxman, *supra* note 43, at 22–27.
48. There is a further question of whether the Enterprise will ever come into existence, given the procedural requirements set forth in the Implementing Agreement.

49. Satya N. Nandan, *Legislative and Executive Powers of the International Seabed Authority for the Implementation of the Law of the Sea Convention,* in *Order for the Oceans,* at 78–80; Bandow, *supra* note 46 at 7, citing UNCLOS, art. 150(h).
50. Bandow, *supra* note 46; Jeremy Rabkin, *The Law of the Sea Treaty: A Bad Deal for America,* Competitive Enter. Inst., June 1, 2006, http://cei.org/studies-issue-analysis/law-sea-treaty-bad-deal-america.
51. We should note, however, that some scholars are skeptical about whether even cash transfers from rich countries to poor countries actually help poor countries. If these transfers are mainly enjoyed by corrupt elites, then the case for redistribution is obviously weakened. See, e.g., William Easterly, *The White Man's Burden: Why the West's Efforts to Aid the Rest Have Done So Much Ill and So Little Good* (2006).
52. The rule is mitigated somewhat by a provision that gives the mining company a right to participate with the Enterprise in a joint venture.
53. See Churchill & Lowe, *supra* note 2, at 239–248.
54. See, e.g., Steven Groves, *Why Reagan Would Still Reject the Law of the Sea Treaty,* Heritage Foundation, October 24, 2007, http://www.heritage.org/Research/internationalorganizations/wm1676.cfm.
55. Cf. Edmund W. Kitch, *The Nature and Function of the Patent System,* 20 J.L. & Econ. 265 (1977) (describing the mineral prospecting system in the American west and the analogy to patent law).
56. See also *Agreement for the Implementation of the Provisions of the United Nations Convention on the Law of the Sea of 10 December 1982 Relating to the Conservation and Management of Straddling Fish Stocks and Highly Migratory Fish Stocks,* U.N. Doc. A/CONF.164/37 (Sept. 8, 1995) (including art. 8(4), which conditions the right to fish on participation in the regulatory system).

18. International Trade

1. This chapter draws significantly on Alan O. Sykes, *International Law,* in *Handbook of Law and Economics* (A. Mitchell Polinsky & Steven Shavell eds., 2007).
2. Consumer surplus is the difference between what consumers are willing to pay for a good and the price that they must actually pay. If a consumer can buy a sandwich for $3.00 for which she would have paid as much as $5.00, the consumer earns a surplus of $2.00.
3. Producer surplus is the difference between the price received for a good and the (marginal) cost of producing it. If a producer receives $5.00 for a good that cost $2.00 to produce, the producer surplus is $3.00. Producer surplus is essentially a measure of economic profit.
4. The classic reference is Harry Johnson, *Optimum Tariffs and Retaliation,* 21 Rev. Econ. Stud. 142 (1953–1954).
5. Under conditions of imperfect competition, however, export subsidies may emerge from the pursuit of national welfare by individual states, as suggested by the considerable literature on "strategic trade policy."
6. See Gene M. Grossman & Elhanan Helpman, *Protection for Sale,* 84 Am. Econ. Rev. 833 (1994).

7. Some readers may note that this externality is "pecuniary" in that it is transmitted through prices. Pecuniary externalities do not cause economic efficiency in competitive markets, but the problem here is that the relevant markets are not competitive. By hypothesis, nations are "large" and possess monopoly and monopsony power over export and import prices.
8. For a thorough and rigorous exposition, see Kyle Bagwell & Robert W. Staiger, *The Economics of the World Trading System* (2002). The terms of trade theory is not the only story in the literature about the role of trade agreements. One other prominent account, the "domestic commitments theory," suggests that some trade agreements may be motivated not by international externalities but by time consistency problems in domestic politics. Here governments are imagined to have some preferences over investments in various sectors. Suppose, for example, that governments wish to see investment only in sectors that are globally competitive. But suppose both producers and governments know that once investments are sunk, governments will succumb to political pressure to protect them. Following an investment in a sector that is not competitive, for example, governments may protect it from foreign competition with tariffs. In anticipation of this behavior, producers will distort their investments away from the government's preferred pattern. Government may thus benefit from devices that commit it to eschew measures such as tariffs in the future, and it is conceivable that a commitment to free (or freer) trade under a trade agreement might be valuable for this purpose—the government's promise not to use tariffs becomes more credible because of the international sanction that would follow breach of the agreement. For a formal model along these lines, see Giovanni Maggi & Andres Rodriguez-Clare, *The Value of Trade Agreements in the Presence of Political Pressures,* 106 J. Pol. Econ. 574 (1998).
9. Book-length treatments of the WTO/GATT system from legal, economic, and political science perspectives include John H. Jackson, *The World Trading System* (2d ed. 1997); Kyle Bagwell & Robert W. Staiger, *The Economics of the World Trading System* (2002); Michael J. Trebilcock & Robert Howse, *The Regulation of International Trade* (3d ed. 2005); Michael Trebilcock, *Understanding Trade Law* (2011); and John H. Barton, Judith L. Goldstein, Timothy E. Josling, & Richard H. Steinberg, *The Evolution of the Trade Regime: Politics, Law, and Economics of the GATT and the WTO* (2006).
10. For a contrarian perspective, see Andrew K. Rose, *Do We Really Know That the WTO Increases Trade?,* 94 Am. Econ. Rev. 98 (2004). A strong challenge to Rose's empirics is to be found in Judith Goldstein, Douglas Rivers, & Michael Tomz, Comment, *Do We Really Know That the WTO Increases Trade?* 97 Am. Econ. Rev. 2005 (2007).
11. See Henrik Horn & Petros C. Mavroidis, *Economic and Legal Aspects of the Most Favored Nation Clause,* 17 Eur. J. Pol. Econ. 233 (2001); Warren F. Schwartz & Alan O. Sykes, *The Economics of the Most Favored Nation Clause,* 16 Int'l Rev. L. & Econ. 27 (1996); Kyle Bagwell & Robert W. Staiger, *Multilateral Trade Negotiations, Bilateral Opportunism and the Rules of GATT,* 67 J. Int'l Econ. 268 (2005).
12. See Giovanni Maggi, *The Role of Multilateral Institutions in International Trade Cooperation,* 89 Am. Econ. Rev. 190 (1999).
13. See generally Robert Z. Lawrence, *Regionalism, Multilateralism, and Deeper Integration* (1996); Jagdish Bhagwati & Arvind Panagariya, *The Economics of Preferential Trade Agreements* (1996); *Analyzing Preferential Trading Agreements: Alternative Approaches*

(Jagdish Bhagwati, Pravin Krishna, & Arvind Panagariya eds., 1997); T. N. Srinivasan, *Nondiscrimination in GATT/WTO: Was There Anything to Begin with and Is There Anything Left?*, 4 World Trade Rev. 69 (2005).

14. If the arrangement is a customs union, article XXIV does require compensation if the new common external tariff violates a tariff commitment previously made by a member state (e.g., if after Turkey joins the EU, it raises its tariff on widgets above the level it had previously promised to some non-EU trading partner, the EU must compensate that partner). But this compensation obligation is incomplete (it does nothing to compensate for the increase in market power enjoyed by the trading bloc, for example), and its efficacy in practice has proven questionable. Moreover, when the preferential arrangement is a free trade area, members do not alter their tariffs on imports from nonmembers at all, and no compensation is required.

15. Under a liability rule, an actor may take an action that injures another as long as that actor pays a price to compensate the injured party ex post. An example would be a system in which a polluting factory was allowed to pollute but required to pay damages to entities harmed by the pollution in a lawsuit. Under a property rule, by contrast, an actor that wishes to undertake an activity that injures another actor must first obtain permission from that actor. For example, if a polluting factory is subject to an injunction that shuts it down unless those harmed by pollution agree to lift the injunction (no doubt for a price), the system involves a property rule.

16. Kyle Bagwell & Robert W. Staiger, *A Theory of Managed Trade*, 80 Am. Econ. Rev. 779 (1990).

17. Alan O. Sykes, *Protectionism as a "Safeguard": A Positive Analysis of the GATT "Escape Clause" with Normative Speculations*, 58 U. Chi. L. Rev. 255 (1991).

18. See Tracy Epps, *International Trade and Health Protection: A Critical Assessment of the WTO's SPS Agreement* (2008); Robert Howse, *Democracy, Science, and Free Trade: Risk Regulation on Trial at the WTO*, 98 Mich. L. Rev. 2329 (2000).

19. We note in passing that regulatory protection can be an especially wasteful form of protection. Suppose, for concreteness, that an importing nation wishes to protect its grain industry and that it has a target for the domestic grain price. Assume that this target price can be achieved with a tariff of t per bushel of grain, which will limit grain imports to the quantity B and result in tariff revenue to the importing nation of tB. Alternatively, the importing nation can enact a regulation that requires foreign grain producers to incur additional costs of production (for example, the cost of testing all export shipments for the presence of some ostensibly dangerous pest or chemical). Let the additional cost per bushel of grain exports be t under this regulation, and assume that no tariff will be imposed in this alternate scenario. Assume further that the ostensible health or safety basis for the regulation is pretense and that the sole motivation for the regulation is to achieve protection. From the standpoint of the grain industry in the importing nation, both approaches are equivalent in their ability to achieve the target domestic price. Likewise, both measures will have the same effect on the terms of trade, because net purchases from abroad will be the same and thus equilibrium world prices will be the same. But the two approaches are not equivalent in welfare terms—under the regulatory approach to protection, the tariff revenue tB, which is earned by the government under a tariff and available to be spent on socially constructive projects, is

transformed into pure loss with regulatory protection in the absence of any bona fide health or safety justification. See Alan O. Sykes, *Regulatory Protectionism and the Law of International Trade*, 66 U. Chi. L. Rev. 1 (1999).
20. See Warren F. Schwartz & Eugene Harper, *The Regulation of Subsidies Affecting International Trade*, 70 Mich. L. Rev. 831 (1972). A book-length treatment of the problem of defining a "subsidy" is Luca Rubini, *The Definition of Subsidy and State Aid: WTO and EC Law in Comparative Perspective* (2009).
21. See Bagwell & Staiger, *supra* note 8.
22. See Alan O. Sykes, *The Questionable Case for Subsidies Regulation: A Comparative Perspective*, 2 J. Leg. Analysis 473 (2010).
23. See Alan O. Sykes, *Countervailing Duty Law: An Economic Perspective*, 89 Colum. L. Rev. 199 (1989).
24. The history of antidumping law, and its putative but shaky antitrust justification, is discussed in Alan O. Sykes, *Antidumping and Antitrust: What Problems Does Each Address?*, in *Brookings Trade Forum* 1 (Robert Z. Lawrence, ed., 1998).
25. See generally John J. Barcelo, *The Antidumping Law: Repeal It or Revise It*, 1979 Mich. Y.B. Int'l Leg. Stud. 53 (1979); Richard Boltuck & Robert E. Litan, *America's "Unfair" Trade Laws*, in *Down in the Dumps* (Richard Boltuck & Robert E. Litan eds., 1991).
26. See generally *GATS 2000* (Pierre Sauve & Robert Stern eds., 2000); Aaditya Mattoo & Pierre Sauve, *Domestic Regulation and Services Trade Liberalization* (2003); Bernard H. Hoekman, *Liberalizing Trade in Services: A Survey* (2006).
27. See Alan Deardorff, *Welfare Effects of Global Patent Protection*, 59 Economica 35 (1992); Alan Deardorff, *Should Patent Protection Be Extended to All Developing Countries?*, 13 World Econ. 497 (1990).
28. See also Suzanne Scotchmer, *The Political Economy of Intellectual Property Treaties*, 20 J.L. Econ. & Org. 415 (2004).
29. See Robert E. Hudec, *Enforcing International Trade Law: The Evolution of the Modern GATT Legal System* (1993); John H. Jackson, *Restructuring the GATT System* (1990); Alan O. Sykes, *Constructive Unilateral Threats in International Commercial Relations: The Limited Case for Section 301*, 23 L. & Pol'y in Int'l. Bus. 263 (1992).
30. Bagwell & Staiger, *supra* note 8.
31. See Giovanni Maggi & Robert W. Staiger, *The Role of Dispute Settlement Procedures in International Trade Agreements*, 126 Q. J. Econ. 475 (2011).
32. See Alan O. Sykes, *Public versus Private Enforcement of International Economic Law: Standing and Remedy*, 34 J. Leg. Stud. 631 (2005), contrasting the absence of private rights of action under trade agreements with the availability of such actions under investment agreements.
33. Warren F. Schwartz & Alan O. Sykes, *The Economic Structure of Renegotiation and Dispute Settlement in the World Trade Organization*, 31 J. Leg. Stud. S179 (2002). The hypothesis that the "substantial equivalence" standard for retaliation serves to facilitate efficient breach has been criticized by a number of commentators. See various essays contained in *The Law, Economics and Politics of Retaliation in WTO Dispute Settlement* (Chad Bown & Joost Pauwelyn eds., 2010); Simon Schropp, *Trade Policy Flexibility and Enforcement in the WTO* (2009); Robert Z. Lawrence, *Crimes and Punishments: Retaliation under the WTO* (2003). The various arguments are summarized and critiqued in

Alan O. Sykes, *The WTO Dispute Resolution Mechanism: Ensuring Compliance?*, in *The Oxford Handbook on the World Trade Organization* (Martin J. Daunton, Amrita Narlikar, & Robert M. Stern eds., forthcoming).

19. International Investment, Antitrust, and Monetary Law

1. For a much more detailed history of international investment law, see Jeswald W. Salacuse, *The Law of Investment Treaties* (2010).
2. See UNCTAD, *Latest Developments in Investor-State Dispute Settlement*, IIA Issues Note No. 1 (2010), http://www.unctad.org/en/docs/webdiaeia20103_en.pdf.
3. This is the essential argument in Andrew T. Guzman, *Why LDCS Sign Treaties That Hurt Them: Explaining the Popularity of Bilateral Investment Treaties*, 38 Va. J. Int'l L. 639 (1998).
4. This argument may be found in Ryan J. Bubb & Susan Rose-Ackerman, *BITs and Bargains: Strategic Aspects of Bilateral and Multilateral Regulation of Foreign Investment*, 27 Int'l Rev. L. & Econ. 291 (2007).
5. For a recent compendium of a number of the better-known studies, see *The Effect of Treaties on Foreign Direct Investment: Bilateral Investment Treaties, Double Taxation Treaties, and Investment Flows* (Karl P. Sauvant & Lisa E. Sachs eds., 2009). See also Tod Allee & Clint Peinhardt, *Contingent Credibility: The Impact of Investment Treaty Violations on Foreign Direct Investment*, 65 Int'l Org. 401 (2011).
6. For a more extensive discussion of why private rights of action are available under investment treaties but not trade treaties, see Alan O. Sykes, *Public vs. Private Enforcement of International Economic Law: Standing and Remedy*, 34 J. Leg. Stud. 631 (2005).
7. See Salacuse, *supra* note 1.
8. Metalclad Corp. v. United Mexican States, 40 I.L.M. 36 (2001).
9. See Vicki Been & Joel Beauvais, *The Global Fifth Amendment: NAFTA's Investment Protections and the Misguided Quest for an International Regulatory Takings Doctrine*, 78 N.Y.U. L. Rev. 30 (2003).
10. For a sampling, see Frederic M. Scherer, *Competition Policies for an Integrated World Economy* (1994); *Competition Laws in Conflict: Antitrust Jurisdiction in the Global Economy* (Richard A. Epstein & Michael S. Greve eds., 2004); Andrew Guzman, *Antitrust and International Regulatory Federalism*, 76 N.Y.U. L. Rev. 1142 (2001); Andrew Guzman, *Is International Antitrust Possible?*, 73 N.Y.U. L. Rev. 1501 (1998); Eleanor Fox, *Competition Law and the Millennium Round*, 2 J. Int'l Econ. L. 665 (1999); Diane P. Wood, *Antitrust at the Global Level*, 72 Un. Chi. L. Rev. 309 (2005).
11. We thank Ronald MacKinnon for useful conversations on this subject.
12. We are keeping the terminology as simple as possible. Some accounting descriptions distinguish "capital" and "financial" transactions from current account transactions, while others break capital transactions into private and government. We lump all non-current account transactions into what we term the *capital account*.
13. For a more detailed discussion of national income accounting on these points, see Paul R. Krugman, Maurice Obstfeld, & Marc J. Melitz, *International Economics* ch. 13 (9th ed. 2012).
14. See Richard N. Cooper, *"The Gold Standard,"* in *The International Monetary System: Essays in World Economics* (1987).

15. See, e.g., Barry Eichengreen, *Golden Fetters: The Gold Standard and the Great Depression, 1919–1939* (1992).
16. For a much more detailed history of the IMF, see Kenneth W. Dam, *The Rules of the Game: Reform and Evolution in the International Monetary System* (1981).
17. See *id.* at 88–93.
18. See, e.g., Ronald McKinnon, *Why China Should Keep Its Exchange Rate Pegged to the Dollar: A Historical Perspective from Japan,* 10 Int'l Fin. 43 (2007).
19. Milton Friedman, *Markets to the Rescue,* Wall St. J., Oct. 13, 1998.
20. See the collection of commentaries in *The International Monetary Fund: Financial Medic to the World?* (Lawrence J. McQuillan & Peter C. Montgomery eds., 1999).
21. *Id.*
22. *Id.*
23. This section draws on Robert W. Staiger & Alan O. Sykes, *"Currency Manipulation" and World Trade,* 9 World Trade Rev. 583 (2010).
24. See Ronald McKinnon, *China's Exchange Rate and Fiscal Expansion,* Stan. Inst. Econ. Pol'y Research, March 2009, http://siepr.stanford.edu/publicationsprofile/1901; Ronald McKinnon, *Why Exchange Rate Changes Will Not Correct Global Trade Imbalances,* Stan. Inst. Econ. Pol'y Research, June 2010, http://www.stanford.edu/~mckinnon/ . . . /Policy%20Brief%2006_2010%20v21.pdf.
25. For a detailed legal analysis, see Claus D. Zimmerman, *Exchange Rate Misalignment and International Law,* 105 Am. J. Int'l L. 423 (2011).
26. This observation offers a reason why some policymakers suggest that the WTO should address the matter, a possibility that is considered at length in Staiger & Sykes, *supra* note 23.
27. See Robert Mundell, *A Theory of Optimal Currency Areas,* 51 Am. Econ. Rev. 657 (1961).
28. A modern and accessible treatment is provided in Krugman, Obstfeld, & Melitz, *supra* note 13, ch. ?, which argues that Europe is not an optimal currency area.

Acknowledgments

We thank Jack Goldsmith and an anonymous referee for their comments on an earlier version of this book. Dawood Ahmed, Ellie Norton, and Greg Pesce provided helpful research assistance. Eric Posner thanks the Microsoft Fund and the Russell Baker Scholars Fund at the University of Chicago Law School for financial assistance.

Some of the themes/ideas in this book were developed/discussed in the following works: Eric A. Posner & Alan O. Sykes, *Optimal War and Jus ad Bellum,* 93 Georgetown L.J. 993 (2005); Posner & Sykes, *An Economic Analysis of State and Individual Responsibility under International Law,* 9 Amer. L. & Econ. Rev. 72 (2007); Posner & Sykes, *Economic Foundations of the Law of the Sea,* 104 Amer. J. Inter'l L. 569 (2010); Posner & Sykes, *Efficient Breach of International Law: Optimal Remedies, "Legalized Noncompliance," and Related Issues,* 110 Mich. L. Rev. 243 (2011); Posner, *Terrorism and the Laws of War,* 5 Chi. J. Int'l L. 423 (2005); Sykes, *International Law,* in 1 *Handbook of Law and Economics* (A. Mitchell Polinsky & Steven Shavell eds., 2007).

Index

Abu Ghraib prison abuses, 107
Abuse of dominance jurisprudence, antitrust laws and, 301–302
Act of God provisions, in international trade agreements, 272–273
Adjudication, by international institutions, 96–97
Afghanistan, recognition of sovereignty in, 45–47
Agency costs: delegation to international institutions and, 83–85; principal as agent, 117–119; state responsibility and, 116–117; vicarious liability and, 113–115
Aggression: crime of aggression, recognition of, 216–217; imminence requirement and targets of, 179–180; preemptive war and self-defense against, 177–189; "serious breaches" remedies and, 137–138
Agreement on Technical Barriers to Trade, 275
Agreement on the Application of Sanitary and Phytosanitary Measures, 275, 287
Agreement on Trade Related Aspects of Intellectual Property Rights, 266–267
Air Service Agreement arbitration, 135–136
Akayesu, Jean-Paul, 217
Al-Bashir, Omar, 107–108
Aliens: international law protecting, 155–158; investment law and rights of, 290–292. *See also* Immigration law
Alien Tort Statute (U.S.): corporate liability and, 338n10; international forum shopping and, 144–146; investor-state dispute settlement and, 294–296; state responsibility and, 124, 212
Al Qaida: U.S. torture of members of, 107; war on terror and, 196–197
Altruism, humanitarian intervention and, 188–189
Ambassadorial immunity, customary international law and, 50–53
Amnesty International, 108
Antidumping policy, international trade and, 277–278

Antimonopoly agreements: core bargains in, 21–24; deep seabed mining and, 252–257
Antitrust law: antidumping policies and, 278; extraterritorial jurisdiction and, 149–152; international laws, 297–302
Arbitration: antitrust laws and, 302; international institutions for, 96–101, 334n10; Law of the Sea Tribunal and, 109; limits of, 100–101; reduction of war and, 171; restitution and reparations and, 135–136. *See also* Dispute resolution
Archipelagos, law of the sea concerning, 246–248
Arctic Ocean, melting of, 250–251
Asian debt crisis, 321
Asian values debates, human rights and, 206–207
Asylum seeking, extraterritorial jurisdiction and, 147
Austro-Hungarian Empire, 163
Authoritarian regimes: human rights treaties and, 73, 202–206; sovereign debt and, 159–162; sovereignty principle and, 177; state responsibility in, 119

Bagwell, Kyle, 284, 349n8
Balance of payments: exchange rate policies and, 303–306; par value and, 311–313
Bankruptcy process, bailouts and, 321
Bargaining: core of, international agreements and, 21–24; incomplete contracts and, 25–26
Baring, Alexander, 173
Baseline definition, law of the sea and, 245–248
Bays, law of the sea concerning, 246–248, 346n24
Beef hormones, European prohibition of: dispute resolution system and, 286–287; domestic constraints on trade agreements and, 273–275
Belgium, EU membership and, 92–94
Belligerent acts, nineteenth-century warfare and, 172–174

357

Bilateral agreements: antitrust law and, 299–302; customary international law and, 59–60; externalities and, 23–24; international trade and, 268–271; reservations concerning, 73–74; soft law and, 76–77; treaties as, 63

Bilateral investment treaties (BITs): developing countries and, 292–294; investment law and, 291–292

Blockades, nineteenth-century warfare and, 172

Bond posting, contract enforcement and, 33–34

Border disputes, arbitration proceedings for, 98

Bretton Woods system, international monetary law and, 310–313

Bribery: international contracts and, 32; odious debt doctrine and, 160–162

Budget constraints, economic theory and, 12–15

Bush, George H. W., 89–90

Bush, George W., 69, 184–186

Calvo Doctrine, investment law and, 290–292

Cambodia, tribunal for, 96

Canada: antidumping policies in, 277–278; nineteenth-century warfare and, 172–173; Northwest Passage dispute and, 247–248; Trail Smelter case in, 227–229

Capital account transactions: currency convertibility and, 307–308; currency manipulation and, 321–324; current account transactions as, 352n12; exchange rates and balance of payments and, 304–306

Capital costs, investment law and, 288–297

Cartel practices, antitrust laws and, 297–302

Central African Republic, 107

Chile, sovereign debt and, 161–162

China: climate treaties and, 231–232; currency convertibility in, 307–308, 314; currency manipulation in, 321–324; developmental rights championed by, 207; sovereign debt and, 161–162; Sudan and, 108; United Nations membership and, 86–90

Chlorofluorocarbon use, environmental international law and, 229–230

"Choice of law" principles, international forum shopping and, 144–146

Civil penalties, state responsibility vs. individuals and, 209–212

Civil War (U.S.), 85

Climate treaties: environmental international law and, 230–232; multilateral agreements for, 65–67; sovereignty issues and, 46–47

Clinton, William, 69

Coase, Ronald, 21

Coastal states' jurisdiction, law of the sea and, 244–248, 346n7

"Cod war," exclusive economic zones and, 249

Cold war era: human rights in, 199–202; United Nations and, 86–90

Collective action problems: economic theory and, 14; environmental international law and, 229–230; human rights treaties and, 203–206; universal treaties and, 66–67

Collective self-defense principle, 187–188

Colonialism: customary international law and, 59–60; investment law and history of, 290–292; succession issues and collapse of, 47–49; theory of statehood and, 15

Comity: antitrust law and, 299–302; customary international law and role of, 56–57, 333n7 (chap. 5); extraterritorial jurisdiction and, 150–152

Command responsibility doctrine, international criminal law and, 217–218

Commission on Human Rights, 110–111

Commission on the Limits of the Continental Shelf, 249–250

Committee Against Torture, 111

Committee on Economic, Social and Cultural Rights, 111

Committee on the Elimination of Discrimination Against Women, 111

Committee on the Elimination of Racial Discrimination, 111

Committee on the Rights of the Child, 111

Common heritage principle, deep seabed mining and, 251–257

Common pool problems: environmental law and, 226; law of the sea and, 234–241

Communism, human rights and, 199–202

Compensation requirements, investment law and, 296–297

Competing claims, law of the sea and, 237–239

Compliance in international law: inefficiencies in, 127–129; retaliatory noncompliance, 127–128

Conditionality authority of IMF, economic bailouts and, 318–319

Conscious parallelism, antitrust laws and, 301–302

Consensus rule: antitrust laws and, 299–302; dispute resolution and, 281–287

Consent doctrine: customary international law and role of, 56–57, 61–62; treaties and, 67–68

Constitution. *See* United States Constitution

Constitutive theory, recognition of statehood and, 42–49

Consumer surplus: defined, 348n2; free trade *vs.* protectionism, 263–266
Contiguous zone, law of the sea and, 244–248
Continental shelf: customary international law and sovereignty of, 60–62; law of the sea and, 239, 248–250
Contract law: bribery and, 32; economic theory and, 13–15; efficient breach in, 25–26, 128–129; enforcement and dispute resolution, 26–36; incomplete contracts, 24–25; international law as, 24–26; remedies and, 127–129; renegotiation and modification principles, 25–26; reputation and, 32–33; retaliatory noncompliance in, 127–128; sanctions and, 30–32; treaties compared with, 67
Control tests, vicarious liability and, 115
Convention on Long-Range Transboundary Air Pollution, 229
Convention on the Elimination of All Forms of Discrimination against Women, 111
Convention on the Elimination of All Forms of Racial Discrimination, 111
Convention on the Prevention and Punishment of the Crime of Genocide, 74–75
Convention on the Prohibition of Military or Any Other Hostile Use of Environmental Modification Techniques, 70–71
Convention on the Rights of the Child, 111
Coordination game, dispute resolution and, 34–35
Copyright protection, trade-related aspects of, 280–281
Corporations: extraterritorial jurisdiction and, 150–152; international forum shopping by, 144–146; liability of, 113–117, 210–212, 338n10; rational choice and behavior of, 14–15
Corruption, odious debt doctrine and, 160–162
Council of Ministers (EU), 93
Council of the Seabed Authority, 254–257
Countermeasures, ILC guidelines concerning, 132–134
Court enforcement of international law: domestic law and, 140–142; overview of, 9–10, 96–97, 101–103; reduction of war and, 171; regional human rights courts, 109–110; weakness of, 79. *See also* Judicial opinions; specific courts, e.g., International Court of Justice
Covention Against Torture, 111
Crimean War, 172

Crime of aggression, recognition of, 216–217
Crimes against humanity, recognition of, 216–217
Croatia, international recognition of, 42
Cross-border pollution: externalities of, 19–20, 225–226; state responsibilities concerning, 226–227
Cross-border transactions, exchange rate policies and balance of payments and, 303–306
Cross-licensing agreements, antitrust law and, 298–302
Currency convertibility: floating currencies and, 313–314; gold standard and, 309–310; manipulation of, 321–324; monetary law and, 302–303, 306–308. *See also* Exchange rate policies
Customary international law: alien protection and, 156–158; ambassadorial immunity and, 50–52; basic principles of, 50–54; bilateralism *vs.* multilateralism in, 59–60; enforcement and changes in, 60–62; environmental law and, 227–229; human rights treaties and, 158; international disagreements about, 80; investment law and, 290–292; *jus cogens* and, 57–59; origins of, 8–10; state practice and consent and, 54–57; treaties and, 64–67; United States domestic law and, 143–144
Customs unions, trade discrimination and, 271, 350n14

Death penalty, international debate concerning, 220–221
Declaration of the Rights of Man (France), 199
Declarations concerning treaties, 71–72
Declarative theory, recognition of statehood and, 41–49
Deep seabed mining: law of the sea and, 251–257; technological advancements in, 60–62. *See also* Seabed resources
Defamation of religion, human rights and, 206–207
Default terms, economic theory and, 13
Delegation to international institutions: domestic benefits and costs of, 82–83; international benefits and costs of, 84–85
Democracies, state responsibility in, 117–118
Democratic Republic of Congo, 107
"Demonstration effect" of human rights, 208
Detection of breaches of law, difficulty of, 131

Index

Deterrence: imminence requirement and, 179–180; state responsibility *vs.* individual liability and, 210–212; use of force against rogue states *vs.,* 178–179

Devaluation of currency, exchange rate policies and, 315–318

Developing countries: climate treaties and, 231–232; deep seabed mining and, 252–257, 348n51; human rights treaties and, 202–207; intellectual property protection, trade-related issues for, 280–281; investment treaties and, 292–294; protection of aliens and, 157–158; WTO dispute resolution system and, 287

Discrimination: domestic nondiscrimination legislation, trade constraints from, 274–275; in services trade agreements, 278–280; in trade agreements, 269–271; trade in services and, 279–280

Dispute resolution: arbitration proceedings, 96–101; in contracts, 26–36; coordination game and, 34–35; information revelation and, 34–35; International Court of Justice and, 101–102; international trade and, 281–287; investor-state disputes, logic of, 294–295; WTO system for, 10–11, 66, 108–109, 281–287. *See also* Arbitration

Doha Round negotiations, antitrust law and, 299

Domestic law: antitrust law and, 298–302; arbitration proceedings and, 96–98, 100–101; commitment to international trade agreements, 20, 349n8, 350n19; constraints on international trade agreements in, 273–275; contract law, 127–129; corporate liability in, 113–115; customary international law and, 143–144; delegation to international institutions and, 82–83; extraterritorial jurisdiction and, 146–152; international forum shopping and, 144–146; international law and, 7–10, 20, 139–152; investment law and, 289–297; law of the sea and, 235–237; in monist and dualist states, 140–142; piracy and, 212–214; recognition of government institutions and, 44–47; remedies in, 126, 137–138; trade agreements and, 20, 273–275, 349n8, 350n19; trade subsidies and, 276–277; treaties and judicial enforcement and, 142–143; use of force authorization, 178–179

Dual criminality, political crimes and, 220–221

Dualist states, domestic and international law intersection in, 140–142

Dumping practices, international trade agreements and, 277–278

Economic welfare, defined, 330n6

"Effects test," extraterritorial jurisdiction, 149

Efficient breach: dispute resolution in international trade and, 287, 351n33; of incomplete contracts, 25–26; international law and, 128–129; nomenclature concerning, 336n4 (chap. 9); remedies, effect on, 127–132

El Salvador, U.S. defense of, 124–125, 187–188

Enforcement of international law, 26–36; antitrust laws, 300–302; bribery, 32; dispute resolution as information revelation, 34–35; extraterritorial jurisdiction, 149–152; hostage exchange and bond posting, 33–34; human rights treaties and, 204–206; investment law disputes, enforceability of awards, 295; multilateral trade agreements as tool for, 270–271; mutual threats of defection, 27–30; reputation and, 32–33; sanctions (unilateral/multilateral), 30–32. *See also* Use of force

Environmental international law: application to states, 226–227; climate treaties and, 230–232; externalities in, 225–226; Montreal Protocol and, 229–230; multilateral treaties, 65–67; mutual defection strategies and, 27–31; overview of, 10, 225–232; *sic utere tuo ut alienum non laedas* norm in, 227–229; treaties concerning, 70–71

Environmental Protection Agency (EPA), delegation to international institutions by, 82–84

Equal treatment principle, protection of aliens and, 157–158

Equidistance rule, law of the sea and, 250–251

Ethnic cleansing: in Rwanda, 105; in Yugoslavia, 104–106. *See also* Genocide

European Central Bank, Eurozone debt crisis and, 325–327

European Coal and Steel Community (ECSC), 92

European Commission, 93–94

European Council, 93

European Court of Human Rights (ECtHR), 109–110

European Court of Justice (ECJ), 81, 93–94

European Economic Community (EEC), 92

European Parliament, 93

European Union (EU): benefits and limitations of, 93–94; executive power delegation by, 82, 84; human rights treaties and, 203–206; international law and role of, 94–96; judicial delegation by, 81; monetary integration and Eurozone debt crisis and, 324–327;

organization and function of, 92–96; regional powers of, 87; trade agreements and, 350n14; treaties of, 80–81; United States transactions with, 303–306
Eurozone debt crisis: emergence of, 94; European monetary integration and, 324–327
Exchange rate policies: balance of payments and, 303–306; cooperative behavior concerning, 315–318; currency convertibility and, 306–308; gold standard and, 308–310; history of, 308; history of international cooperation concerning, 314–318; monetary law and, 303; risk assessment and avoidance, 309–310, 315–318. *See also* Currency convertibility; Fixed exchange rates; Foreign exchange
Exclusive economic zones (EEZs): continental shelf and, 248–250; deep seabed mining and, 251–257; division and equidistance rule and, 250–251; fisheries and, 257–258; high seas and, 241–244
Expectation damages rule, dispute resolution and, 286–287
Export cartels, antitrust law and, 297–302
Export policies: currency convertibility and, 306–308; currency devaluation and, 315–318; exchange rates and balance of payments and, 303–306
Export subsidies: antidumping policies and, 277–278; imperfect competition and, 348n5; WTO and, 275–277
Expropriation of foreign assets, sovereign debt and, 159–162
Externalities: cooperative behavior and, 21–24; in environmental international law, 225–226; European monetary integration and Eurozone debt crisis, 324–327; extraterritorial jurisdiction and, 148–152; free trade *vs.* protectionism and, 265–266; internalization of, in trade agreements, 274–275; international agreements and, 17–20, 23–24; in investment law, 289–297; law of the sea and, 234–241; monetary cooperation and, 315–318; negative and positive, 13–14; in trade agreements, 263–265, 268–271, 273–275; WTO dispute resolution system and, 285–287
Extradition treaties: bilateralism in, 63; cooperative behavior in, 64–67; extraterritorial jurisdiction and, 148–152; international criminal law and, 218–222; political crimes and, 219–220; reciprocity and, 219; reservations concerning, 74; specialty rule and, 221; U. S. enforcement of, 143
Extraterritorial jurisdiction: antitrust laws, 300–302; intersection of domestic and international law and, 146–152, 338n10

Failed states: international institutions and, 80; international law and role of, 7; state responsibility *vs.* individual liability in, 211–212. *See also* Rogue states
Fair and equitable treatment principle, investment law and, 296–297
"Fair value" principles, antidumping policies and, 277–278
Federal Reserve system, IMF and, 320–321
Fishing industry: environmental international law and, 226–227; high seas rules and, 243–244; law of the sea and, 234–241, 257–258; treaties concerning, 64–67
Fixed exchange rates: Bretton Woods and IMF and, 310–313; gold standard and, 308–310; international cooperation concerning, 316–318
Flag rules on high seas, sovereignty issues and, 243–244
Floating currencies: externalities concerning, 316–318; international cooperation concerning, 314–318; monetary law and, 313–314
Force majeure principle, in international trade agreements, 272–273
Foreign corporations: extraterritorial jurisdiction and, 150–152; international forum shopping by, 144–146
Foreign debt, international law concerning, 159–162
Foreign exchange: currency manipulation in, 321–324; European monetary integration and Eurozone debt crisis, 324–327; exchange rate policies and balance of payments and, 303–306. *See also* Currency convertibility; Exchange rate policies
Foreign investment, international law concerning, 288–297
Foreign property, protection of: ambassadorial immunity and, 50; protection of aliens and, 155–158
Forum non conveniens doctrine, international forum shopping and, 145–146
France: Air Service Agreement arbitration and, 135–136; Declaration of the Rights of Man in, 199; EU membership and, 92–94; Kellogg-

France (*continued*)
Briand Pact and, 173–174; monist state structure in, 140–141; nineteenth-century warfare by, 172

Freedom of the seas principle: customary international law and, 50; extraterritorial jurisdiction and, 147; high seas and, 241–244; piracy and, 212–214; sovereignty over continental shelf and, 60–62; state practice and consent and, 54–57; in treaties, 64–67

Free on board pricing, antidumping policies and, 277–278

Free rider problems: bribery and, 32; international agreements, 23–24; law of the sea and, 235–241; multilateral treaties, 64–67; piracy and, 213–214; "serious breaches" remedies and, 138

Free trade: currency convertibility and, 306–308; political economy of protectionism *vs.*, 263–266; tariff violations and, 350n14

Friedman, Milton, 318

Friendship, commerce, and navigation (FCN) treaties, investment law and, 291–292

Gaddafi, Moammar, 108

Game theory: coordination game, 34–35; motivations for war and, 169–171; mutual defection and, 27–31; reputation and, 32–33; two-period scenario for preemptive attack and, 181–182

General Agreement on Tariffs and Trade (GATT), 95–96, 108–109; antidumping policies in, 277–278; dispute resolution and, 281–287; domestic law and, 273–275; escape clause in, 271–273; legal architecture of, 266–267; most favored nation obligation, 269–271; renegotiation provisions for, 271–273; services trading and, 278–280; "tariffication" policies and, 267–268; WTO as successor to, 263

General Agreement on Trade in Services (GATS), 266–267, 278–280

General Assembly (United Nations): human rights treaties and, 201–202; international law and, 10–11; investment law resolutions and, 291–292; origins of, 86; resolutions issued by, 81; soft law and treaties of, 76–78; structure and function of, 91–92

Geneva Convention, 190, 195, 215; revisions to, 344n5 (chap. 15)

Genocide: command responsibility doctrine and, 217–218; as international crime, 215–217; as natural law violation, 59; "serious breaches" remedies and, 137–138. *See also* Ethnic cleansing

Genocide Convention, 202, 207, 215

Geographic barriers, theory of statehood and, 17

Germany: EU membership and, 92–94; investment law and, 291–292; laws of war and, 192–194; nineteenth-century warfare in states of, 172; postwar monetary policies and, 310–313; recognition of Croatia by, 42; Security Council reforms and, 90

Global calculus for preemptive war, 184

Globalization: economics and international law, recent trends in, 4–5; and intellectual property protection, trade-related issues, 280–281; intellectual property rights and, 280–281; legal architecture of world trade and, 266–267

Global warming, climate treaties and, 230–232

Gold standard: Bretton Woods system and, 310–313; exchange rate policies and, 308–310

Great Britain: currency devaluation in, 312–313; dualist state structure in, 140–141; laws of war and, 192–194; nineteenth-century warfare by, 172–173

Greece, Eurozone debt crisis and, 325–327

Grossman, Gene, 265

Grotius, Hugo, 191

Hague Convention, 190

Hague Peace Conference, 173

Hegemon concept: international agreements and, 24; preemptive self-defense and, 186

Helpman, Elhanan, 265

Helsinki Protocol, 229

High seas rules: fisheries and, 257–258; law of the sea and, 239, 241–244

Holmes, Oliver Wendell, 9–10

Hostage exchange, contract enforcement and, 33–34

Hull, Cordell (Hull formula), 291–293

Humanitarian intervention: conduct of war and, 191–197; in international law, 10; justified war principles and, 176–177; preemptive war and, 177–189; warfare and, 171. *See also* Use of force; War

Human rights, in international law: alien protection and, 156–158; background theories of, 199; challenges to enforcement of, 206–207; countermeasures and, 133–134; empirical effects of treaties, 207–208; evolution of, 200; international committees,

commissions, and quasi-tribunals and, 82; international courts for, 96; international forum shopping and, 144–146; negative and positive rights, 200–202; overview of, 10, 198–208; protection of aliens treaties and, 158; regional human rights courts, 109–110; sovereignty and, 198; treaties concerning, 63, 66–67, 72–73, 202–206
Human Rights Committee, 111
Human Rights Council, 110–111
Hussein, Saddam, 89–90, 184–186

Immigration law: alien protection and, 155–158; extradition treaties and, 64–67; extraterritorial jurisdiction and, 147; law of the sea and, 240–241; trade in services and, 279–280. *See also* Aliens
Imminence requirement for self-defense, 179–181, 185–186, 340n15
Immunity principles: ambassadorial immunity, 50–53; countermeasures restrictions and, 133–134; state officials and, 122–125
Imperialism: impact of World War I on, 163; origins of United Nations and ideology of, 87; succession issues and collapse of, 47–49
Import policies: antidumping policies and, 277–278; currency convertibility and, 306–308; currency devaluations and, 315–318; exchange rate policies and balance of payments and, 303–306; investment treaties in developing countries and, 292–294; subsidies and, 276–277; in WTO/GATT system, 267–268
Incarceration, economics of, 209–212
Income distribution, economic theory and, 13
Incomplete contracts, international law as, 24–25
Indirect expropriation principle, investment law and, 296–297
Inflation: Bretton Woods system and, 311–313; gold standard and, 309–310
Injury test, antidumping policies and, 277–278
Inland waters: fisheries and, 257–258; law of the sea and, 244–248
Innocent passage, right of, law of the sea and, 245–248
Insurgencies, state responsibility in acts of, 125
Intellectual property: antitrust law and, 298–302; trade-related aspects of, 280–281; world trade agreements and, 266–267
Interest groups: government scale of activity and, 120; human rights treaties, 203–206; preemptive war and, 183–184, 340n13

Interest rates, international monetary policies and, 317–318
Intergovernmentalism, European Union as example of, 93
"Internal economy" of ships, sovereignty concerning, 246–248
International agreements: coordination game and, 34–35; economics and, 21–24; enforcement and dispute resolution in, 26–36; hostage exchange and bond posting, 33–34; international law and, 8–10; mutual threats of defection in, 27–31; reputation and, 32–33
International Centre for Settlement of Investment Disputes (ICSID), 292, 295
International Court of Justice (ICJ): collective self-defense considered by, 187–188; customary international law and, 59–60; equidistance rule cases and, 251; functions of, 80; General Assembly role in, 91–92; international law and, 10–11; jurisdiction of, 81–82; Law of the Sea Tribunal and, 109; limitations of, 102–103; performance shortcomings of, 102; structure and function of, 96–97, 101–102; treaty disputes and, 75
International Covenant for Economic, Social and Cultural Rights, 111, 201–202
International Covenant on Civil and Political Rights (ICCPR), 72–73, 111, 201–202, 206
International Criminal Court (ICC): aggression defined by, 216; extradition treaties and, 218; indictments against Uganda by, 214; international law and, 10–11; Rome Statute and creation of, 69; structure and function, 96–97, 106–108; treaty provisions of, 72
International Criminal Tribunal for Rwanda, 96, 105–106
International Criminal Tribunal for the Former Yugoslavia (ICTY), 96, 103–106
International delegation, functions of, 80–82
International institutions: adjudication proceedings, 96; antitrust law and, 298–302; arbitration proceedings, 96–101; committees, commissions, and quasi-tribunals, 82, 110–112; criminal tribunals, 103–108; deficiencies of, 79–80; delegation of issues to, benefits and costs of, 81–82, 84–85; delegations, 80–82; domestic benefits and costs of delegation, 82–83; international law and, 9–11, 79–112; predecessors to the United Nations, 85–86; soft law and, 76; sovereignty issues and, 40; survey of, 86–96, 101–103,

International institutions (*contined*) 108–109; tribunals, 109–110. *See also* specific international institutions, e.g., United Nations

International Labor Organization, 79, 81, 110

International law: domestic law intersection with, 7–10, 20, 139–152; economic analysis of, 12–36; fundamentals of, 6–11; preemptive self-defense in, 184–186; recent research on, 3–5. *See also* Customary international law; Environmental international law

International Law Commission (ILC): environmental law and, 228–229; general remedial principles of, 132–138; remedies draft rules of, 126; state responsibility provisions, 121–125

International Maritime Organization, 346n9

International Monetary Fund (IMF), 79, 81; Bretton Woods and fixed exchange rates and, 310–313; conditionality authority, par value and, 311–313; currency convertibility rules of, 306–308; currency manipulation and, 321–324; current policies and systems of, 313–314; mission of, 318–321; monetary law and Articles of, 302–324

International Tribunal for the Law of the Sea (ITLOS), 71–72, 96–97, 109, 135–136

International tribunals: establishment of, 96; survey of, 102–112

Internet law, extraterritorial jurisdiction and, 147

Interstate wars, chronology of, 163–168

Investment law: developing countries and, 292–294; history of, 290–292; international aspects of, 288–297; investor-state dispute settlement, logic of, 294–295; remedies in, 126; substantive law controversies, 295–297

Iran, Tehran Hostages case in, 124–125

Iraq: invasion of Kuwait by, 40, 88–90, 175, 187–188; U.S. abuse of prisoners in, 194–195; U.S.-led invasion of, 175, 183–186, 340n14

Ireland, EU membership and, 92–94

Islamic values, human rights and, 206–207

Israel, human rights abuses in, 111

Issue linkage, international agreements and, 22–24

Italy, EU membership and, 92–94

Japan, Security Council reforms and, 90

Judicial delegation, by international institutions, 81–82

Judicialization, arbitration and, 100–101

Judicial opinions: as source for international law, 8–10; U.S. enforcement of treaties and, 142–143. *See also* Court enforcement of international law

Jurisdiction: of continental shelf, 248–250; deep seabed mining and, 255–257; extraterritorial jurisdiction, 146–152; in high seas, 241–244; international forum shopping and, 145–146; intersection of domestic and international law and, 140–152; law of the sea and issues of, 235–237, 240–241; piracy and role of, 212–214

Jus ad bellum: authorization for, 179; warfare and, 171. *See also* Use of force

Jus cogens principle: customary international law and, 57–59; "serious breaches" remedies and, 137–138

Jus in bello principle, warfare and, 171

Just war theory, evolution of, 176–177

Kaldor-Hicks criterion, economic theory and, 13

Kellogg-Briand Pact, 173–174

Kontorovich, Eugene, 332n4 (chap. 5)

Korean War, 87–88, 175, 194

Kosovo, NATO air strikes in: as humanitarian intervention, 189, 342n3; UN Charter rules and, 175

Krugman, Paul, 320–321

Kurdish ethnic group, sovereignty recognition for, 45–47

Kuwait, Iraq invasion of, 40, 88–90, 175, 187–188

Kyoto Accords, 69, 231–232

Kyoto Clean Development Mechanism, 232

Land mines: conduct of war and outlawing of, 190–191. *See also* Sea mines

"Last-in-time" rule, intersection of domestic and international law and, 140–142

Latin America: debt crisis in, 321; sovereign debt in, 161–162

"Law in action," laws of war and, 342n8

Law of the sea: adjudication concerning, 96–97, 109; continental shelf and Exclusive Economic Zone, 248–250; deep seabed provisions, 251–257; distant resources and high seas issues in, 239–240; division and the equidistance rule, 250–251; economics of, 234–241, 345n3; fisheries, 257–258; government and international cooperation role in, 235–237; high seas provisions in, 241–244; importance of, 233–234; inland

waters, territorial seas, and contiguous zone, 244–248; overview of, 233–259; proximity issues and competing claims in, 237–239; resource distribution, 258–259. *See also* International Tribunal for the Law of the Sea
Law of treaties, treaty interpretation and, 67–69
Laws of war: combat tactics restrictions, 192; conduct of war and, 190–197; customary international law and, 50; "law in action" and, 342n8; self-defense and preemptive attacks in, 177–189; state practice and consent and, 54–57; symmetry and reciprocity in, 192–195; United Nations and, 85–92; war on terror and, 195–197. *See also* Use of force; War
League of Nations, 85–86, 173–174
Legal principles: alien protection and, 156–158; economic theory and, 13–15; general remedial principles, 132–138; international institutions and, 79–80; international law based on, 8–10; investment law and, 289–297; soft law and, 76–77; world trade and architecture of, 266–267. *See also* specific principles, e.g. *Jus cogens* principle
Lex loci delictus rule, international forum shopping and, 145–146
Libya: human rights abuses in, 111; invasion as humanitarian intervention, 189; recognition of sovereignty for, 46; Security Council resolution concerning, 108, 175
Luxembourg, EU membership and, 92–94

Maastricht Treaty, 324
Macroeconomic stabilization: currency convertibility and, 306–308; externalities and, 316–318; gold standard and, 309–310
Mallén, Francisco, 123–124
Managed float: currency convertibility in, 313–314; international cooperation concerning, 314–318
Mandatory jurisdiction: arbitration and, 100–101; International Court of Justice and, 101–102
Mercosur, antitrust law and, 299–302
Mergers of corporations, antitrust law and, 297–302
Metaclad case, as substantive investment law dispute, 295–297
Mexico: investment law and U.S. dispute of, 290–292; *Metaclad* case and, 295–297
Military force: command responsibility doctrine and, 217–218; as countermeasure, 133–134; enforcement and dispute resolution of international contracts and, 26–36; international agreements and, 23–24; law of the sea and, 235–241; motivations for war and, 168–171; war crimes and use of, 215–217. *See also* Use of force; War
Minimum standards principle: investment law and, 290–292; protection of aliens and, 156–158
Misalignment principle, currency manipulation and, 322–324
Monetary aid: exchange rate policies and balance of payments, 303–306; human rights treaties and, 202–206; IMF bailouts as, 318–321; international agreements and, 21–22
Monetary damages: private investors' claims for, 294–295; reparations as, 134–136
Monetary law: Bretton Woods, IMF, and fixed exchange rates and, 310–313; currency convertibility and, 306–308; currency manipulation and, 321–324; European monetary integration and Eurozone debt crisis, 324–327; exchange rates and balance of payments and, 303–306; gold standard and, 308–310; government management of exchange rates and, 308; history of international cooperation and, 314–318; international aspects of, 302–324
Monetary penalties: individual civil and criminal sanctions *vs.* state actions and, 209–212; state responsibility and, 117–118; vicarious liability and, 113–115
Monist states, intersection of domestic and international law in, 140–142
Monopolies: core bargains concerning agreements on, 21–24, 330n10; in deep seabed mining, 252–257. *See also* Antimonopoly agreements; Antitrust law
Montreal Protocol on Substances That Deplete the Ozone Layer, 72, 229–230
Most favored nation (MFN) obligation: dispute resolution and, 287; legal architecture of, 266; trade agreements and, 269–271
Multilateral agreements: customary international law and, 59–60; externalities and, 23–24; Extradition treaties, 74; international committees, commissions, and quasi-tribunals and, 82; law of the sea and, 237–241; for sanctions, 30–32; soft law and, 76–77; trade agreements as, 268–271; treaties as, 63, 65–67

Multinational corporations: antitrust law and, 297–302; extraterritorial jurisdiction, 150–152
M/V "Saiga" case, 135–136
Myanmar, human rights abuses in, 111–112

Nash equilibrium: dispute resolution and, 284–287; free trade *vs.* protectionism and, 265–266; intellectual property rights and, 281; international externalities and, 19–20; prisoner's dilemma game and, 29–31, 330n7; renegotiation of trade agreements and, 273
National income accounting, exchange rates and balance of payments and, 304–306
Nationalism, human rights and, 199
Nationality jurisdiction, 149
National treatment obligations, investment law and, 290–292
NATO air strikes in Kosovo: as humanitarian intervention, 189, 342n3; UN Charter rules and, 175
Natural law, *jus cogens* norms and, 59
Navigational issues, law of the sea and, 237–241
Negative rights, defined, 200–202
Neoclassical economics, free trade *vs.* protectionism and, 263–266
Netherlands: EU membership and, 92–94; objections to treaty reservations by, 75
Neutrality: arbitration proceedings and, 99–100; nineteenth-century warfare and, 172–173
New York Convention on the Enforcement of Foreign Arbitral Awards, 334n10
Nicaragua, U.S.-led insurgency in, 124–125, 187–188
Nonlegal agreements: treaties as, 63. *See also* Soft law
Nonpecuniary externalities, 17–18, 330n5; environmental law and, 226
Nonrivalrous consumption, public good and, 330n4
Non-self-executing treaties, 142–143
Nonviolation nullification or impairment principle, WTO subsidies and, 275–277
Norms: customary international law and, 53–54, 332n4 (chap. 5); *jus cogens* norms, 57–59; state practice and consent and, 54–57; technological advancements and formation of, 60–62; trade subsidies based on, 275–277; in treaties, 63–67, 70
North American Free Trade Agreement (NAFTA): antitrust law and, 299–302; cooperative behavior and, 63; court system, 96; investor protection and, 292; *Metaclad* case and, 295–297; private actors' rights not protected in, 294–295
North Atlantic Treaty Organization (NATO), legal immunity for members of, 105
Northwest Passage dispute, 247–248
Notification requirement, antitrust law and, 299–302
Nuremberg Tribunal, 96, 103, 216–218

Obama, Barack, 107
Occupation, law of, 194–195
Odious debt doctrine: recognition of government institutions and, 45–47; sovereign debt and, 159–162
Open access regime, law of the sea and, 237–239, 346n10
Opportunity costs, state responsibility and role of, 118
Optimal currency theory, 325–327
Organization for Economic Cooperation and Development (OECD), antitrust law and, 299–302
Ostrom, Elinor, 235
Ottoman Empire, 163
Overlapping jurisdiction: antitrust law and, 298–302; division and equidistance rule and, 250–251; high seas rules and, 243–244
Ozone layer, environmental international law and, 229–230

Paqueta Habana case, state practice and consent and, 54–57
Pareto criterion, economic theory and, 13, 330n7
Patent protection, trade-related aspects of, 280–281
Peace treaties, coercive and noncoercive, 68
Pecuniary externalities, 17–18, 330n5; international trade and, 349n7
People's Republic of China, sovereignty of, 42–47, 332n7
Performance costs, efficient breach in contracts and, 128–129
Permanent Court of International Justice (PCIJ), 101, 173–174, 292
Persistent objector exception, customary international law and, 56–57
Piracy: high seas rules and, 243–244; international law and, 212–214; law of the sea and, 235–241; state responsibility *vs.* individual liability for, 211–212
Poaching, law of the sea and, 240–241

Political crimes, extradition treaties and, 219–220
Pollution: as collective action problem, 14; cross-border pollution, 19–20, 225–226; in environmental international law, 225–226; government institutions and reduction of, 83; intersection of international and domestic law concerning, 147; mutual threats of defection concerning, 27–28; of oceans, 346n6; treaties concerning, 63, 65, 74
Positive externalities, economic theory and, 14
Positive rights, defined, 200–202
Positivism, state consent and, 59
Preemptive war: humanitarian intervention as grounds for, 188–189; in international law, 184–186; private calculus of states on gains of, 182; proportionality requirement for, 187; self-defense as grounds for, 177–189; social calculus concerning, 183–184; timing of attack and, 179–181; two-period scenario for, 181–182
Preferences: economic theory and, 12–15; of states, 18–20
Prescriptive jurisdiction, 148–149; antitrust law and, 297–302
Price fixing, antitrust laws and, 301–302
Prices: antidumping policies and, 277–278; economic theory and, 12–15; exchange rate policies and, 315–318; vicarious liability and, 114–115
Prisoner's dilemma: mutual threats of defection and, 28–31; reputation and, 33; retaliatory noncompliance and, 127–128
Prisoners of war (POWs): coercive interrogation of, 196–197; exchanges of, 342n12; laws of war and, 191–195; war crimes charges against, 215–217
Private actors and actions: antidumping policies and, 277–278; as arbitrators, 98; consumption by, sovereign debt and, 159–160; cooperative behavior and, 64; criminal international law and acts of, 222; domestic arbitration of international violations by, 121–125, 139; enforcement and dispute resolution involving, 26–36; as government officials, 44; investment law and protections for, 289–292; investor-state dispute settlement and, 294–295; law of the sea provisions concerning, 251–255; in monist vs. dualist states, 141–144; resource exploitation by, international environmental law concerning, 226, 234–237; state responsibility for acts by, 121–125; tort law and acts of, 123–124; WTO denial of standing for, 286–287
Private citizens, responsibilities of, 121–125
Producer surplus, 263–265, 348n2
Property rules: aliens and, 156–158; incomplete contracts and, 26, 331n14; investment law and, 289–297; law of the sea concerning, 239; sovereignty and foreign property ownership, 155; in trade agreements, 272–273, 350n15
Proportionality requirement for preemptive war, 187
Protectionism: investment law and, 289–297; political economy of, free trade vs., 263–266; regulatory protection, 350n19; WTO/GATT reduction of, 267–268. *See also* Free trade
Proximity issues, law of the sea and, 237–239, 259
Public good: defined, 330n4; economic theory and, 14; odious debt doctrine impact on, 160–162; theory of statehood and, 16–17

Ratification of treaties, procedures for, 68–69
Rational choice theory: economic theory and, 14–15; international law and, 4–5; war and, 168–171
"Reasonable period of time" principle, WTO dispute resolution system and, 282–287
Reciprocity: extradition treaties and, 219; extraterritorial jurisdiction and, 151–152; human rights treaties and, 73; laws of war and, 192–195; retaliatory noncompliance and, 128; treaty reservations concerning, 71–72; war on terror and, 197; WTO/GATT tariffication and, 267–268
Recognition of sovereignty: government institutions, 43–47; statehood and, 41–43
Regionalism, international trade and, 268–271
Regulatory takings, investment law and, 296–297
Religion, human rights and values of, 206–207
Religious terrorism, laws of war and, 342n11
Remedies in international law, 126–138; apportionment of liability, 136; compliance inefficiencies and, 127–129; countermeasures, 132–134; general legal principles, 132–138; international forum shopping and, 145–146; investment law violations, 294–295; legal sources on, 336n1; reparations and restitution, 134–136; retaliatory noncompliance and, 127–132; "serious breaches" obligations, 136–138

Renegotiation: of incomplete contracts, 25–26; international sanctions and, 31–32; of trade agreements, 271–273
Reparations, ILC provisions concerning, 134–136, 337n16
Reputation, international contracts and role of, 32–33
Reservations concerning treaties, 70–76; non-bilateral obligations and, 73–74; objections to, 74–75
Resource mobility, law of the sea and, 235–237, 239–241. 258–259, 348n21
Restitution, ILC provisions concerning, 134–136
Retaliatory noncompliance: breach of contract through, 127–128; impact on remedies of, 127–132
Right of Passage over Indian Territory (Portugal v. India), 59–60
"Right to transit passage," law of the sea and, 247–248
Rogue states: imminence requirement concerning, 179–180; use of force against, 178–179. *See also* Failed states
Rome Statute, 69, 107–108, 216
Roosevelt, Eleanor, 200
Roosevelt, Franklin Delano, 86–87
"Rule of law": reservations concerning treaties and, 70–77; treaties and principles of, 67
Russia: climate treaties and, 231–232; exclusive economic zone dispute and, 250–251; impact of World War I on, 163; nineteenth-century warfare by, 172; recognition of sovereignty for, 46. *See also* Soviet Union

Sachs, Jeffrey, 321
Saint Vincent, M/V "Saiga" case and, 135–136
Sanctions: consensus rule regarding, 282–287; dispute resolution and, 283–287; domestic commitment and impact of, 20; history of, 85–86; human rights treaties and, 204–206; impact on remedies of, 130–132; individual liability *vs.* state responsibility and, 209–212; international contracts and, 30–32; state responsibility and, 118–119, 209–212; use of force against rogue states *vs.*, 178–179
Scope of employment: state responsibility and, 122–125; vicarious liability and, 115, 335n1
Seabed resources: laws of the sea and, 239. *See also* Deep seabed mining
Sea mines: laws of war and, 192–195. *See also* Land mines

Second-best circumstances, trade subsidies and, 276–277
Security Council (United Nations): International Court of Justice and, 101–102; International Criminal Court and, 106–108; international criminal tribunals and, 104–106; international law and, 10–11, 79; legislative activities of, 81; origins of, 86; power over international institutions of, 91–92; reform of, 90–92; sovereignty issues for members of, 40–41; structure of, 86–90; UN Charter provisions concerning, 174–176; use of force authorization by, 179, 185–186
Self-defense: collective self-defense, 187–188; imminence requirement for, 179–181; nineteenth-century warfare and principles of, 172–174; preemptive war and, 177–189; proportionality requirement, 187
Self-determination: declarative and constitutive theory and, 43; international law and role of, 7
Self-executing treaties, 142–143
Self-help principles: customary international law and, 52–53; dispute resolution and, 282–287
Self-interest, economic theory and role of, 12–15
Services, international trade in, 278–280
Sic utere tuo ut alienum non laedas maxim, environmental law and, 227–229
Sierra Leone, tribunal for, 96
Signatures on treaties, procedures for, 68–69
Singapore, sovereign debt and, 161–162
Single monetary policy, Eurozone debt crisis and, 325–327
Slavery, as international crime, 215–217
Smoot-Hawley tariffs, 267
Smuggling: high seas rules and, 243–244; law of the sea and, 240–241
Socialism, human rights and, 199–202
Soft law, treaties and, 76–77
Somalia, human rights intervention in, 205–206
Sources, doctrine of, international law based on, 8–10
South Korea, sovereign debt and, 161–162
Sovereign debt: Eurozone debt crisis and, 324–327; exchange rates and balance of payments and, 304–306; IMF bailouts and, 318–321; international law concerning, 159–162
Sovereignty: customary international law and, 60–62; definitions of, 39–40; extraterritorial jurisdiction and, 146–152; foreign property

ownership and, 155; high seas rules and, 243–244; human rights and, 198; "internal economy" of ships and, 246–248; international law and, 17–20; law of the sea and, 240–241; origins of United Nations and, 87–90; presumptive ban on war and, 176–177; protection of aliens and, 155–158; statehood attributes and, 39–49; statehood theory and, 15–17; succession issues and, 47–49

Soviet Union: collapse of, 103–104, 201, 206; United Nations and, 86–90. *See also* Russia

Spanish-American War, Paqueta Habana case during, 54–57

"Special agreement" cases, International Court of Justice and, 101–102

Special drawing right (SDR), monetary law and, 312–313

Staiger, Robert W., 284, 349n8

Standstill rules, bailouts and, 321

State officials, responsibilities of, 121–125

State responsibility: acts of private citizens and, 124–125; civil and criminal sanctions, individual responsibility *vs.*, 209–212; corporate liability compared with, 113–115; government scale of activity and, 119–121; individual responsibility *vs.*, 121–125, 209–212; insurgencies and, 125; international law and, 113–126; International Law Commissions' provisions concerning, 121–125; of state officials *vs.* private citizens, 121–125; states' "principal" and, 117–119; vicarious liability and, 116–117

States and statehood theory: alien protection and, 155–158; countermeasures restrictions and, 133–134; customary international law and role of, 50–57; delegation to international institutions, 81–82, 84–85; domestic commitment to, 20; economics and role of, 12, 15–17; environmental law and, 226–227; externalities and, 17–20; extraterritorial jurisdiction and, 146–152; human rights treaties and norms of, 72–73, 202–206; incomplete contracts and, 24–25; international law and role of, 6–10, 17–20, 209; intersection of domestic and international law in, 140–152; interstate wars, chronology of, 163–168; investor-state dispute settlement and, 294–295; *jus cogens* norms and, 57–59; law of the sea and, 233–234; monist and dualist states, 140–142; motivations for war and, 168–171; objections to treaty reservations and, 75–76; piracy and role of, 213–214; principal in, responsibilities of, 117–119; recognition of, 41–49; restitution and reparations by, 134–136; soft law and treaties of, 77–78; sovereignty and attributes of, 39–49; state practice and consent and, 54–57; succession issues in, 47–49; treaty consent and, 67–68. *See also* Government institutions

Statute of the ICJ, 101

Stockholm Chamber of Commerce, 292

Stockholm Declaration on the Human Environment, 228–229

Straits, law of the sea concerning, 246–248

Strategic Arms Limitation Talks (SALT), 25–26

Submarine warfare, laws of war and, 192–195

Subsidies, international trade and, 275–277

Substantial equivalence standard: dispute resolution and, 285–287, 351n33; renegotiation of trade agreements and, 272–273

Succession issues, sovereignty and, 47–49

Sudan: human rights abuses in, 111; International Criminal Court and, 107–108

Summers, Lawrence, 320–321

Superior orders doctrine, war crimes and, 218

Supranationalism, European Union as example of, 93

Supreme Court. *See* United States Supreme Court

Taiwan: sovereignty of, 42–43, 44–47, 332n7; United Nations membership and, 86–90

"Takings clause" (Fifth Amendment, U.S. Constitution), 289–297

Takings concept, government scale of activity and, 120

Taliban government, recognition of, 45–47

Tariffs: antidumping policies and, 277–278; discriminatory practices concerning, 268–271; free trade *vs.* protectionism, 263–266; multilateral, bilateral, and regional agreements concerning, 268–271; regulatory protection impact on, 350n19; renegotiation of agreements concerning, 271–273; services trade policies and, 278–280; subsidies in trade agreements *vs.*, 275–277; trade liberalization and, 266–267; WTO/GATT tarrification commitments and, 267–268

Tehran Hostages case: countermeasures restrictions in, 133–134; state responsibility in, 124–125

Territorial issues: customary international law and, 59–60; declarative and constitutive

Territorial issues (*continued*)
theory and, 43; extraterritorial jurisdiction and, 146–152; law of the sea and, 235–241; piracy and, 214; restitution and, 134–136; territorial sea, 50, 244–248, 257–258

Territorial sea: fisheries and, 257–258; law of the sea and, 244–248

Terrorism, war on, 195–197

"Three-year free pass," in WTO dispute resolution system, 284–287

Time consistency problem: dispute resolution and, 282–287; domestic commitment and, 20; investment law and, 289–297

Tito, Osip Broz, 104

Tokyo Round Antidumping Code, 277

Tort law: individual liability under, 209; international forum shopping and, 144–146; level of damages in, 337n8; state responsibility and, 113–115, 123–125

Torture Convention, 206–207

Torture practices: *jus cogens* norms and, 58–59; treaties outlawing, 206–207

Trade agreements: antidumping policy and, 277–280; balance of payments and, 303–306; bargain adjustments over time, 271–273; dispute resolution, 281–287; domestic law constraints, 273–275, 350n19; exchange rate policies and, 303–306, 315–318; "free trade" and protectionism, 263–266; intellectual property and, 280–281; international law and, 263–287, 349n8; legal architecture of world trade, 266–267; multilateralism, bilateralism, regionalism, and trade discrimination, 268–271; nineteenth-century warfare and, 172–174; preemptive war and, 183–184, 340n13; remedies in, 126; reservations concerning, 71–72; subsidies in, 275–277; tariffs and, 266–268; treaties as, 65–67. *See also* Free trade; Tariffs

Trade deficits and surpluses, 304–306

Trade discrimination, international trade and, 268–271

Trade diversion, bilateral agreements and, 268–269

Trademark protection, trade-related aspects of, 280–281

Trade Related Aspects of Intellectual Property (TRIPs), Agreement on, 22, 280–281

Trail Smelter case, 227

Transaction costs: economic theory and, 13; international agreements, 22–24

Treaties: alien protection in, 158; bilateralism in, 63; climate treaties, 230–232; cooperative behavior through, 63–67; customary international law and, 50–54; declarations and understandings in, 71–72; disagreements about interpretation, 67–69, 74–76, 80; of European Union, 80–81; human rights treaties, 66–67, 72–73, 158, 202–208; international law and role of, 8–10, 63–78; investment law and, 291–297; judicial enforcement in United States of, 142–143; *jus cogens* norms in, 58–59; monist and dualist states and enforcement of, 140–142; multilateralism in, 63; objections to reservations, 74–76; public goods in, 73–74; recognition of government institutions and, 44–47; renegotiation, modification, and efficient breach of, 25–26; reservations concerning, 70–76; retaliatory noncompliance and, 131–132; signature and ratification, 68–69; soft law in, 76–78; state practices in, 57; substantive investment law controversies, 295–297; termination of, 69–70; universal treaties, 66–67; validity and interpretation of, 67–69

Treaty of Versailles, 85–86

Truman, Harry S., 60–62

Turkey: EU membership and, 94; nineteenth-century warfare in, 172

Uganda, 107, 214

Understandings concerning treaties, 71–72

Unfair advantage concept, currency manipulation and, 321–324

Unilateral preemptive force: as humanitarian intervention, 189; pretexts for, 185–186

Unilateral sanctions: dispute resolution and, 282–287; international contracts and, 30–32

United Nations: authorization of war by, 179, 185–186, 341n21; committees, commissions, and quasi-tribunals of, 110–112; institutional functions of, 79; International Court of Justice and, 91–92, 96, 101–102; international law and, 9–11; investment law and resolutions by, 291–294; Law of the Sea convention and, 109; origins of, 86–90, 174–175; predecessors to, 85–86; reform of, 90–92; soft law and treaties of, 76; sovereignty issues for members of, 40–41; treaties sponsored by, 63, 66–67. *See also* General Assembly (United Nations); Security Council (United Nations)

United Nations Charter, 174–175; self-defense defined in, 179–180
United Nations Children's Fund, 86
United Nations Climate Summit, 231–232
United Nations Commission on International Trade Law, 292
United Nations Conference on Trade and Development, 292
United Nations Convention on the Law of the Sea (UNCLOS): basic provisions of, 241–259; continental shelf and Exclusive Economic Zone, 248–250; deep seabed provisions, 251–257; distant resources and high seas issues in, 239–240; division and the equidistance rule, 250–251; fisheries, 257–258; high seas provisions in, 241–244; importance of, 233–234; inland waters, territorial seas, and contiguous zone, 244–248; proximity issues and competing claims in, 237–239; resource distribution, 258–259
United States: abuse of POWs by, 194–195; currency convertibility in, 307–308; customary international law, 143–144; deep seabed mining issues and, 254–257; European transactions with, 303–306; exchange rates and balance of payments in, 304–306; hegemony of, 186; human rights treaties and, 72–73, 202–206; International Criminal Court, opposition in, 106–107; international forum shopping in, 144–146; intersection of domestic and international law in, 140–152; Iraq invasion led by, 175, 183–186, 340n14; Kellogg-Briand Pact and, 173–174; *Metaclad* case, 295–297; monetary expansion in, 311–313; nineteenth-century warfare by, 172–173; Northwest Passage dispute and, 247–248; objections to treaty reservations by, 74–76; recognition of sovereignty by, 42–47; Soviet Union and, 86–90; treaties and judicial enforcement in, 142–143; UNCLOS opposition in, 233–234; WTO dispute resolution system and, 282–287
United States Bill of Rights, 199
United States Constitution: enforcement of international law, 140; Fifth Amendment to, investment law and, 289–297
United States Diplomatic and Consular Staff in Tehran case, 133–134
United States Supreme Court: Paqueta Habana case, 54–57, 333n7 (chap. 5); rejection of international rulings by, 81–82; U.S. enforcement of treaties and, 142–143
Universal Declaration of Human Rights, 111, 200–201
Universal jurisdiction: piracy and, 213–214; rationale for, 215–217
Universal treaties, principles of, 66–67
Unlicensed broadcasting, high seas rules and, 243–244
Uruguay Round, 275, 281
Use of force: collective self-defense principle and, 187–188; delaying of, 183–184, 340n15; humanitarian intervention as grounds for, 188–189; international institutions and, 80; international law and, 10, 163–189; private calculus on benefits of, 182; proportionality requirement for, 187; against rogue states, 178–179; self-defense and preemptive war as grounds for, 177–189; social calculus on benefits of, 183–184; timing of preemptive attacks, 179–181. *See also* Enforcement of international law; Military force; War

Vatican City, sovereignty of, 42
Vicarious liability: basic principles of, 113–115, 335n1; command responsibility as, 217–218
Vienna Convention on Treaties: contract law and, 24–25; *jus cogens* norms in, 58; law of treaties in, 67–69; signature and ratification principles in, 69; termination of treaties under, 69–70
Vietnam War, UN Charter rules and, 175

War: conduct of, 190–197; customary international law and, 50; government scale of activity and, 120–121; human rights as justification for, 198; international law and reduction of, 171; nineteenth-century regulation efforts concerning, 171–173; presumptive ban on, 176–177; private calculus of states concerning, 182; proportionality requirement, 187; protection of aliens and, 158; self-defense and preemptive war, 177–189; state practice and consent and, 54–57; state responsibility *vs.* individual liability during, 211–212; timing of preemptive attacks, 179–181; two-period scenario for preemptive attack in, 181–182; UN Charter and laws of, 174–175; United Nations and, 85–92; use of force and,

163–189; World War I and consequences of, 173–174. *See also* Laws of war; Military force; Use of force

War crimes: command responsibility and, 217–218; modern international trends concerning, 215–217; superior orders doctrine and, 218

War on terror, laws of war and, 195–197

Weapons of mass destruction (WMD): dismantling of, 89–90; preemptive war and threat of, 183–186

Webb-Pomerene Act, 151–152

Webster, Daniel, 173

Webster-Ashburton Treaty, 173, 179, 187

World Bank, 79, 81, 292

World Health Organization (WHO), 79, 110

World Trade Organization (WTO): activities of, 79; Antidumping Agreement, 277–278; antitrust law and, 299–302; Appellate Body of, 282–287; arbitration proceedings and, 99; denial of standing for private actors in, 286–287; Dispute Settlement Understanding of, 10–11, 66, 96, 108–109, 281–287; domestic law and, 273–275; efficient breach violations and, 336n4 (chap. 9); escape clause in provisions of, 271–273; European Union and, 95; forums provided by, 81; growth of, 263; intellectual property rights and, 280–281; investor provisions and, 292; legal architecture of, 266–267; obligations of treaties by, 132; renegotiation provisions for, 271–273; services trading and, 278–280; subsidies system in, 275–277; "tariffication" policies and, 267–268; tariff reduction agreements, 22–23; Trade Related Aspects of Intellectual Property (TRIPs) Agreement, 22

World War I: destructiveness of, 163; formation of Yugoslavia and, 104–106; gold standard's demise and, 310; "law in action" during, 342n8; League of Nations and, 85

World War II: containment theory in aftermath of, 176–177; currency convertibility following, 307–308; decline of nationalism and, 199; destructiveness of, 163; formation of United Nations and, 85–86; human rights law and, 200; investment law after, 291–292; laws of war during, 191–194; superior orders doctrine and, 218; war crimes during, 217–218

Yamashita case, 217–218

Yoo, John, 340n15

Yugoslavia: collapse of, 103–106; Croatia independence from, 42

Zimbabwe, human rights in, 203